To David:

Glad that we've met.

I look forward to many m

conversations.

Yours, [signature]

Oxford 15/11/2007

The UN Security Council and Informal Groups of States

The UN Security Council and Informal Groups of States:
Complementing or Competing for Governance?

JOCHEN PRANTL

OXFORD
UNIVERSITY PRESS

OXFORD
UNIVERSITY PRESS

Great Clarendon Street, Oxford OX2 6DP

Oxford University Press is a department of the University of Oxford.
It furthers the University's objective of excellence in research, scholarship,
and education by publishing worldwide in

Oxford New York

Auckland Cape Town Dar es Salaam Hong Kong Karachi
Kuala Lumpur Madrid Melbourne Mexico City Nairobi
New Delhi Shanghai Taipei Toronto

With offices in

Argentina Austria Brazil Chile Czech Republic France Greece
Guatemala Hungary Italy Japan Poland Portugal Singapore
South Korea Switzerland Thailand Turkey Ukraine Vietnam

Oxford is a registered trade mark of Oxford University Press
in the UK and in certain other countries

Published in the United States
by Oxford University Press Inc., New York

British Library Cataloguing in Publication Data

Data available

Library of Congress Cataloging in Publication Data

Data available

Typeset by SPI Publisher Services, Pondicherry, India
Printed in Great Britain on
acid-free paper by
Biddles Ltd., King's Lynn

ISBN 0-19-928768-6
978-0-19-928768-0

To my parents
Irmela and Helmuth Prantl
with love

Contents

Acknowledgements

This book could not have been written without the help of a large group of colleagues, mentors, and friends indeed. It is based on my doctoral thesis which I have written at Oxford and Yale. I am greatly indebted to both Adam Roberts and Bruce Russett, who encouraged me early on to embark on this endeavour. The project received financial support from the Economic and Social Research Council, United Kingdom (Grant No. R42200024335), and the Centre for International Studies, University of Oxford. The UN Studies Program at Yale University was a frequent host and home over recent years.

Informal processes are by its nature difficult to identify, and the phenomenon this book seeks to explain is itself elusive. In consequence, the study of informal *ad hoc* groupings of states requires a wide array of interviews. It is therefore certainly more than just an act of courtesy that I would like to express my sincere gratitude to the numerous decision-makers and officials in national administrations, permanent missions to the United Nations as well as in the Secretariat at UN Headquarters, who were willing to share their expertise on the workings of informal groups. In many cases, they discussed with me off the record and on the condition of anonymity. Not all of them are therefore identified in the text. However, I have listed the names of interviewees in the annex of the book.

At Oxford, I am particularly grateful to my former supervisor and now colleague Neil MacFarlane for his great support and advice. He not only encouraged but also challenged and inspired me throughout this endeavour. His superb supervision made my 'Oxford experience' truly exceptional. Mats Berdal gave me invaluable advice until he left to assume the position of Academic Director at IISS, and later Professor for Security and Development at King's College. Marrack Goulding was patient enough to share his deep knowledge about the workings of the UN conflict resolution machinery. Andy Hurrell has been extremely supportive in facilitating my start into postdoctoral academic life and studying further the anatomy of informal governance.

At Yale, I was privileged to work in a world-class research environment and to meet many colleagues who made this stay an unforgettable experience.

Acknowledgements

I am extremely grateful to Bruce Russett for his invitation to assume a visiting fellowship in the UN Studies Program at Yale and for his critical advice. I owe him very much. Throughout this project, Jim Sutterlin shared his rich experience in the US State Department and on the 38th floor at UN Headquarters, providing me with very useful intellectual guidance. I also felt privileged to work with Jean Krasno, who has been the first scholar analysing the workings of *ad hoc* arrangements such as the group of friends in her contribution to the Carnegie Commission's report 'Preventing Deadly Conflict', published in 1997.

The Policy Planning Unit in the Department of Political Affairs at UN Headquarters was kind enough to accept me as external consultant in fall/winter 2002, which allowed me to gain additional insights from the UN Secretariat's perspective. I have to thank the Head of Unit, Tapio Kanninen, for facilitating this stay. Karl Kaiser was kind enough to invite me for a stay as visiting scholar of the German Council on Foreign Relations in 2000. I am very grateful for this invitation as well as his long-term support and encouragement. I also wish to thank Richard Caplan, Sam Daws, Kurt Gaubatz, Hans-Peter Kaul, Edward Luck, David Malone, James Mayall, Roger Morgan, Joseph Nye, Hans-Peter Schwarz, Avi Shlaim, and Ngaire Woods for their comments and criticism at various stages of the project.

Some parts of the book have been first published elsewhere. Portions of Part I appeared as a coauthored contribution in *The United Nations: Confronting the Challenges of a Global Society*, edited by Jean E. Krasno (Boulder, CO: Lynne Rienner, 2004). A summary of the book's findings was published in *International Organization*, 59/3 (2005). I gratefully acknowledge the permission to reprint relevant sections.

Last, but certainly not least, I owe my warmest thanks to my wife Anja for her love, friendship, unfailing encouragement, patience, and humour. However, I would not have met her without the help of my parents, Irmela and Helmuth. This book is therefore dedicated to them, with deep gratitude for supporting me in all the ways that matter.

Abbreviations

ACTORD	Activation Order
ACTREQ	Activation Requirement
ACTWARN	Activation Warning
ANC	African National Congress
AU	African Union
CIS	Commonwealth of Independent States
CMN	Total-Compagnie minière et nucléaire
CCP	Consultative and Co-ordination Process in New York relating to the work of the Contact Group
CDG	Consultation and Drafting Group
CDM	Consolidated Diamond Mines
CIA	Central Intelligence Agency
CIVS	International Verification and Follow-up Commission
COPAZ	National Commission for the Consolidation of Peace
CSCE	Conference on Security and Cooperation in Europe
EC	European Community
ECOMOG	Economic Community of West African States Monitoring Group
ECOWAS	Economic Community of West African States
EU	European Union
FDI	foreign direct investment
FMLN	Frente Farabundo Martí para la Liberación Nacional
FNLA	National Front for the Liberation of Angola
Frelimo	Frente de Libertação de Moçambique
FRY	Federal Republic of Yugoslavia
G-8	Group of Eight
G77	Group of 77
GAOR	General Assembly Official Records
GDP	Gross domestic product
GOES	Government of El Salvador
IAEA	International Atomic Energy Agency
ICJ	International Court of Justice
ICFY	International Conference on former Yugoslavia
ICRC	International Committee of the Red Cross
IFOR	Implementation Force
IMF	International Monetary Fund
IO	International Organizations

Abbreviations

KFOR	Kosovo Force
MPLA	Popular Movement for the Liberation of Angola
NAM	Non-Aligned Movement
NATO	North Atlantic Treaty Organization
Nepad	New Partnership for Africa's Development
NGO	Non-Governmental Organization
OAS	Organization of American States
OAU	Organization of African Unity
OIC	Organization of Islamic Conferences
ONUC	United Nations Operation in the Congo
ONUMOZ	United Nations Operation in Mozambique
ONUSAL	United Nations Observer Mission in El Salvador
OP	Operative paragraph
OSCE	Organization for Security and Cooperation in Europe
OSZE	Organisation für Sicherheit und Zusammenarbeit in Europa
P-3	Three Western permanent members of the UN Security Council
P-5/P5	Five permanent members of the UN Security Council
PAC	Pan African Congress
Renamo	Resistência Nacional de Moçambique
RES	Resolution
RTZ	Rio Tinto Zinc Corporation Ltd.
SC	Security Council
SFOR	Stabilization Force
SFRY	Socialist Federal Republic of Yugoslavia
SPD	Sozialdemokratische Partei Deutschlands
SWAPO	South West Africa People's Organization
TEU	Treaty of the European Union
TNC	Transnational Corporation
UCK	Ushtria Çlirimtare e Kosovës (Kosovo Liberation Army)
UN	United Nations
UNAMIR	United Nations Assistance Mission for Rwanda
UNEF	United Nations Emergency Force
UNITA	National Union for the Total Independence of Angola
UNITAF	Unified Task Force (Somalia)
UNITAR	United Nations Institute for Training and Research
UNMIK	United Nations Interim Administration Mission in Kosovo
UNO	United Nations Organization
UNOGIL	United Nations Observation Group in Lebanon
UNOMIG	United Nations Observer Mission in Georgia
UNPREDEP	United Nations Preventive Deployment Force (Macedonia)
UNPROFOR	United Nations Protection Force
UNRWA	United Nations Relief & Works Agency
UNTAG	United Nations Transition Assistance Group

UNTSO	United Nations Truce Supervision Organization
WTO	World Trade Organisation

The theory of the divorce between the spheres of politics and morality is superficially attractive, if only because it evades the insoluble problem of finding a moral justification for the use of force. But it is not ultimately satisfying. Both non-resistance and anarchism are counsels of despair, which appear to find widespread acceptance only where men feel hopeless of achieving anything by political action; and the attempt to keep God and Caesar in watertight compartments runs too much athwart the deep-seated desire of the human mind to reduce its view of the world to some kind of moral order.[1]

Edward Hallett Carr

---

[1] Edward Hallett Carr, *The Twenty Years' Crisis 1919–1939. An Introduction to the Study of International Relations*, 2nd edn., reissued with a new preface (London: Macmillan, 1981), 94.

Introduction

The US invasion in March 2003 aiming at Iraq's disarmament and the change of its regime without explicit authorization of the UN Security Council (SC) has revived discussions about the potential and limits of this international institution.[2] Some scholars concluded that the SC fails to meet its primary responsibility for the maintenance of international peace and security, because the international system has transformed in a way which is 'incompatible' with the original design of the United Nations (UN).[3] 'The SC is dead. Long live the Council!', may be the provocative summary of the periodically recurring exchange of arguments between opponents and proponents of the Council that is often based on a superficial analysis of its actual workings and a misreading of its functions.[4] While it is certainly true that the Council is challenged by structural constraints that will not disappear, even in case of formal adaptations, conclusions of failure seem to be premature. Analysis of the Council's workings should not exclusively focus on levels of formal cooperation. In order to gain a proper understanding of the variables that define its performance, we need firstly to extend our analysis to levels of informal cooperation, as epitomized in the plethora of *ad hoc* groupings of states gathering outside the Council's chambers. Those informal settings

[2] Institutions shall be understood as a 'set of rules that stipulate the ways in which states should cooperate and compete with each other'; John J. Mearsheimer, 'The False Promise of International Institutions', *International Security*, 19/3 (1994/95), 8; also John J. Mearsheimer, *The Tragedy of Great Power Politics* (New York: W. W. Norton, 2001), 14–22.

[3] Michael J. Glennon, 'Why the Security Council Failed', *Foreign Affairs*, 82/3 (2003), 18.

[4] David Malone, for example, points to the lack of 'a sound understanding of what the Security Council is good at and what it is bad at'. David M. Malone, 'Introduction', in David M. Malone (ed.), *The UN Security Council: From the Cold War to the 21st Century* (Boulder, CO: Lynne Rienner, 2004), 1.

Table 1.

Period	Conflict Setting
1950s	Sinai (1956); Lebanon (1958)
1960s	Congo (1960)
1970s	Namibia (1972; 1977)
1980s	El Salvador (1989)
1990s	Cambodia (1990); Angola (1991); Haiti (1992); Western Sahara (1993); Guatemala (1994); Suriname (1994); Bosnia and Herzegovina (1994); Georgia/Abkhazia (1994); Afghanistan (1994); Tajikistan (1995); Sierra Leone (1998); Central African Republic (1998); Kosovo (1999); East Timor (1999); Guinea-Bissau (1999); Democratic Republic of the Congo (1999)
2000–	Ethiopia and Eritrea (2000); Sudan (2002); Somalia (2002); Liberia (2002); Iraq (2003); Great Lakes Region of Africa (2003); Uganda (2004)

Source: UN documents; Jochen Prantl and Jean E. Krasno, 'Informal Groups of Member States', in Jean E. Krasno (ed.), *The United Nations: Confronting the Challenges of a Global Society* (Boulder, CO: Lynne Rienner, 2004), 342 *et seq.*

emerged very early in UN history and proliferated in the post-bipolar era.[5] Secondly, we must not underestimate the importance and persistence of the 'symbolic life'[6] of the SC, which exerts a strong pull on UN member states to seek its blessing, though sometimes *post hoc.*

The Argument

This book seeks to establish the importance of informal groups of states in the making of peace. More precisely, it grasps the dynamics between informal institutions and the UN SC in the resolution of conflict. Informal groups matter. Questions arising from this hypothesis include: (*a*) When and why do they matter? (*b*) How do they matter? (*c*) And under what circumstances do they not matter? Analysis also entails examination of the effects of informal groups on governance of and in the UN SC: do informal groups complement or compete for SC governance?[7] It touches upon wider questions that are at the heart of the discourse over the extent to which international organizations (IOs) are able to adapt to systemic change.

[5] See Table 1.

[6] Ian Hurd, 'Legitimacy, Power, and the Symbolic Life of the UN Security Council', *Global Governance*, 8/1 (2002), 35–51; see also the account by the same author on why legitimacy matters to international institutions: Ian Hurd, 'Legitimacy and Authority in International Politics', *International Organization*, 53/2 (1999), 379–408.

[7] Governance shall be understood here as 'the processes and institutions, both formal and informal, that guide and restrain the collective activities of a group'; Robert O. Keohane and Joseph S. Nye, 'Introduction', in Joseph S. Nye and John D. Donahue (eds.), *Governance in a Globalizing World* (Washington, DC: Brookings Institution Press, 2000), 12.

The UN with its nearly universal membership becomes a prism through which to view this transformation. In 1995, then UN Secretary-General Boutros Boutros-Ghali explained in a speech:

'[T]he increasing complexity of operations has led, on the political side, to the intensification of peacemaking efforts. Thus, a new concept, that of 'Friends of the Secretary General', 'International Conferences', or 'Contact Groups' means that, while the UN peacekeepers are on the ground, intense diplomatic efforts continue with many parties to a conflict in order to reach a political settlement.'[8]

Friends of the Secretary-General and Contact Groups are diplomatic devices operating with no formal mandate from the SC or the General Assembly. By name, a Group of Friends is a gathering of like-minded UN member states supporting the implementation of good offices, peacemaking, and peacekeeping mandates entrusted to the Secretary-General. They are genuinely an effort 'to redress the balance between the public and private procedures of the UN,' by creating a platform for quiet diplomacy in the process of peacemaking on a consensual basis.[9] Like-minded countries that constitute a Group of Friends lend leverage to the peacemaking efforts taken by the Secretary-General and help to keep the parties to a conflict engaged throughout the process.[10] In contrast, Contact Groups are rather self-selected *ad hoc* coalitions of able and willing countries, working separately from the Council and outside the UN framework. They may either operate within the objectives of the Organization or act according to their own agenda. In ideal terms, Groups of Friends may suggest a stronger involvement of the UN than Contact Groups, although the dividing line is much more blurred in practice. These groups may be categorized as '*ad hoc* settings', as other scholars have done before.[11] Here, they are subsumed under the term of 'informal groups of states'. In essence, the formation of groups occurs *ad hoc*, and the meeting structure is informal. Informal groups of states have taken over specific tasks in the field of management and resolution of conflicts, including the negotiation and implementation of peace agreements, not only in

---

[8] UN Doc SG/SM/5624, May 1, 1995.

[9] Dag Hammarskjöld, 'The Element of Privacy in Peacemaking, Address at Ohio University, Athens, Ohio, February 5, 1958', in Andrew W. Cordier and Wilder Foote (eds.), *Public Papers of the Secretaries-General of the United Nations*, Vol. IV: *Dag Hammarskjöld, 1958–60* (New York: Columbia University Press, 1974), 27.

[10] See Jochen Prantl and Jean E. Krasno, 'Informal Groups of Member States', in Jean E. Krasno (ed.), *The United Nations: Confronting the Challenges of a Global Society* (Boulder, CO: Lynne Rienner, 2004), 335.

[11] See Sydney Bailey and Sam Daws, *The Procedure of the UN Security Council*, 3rd edn. (Oxford: Oxford University Press, 1998), 72.

those cases when UN peacekeepers have already been on the ground. However, it is less obvious to what extent they influence governance in and of the SC, which still provides, though sometimes *post hoc*, the framework for action. As such action is usually based on recommendations of the Secretary-General, the role of the Secretariat constitutes a subset of the question of SC governance.

This book concentrates on the role of Groups of Friends of the UN Secretary-General and of Contact Groups, including the Group of Eight (G-8), within the crisis settings of Namibia, El Salvador, and Kosovo. Informal groups of states appear as part and parcel of SC governance. Exploring the role of informal groups contributes to a better understanding of such processes and institutions that define the performance of the Council.[12] The study sets forth three main arguments. Firstly, informal groups of states may serve as agents of incremental change. They are part and parcel of the increasing demands on the UN to adapt to the new security environment of the post-bipolar world, without formally changing the constitutional foundation of the Organization. Secondly, ancillary to the previous point, *ad hoc* groupings may narrow the operational and participatory gap growing out of the multiple strategic incapacities that prevents the Council from formulating an effective response to crisis situations. They enhance SC governance if they strike a balance between the competing demands of inclusiveness, efficiency, informality, transparency, and accountability. Thirdly, the post-Cold War era has fostered an environment where the substance of conflict resolution and the process of its legitimation have become increasingly decoupled. The former tends to be delegated to informal groups of states, while the SC provides the latter. The successful merger of right process and substantive outcome may strengthen the legitimacy of the Council and make actions taken by informal settings more acceptable.

Why Informal Institutions?

Informal groups of states are an integral, though widely neglected, part of the development of UN constitutional practice. In essence, they are another variation on the collective security scheme, as originally

---

[12] It is not the aim of this study to provide an encyclopaedic overview on all possibilities of informal influence on decision-making in the UN Security Council. While other players such as the African Union, the European Union, the G-77, the Non-aligned movement, or the Organization of American States are important, they do not match the criteria of informal groups of states. These international institutions are neither informal nor *ad hoc*.

envisaged by the founders of the UN: 'The term "collective security" normally refers to a system, regional or global, in which each participating state accepts that the security of one is the concern of all, and agrees to join in a collective response to aggression.'[13] Although the UN was originally supposed to have a system of collective security at its core, the Organization has failed to establish such a system from its establishment in 1945. Instead, one could observe the development of certain variations on the theme of collective security, such as the tendency towards regional alliances and multilateral military interventions, UN authorizations of military enforcement activities by states, and peacekeeping operations under UN auspices.[14]

Informal groups of states affect the triangular relationship between the SC, the Secretariat and, to a lesser extent, the General Assembly. Yet it is still unclear whether and how their activities translate into influence on decision-making in the Council, as the Charter does not have any provisions at its disposal that would grant these *ad hoc* groupings formal access to Council consultations. The performance of Groups of Friends, Contact Groups, or even the Group of Eight (G-8) shows strong evidence that they are able to exert considerable influence on an informal level. In this context, influence is to be defined as 'the modification of one actor's behavior by that of another'.[15] This includes the modification or, in the extreme case, the hijacking of SC decision-making by *ad hoc* groupings. The phenomenon of influencing different stages of SC decision-making by informal groups of states shall be defined as *informal influence*. Such influence is usually derived from their activities as stakeholders in a conflict. Participants in informal settings tend to be well positioned to activate or advise the Council on matters related to the conflict setting. Informal influence on SC decision-making does not occur on a permanent basis, but differs significantly from case to case. It takes place on different levels and varies in its extent.

The influence of these *ad hoc* groupings ranges from consultations with members of the SC to a much stronger involvement, which comes close to a kind of informal membership.[16] Under certain circumstances, informal

---

[13] Adam Roberts, 'The United Nations: Variants of Collective Security', in Ngaire Woods (ed.) *Explaining International Relations Since 1945* (Oxford: Oxford University Press, 1996), 309.
[14] Ibid.
[15] Robert W. Cox and Harold K. Jacobson, 'The Framework for Inquiry,' in Robert W. Cox and Harold K. Jacobson (eds.) *The Anatomy of Influence. Decision-Making in International Organization* (New Haven, CT: Yale University Press, 1973), 3.
[16] Ian Hurd has offered a useful starting point to elaborate on the concept of informal membership. However, the terminology is quite problematic since it suggests a 'quasi-

membership even implies the capacity to prevent decisions being taken, in essence, an *informal veto*. In addition to their core functions of designing a multiparty response to conflicts, supporting (UN-led) negotiations or assisting in the implementation of peace agreements, informal groups may pre-negotiate and pre-formulate pending SC resolutions and statements in such a precise manner that substantial change is almost impossible in subsequent stages when the matter comes under official consideration in the Council. For the participant in informal groups of states, the probability of making a difference may increase, since decisions taken are usually based upon consensus. Although there is no formal vote taken, negotiations are characterized by the will of its members to arrive at a common position. Members of informal groups of states therefore tend to have a considerably higher potential of leverage than non-permanent members of the Council. Informal groups of states played various roles— with greater or lesser impact—in conflicts such as Afghanistan, Angola, Cambodia, Central African Republic, East Timor, Ethiopia and Eritrea, El Salvador, Georgia, Guatemala, Guinea-Bissau, Haiti, Mozambique, Namibia, Sierra Leone, Suriname, Uganda, Western Sahara, and former Yugoslavia.[17]

This should not obscure the fact that all too often the UN Security Council plays only a marginal role in the management of conflicts, while at the same time power projection by single states and alliances without any significant Council involvement remains quite a common phenomenon. Given the extent to which single states in cooperation with the Contact Group on former Yugoslavia (and the G-8, as well as the Quint on Kosovo) defined the chain of events, those cases are clear examples of the limits of the SC in the field of conflict management. The primary responsibility for the maintenance of international peace and security was almost fully overtaken by the Contact Group and in subsequent stages by the G-8, Quint, and Troika. Nevertheless, the UN Security Council *is* sought as legitimizer of state action, which is one of its most important functions. Even in those cases where the SC has been prima facie bypassed, action by coalitions of the willing or regional actors has often been explicitly or implicitly approved in a kind of *post hoc* ratification (e.g. in cases

membership' on the Council, which covers only one end of the spectrum where influence on SC decision-making is particularly strong. Empirical evidence points however to a much more diverse picture; see Ian Hurd, 'Security Council Reform: Informal Membership and Practice', in Bruce Russett (ed.). *The Once and Future Security Council* (New York: St. Martin's Press, 1997), 135–52.

[17] See Table 1.

such as regional action by the Economic Community of West African States (ECOWAS) in Liberia and Sierra Leone). In situations where the SC body is or appears to be deadlocked, *ad hoc* groupings acting without the explicit mandate of the Council may provide the platform to re-involve the UN, as the case study on Kosovo will demonstrate later.

While Article 24 of the UN Charter allocates primary, though not exclusive, responsibility for the maintenance of international peace and security to the SC, Groups of Friends and Contact Groups increasingly complement or even compete with the original functions of the Council as provided for in the Charter. Although Groups of Friends and Contact Groups constituted an important element in the history of UN peacekeeping after the breakdown of the bipolar system, they are not entirely new. Predecessors of the Group of Friends can already be found in the 1950s when Dag Hammarskjöld established Advisory Committees of key UN member states to obtain necessary support for implementing mandates entrusted to him by the General Assembly or the SC. The term Group of Friends was originally coined in the context of the El Salvador peace process in 1989. As far as the Contact Group is concerned, a similar core group had already been established for Namibia in 1977. Despite the fact that the majority of Groups of Friends work under the label of Friends of the Secretary-General, especially at later stages, they were, in fact, self-constituted rather than selected by the Secretary-General. Even if a group constitutes itself under the label Friends of the Secretary-General, it does not necessarily imply that the Secretariat has a strong voice in related peacemaking efforts.

Informal groups of states reflect the fact that the SC is often incapable of effective crisis management. Reasons for these limits are structural to some extent: only a few states serving on the Council have the necessary resources—given, for example, the size of their Permanent Missions—to deal in depth with the plethora of conflicts placed on the daily agenda. Moreover, the breakdown of the bipolar system widened and, for a certain time, overstrained the role of the SC leading to a problem of overload, as it had to manage simultaneously more and more complex crises. UN member states have been facing hard choices regarding which conflicts to address and how to respond to them. In addition to problems of overload, it was often sheer lack of interest or disagreement of the Five Permanent Members of the UN SC (P-5) that prevented the Council from effective crisis response. The situation has been exacerbated by the fact that the current formal composition of the permanent membership of the SC still mirrors the situation of 1945 without taking into account the shifts in relative power among the actors of the international system which have occurred since then. In consequence, the perception of both the capacity and the limits of the SC has had a catalytic effect on the creation of informal structures.

The Analytical Framework

Underlying this book are the following four main guiding questions. Firstly, what are the parameters that define the dynamics between informal groups of states and the UN Security Council? Secondly, what triggered the emergence and proliferation of informal groups? The question also takes into account the role of the P-5 in this development. Thirdly, what are the main factors that determine their informal influence in practice? This question involves a closer examination of who decides on both the composition of informal groups of states and which groups are recognized. Furthermore, it includes an analysis of how the work of informal arrangements is affected by structural conditions such as 'the current international climate' that affect patterns of (non-) cooperation between the major powers, or the great powers' interest in or benign neglect of a specific conflict situation. Finally, how do informal groups of states affect governance in and of the SC?

To explore these questions, the study adopts a predominantly rationalist theoretical approach.[18] Although such a framework has been designed by scholars to assess the actual workings of international institutions, this approach clearly has its limits. It is therefore my primary concern here to establish the importance of informal groups of states as empirical phenomena rather than following a single line of international relations theory. International Organisations (IOs) are complex settings, which cannot be analysed through the exclusive lens of the rationalist research agenda.[19] Such an approach would face the danger of what Walter Lippmann has called the murder of a beautiful theory by a gang of brutal facts.[20] Instead, it is preferable to develop a synergistic approach that employs theoretical strands in a complementary rather than competitive

---

[18] See Barbara Koremenos, Charles Lipson, and Duncan Snidal (eds.), *The Rational Design of International Institutions* (Cambridge: Cambridge University Press, 2004).

[19] For example, one may gain important insights by applying a constructivist approach treating IOs as bureaucracies to explain their autonomy, including their propensity for self-defeating behaviour; see Michael Barnett and Martha Finnemore, 'The Politics, Power, and Pathologies of International Organizations', *International Organization*, 53/4 (1999), 699–732; also Michael Barnett and Martha Finnemore, *Rules for the World: International Organizations in Global Politics* (Ithaca, NY: Cornell University Press, 2004).

[20] Walter Lippmann, *Public Opinion* (New York: Simon & Schuster, 1922), 10.

manner. I identify the causal mechanisms that contribute to the formation of informal groups of states by borrowing from insights of theories of agency and delegation. Agency theory helps to understand the development of institutions under conditions of systemic change, which alters agency relationships.[21] At the same time, and this is particularly relevant for explaining the workings of Groups of Friends of the UN Secretary-General, we also need to integrate a constructivist element in the analytical framework to fully appreciate the autonomous role of IOs' bureaucracies in this process, that is, the UN Secretariat.

In order to grasp the dynamics between informal groups of states and the SC, the analytical framework is further complemented by adapting Albert Hirschman's typology of exit, voice, and loyalty [22] Such an analytical framework provides us with explanatory leverage to analyse institutional effects of the UN SC under conditions of systemic change. Exit signifies the option of leaving the UN framework, either partially or completely, in order to escape from the structural constraints of the UN. Exit is partial if it occurs within the objectives of the UN, for example, by acting under the umbrella of an SC resolution. I illustrate this further in the case of Namibia. Exit is complete if it occurs outside UN objectives. This may take the form of (temporarily) bypassing the UN, as has been the case during the Kosovo and Iraq wars in 1999 and 2003 respectively. Voice constitutes the possibility for stakeholders in a conflict (as well as the UN Secretariat) to articulate their interests before the SC and to have informal influence on its decision-making. This is particularly relevant in those cases where stakeholders are not being represented on the Council, as I demonstrate in the case study on El Salvador. The decision to opt either for exit or voice is informed by the conflict setting. Underlying the notion of loyalty is the interest-based argument that achieving legitimacy eventually buttresses the position of (groups of) states. Loyalty displays four distinctive functions. First, it exerts a pull on UN member states towards compliance with the objectives of the Organization. Second, it may push those players acting outside the UN framework to seek (*post hoc*) legitimation by the UN SC. Third, it activates the voice option. Fourth, loyalty may contain the extent of exit and limit the damage created by the marginalization of the Organization.

---

[21] Robert O. Keohane and Lisa L. Martin, 'Institutional Theory as a Research Program', in Colin Elman and Miriam Fendius Elman (eds.), *Progress in International Relations Theory: Appraising the Field* (Cambridge, MA.: MIT Press, 2003), 102–4.
[22] See Albert O. Hirschman, *Exit, Voice, and Loyalty: Responses to Decline in Firms, Organizations, and States* (Cambridge, MA: Harvard University Press, 1970).

It is important to understand that this analytical framework differs from Hirschman's typology in one important respect. The classical exit option implies that if a customer is dissatisfied with the quality of the product or the service provided by a firm, then he or she may buy the product from a competitor. This is different in the case of the UN, as there are no peer competitors around. This is neither to suggest that the UN has a monopoly in maintaining international peace and security nor is this to argue that the Organization is the exclusive provider of legitimacy. However, with its nearly universal membership, the UN enjoys an unparalleled comparative advantage in providing a forum for achieving the broadest possible international acceptance for state action taken. Procedural legitimacy is one of the most important products the UN has to sell. The termination of UN membership is therefore an extremely unlikely option, as the political cost for implementation would be considerable.[23] Loyalty matters. In the absence of loyalty, exit would be essentially costless.

Informal Institutions: So What?

How do the findings of this book impact on our understanding of international relations theory? The answer to this question becomes a bit clearer when we analyse how international institutions cope with the problem of adjustment. As organization theory has illustrated, there are considerable constraints on initiating a formal adaptation process to respond to both changes in the relative power of states and the demands of a changed security environment.[24] Formal organizations reflect the institutionalization of the distribution of their member states' relative influence and power over governance at a certain point of time. Such institutionalization tends to result in the maintenance of the status quo, given the sunk costs and a high degree of risk aversion to initiate adaptations in response to changes in structural variables. While some scholars have taken the SC as an example to illustrate the stability of institutions,[25] others have claimed that the Council is an unstable system because there are no mechanisms to adapt its hierarchy of influence in response to

---

[23] Even the US intervention in Iraq in March 2003 constituted a case of temporary exit only.

[24] Robert O. Keohane, *After Hegemony: Cooperation and Discord in the World Political Economy* (Princeton, NJ: Princeton University Press, 1984), 100–3.

[25] Keohane and Martin, 100–2.

external changes.[26] We need to qualify both views. On the one hand, the SC is indeed affected by systemic change, with consequences for its decision-making, effectiveness, and representativeness. In effect, systemic change endangers organizational stability. However, does this inevitably lead to the conclusion that the Council is unstable? Not necessarily. Empirical evidence is much more diverse than these two propositions suggest. Informal groups of states provide a bridge to solve this puzzle. These groups may be instrumental in incrementally adapting the SC to systemic change without formally altering its structure and composition. At the same time, they may alleviate unanticipated effects.[27] In consequence, these *ad hoc* mechanisms may accommodate the potential to serve as a stabilizing element for international institutions in transition.

The book's findings that are related to the dynamics between informal groups of states and the SC, may force a re-examination of Kenneth Abbott's and Duncan Snidal's proposition that centralization and independence are key functional characteristics of IOs, which provide a powerful incentive for states to act through formal IOs.[28] Empirical evidence presents a much more complex picture. It demonstrates that informal groups of states in fact decentralize the workings of the SC, with the effect of ameliorating its structural deficiencies. Seen from the perspective of agency theory, those findings have a direct impact on our understanding of the nature of delegation to IOs, including the relationship between principal and agent.[29] The findings explain two puzzles: first, why states continue to delegate certain tasks and responsibilities to IOs despite the

---

[26] See Patrick A. McCarthy, 'Positionality, Tension, and Instability in the UN Security Council', *Global Governance*, 3/2 (1997), 147–69; and Glennon, 'Why the Security Council Failed'.

[27] On the problem of unanticipated effects of international institutions, see Giulio M. Gallarotti, 'The Limits of International Organization: Systematic Failure in the Management of International Relations', *International Organization* 45/2 (1991), 183–220.

[28] Kenneth W. Abbott and Duncan Snidal, 'Why States Act Through Formal International Organizations', *Journal of Conflict Resolution*, 42/1 (1998), 8.

[29] On the delegation of tasks to IOs and the related issue of IO autonomy, see, for example, Barnett and Finnemore, 'The Politics, Power, and Pathologies of International Organizations'; also Barnett and Finnemore, *Rules for the World*; Darren Hawkins, David A. Lake, Daniel Nielson, and Michael J. Tierney, *Delegation Under Anarchy: States, International Organizations, and Principal-Agent Theory*, Working Paper, Program on International Organization & Change. Available at: *http://www.internationalorganizations.org/Delegation_Under_Anarchyv_8.26.pdf*; Koremenos, Lipson, and Snidal (eds.), *The Rational Design of International Institutions*; Mark Pollack, 'Delegation, Agency, and Agenda-Setting in the European Community', *International Organization* 51/1 (1997), 99–134; and David A. Lake and Mathew D. McCubbins, *Delegation to International Agencies*, Working Paper (San Diego, CA: University of California, 2004). Available at: *http://weber.ucsd.edu/~dlake/Working%20Papers/mclake-delegation%20Draft%202.1.pdf*.

limits of the institutional problem-solving capacity; and, second, how 'delegation in reverse', that is, re-delegating tasks away from IOs to other agents such as informal groups of states, can ultimately enhance IO governance. We must therefore reconsider Abbott's and Snidal's claim that the functions of centralization and independence enhance efficiency.[30] Contrary to them, it is argued that decentralization through the establishment of informal groups of states allows UN member states to achieve policy goals that would be unattainable in a centralized setting. However, centralization still matters. Analysis of the dynamics between informal groups of states and the SC suggests that the main benefits of centralization lies in the procedural legitimation of member states' actions, which remains one of the most important functions of IOs.[31]

Andrew Hurrell has uncovered the inadequacy of traditional strategies of reconciling order and justice in international security, illustrating tensions at the systemic level between the need for concentrations of power and shared principles of justice.[32] He also pointed to the problem for weaker states in capturing the joint gains of institutions while keeping the powerful both engaged and constrained.[33] These tensions are epitomized in the dynamics that characterize the relationship between Concert-type arrangements such as Contact or Core Groups and formal IOs. In a nutshell, informal arrangements appear as a flexible mechanism, creating the possibility of exit from inflexibility by providing voice for stakeholders in conflicts. At the same time, those states serving as non-permanent members are likely to gain a greater voice via participation in informal groups than on the Council proper. They enhance their possibility of influence. Given the wide-ranging structural deficiencies of the UN to develop an effective crisis response, these groups may serve as a tool to close the operational gap resulting from those incapacities. In effect, they may be instrumental in preventing complete exit, that is, boycotting the Organization and conducting conflict management outside the UN frame-

---

[30] Abbott and Snidal, 'Why States Act Through Formal International Organizations', 9.

[31] It is important in this regard to distinguish between *procedural* and *output* legitimacy. While procedural legitimacy refers to the creation of broad acceptance through public discourse over and through the formal decision-making leading towards a specific course of action, output legitimacy refers to the creation of acceptance through the outcomes a course of action itself is able to produce.

[32] See Andrew Hurrell, 'Order and Justice in International Relations: What is at Stake?', in Rosemary Foot, John Lewis Gaddis, and Andrew Hurrell, (eds.), *Order and Justice in International Relations* (Oxford: Oxford University Press, 2003), 24–48.

[33] See Andrew Hurrell, 'Power, Institutions, and the Production of Inequality', in Michael Barnett and Raymond Duvall, (eds.), *Power in Global Governance* (Cambridge: Cambridge University Press, 2005), 33–58.

work. At the same time, the possibility of exit may eventually maintain the overall loyalty of member states towards the UN. In the last resort, informal groups of states are responses to UN decline, whereas exit and voice appear as the cheaper option than a complete overhaul of the Organization's foundations, that is the revision of the UN Charter. The enlightened use of those groups by UN member states in cooperation with the Secretariat may eventually strengthen the crisis response capabilities of the UN.

The Structure of the Book

To explore the issues outlined previously the study has been divided into two parts. Part I opens with defining parameters of the relationship between informal groups of states and the SC. The first part of the study traces the process of the emergence and proliferation of informal groups, setting forth the main arguments of the book. Although these groupings have been convened for different reasons and under varying circumstances, there are patterns to the phenomenon. The evidence of these groupings has certain implications for SC governance, which are summarized as hypotheses in the concluding chapter of the first part. Part I places informal groups into the historical context of UN crisis response, elaborating on their emergence in the 1950s, and their proliferation in the post-Cold War era. The set of parameters that emerge from Part I provides the analytical framework for setting up a structured and focused comparison of specific cases in the second part of the study.

Part II tests the main arguments by adopting the analytical framework of exit, voice, and loyalty. It illustrates how conflict settings inform the decision to opt for either exit or voice. The second part adduces empirical evidence to support the argument of the study. Part II elaborates in detail on the questions of 'When do informal groups matter?' and 'How do they matter?' In order to demonstrate the significance of these groups, analysis must focus on instances that reflect variations in the structural conditions under which *ad hoc* groupings operate. In general, the selection of cases must reflect, firstly, geographical variety. Secondly, they must include varying types of conflicts and varying degrees of conflict intensity. Thirdly, cases must also reflect a varying degree of direct UN involvement at the levels of the Secretariat and the Council. Fourthly, they must reflect temporal variety, involving crises that occurred before, during, and after the breakdown of the bipolar system. In particular, the selection of case studies reflects a special interest in precedent cases. The cases of Namibia and El

Salvador constitute precedent cases that illustrate the contextual and situational parameters contributing to the establishment of the Contact Group and the Group of Friends of the Secretary-General respectively. Both informal devices served as a model that would be applied in subsequent crisis settings. The Kosovo case illustrates structural conditions under which the SC had to operate at the end of the 1990s. The crisis demonstrated the changing role of the SC, with the functions of diplomatic problem-solving and collective legitimation becoming separate from one another. The Kosovo case demonstrates that the UN Security Council, even in those cases when it has become bypassed, continues to exert a strong pull on the players to seek *post hoc* legitimation for actions taken outside the UN framework.

The empirical agenda entails the examination of periods where the perception of the potential and limits of the UN varied significantly. The cases allow in-depth study of the role and performance of informal groups operating under varying structural conditions of conflict settings that affected ways and means of crisis response, such as patterns of cooperation between great powers and the degree to which the UN became involved in the resolution of conflicts. Despite variations in geography, type and intensity of conflict, time, and UN involvement, the conflict settings share the common pattern that they had major regional implications, which fostered the willingness among stakeholders to coordinate peace-making efforts.

Participation of informal groups in conflict settings is analysed with specific regard to their impact on SC governance. The cases illustrate how states without a seat on the Council may benefit from a certain kind of de facto involvement in decision-making by virtue of their influence on and informal consultations with Council and Secretariat members. While membership on the Council provides the possibility to shape the formalized processes that guide the activities of the Council, participation in *ad hoc* groupings offers a platform to exert influence on an informal level. SC governance is defined by the interaction of both formal and informal processes. Such processes may be either complementary, or they may stand in stiff competition. With the Council as the common point of reference, the comparative analysis allows us to extract distributions and patterns of influence revealed in the three case studies.

The first case study examines the role of the Group of Three and the Western Contact Group in negotiating an agreement for the independence of Namibia in 1990. The emergence of the Contact Group coincided with the non-permanent Council membership of Canada and the Federal

Republic of Germany in 1977–8. At this time, several General Assembly resolutions had been adopted under massive pressure from the Organization of African Unity (OAU), criticizing the attitude of Western countries towards apartheid in general, and their stance towards the situation in Namibia and Rhodesia in particular. From this perspective, the joint activities of the five Western members of the Council—Canada, France, Germany, the United Kingdom, and the United States—may therefore be seen as an exit strategy to develop a constructive response to (and to escape from) that pressure. The coincidence of five like-minded Western countries serving on the Council opened the gate for a concerted approach. The case is worth considering especially for four reasons. Firstly, the conflict sheds some light on the working of informal groups of states well before the breakdown of the bipolar system, differing in this regard from the other case studies that fall into the transitional or post-bipolar period. Secondly, the UN had tested several approaches over the years to grapple with the long-standing problem, including the establishment of the so-called Group of Three, which constituted a de facto group of friends, without using that label.[34] Given the lack of success, this grouping had discontinued mediation efforts at the end of 1973. Analysing its failure may offer some additional insights as to why the Western Contact Group turned out to be more successful from 1977 onwards. Thirdly, the multi-party response of an informal *ad hoc* grouping of able and willing countries in cooperation with the UN, working *outside* the UN framework but within the objectives defined by the SC, stands as an early model for using the disparate capacities of the UN and its member states towards a common goal. Fourthly, it amply illustrates the difficult relationship between the US hegemon and its Western partners. The re-delegation of tasks to informal arrangements operating within the objectives of a resolution or mandate of the Council but outside its formal structures may help to capture the joint gains of the institution while keeping the powerful both engaged and constrained. Such re-delegation may help to manage the relationship between hegemon, international institution, and weaker states.[35] At the same time, and this is particularly prevalent in the Namibia case, weaker states may expose a high degree of acquiescence to the policies of the hegemon to avoid its defection.

The second case study focuses on the Group of Friends of the Secretary General on El Salvador, which was the first group operating under such a

---

[34] Initially, the Group of Three comprised Argentina, Somalia, and Yugoslavia.
[35] For an astute analysis of this relationship, see Hurrell, 'Power, Institutions, and the Production of Inequality'.

label.[36] Contrary to the first case study, where the Western Contact Group led the negotiation process *outside* the UN framework, in the case of El Salvador, the UN took over the leading role as intermediary to reach a negotiated political solution to the conflict. Consequently, the process rested firmly *inside* the UN framework. Established in December 1989, the informal group served as a means at the disposal of the Secretary-General and his representatives to support the UN's efforts to mediate an agreement between the conflicting parties, that is the government of El Salvador and the rebel forces, the Frente Farabundo Martí para la Liberación Nacional (FMLN). The *ad hoc* group of like-minded countries was needed to enhance his voice vis-à-vis the SC. The Group of Friends was instrumental to balance against the might of the permanent members of the SC, and the United States in particular. The Secretary-General, as the chief administrative officer of the Organization, has only very limited capabilities on his own to pressure the parties to act. The Friends of the Secretary-General on El Salvador somewhat revived the concept of the advisory committees that had been established in the 1950s and 1960s. The case study elaborates in detail on the reasons why such a concept re-emerged in 1989. The breakdown of the bipolar system created the permissive political context for a leading role of the UN, with the United States and the Soviet Union as guardians of the process in the background. Given the relative success of the Group of Friends of the Secretary-General on El Salvador, the concept became a model that was applied to other crisis settings. It raised the question of the extent to which the concept can be applied as a ready-made strategy to other conflict situations.[37]

The third case study concentrates on the performance of the Quint,[38] the G-8,[39] and the Troika[40] during the Kosovo war in 1999. The Kosovo

[36] The group comprised Colombia, Mexico, Spain, and Venezuela, later joined by the United States. At that stage, the Friends became known as the '4+1'.

[37] Looked at from the perspective of international relations theory, this case sheds light on the role of international organizations as active agents. It illustrates the tensions between what people want and what states want, which has been a serious shortcoming in the work of international relations scholars thus far; see Barnett and Finnemore, *Rules for the World*. At the same time, the case shows that the constructivist and principal-agent analyses are mutually enforcing rather than exclusive.

[38] The Quint comprised the five key allies within the North Atlantic Treaty Organization (NATO), namely, France, Germany, Italy, the United Kingdom, and the United States. They coordinated positions and cooperated to maintain the coherence of the Atlantic Alliance.

[39] The G-8 comprises Canada, France, Germany, Italy, Japan, the United Kingdom, the United States, and Russia.

[40] The Troika consisted of then President of Finland Martti Ahtisaari as EU Envoy, Russian Envoy Victor Chernomyrdin, and then US Deputy Secretary of State Strobe Talbott. The trilateral diplomacy was intended to close the various gaps that existed between efforts made by the European Union, the G-8, NATO, and the United Nations.

case fostered a discussion that circled around the question of which institution is in charge of international peace and security.[41] Furthermore, the question whether informal groups are complementing or competing with SC governance stands at the centre of the analysis. The Kosovo case is an extreme example that illustrates the devolution of the substance of crisis management to informal settings. The G-8 and the Troika conducted conflict management *outside* the UN framework on the diplomatic track, while NATO sustained the pressure with air strikes on the military track. The use of force occurred notably without explicit SC authorization, since the Council was, or appeared to be, deadlocked at that time. Despite a complete shift of governance to the G-8, Quint, and the Troika, which reflected a marginalization of the SC, it was however the prospect of re-involving the UN that turned out to be a sine qua non for bringing the Kosovo war to an end. The informal agreement upon a UN resolution on the G-8 level, formally adopted by the Council as SC Resolution 1244, appeared as a kind of *post hoc* ratification of action that had already been taken outside the UN framework. The importance of the SC as legitimizer of state action therefore has to come under scrutiny. Furthermore, the Kosovo case illustrates what various informal groups can contribute at different stages to the resolution of a conflict. While the G-8 and the Troika played the leading role in finding a diplomatic formula to end the war, implementation of the agreement became embedded in a much larger process, as epitomized in the Group of Friends of Kosovo. The Friends of Kosovo should assist the Secretary-General in, and secure the broadest possible support for, implementing the civilian part of the far-reaching mandate entrusted to the UN. Secretary-General Kofi Annan had established such a group shortly after the adoption of SC Resolution 1244. The analysis of the Friends of Kosovo helps to understand how this informal grouping facilitated the re-involvement of the UN to become engaged in the transition of the Kosovo conflict from war to peace.

The final part provides a summary of the causes of informal groups of states and their effects on the workings of the SC.

With regard to the case studies it is important to note that the focus of the analysis rests less upon the various crises per se but rather on the influence of informal groups on the decision-making process of the SC at UN Headquarters in New York. The focus rests therefore upon the dynamics between

---

[41] See Winrich Kühne and Jochen Prantl (eds.), *The Security Council and the G8 in the New Millennium: Who is in Charge of International Peace and Security?*, Report of the 5th International Berlin Workshop (Ebenhausen, Germany: Research Institute for International Affairs, 2000).

informal arrangements and the SC rather than the role of the informal groups as part of the respective negotiations strategies. Although a broad picture of the conflict situation on the ground is clearly important, the book is primarily concerned with the effect of informal groups on SC governance. The analysis does not therefore provide an in-depth examination of every single event related to the selected crises. Domestic policies of the key actors are also of secondary concern. There are a considerable number of studies examining the role of the UN as an international institution before and after the breakdown of the bipolar system.[42] Those publications include analyses on the procedure, decision-making processes, and historical development of the SC.[43] The focus on the role and performance of the Council within specific crises tends to remain underexposed.[44] Only a few studies examine the interaction between Groups of Friends or Contact Groups and the Council, including their effects on SC governance.[45] Various articles and papers point at the general importance

---

[42] See Inis L. Claude, *Swords into Plowshares. The Problems and Progress of International Organization*, 3rd edn. (New York: Random House, 1964); Mahdi Elmandjra, *The United Nations System: An Analysis* (London: Faber and Faber, 1973); H.G. Nicholas, *The United Nations as a Political Institution*, 5th edn. (Oxford: Oxford University Press, 1975); Karen A. Mingst and Margaret P. Karns, *The United Nations in the post-Cold War era*, 2nd edn. (Oxford: Westview Press, 2000); Adam Roberts and Benedict Kingsbury (eds.), *United Nations, Divided World. The UN's Roles in International Relations*, 2nd edn. (Oxford: Clarendon Press, 1993); Adam Roberts and Benedict Kingsbury, *Presiding over a Divided World. Changing UN Roles, 1945–1993*, International Peace Academy, Occasional Paper Series (Boulder, CO: Lynne Rienner, 1994); Bruno Simma (ed.), *The Charter of the United Nations: A Commentary*, 2nd edn. (Oxford: Oxford University Press, 2002); Jean E. Krasno (ed.), *The United Nations: Confronting the Challenges of a Global Society* (Boulder, CO.: Lynne Rienner, 2004); Thomas G. Weiss, David P. Forsythe, and Roger A. Coate, *The United Nations and Changing World Politics*, 4th edn. (Boulder, CO: Westview Press, 2004).

[43] Those studies on the politics of the UN Security Council and its decision-making processes include Bailey and Daws, *The Procedure of the UN Security Council*; Sydney D. Bailey, *Voting in the Security Council* (Bloomington, IN: Indiana University Press, 1969); Francis Delon, 'La concertation entre les membres permanents du Conseil de sécurité', *Annuaire français de droit international*, 39 (1993), 53–69; Hague Academy of International Law (ed.), *The Development of the Role of the Security Council* (Dordrecht, The Netherlands: Martinus Nijhoff, 1993); Richard Hiscocks, *The Security Council: A Study in Adolescence* (London: Longman, 1973); David Malone, 'The Security Council in the post-Cold War era,' in Muthia Alagappa and Takashi Inoguchi (eds.), *International Security Management and the United Nations* (Tokyo/New York/ Paris: United Nations University Press, 1999), 394–408; Alexandre Novosseloff, 'Le processus de décision au sein du Conseil de sécurité des Nations Unies: Une approche historique', *Revue d'histoire diplomatique*, 109/3 (1995), 273–304; Michael C. Wood, 'Security Council Working Methods and Procedure: Recent Development', *The International and Comparative Law Quarterly*, 45/1 (1996), 150–61.

[44] A notable exception is the recently edited volume by David M. Malone (ed.), *The UN Security Council: From the Cold War to the 21st Century* (Boulder, CO.: Lynne Rienner, 2004).

[45] David Malone describes in some detail the activities of the Friends of the Secretary-General on Haiti and their interaction with decision-making in the Council; see David Malone, *Decision-Making in the UN Security Council: The Case of Haiti, 1990–1997* (Oxford: Oxford University Press, 1998); see also the general account on the role of Groups of Friends by Teresa

of informal groups, either as a diplomatic device that supports efforts by the UN to manage the making of peace on a consensual basis[46] or as a means to coordinate strategies vis-à-vis the parties and the implementing agencies in the crucial stage of the implementation of peace agreements.[47] Furthermore, there is a remarkable lacuna of academic work that examines the performance of informal groups in specific crisis settings.[48] As for the case studies, several publications cover to a greater or lesser extent the involvement of the UN in Namibia,[49] El Salvador.[50] and Kosovo.[51] Yet there is no comparative analysis of the various efforts of informal

Whitfield, 'Groups of Friends', in Malone (ed.), *The UN Security Council*, 311–24; for an analysis of the causes and effects of informal groups of states on SC governance, see Jochen Prantl, 'Informal Groups of States and the UN Security Council', *International Organization*, 59/3 (2005), 559–92.

[46] For example, see Michael Doyle, 'War Making and Peace Making: The United Nations' Post-Cold War Record', in Chester A. Crocker, Fen Osler Hampson, and Pamela Aall, (eds.), *Turbulent Peace: The Challenges of Managing International Conflict* (Washington, DC: United States Institute of Peace Press, 2001), 529–60.

[47] See Stephen John Stedman, Donald Rothchild, and Elizabeth M. Cousens (eds.), *Ending Civil Wars: The Implementation of Peace Agreements* (Boulder, CO: Lynne Rienner, 2002); Bruce D. Jones, *The Challenges of Strategic Coordination: Containing Opposition and Sustaining Implementation of Peace Agreements in Civil Wars*, IPA Policy Paper Series on Peace Implementation (New York: International Peace Academy, June 2001); Stephen John Stedman, *Implementing Peace Agreements in Civil Wars: Lessons and Recommendations for Policymakers*, IPA Policy Paper Series on Peace Implementation (New York: International Peace Academy, May 2001).

[48] Notable exceptions are, *inter alia*, Alvaro de Soto, 'Ending Violent Conflict in El Salvador,' in Chester Crocker, Fen Osler Hampson, and Pamela Aall (eds.), *Herding Cats. Multiparty Mediation in a Complex World* (Washington, DC: United States Institute of Peace Press, 1999), 345–85; Michael W. Doyle, Ian Johnstone, and Robert Orr (eds.), *Multidimensional Peacekeeping: Lessons from Cambodia and El Salvador* (New York: International Peace Academy, 1995); Vivienne Jabri, *Mediating Conflict: Decision-making and Western Intervention in Namibia* (Manchester: Manchester University Press, 1990); Margaret P. Karns, 'Ad Hoc Multilateral Diplomacy: The United States, the Contact Group, and Namibia', *International Organization*, 41/1 (1987), 93–123; David M. Malone, *Decision-Making in the UN Security Council*; Stewart Eldon, 'East Timor', in Malone (ed.), *The UN Security Council*, 551–74.

[49] See G. R. Berridge, 'Diplomacy and the Angola/Namibia accords,' *International Affairs*, 65/3 (1989), 463–79; Chester Crocker, *High Noon in South Africa: Making Peace in a Rough Neighborhood* (New York/London: W. W. Norton, 1992); Jabri, *Mediating Conflict*; Karns, 'Ad Hoc Multilateral Diplomacy'; Herbert Weil and Mathew Braham (eds.), *The Namibian Peace Process: Implications and Lessons for the Future* (Freiburg: Arnold Bergstraesser Institut, 1994).

[50] See Alvaro de Soto, 'Ending Violent Conflict in El Salvador'; Michael W. Doyle, Ian Johnstone and Robert Orr (eds.), *Multidimensional Peacekeeping*; Ian Johnstone, *Rights and Reconciliation: UN Strategies in El Salvador* (London: Lynne Rienner, 1995); Tricia Juhn, *Negotiating peace in El Salvador: Civil-Military Relations and the Conspiracy to End the War* (Basingstoke: Macmillan, 1998); Barbara Messing, 'El Salvador', in Melanie C. Greenberg, John H. Barton, and Margaret E. McGuinness (eds.), *Words Over War: Mediation and Arbitration to Prevent Deadly Conflict* (Oxford: Rowman & Littlefield, 2000), 161–81.

[51] See Albrecht Schnabel and Ramesh Thakur (eds.), *Kosovo and the Challenge of Humanitarian Intervention: Selective Indignation, Collective Action, and International Citizenship* (Tokyo: United Nations University Press, 2000); Madeleine Albright, *Madam Secretary: A Memoir* (New York: Miramax Books, 2003); Strobe Talbott, *The Russia Hand* (New York: Random House, 2002); Ivo H. Daalder and Michael E. O'Hanlon, *Winning Ugly: NATO's War to Save*

groups of states within selected crises proper.[52] It is hoped that this book contributes to fill the gap.

Kosovo (Washington DC: Brookings Institution Press, 2000); Independent International Commission on Kosovo, *The Kosovo Report* (Oxford: Oxford University Press, 2000); Günther Joetze, *Der letzte Krieg in Europa? Das Kosovo und die deutsche Politik* (Munich: DVA, 2001); Oleg Levitin, 'Inside Moscow's Kosovo Muddle', *Survival*, 42/1 (2000), 130–40; Adam Roberts, 'NATO's "Humanitarian War" over Kosovo', *Survival*, 41/3 (1999), 102–23; Marc Weller, *The Crisis in Kosovo 1989–1999, International Documents and Analysis*, 1 (Cambridge: Documents & Analysis Publishing, 1999).

[52] As for the Groups of Friends, Jean Krasno has contributed a paper to the final report of the Carnegie Commission of Preventing Deadly Conflict (1997) that offers a useful starting point in this regard, see Jean E. Krasno, *The Group of Friends of the Secretary-General: A Useful Diplomatic Tool* (Washington, DC: Carnegie Commission on Preventing Deadly Conflict, 1996); see also more recently Jochen Prantl and Jean E. Krasno, 'Informal Groups of Member States', in *The United Nations: Confronting the Challenges of a Global Society*, 311–57; on the Groups of Friends, see also the chapter by Whitfield, 'Groups of Friends'.

Part I

Informal Groups of States and the Security Council: Grasping the Dynamics

Sed quis custodiet ipsos custodes?

Juvenal (*Satirae*, VI: 347–8)

'The question "Who governs?" directly implies the question "Who is likely to benefit most and who least from a particular form of government?" '[1] The notion of governance, as it is used in the following, encompasses both formal and informal processes and institutions defining the activities of a group.[2] Informal groups of states shall therefore be understood as part and parcel of governance of the UN Security Council (SC). The central aim of Part I is to provide a deeper understanding of SC governance by exploring the relationship between informal groups and the Council under Cold War and post-Cold War conditions. It has a twofold task: firstly, tracing the process that led to the emergence and proliferation of informal settings; and secondly, establishing an analytical framework that allows grasping the dynamics between informal groups of states and the SC. In order to understand the rationale behind the formation of *ad hoc* groupings, Chapter 1 takes a closer look at the institutional setting of the United Nations (UN). Underlying is the assumption that the SC can best be described as a *Janus*-faced structure of both an open system and a closed shop. This notion reflects its sensitivity towards external change while the restrictive provisions of the Charter constrain the possibilities of formal adaptation. Looking into the history of UN crisis response reveals the development of certain variations on the collective security scheme as originally envisaged by the UN Charter. These variants include the tendency to utilize (*a*) regional military alliances (or coalitions of able and willing countries) for multilateral action, (*b*) the delegation of enforcement powers from the SC to (coalitions of) states, or (*c*) the establishment of peacekeeping operations under UN authority.[3] Chapters 2 and 3 introduce informal groups of states as a fourth variation, analysing their emergence in the 1950s and proliferation in the post-bipolar era. Chapter 4 draws some conclusions by

---

[1] Cox and Jacobson, 'The Framework for Inquiry', 371.
[2] See Keohane and Nye, 'Introduction', 12.
[3] See Roberts, 'The United Nations: Variants of Collective Security , 309–36.

fitting the findings into the wider perspective of SC governance and institutional change.

What triggered the emergence of informal groups of states? Why did they proliferate in the 1990s? How can the dynamics between informal arrangements and SC best be captured? How do informal groups affect SC governance? Part I offers five central arguments. Firstly, the emergence of advisory committees in the 1950s has to be seen against the background of great power tensions in the SC. When the lack of unanimity of the permanent members prevented the Council from assuming its responsibilities according to Article 24, the General Assembly took charge by recommending collective measures. When the SC however was able to act, its resolutions and mandates entrusted to the Secretary-General often reflected a political compromise based on the lowest common denominator among its members. Especially the two advisory committees established in the context of crises at the Suez Canal (1956–67) and in the Congo (1960–4) reflect the different political background against which these committees operated. With the establishment of the first UN peacekeeping force—United Nations Emergency Force (UNEF I)—governance shifted from the paralysed SC to the General Assembly and the Secretary-General respectively. The application of the Uniting-for-Peace procedure during the Suez crisis affected Council governance in a way that increased the reluctance of permanent members to cast their veto in order to keep the operation under the control of this body. At the same time, the price for preventing a stalemate was the agreement upon ambiguous diplomatic formulas that left the clarification of the mandate to the Secretary-General. Confronted with the challenge not to antagonize the great powers in the execution of the delegated authorities by the General Assembly or the SC, the Secretary-General aimed at reducing his vulnerability by establishing advisory bodies, designed to share the burden of implementing the mandates entrusted to him by the principal organs of the Organization.

Secondly, the establishment of UNEF II (1973–9) reshifted governance from the General Assembly and the Secretary-General back to the Council. With the SC returning into the driving seat, the rationale for constituting advisory bodies as a means to assist the Secretary-General in the performance of his functions faded. The clarification of the peacekeeping doctrine and the adoption of clearer mandates alleviated the pressure on the establishment of further informal *ad hoc* groupings.

Thirdly, the proliferation of Groups of Friends and Contact Groups in the post-bipolar era must be analysed in the context of the mounting pressure on the UN and the international community to respond to more and more complex crises than ever before. Opting for exit or voice, as epitomized in the establishment of those informal devices, occurred in response to systemic change.

Fourthly, given the current architecture of SC governance, Groups of Friends and Contact Groups appear as agents of incremental change, without formally changing the constitutional foundation of the Organization. Employing the exit or voice option may close the operational and participatory gap growing out of the multiple strategic incapacities that prevent the Council from formulating an effective response to crisis situations.

Fifthly, it will be argued that the post-Cold War era has permitted a political context that fostered devolution of the substance of crisis management to informal groups of states, whereas the SC provides—at least in most cases—the form, that is the legitimation for state action. The functions of diplomacy and its collective legitimation become decoupled. Loyalty is exerting a pull on those players acting outside the UN framework to seek (*post hoc*) approval by the SC. Underlying this analysis is the interest-based argument that achieving legitimacy eventually buttresses the position of (groups of) states.

1

Janus-faced Structure of the Security Council: Open System and Closed Shop

The UN Security Council (SC) can best be described as a *Janus*-faced structure of both an open system and a closed shop, given its sensitivity towards changes in the international system while facing considerable constraints to adapt itself internally given the restrictive provisions of the UN Charter. This chapter places informal groups of states into the wider context of the SC's so-called 'informal consultations other than consultations of the whole'.[1] In order to address the *Janus*-faced structure of the Council, it proceeds on three levels of analysis, examining (a) the role of great powers in international organizations, (b) the role and function of the SC according to the Charter of the UN, and (c) the 'constitutional practice' of the Council, elaborating on certain variants of the collective security scheme as envisioned in the Charter.

Governance in the SC comprises the following dimensions. Firstly, it involves the formal process of decision-making according to the UN Charter and the Council's Provisional Rules of Procedure. Secondly, it involves the actual process of decision-making that is characterized by the established practice of holding informal consultations (of the whole) before decisions are being taken in formal meetings of the Council. With no official records kept, they form an essential part of the SC's the

---

[1] Bailey and Daws, *The Procedure of the UN Security Council*, 6. Although the term is vague, it may serve as a useful distinction between the Council's consultations of the whole, taking place in the consultation room opposite the SC Chamber, and the various other bi- and multilateral informal meetings outside this Chamber, involving both members and non-members of the Council.

decision-making.[2] Neither the Charter nor the Rules of Procedure refer to those meetings. And finally, it involves the informal consultations other than consultations of the whole, under which informal groups of states may be gathered.

The SC is the master of its Rules of Procedures, with a plethora of possibilities to convene bi- and multilateral meetings on an informal level, as Davidson Nicol has succinctly summarized:

> If bilateral they may involve the President and one other party who may or may not be a member of the Security Council, they may involve two members of the Security Council, or they may involve one member of the Security Council and one other party who may or may not be a member of the Security Council. If multilateral, they may involve the President and some other members of the Council; the President and some non-members of the Council; the President and parties to a dispute; the President and representatives of some regional groups; the President and Secretariat officials possibly including the Secretary-General; the President and representatives of liberation movements; or they may involve the President and a mix of two or more of these categories. They may involve one or more members of the Security Council and persons in one or more of the above categories with or without inclusion of the President.[3]

As these examples illustrate, members and non-members of the SC including the Secretariat consult and coordinate their policies in various informal settings, though some formulas tend to be more institutionalized than others.[4] These include regular meetings between the five permanent members of the Council (P-5)[5] or the three Western permanent members (P-3)[6] respectively. Other groupings are the Non-Aligned Security Council Caucus, that is, countries of the Non-Aligned Movement (NAM)[7] elected to the Council. Furthermore, in 1994, the NAM and the Group of 77 (G-77),[8] another coordinating mechanism of developing countries, established a

---

[2] 'The informals are virtually formal', is the assessment of the representative of an elected member serving on the Council in the period of 2000–1, UN Doc S/PV.4445, 21 December 2001.

[3] Davidson Nicol, *The United Nations Security Council: Towards Greater Effectiveness* (New York: UNITAR 1982), 77.

[4] See Anthony Aust, 'The Procedure and Practice of the Security Council Today', in Hague Academy of International Law (ed.), *Peacekeeping and Peacebuilding: The Development of the Role of the Security Council* (Dordrecht, The Netherlands: Martinus Nijhoff, 1993), 365–74.

[5] The permanent members of the SC include China, France, Russia, the United Kingdom, and the United States.

[6] The P-3 comprises France, the United Kingdom, and the United States.

[7] The NAM comprises 115 members. The movement provides a platform for representing the interests of developing countries. Available at: www.nam.gov.za/background/background.htm.

[8] The G-77 owes its name to the seventy-seven founding members that established the organization in 1964. Being the largest gathering of developing countries in the UN, the membership of the G-77 has increased to 133 countries. Available at: www.g77.org

Joint Coordinating Committee to enhance the cooperation between the two groupings in New York. Those members on the Council that neither belong to the P-5 nor the Non-aligned constitute the so-called Non-non-aligned group. Given the fluid composition of this loose gathering, the Non-non-aligned does not constitute a group as such, although countries do cooperate on certain matters. Regional organizations such as the European Union (EU), the African Union (AU),[9] and the Organization of the Islamic Conference (OIC) may coordinate their policies on matters under consideration in the Council. Respective members bring their joint positions into the Council's decision-making process. The EU in particular has established a high level of cooperation and coordination, even though France and the United Kingdom have been quite reluctant to comply fully with the words and spirit of Article 19.2 of the Treaty of European Union (TEU). It requires them to 'ensure the defence of the positions and the interests of the Union, without prejudice to their responsibilities under the provisions of the United Nations Charter'. The coherence of EU member states tends to be much stronger on General Assembly than SC affairs.

Informal meetings of the SC may also convene in a rather *ad hoc* setting. These include consultations under the so-called Arria formula, named after Diego Arria, the then Venezuelan Ambassador who devised it and chaired the first meeting under this format in 1993. It is an informal arrangement under which Council members and non-members may gather. Having proliferated over recent years, meetings involve furthermore consultations with non-state actors being party to a conflict, also with Non-governmental Organizations (NGOs) such as Amnesty International, Human Rights Watch, Oxfam, or *Médecins sans Frontières*, or various think tanks such as the International Crisis Group or the International Peace Academy.[10] Other *ad hoc* meetings may include informal consultations of so-called drafting groups, convening on expert level, to negotiate the specific wording of a pending Council resolution or Presidential statement.[11]

Groups of Friends, Contact and Core Groups may be summarized under the rubric of '*ad hoc* settings'.[12] However, Groups of Friends and

---

[9] In 2002, the AU replaced the Organization of African Unity (OAU). The AU held its inaugural summit in Durban, South Africa, 28 June–10 July 2002.

[10] See Bailey and Daws, *The Procedure of the UN Security Council*, 73 *et seq.*; see also the useful summary available on the website of the Global Policy Forum, New York. Available at: www.globalpolicy.org/security/mtgsetc/ arria.htm.

[11] See Hans-Peter Kaul, 'Arbeitsweise und informelle Verfahren des Sicherheitsrates: Beobachtungen eines Unterhändlers', *Vereinte Nationen*, 46/1 (1998), 11.

[12] See Bailey and Daws, *The Procedure of the UN Security Council*, 72.

Contact Groups obviously differ from the above-mentioned informal groupings in some important aspects. By name, Groups of Friends are first and foremost created to support the implementation of peacemaking and peacekeeping mandates entrusted to the Secretary-General, while Contact Groups are self-selected *ad hoc* coalitions of able and willing countries, working separately from the Council. This broad division line is however blurred when looking at empirical evidence. Both groupings may meet away from UN headquarters on various levels in different compositions. Since one of their primary functions is helping to manage 'the making of peace on a consensual basis',[13] they seem to form—at first sight—a different category. However, in their specific functions as agenda-setter of the Council or drafting group, preparing SC resolutions and Presidential Statements, they still fit under the heading of SC *ad hoc* settings.

Pointing to the various possibilities of informal meetings, bi- and multilateral settings of members and non-members of the Council, demonstrates that Groups of Friends and Contact Groups are by no means exclusive instruments to exert influence on SC decision-making. However, the analysis will elaborate on the circumstances that triggered the emergence of informal groups of states and the reasons why these groupings have gained considerable importance in the post-Cold War era. Placing informal groups of states into the wider context of SC *ad hoc* settings opens the gate to a closer examination of the degree to which those groupings complement or compete with Council action. Such analysis will set the parameter to define the answer to the question of 'Who governs?'.

1.1 Role of Great Powers

Since the end of the eighteenth century, it seems to be a common pattern for great powers after the cessation of major wars to remodel the international order according to their lessons learned, aimed at preventing the outbreak of future conflicts.[14] The search for international order after World War II continued this tradition. However, it differed in one

---

[13] Doyle, 'War Making and Peace Making', 540.

[14] See Francis Harry Hinsley, 'Peace and War in Modern Times', in Raimo Väyrynen (ed.), *The Quest for Peace. Transcending Collective Violence and War among Societies, Cultures and States* (London: Sage, 1987), 63–79.

important respect. While the Covenant of the League of Nations differentiated between *bellum iustum* and *bellum iniustum*, the Charter of the UN tried to contain the *ius ad bellum* via several provisions and, for the first time, outlawed war as a means of policy.[15]

The maintenance of international peace and security should be one of the primary functions of the UN in general and the SC in particular. Founded on the belief that aggression could be countered by the collective will of powerful states, the UN founding fathers perceived the Organization as the centre of military action, or at least its legitimation. However, the functions allocated to the UN never implied that the Organization would have a monopoly on the use of force. The possibility of casting a veto should involve the five members of the former Grand Alliance (namely China, France, the United Kingdom, the United States, and Russia) only in those conflicts where they were not immediately affected, for example in disputes between smaller states.[16]

Furthermore, it had been clear from the very beginning that the UN could work effectively only if the five victorious powers of World War II were able and willing to cooperate in the future. Their solidarity has been, therefore, a precondition to the functioning of the SC. Writing his final report in 1945 on the UN Conference on International Organization in San Francisco, US Secretary of State Edward Stettinius stated: 'It was taken as axiomatic at Dumbarton Oaks, and continued to be the view of the Sponsoring Powers at San Francisco, that the cornerstone for world security is the unity of those nations which formed the core of the grand alliance against the Axis'.[17]

From this point of view, the conception rejuvenated the idea of the nineteenth century great power concert.[18] Furthermore, it reflected President Franklin Delano Roosevelt's vaguely defined concept of the four world policemen who should have the primary responsibility for maintaining and enforcing international peace and security.[19] Ideas on the

---

[15] The right of individual and collective defence as later embodied in Article 51 remained unaffected; ibid., 67.

[16] See Francis Harry Hinsley, *Power and the Pursuit of Peace: Theory and Practice in the History of Relations between States* (Cambridge: Cambridge University Press, 1963), 340.

[17] Quoted in James S. Sutterlin, 'The Past as Prologue', in Bruce Russett (ed.), *The Once and Future Security Council* (New York: St Martin's Press, 1997), 3.

[18] See Herbert George Nicholas, *The United Nations as a Political Institution*, 5th edn. (Oxford: Oxford University Press, 1975), 19.

[19] See Georg Schild, *Bretton Woods and Dumbarton Oaks. American Economic and Political Postwar Planning in the Summer of 1944* (Basingstoke: Macmillan, 1995), 22; Townsend Hoopes and Douglas Brinkley, *FDR and the Creation of the U.N.* (New Haven, CT: Yale University Press, 1997), 43–54.

conception of the SC had already been developed during World War II, whereby the overall approach appeared much more down-to-earth than the somewhat lofty model of the League of Nations. It emphasized the political responsibility of the great powers and their allocated function to maintain order.[20] At the same time, it reflected the lessons learned of a misguided policy, as Edward Hallett Carr has observed in his analysis of international relations between 1919 and 1939:

Periods of crisis have been common in history. The characteristic feature of the twenty years between 1919 and 1939 was the abrupt descent from the visionary hopes of the first decade to the grim despair of the second, from a utopia which took little account of reality to a reality from which every element of utopia was rigorously excluded.[21]

One might conclude, consequently, that the fine-tuned balance between utopia and reality ought to be the defining moment for the future development of the UN SC. On the one hand, the Charter of the UN formulated high hopes 'to save succeeding generations from the scourge of war'.[22] On the other hand, it acknowledged the fact that if there should be any realistic chance to live up to those high expectations the great powers had to be granted special privileges in order to keep engaged. In case of an institutional deadlock, the Charter offered, furthermore, the possibility of exit via the right of individual or collective defence to conduct conflict management outside the Organization: 'Article 51 "turned the veto inside out"...by recognizing that a majority of powers cannot be prevented from cooperating to pursue *outside* an international organization a policy which the unanimity rule prevents them from pursuing *inside* the organization'.[23]

Based upon this interpretation of Article 51, one might argue that such cooperation may include the building of *ad hoc* coalitions of able and willing countries. Looking from this angle, informal groups of states do not infringe on existing Charter provisions, but can be directly derived from them. However, Article 51 cannot be interpreted as a blank cheque to bypass the UN. It is not an invitation for unilateral action by single states, since there is a clear, although not clearly defined, reference that—in Martin Wight's words—'a majority of powers cannot be prevented' from conducting conflict management outside the Organization.

---

[20] See Jürgen Heideking, 'Völkerbund und Vereinte Nationen in der internationalen Politik', *Aus Politik und Zeitgeschichte*, 36/83 (1983), 3–16.

[21] Carr, *The Twenty Years' Crisis 1919–1939*, 207.

[22] See Preamble of the Charter of the United Nations.

[23] Martin Wight, *Power Politics* (London: Leicester University Press, 1978), 218.

The key to understanding this provision lies less in the futile exploration of the question of how many states are needed to get this very majority, but rather in the interpretation that a minority of one or two countries should not be able to stop a majority of like-minded states from taking action. Should members exert their right of individual or collective self-defence, the actions taken entail, however, a clear time horizon. The Charter grants the possibility to act until the SC has agreed upon the measures to restore international peace and security.[24] The UN SC, therefore, shall come into play at the earliest possible stage.

The possibility of veto was perceived as a kind of reinsurance, providing the great powers with the option of an exit to preserve their vital national interests. Furthermore, the five victorious powers were granted the privilege of permanent membership on the SC, whereas the other (non-permanent) members should be elected for a term of two years, without being eligible for immediate re-election. The veto power in combination with the restrictions of Charter revision hermetically sealed their privileges under the conditions of 1945. However, it has not been a new phenomenon to think about the allocation of special privileges and duties within a group of states characterized by an asymmetric power structure. It already existed in 1685 when the Advocate Samuel Pufendorf observed in his opus *De Jure Naturae et Gentium Libri Octo*:

Another consideration is that it would often involve great injustice in a system of confederates for the vote of a majority to bind the rest when there is a great difference in resources, and so one contributes more to the common safety than another. For despite the fact that those who contribute in proportion to their wealth appear to bear equal burdens, it may frequently happen that one man is readier to expose his own modest fortune to risk than another his, a large one. Thus supposing that one state of a system contributes more to the common defence than all the others together, it would be manifestly unjust for it to be possible for the rest to force such a state to undertake something that would devolve the chief burden upon it. But yet for the votes of each state to weigh in proportion to its contribution to the society would grant such a powerful state sovereignty over the rest.[25]

This fundamental problem of international relations has not significantly changed even three centuries later. UN membership is composed of a large group of states that have only limited capacities to contribute to the aims of the Charter. At the same time, there is a minority of states having more

---

[24] See Bruno Simma, *The Charter of the United Nations. A Commentary*, 2 nd edn. (Oxford: Oxford University Press, 2002), 788–806.

[25] Quoted in Bardo Fassbender, *UN Security Council and the Right of Veto: A Constitutional Perspective* (The Hague: Kluwer Law International, 1998), 17.

resources than the majority of other states taken together. While only a few members have the capacity for a credible projection of power, this minority, however, is not necessarily represented on the SC, for three reasons. First, the composition of the SC, consisting of permanent and non-permanent members, reflects a trade-off between inclusiveness and efficiency. Second, the election of non-permanent members follows the same pattern according to Article 23 of the UN Charter, paying regard to contributions to the maintenance of international peace and security as well as to equitable geographical distribution. Third, the strict provisions regarding Charter amendments—as embodied in Article 109[26]—prevent the adaptation of the SC composition according to shifts in the relative power of UN member states. Informal groups of states may therefore provide a convenient exit strategy to include those countries that have the capacities at their disposal, but no formal voice on the Council to define the chain of action.

Those UN member states with only limited capacities at their disposal generally refer to the principle of equality and sovereignty, while the powerful minority points to its privilege *qua* exposed position and the necessity of having an efficient Organization.[27] This clash of interests was already apparent during the San Francisco Conference in 1945, when forty-nine states were engaged to find a workable mechanism to prevent another world war by an alliance of states for collective security. The structure of the SC reflects this circumstance by differentiating between permanent and non-permanent members, granting China, France, the Soviet Union, the United Kingdom, and the United States the privilege of permanent membership.

In conclusion, the thinking about how to model the international order after World War II had been translated into an institution that mirrored a policy mix of elements of utopia and reality. Firstly, the UN Security Council is composed of a limited number of permanent and non-permanent members (Article 23). Secondly, it has the primary though not exclusive responsibility for the maintenance of international peace and security (Article 24.1). Thirdly, the Council acts on behalf of all UN member states. Furthermore, it defines any threat to or breach of peace,

---

[26] Article 109 reads as follows: 'Amendments to the present Charter shall come into force for all Members of the United Nations when they have been adopted by a vote of two-thirds of the Members of the General Assembly and ratified in accordance with their respective constitutional processes by two-thirds of the Members of the United Nations, including all the permanent members of the Security Council.'

[27] In this context, efficiency however is only vaguely defined.

deciding whether there is an act of aggression (Article 39). Fourthly, it adopts resolutions that are legally binding for all members of the Organization; even non-members can be affected to some extent (Article 2.5, 2.6, Article 25, Article 49). Fifthly, the five permanent members of the SC possess the right of veto in all matters going beyond procedural questions, a privilege acknowledging the asymmetric power structure within the UN. The veto explicitly includes all aspects of Charter revision (Article 27.3, Article 108, Article 109). Sixthly, Article 51 turns the veto inside out and offers via the right of collective or individual self-defence a limited exit strategy to conduct conflict management outside the Organization. Finally, the right to adopt its own Rules of Procedure (Article 30) provides the Council with a flexible instrument to adapt the formula of its meetings according to changing circumstances.

1.2 Variations on the Collective Security Scheme

The system of collective security as agreed upon in San Francisco and embedded in the Charter of the UN faced a deep crisis immediately after its adoption.[28] The ambitious provisions of Chapter VII (Articles 43–8) were not implemented. The most obvious reason was the antagonism between the United States and the Soviet Union, which already foreshadowed the outline of the Cold War. In the SC, this conflict of interests became visible by the increasing number of vetoes cast in formal meetings.[29]

While the Soviet Union had used this privilege from 1946 to 1955 in seventy-five cases, between 1956 and 1965 in twenty-six cases, the United States used it only once up until 1965. Between 1966 and 1975, they cast it in twelve, and from 1976 to 1985 in thirty-four cases. The year 1966 appears as a watershed, since the recomposition of the SC, namely the enlargement of its non-permanent membership from six to ten seats, changed the institutional balance at the expense of Western powers. The action threshold was increased from seven to nine votes. This had the effect that, after 1966, eighty-six percent of all vetoes were cast by the P-3, that is, France, the United Kingdom, and the United States.[30]

---

[28] See Fernand van Langenhove, *La Crise du Système de Sécurité Collective des Nations Unies, 1946–1957* (The Hague: M. Nijhoff, 1958).
[29] See Table 2.
[30] Bailey and Daws, *The Procedure of the UN Security Council*, 228.

Table 2. Number of vetoes cast in the UN Security Council, 1946–2004

Period	China*	France	UK	USA	USSR/Russia	Total
2004	—	—	—	2	1	3
2003	—	—	—	2	—	2
2002	—	—	—	2	—	2
2001	—	—	—	2	—	2
2000	—	—	—	—	—	—
1999	1	—	—	—	—	1
1998	—	—	—	—	—	—
1997	1	—	—	2	—	3
1996	—	—	—	—	—	—
1986–95	—	3	8	24	2	37
1976–85	—	9	11	34	6	60
1966–75	2	2	10	12	7	33
1956–65	—	2	3	—	26	31
1946–55	1	2	—	—	75	78
Total	5	18	32	80	117	252

Source: Bailey and Daws, *The Procedure of the UN Security Council*, 239;
www.globalpolicy.org/ security/data/vetotab.htm

* The Republic of China (Taiwan) occupied the Chinese permanent seat on the Council in the period from 1946 to 1971.

Although these numbers do suggest a paralysis of the SC, scrutiny reveals a more accurate and complex picture. Even for the so-called hot phase of the Cold War, complete stalemate in the Council was not maintained. Sydney Bailey, Inis Claude, and Francis Delon point to a considerable number of cases that support this argument.[31] The causal connection between veto and the incapacity of the SC to act therefore has serious shortcomings in its explanatory power. It is not only the veto that determines an active or passive role for the Council, but other factors like political will or leadership by one single country or groups of states. The reflexive pointing to the veto as a monodimensional explanation of the potential paralysis of the SC all too often distracts from a broader understanding. This brings into question the truism that Articles 43–8 could not be implemented due to Cold War antagonism. The lack of action also reflects a deep-rooted reluctance of governments to become involved in seemingly distant regions and risky military operations without reserving the right to their explicit consent.

The non-implementation of central Articles in the Charter permitted an environment that led, according to Adam Roberts, to three developments

[31] See Bailey, *Voting in the Security Council*; Claude, *Swords into Plowshares*, 140; Delon, 'La concertation entre les membres permanents du conseil de sécurité', 56.

highlighting the inherent flexibility of the UN Charter. These variants of collective security include: (a) the tendency to regional alliances and military action in a multilateral framework, (b) the delegation of the enforcement powers of the SC authorizing (coalitions of) states or regional arrangements to use military force on behalf of the UN, and (c) peacekeeping operations under the authority of the UN.[32] Informal groups of states shall be introduced later as a fourth variant of collective security, caused by, and evolving as part and parcel of, the development of UN crisis response.

1.2.1 Regional Alliances and Multilateral Action

The creation of regional alliances reflects the fact that most states tend to use their forces for military operations on a regional rather than a global level.[33] The San Francisco Conference in 1945 had agreed to include in the UN Charter a special authorization for regional organizations or agencies to deal with security problems that are appropriate for regional action. The final report of Commission III dealing with questions relating to the SC underlined that '[m]embers should make every effort to settle local disputes by regional agencies before referring them to the Security Council'.[34] Those provisions should become later embodied in Chapter VIII of the UN Charter. The development of nuclear weapons in the hands of a few states fostered the trend towards the creation of alliances, which undermined the far more ambitious system of global collective security. With nuclear deterrence as one of the defining moments of the bipolar system, the growing perception of vulnerability led states to align themselves with a nuclear power.[35]

The emergence of several regional alliances after 1945 was also accompanied by the tendency to use force in a multilateral framework rather than to intervene unilaterally. The preference for multilateral action—or what Ruth Wedgwood calls 'technical multilateralism'[36] to keep up appearance of collective action—gained currency. When the United States intervened in the Dominican Republic in 1965, it achieved prior authorization

---

[32] See Roberts, 'The United Nations: Variants of Collective Security', 309.

[33] Ibid., 319; a notable exception of that pattern is the United States.

[34] 'Report of the Rapporteur of Commission III to the Plenary Session', in United Nations, (ed.), *Documents of the United Nations Conference on International Organization, San Francisco, 1945*, III (ed.) (London/New York: United Nations, 1945), 234 *et seq.*

[35] See Adam Roberts, 'The United Nations: Variants of Collective Security', 310.

[36] Ruth Wedgwood, 'Unilateral Action in a Multilateral World', in Stewart Patrick and Shepard Forman (eds.), *Multilateralism and US Foreign Policy: Ambivalent Engagement* (London: Lynne Rienner, 2002), 178.

through a resolution adopted by the Organization of American States (OAS), thereby avoiding a Soviet veto in the UN Security Council. Furthermore, US efforts were flanked by the deployment of an Inter-American Peace Force. Even the Soviet intervention in Czechoslovakia in 1968 was the hidden behind the fig leaf of the multilateral action of the Warsaw Pact, with the participation of Bulgaria, the German Democratic Republic, Poland, and Hungary.[37] The US–American intervention in Grenada in October 1983 was based upon the *placet* of the rather inactive Organization of Eastern Caribbean States. These few post-1945 examples of 'thin multilateralism',[38] which can be further continued *in extenso*, illustrate that multilateral action became the screen behind which the great powers could hide their interests. At the same time, the appearance of legitimate state action gained importance as a means of 'social control',[39] restricting the uncontrolled exercise of power in the conduct of international relations.

Regional alliances can be perceived as both starting point and turning away from the system of collective security. Looking at the development of the international system since 1945, there has not been a ripe moment for implementing such an ambitious scheme. Consequently, despite the examples of thin multilateralism, arrangements of regional security should rather be seen as the best possible, though sub-optimal, rapprochement to the concept of collective security, as envisaged by the Founders of the UN.[40] Regional arrangements remain sub-optimal since they have never been a substitute for the idea of a collective force under UN authority. However, this optimal solution has always been out of reach.

The structural conditions of the post-Cold War era have reinforced this trend towards regionalism in dealing with crisis situations that may endanger the maintenance of international peace and security.[41] It has led to a decentralization of global security, with the stakeholders seeking 'cooperative regional solutions'.[42] The reliance upon regional and sub-regional settings, including informal groups of states constitutes a variant of collective security that 'may cause sleepless nights for some international lawyers, but has often seemed to salve the concerns

[37] See Roberts, 'The United Nations: Variants of Collective Security', 319.

[38] Wedgwood, 'Unilateral Action in a Multilateral World', 178.

[39] Ian Hurd, 'Legitimacy and Authority in International Politics', *International Organization*, 53/2 (1999), 379.

[40] See Roberts, 'The United Nations: Variants of Collective Security', 322.

[41] For a good analysis of this trend, see Michael Pugh and Waheguru Pal Singh Sidhu (eds.), *The United Nations and Regional Security: Europe and Beyond* (Boulder, CO: Lynne Rienner, 2003).

[42] Andrew Hurrell and Louise Fawcett, 'Conclusion: Regionalism and International Order?', in Louise Fawcett and Andrew Hurrell (eds.), *Regionalism in World Politics: Regional Organization and International Order* (New York: Oxford University Press, 1995), 311.

felt by other countries at the singular career of a country with formidable military power'.[43]

1.2.2 Authorization of Military Force

The strongest variant of collective security has been the authorization to use force, thereby delegating the enforcement powers of the SC. This shift of competence developed out of the circumstance that member states could not agree upon the use of force during the Cold War era. The Korean War (1950–3) marked the beginning of the subsequent practice to delegate the enforcement powers of the SC to (coalitions of) states or regional arrangements.[44] After the outbreak of the conflict on 25 June 1950, the SC determined there had been a breach of peace. It called for the immediate cessation of hostilities and demanded the withdrawal of North Korean troops to the 38th parallel.[45]

These far-reaching decisions were possible at this stage since the Soviet Union had conducted an 'empty chair' policy at the time the crisis emerged: it had boycotted virtually all Council meetings in protest because the government in Taiwan instead of Communist Beijing was still holding the seat of China. Consequently, the SC was able to authorize a UN military operation under the unified command of the United States.[46] Not the least due to this unusual activism of the Council, the Soviet Union terminated its boycott in August 1950 and vetoed all subsequent decisions of the Council.[47] Facing complete paralysis, US Secretary of State Dean Acheson submitted an Action Plan to the Western-dominated General Assembly, which was adopted on 3 November 1950, as the so-called 'Uniting-for-Peace' resolution:

[I]f the Security Council, because of lack of unanimity of the permanent members, fails to exercise its primary responsibility for the maintenance of international peace and security in any case where there appears to be a threat to peace, breach of the peace, or act of aggression, the General Assembly shall consider the matter immediately with a view to making appropriate recommendations to Members for collective measures, including in the case of a breach of the peace or acts of aggression the use of armed force when necessary, to maintain or restore international peace and security. If not in session at the time, the General Assembly may meet in emergency special session within twenty-four hours of the request therefore. Such an emergency special session may be called if requested by the Security

---

[43] Wedgwood, 'Unilateral Action in a Multilateral World', 185.
[44] See Hiscocks, *The Security Council*, 163 *et seq.*   [45] Ibid.
[46] See UN Doc S/RES/84 (1950), 7 July 1950, op. 3 and 5.
[47] See Richard Hiscocks, *The Security Council*, 166.

Council on the vote of any seven members, or by a majority of the members of the United Nations.[48]

The General Assembly established furthermore a fourteen-member Peace Observation Commission,[49] which should report on potential threats to international peace and security, thereby entering into competition with the authority of the SC under Article 39 to 'determine the existence of any threat to the peace, breach of the peace, or act of aggression'.

The Uniting-for-Peace procedure constituted a precedent case in the application of UN Charter provisions. The resolution significantly expanded the competence of the General Assembly, while restricting the provisions of Article 24, which had granted the primary responsibility for the maintenance of international peace and security to the Council. The resolution was a gate-opener, providing the General Assembly with the possibility of convening a special session and advising military measures on its own. This revaluation was, however, limited since its vote did not imply a legally binding decision. Consequently, the resolution did not transfer any of the enforcement powers from the Council to the Assembly. Enforcement action under Chapter VII continued to be reserved to the SC. The Uniting-for-Peace resolution pointed to the flexible, if not uncontested, mechanisms of the Charter that allowed the UN to take action even when the SC was blocked. Due to the contentious nature of the decision, this procedure has not been evoked very often.[50] Another emergency special session was convened during the Suez crisis in 1956, when the General Assembly adopted a resolution to send a ten-nation-peacekeeping force to supervise the cessation of hostilities. Such agreement was possible since the interests of the two superpowers converged, acting against the veto of France and Britain, which were directly involved in the conflict. In consequence, this peacekeeping operation had been made possible by invoking the Uniting-for-Peace procedure, whereby the Soviet Union this time deliberately supported the decision taken by the General Assembly.

In conclusion, the delegation of the SC's enforcement powers to (groups of) states marked a significant deviation of the collective security scheme of the UN Charter. While this practice developed against the background of a lack of agreement among permanent members of the SC to use force, the

[48] The title of this resolution stems from its introductory call 'Uniting for Peace'. The resolution was adopted by the General Assembly with fifty-two votes in favour, five against, and two abstentions; UN Doc A/RES/377, 3 November 1950, op. 1.

[49] The fourteen members were China, Colombia, Czechoslovakia, France, India, Iraq, Israel, New Zealand, Pakistan, the Soviet Union, Sweden, United Kingdom, United States, Uruguay; ibid. op. 3.

[50] Ten emergency special sessions have been convened so far; information available at www.un.org/ga/documents/liemsps.htm.

reliance on delegation would continue to be a defining element of peace enforcement actions in the post-Cold War era. It prepared the ground for a scenario in which the Council is most likely to act if (groups of) states signal in advance the political will to bear the financial burdens and to suffer the human costs of such operations.

1.2.3 *Peacekeeping Operations*

The evolution of peacekeeping can be analysed as an *ad hoc* mechanism of the UN, customized out of practice. It also demonstrates another example of the flexibility of the UN Charter. The United Nations Truce Supervision Organization (UNTSO) of 1948 is generally seen as the first peacekeeping operation consisting of unarmed military observers who supervised the ceasefire between Israel and its Arab neighbours in Palestine.[51] The first armed UN operation emerged, however, in October 1956 as the United Nations Emergency Force (UNEF) during the Suez crisis.[52] Peacekeeping, as an instrument of the UN, is not explicitly mentioned in the Charter. Implicitly, it can be derived from Article 33,[53] which allows UN member states, in the context of the pacific settlement of disputes, to use 'other peaceful means of their own choice'.[54] Other scholars define peacekeeping as a subsidiary organ established by either the General Assembly or the SC under Article 22 and 29 respectively.[55]

Originally, UN peacekeeping was characterized by three distinct principles.[56] First, the forces were expected to maintain impartiality between the conflicting parties. Second, and this remained valid up to the early 1990s, the consent of the parties to send UN peacekeeping forces was the *sine qua non* of every operation. Although this principle has been seriously tested in the post-Cold War era, it has not lost its importance. However, consent of the parties is not an independent variable, but 'a function of the alternatives'.[57] It may be induced by a

---

[51] See Marrack Goulding, 'The Evolution of United Nations Peacekeeping', *International Affairs*, 69/3 (1993), 452.

[52] See Brian Urquhart, *Hammarskjöld* (New York: W.W. Norton, 1972), 159–94.

[53] See Roberts, 'The United Nations: Variants of Collective Security', 327.

[54] Measures for the pacific settlement of disputes include, according to Article 33, negotiation, enquiry, mediation, conciliation, arbitration, judicial settlement, resort to regional agencies, or arrangements and other peaceful means of their own choice.

[55] See Simma, *The Charter of the United Nations*, 648–700.

[56] See Roberts, 'The United Nations: Variants of Collective Security', 327.

[57] Kofi A. Annan, 'Challenges of the New Peacekeeping', in Olara A. Otunnu and Michael W. Doyle (eds.), *Peacemaking and Peacekeeping for the New Century* (Lanham: Rowman & Littlefield, 1998), 172.

stick-and-carrot-policy, creating a policy mix of positive incentives and threats of coercion. A third principle was to avoid the use of force. Early peacekeeping forces were allowed to use force only for purposes of self-defence.

The Congo operation in the 1960s showed very quickly that UN peace-keeping tended to move within a grey zone between Chapter VI and VII of the UN Charter. Since 1973, the original doctrine has been changing with the deployment of interposition forces between the Egyptian and Israeli lines after the Yom Kippur War. The possibility to use force was extended to those cases where parties hinder the ability of UN troops to fulfil their mandate.[58] Furthermore, even between 1945 and 1989 peacekeeping has never been exclusively used in inter-state conflicts. UN involvement in intra-state wars, which have become 'normality' after the end of bipolarity, was already taking place in crises like those of the Congo (1960–4) and Cyprus (since 1964).[59] In both cases, the SC decided to send interposition forces without being able to define clear-cut frontlines or without an existing ceasefire between the parties concerned. All too often, the fundamental principles of peacekeeping like impartiality, consent of the conflicting parties, and non-use of force have been put into question. Although UN forces have helped to stabilize conflicts and, indeed, to keep the peace, it has often been overlooked that the long-term presence of peacekeeping forces may reduce the pressure to work towards a solution of the conflict: the tendency to freeze the status quo increases while incentives for any long-term constructive conflict management will decrease.

In conclusion, the evolution of UN peacekeeping formed another innovative element in the constitutional practice of the UN. Peacekeeping, regional alliances, and the delegation of the SC's enforcement powers constitute three variants of collective security emerging against the background that the UN Charter was being challenged by systemic change. In consequence, the UN has never been able to fulfil its functions as originally envisioned by the Founders of the Organization. In the following chapters, informal groups of states will be introduced as a fourth variation on the collective security scheme. Analysis of the emergence and proliferation of informal groups of states allows for setting up a framework to grasp the dynamics between informal settings and the UN Security Council.

---

[58] See Goulding, 'The Evolution of United Nations Peacekeeping', 455.
[59] See Anthony Parsons, *From Cold War to Hot Peace: UN Interventions 1947–1995* (London; New York: Michael Joseph, 1995), 77–93 and 167–82.

2

Emergence of Informal Groups of States

The Secretary-General, as the chief administrative officer of the UN, has always been exposed to the current international political climate in the performance of those functions entrusted to him by the principal organs of the UN according to Article 98 of the Charter. Exposure to political controversy becomes particularly apparent in his relationship to the Security Council (SC) given its primary responsibility for the maintenance of international peace and security. This section argues that the early stages of UN peacekeeping saw a shift of governance from the SC to the Secretary-General and the General Assembly, which fostered the emergence of informal groups of states. The formation of advisory committees reflected the desire of the Secretary-General to strengthen his voice vis-à-vis the SC. This would be a recurring theme in the context of the Group of Friends of the Secretary-General on El Salvador, which will be discussed in the second part of the book. The trend of establishing advisory committees reversed in 1973 when the UN set up the second UN Emergency Force (UNEF II), with governance reshifting to the Council. As will be further illustrated in the case of Namibia, the establishment of the so-called Group of Three in the early 1970s illustrated the weakened role of the Secretary-General vis-à-vis the SC. It also demonstrated the push for exit at that stage, generated by the structural deficiencies of the UN conflict resolution machinery that had been worsening because of systemic change.

Since the SC is a political body, resolutions reflect accordingly a precarious compromise of member states, embodied in a diplomatic formula. If the Council wants to present a united front, the price its members have to pay is an ambiguous language in the resolution, which leaves room for different interpretations.[1] In consequence, disagreement over the interpretation of resolutions adopted by the Council has been a common pattern. Securing compliance is very often left to the Secretariat, without any further guidance for the implementation of a given mandate. The Secretary-General is confronted with the perennial challenge not to antagonize the great powers in the execution of these delegated authorities, especially, though by no means exclusively, in the Cold War period. He must constantly navigate between the Scylla of strictly limiting his role to those functions explicitly mentioned in the UN Charter and the Charybdis of overextending responsibilities by a far-stretching interpretation of Charter provisions. Both extremes are detrimental to his office.

These structural conditions should be kept in mind when tracing the emergence of informal groups of states. They initially emerged as advisory bodies of the Secretary-General during the term of Dag Hammarskjöld. Under his predecessor, an increasingly divided SC had shaken the Organization, as the Korean War made abundantly clear. Then Secretary-General Trygve Lie had supported the United States initiative to circumvent the paralysed SC by referring the matter to the General Assembly, which brought him in open opposition to the Soviet Union. Once the Soviet delegation refused to recognize him as Secretary-General of the UN from February 1951 onwards, having vetoed his re-nomination, Trygve Lie's room to manoeuvre became severely limited.

This has been almost a textbook example of the dangers the Secretary-General faced under Cold War conditions. Once Lie had lost his impartiality in the perception of key states, his office was doomed to remain politically paralysed. Furthermore, the Secretariat had become a base for McCarthyite agitation over spying or subversive American citizens who had allegedly infiltrated the Organization: however, not a single staff member was ever even charged with those accusations.[2] Although the General Assembly had voted to extend his term of office by three years, Lie announced his resignation on 10 November 1952, because of these pressures.[3] In April 1953, when leaving office, the Secretary-General delivered a brief valedictory, hinting at the inherent potential of the Charter, yet to be explored:

The Charter is a flexible instrument, capable of adaptation and improvement, not merely by amendment but by interpretation and practice. I am convinced that the

---

[1] Interview with Neylan Bali, former Director of the Security Affairs Division in the UN Department of Political Affairs, New York, 1 December 2000.

[2] See Nicholas, *The United Nations as a Political Institution*, 56.

[3] See UN Doc A/2253, 10 November 1956.

institutions of the United Nations system can be used by the Member States with far greater effect than in the past for the peace and progress of all those nations willing to cooperate.[4]

Lie's successor in office, Dag Hammarskjöld, would become a master of exploring the as yet uncharted territories of the UN Charter's 'constitutional practice', in that special sense truly a 'Machiavelli of Peace'.[5]

2.1 De-politicizing the Discourse: The Advisory Committee on the Peaceful Uses of Atomic Energy

Hammarskjöld became for the first time exposed to the instrument of an advisory committee in the context of preparing the Atoms for Peace Conference, to be held in Geneva from 8–20 August 1955.[6] The conference responded to a number of proposals brought forward by the Eisenhower administration to achieve arms control.[7] In his statement to the General Assembly on 8 December 1953, the US President had come up with far-reaching proposals for establishing an international atomic energy agency under the aegis of the UN. In December 1954, the General Assembly accordingly adopted a resolution to hold an international technical conference under UN auspices to explore possibilities of sharing technical information in the field of using nuclear energy for peaceful purposes.[8] Under the chairmanship of the Secretary-General, the Advisory Committee on the Peaceful Uses of Atomic Energy prepared the programme of the conference, issued invitations, and provided the necessary staff services. Composed of seven high-level scientists of Brazil, Canada, France, India, the Soviet Union, the United Kingdom, and the United States, the Advisory Committee held three series of meetings with the Secretary-General: from 17 to 28 January 1955, at UN Headquarters, 23–27 May in Paris, and from 3 to 5 August in Geneva.[9] After initial difficulties especially reflecting

---

[4] Andrew W. Cordier and Wilder Foote (eds.), *Public Papers of the Secretaries-General of the United Nations*, vol. I: *Trygve Lie: 1946–53* (New York: Colombia University Press, 1969), 513.

[5] Thomas L. Hughes, 'On the Causes of Our Discontents', *Foreign Affairs*, 47/4 (1969), 660.

[6] See UN Doc A/2967, 14 September 1955, para 3.

[7] In January 1953, Dwight D. Eisenhower had taken office as the thirty-fourth President of the United States.

[8] See UN Doc A/RES/230, 4 December 1954.

[9] The Committee consisted of Nobel Prize winners Sir John Cockcroft of the United Kingdom and I. I. Rabi of the United States. Further representatives were Soviet Academy member D. V. Skobeltzin, Homi Bhabba of India and W. B. Lewis of Canada, both heads of their countries' atomic energy programmes, Bertrand Goldschmidt of France and J. Costa Ribeiro of Brazil; see UN Doc A/2967, 14 September 1955, para 3; UN Oral History Project Interview Transcripts, Brian Urquhart, 15 October 1984; also Urquhart, *Hammarskjöld*, 83.

Cold War tensions between the Soviet and the US–American sides, the Secretary-General managed, as Brian Urquhart recalls, 'to get rid of most of the political advisers on the delegations, after a certain amount of very plain speaking'.[10] Thus, de-politicizing the composition of the Committee resulted in a re-focus of the discussion on scientific issues. The scientific members managed to tone down the political discourse:

They squared off to have the normal heavyweight cold war discussion on this, and Hammarskjöld..., by a really masterly display of good chairmanship and intellectual grasp of the subject, completely derailed the cold war part of it and we had... as long as those people remained in that committee, one of the most constructive, most collegial... and efficient committees I have ever attended.[11]

Still, the sensitive topics under discussion and the composition of the Committee did not provide a great chance to reach unanimity, but members engaged in a full discussion without trying to reach agreement. At the end of each meeting, it had been up to the Secretary-General to present an informal summing up, concluding the thrust of the discussion. Those who disagreed with his conclusion had the opportunity to record as disagreeing, presenting their own point of view, although no member had ever gone on record as dissenting with the Secretary-General.[12]

The success of the first Geneva conference prepared the ground for a follow-up meeting in 1958. Hammarskjöld was keen to continue the Advisory Committee 'as a consultative body for assistance on those atomic matters in which responsibilities may be entrusted to the United Nations Secretariat'.[13] In December 1955, the General Assembly recommended accordingly that the Committee should also prepare the second international conference.[14] The Committee became entrusted with drafting a relationship agreement between the UN and the International Atomic Energy Agency (IAEA).[15] The positive experience of the Advisory Committee the Secretary-General and UN member states had gained led to a further expansion of the Committee's terms of reference, advising him 'on many matters... in the field of peaceful uses of atomic energy or

---

[10] UN Oral History Project Interview Transcripts, Brian Urquhart, 15 October 1984.
[11] Ibid.
[12] This is Hammarskjöld's own assessment, as presented during the first meeting of the later established Advisory Committee on the Congo; see Papers of the Secretaries General, Advisory Committee on the Congo, Verbatim Records, first meeting, 24 August 1960.
[13] UN Doc A/2967, 14 September 1955, para 19.
[14] See UN Doc A/RES/334, 3 December 1955. The second conference was eventually held in Geneva from 1 to 13 September 1958, see UN Doc A/3949, 16 October 1958, para 2.
[15] This agreement was later adopted by General Assembly resolution UN Doc A/RES/1145, 14 November 1957.

in related fields of science, with which the United Nations is, or may later be, concerned'.[16] Furthermore, the Committee was re-christened into United Nations Scientific Advisory Committee, reflecting the expanded mandate.[17]

In conclusion, the Advisory Committee on the Peaceful Uses of Atomic Energy provided the platform for a discourse among equals beyond the political and ideological divide of the Cold War. Based upon this precedent, Hammarskjöld would establish similar committees as a means to assist the Secretary-General in the performance of his functions during crises at the Suez Canal, in Lebanon, and in the Congo.

2.2 Uniting for Peace: The UNEF Advisory Committee

The idea to establish advisory bodies in crisis situations advising the Secretary-General in the performance of his tasks entrusted to him by the SC or the General Assembly therefore did not emerge out of the blue. In the context of the Suez crisis in 1956, when Israel, the United Kingdom, and France had invaded Egypt, the UN responded by setting up an international emergency force whose mandate developed out of the stalemate within the SC. Britain and France had subsequently vetoed two draft resolutions, introduced by the United States and resubmitted in an amended form by the Soviet Union. The blockade situation was overridden by adopting SC resolution 119, which had called an emergency special session of the General Assembly under the Uniting-for-Peace procedure.[18]

It is important to note that the emergency special session had been convened on the initiative of the United States, without the active opposition of the Soviet Union. The flexible evolution of UN constitutional practice during the Cold War must be seen through the lens of US–Soviet interaction.[19] In the early 1950s, the United States actively promoted a greater use of the General Assembly that was being controlled by its allies, while the Soviet Union sought to increase the membership of the Assembly to alter the institutional balance of power. The *ultima ratio* of US policy

---

[16] UN Doc A/3949, 16 October 1958, para 32.

[17] See UN Doc A/RES/1344 (XIII), 13 December 1958.

[18] See UN Doc A/RES/119 (1956), 31 October 1956. This resolution referred to a procedural matter. Consequently, the Council was able to adopt the resolution by an affirmative vote of seven against two, with two abstentions (Australia, Belgium) despite objections of Britain and France.

[19] See John G. Stoessinger, *The United Nations and the Superpowers: United States–Soviet Interaction at the United Nations*, 2nd edn. (New York: Random House, 1970), 176.

was to deflect activities from a veto-prone SC by referring contentious matters to the General Assembly. However, the year 1955 marked a large influx of sixteen new members that had cost the United States its 'automatic majority'. Strengthening the office of the Secretary-General—the organ that seemed to be the least politically contaminated one—offered therefore a convenient exit and ultimately served the US policy. It is against this background that 'the United States encouraged the passage of broadly conceived resolutions that invested the Secretary-General with increasing policy-making responsibilities'.[20] Consequently, governance shifted from the SC to the General Assembly and further to the Secretary-General, with the United States and the Soviet Union as gatekeepers of this process.

UNEF derived its legitimacy therefore not by virtue of an SC mandate, but by a set of resolutions adopted by the General Assembly, thus a deviation from the provisions of the UN Charter. The contentious constitutional basis of the first peacekeeping force, operating in the grey zone between Chapter VI and VII of the UN Charter under a mandate adopted by the General Assembly and not the SC, had far-reaching, long-term implications for the operation. As Brian Urquhart recalls: 'For this reason, both the French and the Russians always regarded it as illegal, and we started a whole peck of trouble right there. This was the first shadow over the whole concept of peacekeeping'.[21]

The emergency force was supposed to stabilize the situation on the ground until a more durable settlement could be achieved, which constituted another deviation. The San Francisco Conference in 1945 had originally foreseen concerted action by the permanent members of the SC. While the great powers would have to give their general support to the operation, they were however effectively excluded from contributing troops to the peacekeeping force.

When the General Assembly decided upon the establishment of an interposition force to be deployed in the theatre based on an agreement between the contending parties, it asked the Secretary-General to set up the force and negotiate its deployment into Egypt. General Assembly Resolution 998 requested Hammarskjöld to submit to the Assembly a plan within forty-eight hours for the setting up of an emergency force to secure and supervise the cessation of hostilities.[22] Hammarskjöld floated the idea of constituting an advisory committee, which, in conjunction with the Secretary-General, would assume political control over UNEF on

[20] Ibid., 177.
[21] UN Oral History Project Interview Transcripts, Brian Urquhart, 20 July 1984.
[22] See UN Doc A/RES/998 (ES-I), 4 November 1956.

behalf the General Assembly, in his second and final report on the plan for an emergency force.[23] UNEF had to lay the foundation for something that had no explicit reference in the Charter, thereby constituting an entirely new concept of UN crisis response, which had to be planned from scratch. Referring to the advice and guidance of like-minded member states seemed to be a promising strategy for the Secretary-General to be able to navigate between Scylla and Charybdis without wrecking the ship. It was obvious that the Secretary-General would not be able to present a full-fledged plan within the short period of two days, but rather guiding principles, which he had set up in close cooperation with Lester Pearson of Canada, Francisco Urrutia of Colombia, Arthur Lall of India, and Hans Engen of Norway.[24]

Besides the Canadian representative who had originated the idea of establishing a force, these countries represented large parts of the General Assembly supporting its decisions being taken. Questions such as the regulations of the force or the policy of the force with regard to self-defence needed further deliberations. In his report, Hammarskjöld had already indicated that a small committee of the General Assembly should deal with those open matters. He stated furthermore that 'this body might also serve as an advisory committee to the Secretary-General for questions relating to the operations'.[25]

General Assembly Resolution 1001 formally constituted the UNEF Advisory Committee, originally composed of seven countries which were to provide troops to UNEF, namely Brazil, Canada, Ceylon, Colombia, India, Norway, and Pakistan; Yugoslavia would join later.[26] However, it included by no means all troop-contributing countries, since the Secretary-General had deliberately tried to keep the Committee small.[27] The composition of the Advisory Committee came under certain criticism during the emergency special session of the General Assembly, since it did not include any country from the Eastern bloc.[28] Poland had therefore pressed for the admission of Czechoslovakia to the Advisory Committee, which was

---

[23] See UN Doc A/3302, 6 November 1956.

[24] See Yale–UN Oral History Project Interview Transcripts, Geoffrey Murray, 10 January 1991. At the time of the crisis, Murray served in the Middle East Section of the European Division, Department of External Affairs, Ottawa.

[25] Ibid.

[26] The resolution was adopted with sixty-four votes in favour, none against, and twelve abstentions; see UN Doc GAOR, First Emergency Special Session, 567th Plenary Meeting, 7 November 1956, para 269.

[27] More than twenty countries had committed troops to the operation. The United States provided logistical support (air and surface transport), notably, at no charge for the UN.

[28] Ibid., para 49–53.

however rejected by the Assembly.[29] In consequence, the Soviet Union and their Eastern satellites abstained in the vote on what would become General Assembly resolution 1001.[30] Other countries such as Indonesia, Iran, and Pakistan, which had volunteered troops to the emergency force equally tried hard to become members on the Advisory Committee, but did not succeed.[31] The Committee had to reflect a trade-off between inclusiveness and efficiency in order to work.

Under the chairmanship of the Secretary-General, the Advisory Committee was to 'undertake the development of those aspects of the planning for the Force and its operation not already dealt with by the General Assembly and which do not fall within the area of the direct responsibility of the Chief of Command'.[32] The Committee constituted therefore a link both to the General Assembly and to the troop-contributing countries. Although not explicitly a subsidiary organ of the General Assembly under Article 22 of the Charter,[33] de facto it had assumed exactly those functions. The resolution empowered the Committee 'to request . . . the convening of the General Assembly and to report to the General Assembly whenever matters arise which, in its opinion, are of such urgency and importance as to require consideration of the General Assembly itself',[34] although it never invoked that authority.

The Committee held forty-four meetings in the period between 14 November 1956 and 31 December 1959. After a long pause due to the smooth running of UNEF, the Advisory Committee was consulted again, for the last time, on 8 May 1967, under the chairmanship of the then Secretary-General U Thant to advise him on the request of Egypt to withdraw UNEF. Meetings were usually announced with one day's notice by letter and telephone. They generally took place in the Secretary-General's conference room. Verbatim records for personal information were provided by the Secretariat after each meeting and distributed to members of the Committee up to nine days later. The records of the meeting were classified as confidential.

---

[29] The amendment proposed by Poland was rejected by thirty-one votes to twenty-three, with fourteen abstentions; ibid., para 263.

[30] Ibid., para 269.

[31] See Yale–UN Oral History Project Interview Transcripts, Geoffrey Murray, 10 January 1991.

[32] UN Doc A/RES/1001 (ES-I), 7 November 1956, op. 6.

[33] Article 22 of the Charter reads as follows: 'The Charter may establish such subsidiary organs as it deems necessary for the performance of its functions.'

[34] UN Doc A/RES/1001 (ES-I), 7 November 1956, op. 9.

By consulting the Committee, the Secretary-General had been able to secure continued feedback of his negotiations with the Egyptian government, without asking the entire General Assembly body for approval of every step. For example, Hammarskjöld had negotiated with President Nasser of Egypt three memoranda on the presence and functioning of UNEF. The low profile of the force, embodied in the restrictive definition of its functions—hardly the kind of take over Britain and France had hoped for and had advocated to their domestic audiences—posed a considerable embarrassment for the two permanent members of the SC. They had asked the Secretary-General therefore not to publish the second and third memoranda in a report to the General Assembly containing those provisions.[35] Hammarskjöld had responded to their request in the affirmative, leaving the two memoranda out on the basis that he had delivered an oral report to the Advisory Committee, as the *ad hoc* executive committee of the General Assembly, 'with a full account of the interpretations given'.[36] Members of the Advisory Committee had actively participated in drafting the final wording of the Secretary-General's report to the General Assembly.[37]

The Secretary-General used the small gathering as an effective tool to legitimize and sanction his quiet diplomacy, thereby circumventing potential criticism from the General Assembly, a large body consisting of eighty member states at this time. Furthermore, by refraining from the publication of the two memoranda, he hoped to keep Britain and France in a cooperative mood, two permanent members of the SC he might need in the future to initiate Council action. The Advisory Committee was consulted in particular on matters relating to regulations for UNEF and the policy of the Force regarding self-defence.[38] Some questions of the operation were delegated to a subcommittee comprising Brazil, India, and Norway, assisting the Secretary-General in his direct negotiations with Egypt, France, and the United Kingdom.[39] On occasion, Hammarskjöld consulted the representatives on the Committee in their personal capacity. Those discussions were strictly held off the record.[40] As Brian Urquhart recalls:

---

[35] See Urquhart, *Hammarskjöld*, 192.
[36] UN Doc A/3375, 20 November 1956, para 2.
[37] See Papers of the Secretaries-General, UNEF Advisory Committee, Verbatim Records, fourth meeting, 20 November 1956.
[38] See UN Doc A/3943, 9 October 1958, para 30.
[39] See Papers of the Secretaries-General, UNEF Advisory Committee, Verbatim Records, fourteenth meeting, 31 January 1957.
[40] For example, parts of the thirteenth, thirty-fourth, and thirty-sixth meeting were held off the record; see Papers of the Secretaries-General, UNEF Advisory Committee, Verbatim Records.

It also allowed Hammarskjöld to say what he thought to a group of government representatives who would then explain things he could not say publicly. There was a very complicated arrangement, for example, about Sharm el Sheikh. . . . One of the points was that the Egyptians could not take over the coastal batteries again, and of course Fawzi,[41] representing a country which had just been invaded by three foreign armies, could not conceivably say publicly that a fourth group of foreigners would be sitting in one of the key strategic locations of Egypt. So Hammarskjöld simply said 'Let me try it this way: I assume . . . that as long as UN troops are stationed in Sharm el Sheikh the Egyptians will find it unnecessary to be there', and Fawzi simply closed his eyes and nodded. Hammarskjöld could not possibly publish that, but he told the advisory committee and the advisory committee was a kind of guarantors' club.[42]

Member states serving on the Committee therefore shared the considerable burden that the General Assembly's resolutions had put upon the shoulders of the Secretary-General, as Hammarskjöld pointed out at the fourth meeting on 20 November 1956:

[T]here is one thing which is very pleasant from my point of view: that the mandate accepted in the resolution providing for this Committee is such that every responsibility in this whole Middle Eastern context that falls on me automatically falls on this Committee.[43]

Even more, Hammarskjöld personally perceived the Committee as a 'cloud of angels'[44] over his head, granting leverage and feedback to the Secretary-General's efforts to implement the resolutions adopted by the General Assembly. This burden-sharing function applied in particular to the early phase of setting up the emergency force when the Secretary-General had the chief responsibility of 'inventing' the first peacekeeping operation of the UN. Within the Advisory Committee, Lester Pearson of Canada expressed in particular concerns that if the UN should not be able to create this precedent successfully, 'then police action by the United Nations in the future would be quite impossible'.[45]

However, it remained unclear to what extent the Secretary-General's perception of the Committee as a means to share the burden of his office was shared by the member states. Advisory Committee member India, especially, seemed to follow its own policy agenda, pursuing on a parallel

[41] Mahmoud Fawzi was Foreign Minister of Egypt from 1952 to 1964.
[42] UN Oral History Project Interview Transcripts, Brian Urquhart, 15 October 1984.
[43] Papers of the Secretaries General, UNEF Advisory Committee, Verbatim Records, fourth meeting, 20 November 1956.
[44] Telephone interview with Sir Brian Urquhart, 7 February 2001.
[45] Papers of the Secretaries-General, UNEF Advisory Committee, Verbatim Records, first meeting, 14 November 1956.

track a kind of behind-the-scene cooperation with Egypt, one of the most interested parties to the conflict. Non-aligned India had played a key role in drafting the resolutions setting up the international emergency force in Egypt. Furthermore, it was to provide the largest contingent to UNEF. The Egyptian government desperately tried to influence from outside the informal consultations of the Advisory Committee in order to get the low profile force it wanted, which under no circumstances should look like another occupation force. Arthur Lall, the then Permanent Representative of India to the UN, concedes that he regularly briefed his Egyptian colleague, Omar Loutfi, after every meeting of the Advisory Committee.[46] In addition, Lall subsequently leaked all verbatim records to the Egyptian representative, who sent them to Cairo to keep his government informed about the state of the informal discussions between Committee members. Both representatives coordinated their positions in advance of those meetings, trying to find a joint agreement which Lall would present accordingly.

The episode around President Gamal Abdel Nasser's request for the final withdrawal of UNEF in May 1967 shows the limited loyalty of Hammarskjöld's 'cloud of angels', whose like-minded attitude lasted only as long as it did not interfere with their perceived national interests, and as long as the burden to share did not become too heavy. The different personalities involved at that stage may also have contributed to the shifting 'like-mindedness' of the grouping. On 18 May 1967, according to the agreement on the presence of UNEF in Sinai, the Advisory Committee convened to advise the Secretary-General on the request to withdraw UNEF. Although the majority of members tended to acknowledge Nasser's legal stance,[47] the Committee members failed to ask for an emergency session of the General Assembly or a meeting of the SC for further action. Furthermore, India and Yugoslavia, the two largest troop contributors, indicated that their ambassadors in Cairo had been informed the day before about Egypt's request for the UNEF withdrawal, and the ambassadors had already agreed to withdraw the contingents.[48] With the Six-Day War already looming, the final decision to withdraw UNEF and the related responsibility fell alone on the then Secretary-General U Thant. As Brian Urquhart recalls:

---

[46] See Yale–UN Oral History Project Interview Transcripts, Arthur Lall, 27 June 1990.

[47] Canada appeared to be the strongest opponent of a withdrawal, calling for further consultations with Egypt; see Papers of the Secretaries General, UNEF Advisory Committee, Verbatim Records, 18 May 1967.

[48] Ibid.

[T]he behaviour of the Canadians, the Americans and the British . . . was absolutely grotesque. . . . It was terrible, because they all went after U Thant, the only person who had (*a*) been to Cairo and (*b*) suggested three perfectly good ways of getting out of it. . . . They all wanted a scapegoat. None of them knew what to do, and so they behaved very badly.[49]

Indeed, U Thant had tried to obtain President Nasser's acceptance to renegotiate the status-of-force agreement. Furthermore, he had approached the Israeli government to move UNEF on to Israeli soil in order to gain some time. Lastly, he had considered appointing a special representative to be sent to the region. All initiatives had been turned down either by the Egyptian or Israeli sides.[50] In his final observation to the report of the Secretary-General on the withdrawal of UNEF, U Thant pointed to the precarious and not uncontested legitimization of the force by a General Assembly mandate, which did not leave much room for manoeuvre if the consent of the host country no longer existed: 'A partial explanation of the misunderstanding about the withdrawal of UNEF is an evident failure to appreciate the essentially fragile nature of the basis for UNEF's operation throughout its existence.'[51]

Nevertheless, the summary study of Secretary-General Hammarskjöld on the experience derived from the establishment and operation of the force during the period of 1956–8, referred to the UNEF Advisory Committee as a useful mechanism, which should be accepted as precedent for the future:

Extensive operations with serious political implications, regarding which, for practical reasons, executive authority would need to be delegated to the Secretary-General, require close collaboration with authorized representatives of the General Assembly. . . . It is useful for contributing countries to be represented on such an advisory committee, but if the contributing States are numerous the size of the committee might become so large as to make it ineffective. On the other hand, it is obviously excluded that any party to the conflict should be a member. Normally, I believe that the same basic rule regarding permanent members of the Security Council which has been applied to units and men in the recent operations should be applied also in the selection of members for a relevant advisory committee.[52]

Based on the Secretary-General's experience with the UNEF Advisory Committee, one can draw the following conclusions: Firstly, advisory committees were seen as most useful in complex crisis situations where

[49] UN Oral History Project Interview Transcripts, Brian Urquhart, 27 June 1984.
[50] See UN Oral History Project Interview Transcripts, Brian Urquhart, 27 June 1984.
[51] UN Doc A/6730, Add. 3, 26 June 1967, para 99.
[52] UN Doc A/3943, 9 October 1958, para 181.

the Secretary-General may have to secure compliance with extensive mandates entrusted to him either by the SC or the General Assembly. Support for the Secretary-General through these *ad hoc* arrangements may have an *inward* and *outward* dimension. *Inward* looking, the support of like-minded states decreases his vulnerability against criticism from the plenary of the General Assembly and the SC, respectively. *Outward* looking, informal groups may support the Secretary-General's efforts by bringing their influence to bear on the parties to a conflict. Secondly, while troop-contributing countries were the 'natural candidates' to be represented on an advisory committee, this did not necessarily imply that all countries providing troops should be selected. The Advisory Committee had to reflect a trade-off between efficiency and inclusiveness. Thirdly, permanent members of the SC, as a rule, would not be considered as members of an advisory committee. Such policy reflected the guidelines the Secretary-General had adopted regarding peacekeeping operations, that is, the Five permanent members of the UN Security Council were not asked to provide troops to a mission in order to prevent an import of the East–West rivalry into the conflict theatre.

Taking into account the structural conditions under which the UNEF Advisory Committee was formed, it is no coincidence that the second United Nations Emergency Force (UNEF II), established in October 1973 to supervise a ceasefire between Egyptian and Israeli forces, would be run without an advisory committee involved. US–Soviet détente had facilitated the agreement upon resolutions that paved the way for the deployment of another peacekeeping force. The structural conditions under which the SC was operating therefore differed completely from the previous case. The United States used the UN as a multilateral instrument to back up its bilateral Middle East policy, allocating to the Council executive functions: the formal decisions taken by this body would legitimize diplomacy conducted outside the Organization. The way the UN was used by a great power to define a response to the crisis in the Middle East took on the character of 'a model of how things should happen',[53] as Brian Urquhart recalls. While UNEF I was set up against the background of governance that had shifted from the SC to the General Assembly and further to the Secretary-General, this time, close US–Soviet cooperation enabled the Council to define a relatively clear response to the crisis on the ground.[54]

---

[53] UN Oral History Project Interview Transcripts, Brian Urquhart, 10 December 1985.

[54] SC resolutions 338 (1973) and 339 (1973), calling upon the parties to agree on a ceasefire within twelve hours and requesting the Secretary-General to dispatch immediately observers to supervise the cessation of conflict, were co-sponsored by the US and Soviet delegation. They entailed however no provisions regarding the implementation of the ceasefire, which should

In addition, the Secretary-General's report outlining the mandate of UNEF II tried to redefine the relationship between the SC, the Secretary-General, and the Force Commander in a way that preserved the day-to-day executive authority of the Secretary-General while the SC held the overall responsibility for the operation.[55] The report had drawn the lessons of previous operations and outlined three key conditions that had to be met for the peacekeeping operation to be effective:

Firstly, it must have at all times the full confidence and backing of the Security Council. Secondly, it must operate with the full co-operation of the parties concerned. Thirdly, it must be able to function as an integrated and efficient military unit.[56]

The UNEF II mandate took a heavy burden off the shoulders of then Secretary-General Kurt Waldheim, thus decreasing his vulnerability, which had been so visible during the terms of office of Dag Hammarskjöld and Sithu U Thant. If the Secretary-General had acted in previous operations like a General, this mandate downsized him to a Secretary of the Organization. The altered institutional balance of power between the Office of the Secretary-General and the SC returning into the driving seat by taking charge of the operation, removed the foundation on which the advisory committees had been based. The clarification of the peacekeeping doctrine at that stage, including the adoption of clearer mandates, alleviated the pressure towards the establishment of further *ad hoc* advisory bodies. Furthermore, the discussion on implementing SC resolution 340, setting up UNEF II, reflected the manifest interest of some permanent members, especially France, in turning back the wheel, that is, regaining the authority lost in the course of UNEF I. The French representative stressed at the meeting the exclusive competence of the Council in matters of keeping peace and maintaining international security under Article 24, thus hinting that it should be the SC rather than the General Assembly or the Secretary-General setting up and, in fact, running such an operation:

We have always, in this respect, considered that the competence of the Council should not be limited simply to the establishment of an international Force, but that the Council should also have control over all operations that might be ordered by it. It is for the Council, in particular, to define the Force's terms of reference, its duration, its size and its composition. The Security Council must also appoint the

be later defined in SC resolution 340 (1973); see UN Doc SCOR, 1747th, 1748th, and 1750th meeting, 21–3 October and 25 October 1973.

[55] See UN Doc S/11052, 26 October 1973, para 3.
[56] Ibid.

commander, decide on the basic directives to be given to that commander, propose the method of financing, and, finally, ensure constant control over the application of its directives. Doubtless, the Security Council is not in a position to direct such a Force on a continuing basis. Hence, it is possible to envisage, in application of Article 29 of the Charter, the establishment of a subsidiary body of the Council whose purpose would be to lessen the Council's work without prejudice, of course, to the primary responsibility conferred upon the Council by the Charter. This committee would be in constant contact with the Secretary-General. It could, for example, propose to the Council the name of a commander and draft basic directives.[57]

The statement revealed some strong misgivings with the broad competence the Secretary-General had been entrusted with in the setting up of UNEF I. It also questioned the role of the Advisory Committee, which was detached from the direct control of the permanent members of the Council. In essence, the statement may be interpreted as an attempt to redefine the answer to the question of 'Who governs?' With the P-5 cooperating,[58] thus regaining control over the chain of events in the course of UN crisis response, the pendulum swung from the General Assembly and the Secretary-General back to the Council.

In conclusion, the UNEF Advisory Committee showed in its early phase the potential of informal groups of states. It had been most useful against the background of a stalemate within the SC that shifted the institutional balance of power in the UN. With the General Assembly applying the Uniting-for-Peace procedure setting the framework of action, the Secretary-General had to implement the far-reaching mandates entrusted to him. In addition, the establishment of UNEF constituted a precedent in the constitutional practice of the UN Charter, increasing even more the vulnerability of the Secretary-General, who had to navigate in virtually uncharted waters. The Advisory Committee, composed of stakeholders, served as a certain kind of counterbalance, thus strengthening the office of the Secretary-General against the diverse General Assembly and the SC respectively. Such committees turned out to be a kind of model soon to be applied to other UN operations, such as in Lebanon and the Congo.

[57] UN Doc SCOR, 1752nd Meeting, 27 October 1973, para 16.
[58] It should be noted that the cooperation between the permanent members remained limited. China, for example, did not participate in the vote on setting up UNEF II, since it opposed the interference of an 'interventionist force'; see UN Doc SCOR, 1750th Meeting, 25 October 1973, para 4.

2.3 Filling a Vacuum: The Advisory Committee on Lebanon

The crisis in Lebanon that broke out in the early summer of 1958 differed entirely in nature from the Suez crisis. The United Nations Observation Group in Lebenon (UNOGIL) had been formed in June 1958 in the context of violent conflict in Lebanon over proposed constitutional changes. The crisis took on an international dimension when Lebanon had accused its Syrian neighbour of interfering in this internal conflict by sending arms and personnel to Lebanon. The Observation Group had been dispatched to discourage illegal infiltration of personnel or supply of arms across the Lebanese borders.[59] The appointment of the Advisory Committee on 24 July 1958 followed an impasse of the SC over a decision on strengthening the Observation Group in Lebanon. The Soviet Union had cast its veto over a draft resolution to make arrangements for expanding UNOGIL, introduced by the Japanese delegation.[60] Furthermore, the Council had adopted a procedural decision to adjourn without setting a date for the next meeting.[61] Later, Council members agreed to call an emergency special session of the General Assembly given the lack of unanimity of its permanent members.[62] At the July meeting, Hammarskjöld had reminded Council members of his remarks originally made on his re-election in September 1957 'that the Secretary-General should be expected to act also without such guidance, should this appear to him necessary in order to fill any vacuum that may appear in the systems which the Charter and traditional diplomacy provide for the safeguarding of peace and security'.[63] Without going into the specifics of the crisis in Lebanon and the role of the advisory body therein, the closer circumstances of its formation grants further insights regarding the rationale of these informal *ad hoc* groupings.

Confronted with the impasse of the SC, Hammarskjöld claimed that he tried to fill a 'vacuum in an informal way'[64] by constituting a mechanism for consultation along the lines of the UNEF Advisory Committee. In the absence of any guidance by SC members, Hammarskjöld asked the representatives of countries serving on the UNEF Advisory Committee, namely Argentina, Brazil, Canada, Ceylon, India, Norway, and Pakistan, to

---

[59] See S/RES/128 (1958), 11 June 1958, op. 1.
[60] See SCOR, 837th Meeting, 22 July 1958, paras 1–9.
[61] Ibid., paras 18–40.
[62] See UN Doc S/RES/129 (1958), 7 August 1958.
[63] UN Doc GAOR, 690th plenary meeting, 26 September 1957, para 73.
[64] Urquhart, *Hammarskjöld*, 286.

act as his consultative group on Lebanon, notably in an 'exclusive personal capacity'.[65] In a deviation from the previous procedure, this time the group was not constituted by virtue of a resolution adopted by the General Assembly, but by the Secretary-General's formal appointment of a 'strictly extra-constitutional group, not unconstitutional at all'.[56]

From this perspective, this Advisory Committee did not act as his consultative forum for the interpretation of mandates, but rather served as a sounding board to bounce off ideas for the strengthening of UNOGIL to prevent a further deterioration of the situation on the ground. The case of the Advisory Committee on Lebanon shows how the Secretary-General used informal *ad hoc* groupings in a very flexible, proactive manner. In his view, the constitution of those grouping could be derived from his authority and responsibilities as Secretary-General without receiving any explicit mandate of the General Assembly or the SC beforehand.

2.4 Interpreting Unclear Mandates: The Advisory Committee on the Congo

The Advisory Committee on Congo was set up amidst serious tensions in the SC over the course of action when the crisis in the former Belgian colony broke in the summer of 1960. Without the agreement of the Congolese government, Belgium had deployed troops into the country to restore law and order. Disorder had broken out following Congo's accession of independence on 30 June 1960. Invoking Article 99 of the Charter for the first time since the foundation of the UN,[67] the Secretary-General decided to bring the matter to the attention of the SC.[68]

During the Suez crisis, the application of the Uniting-for-Peace procedure had affected governance of the SC in a way that altered the pattern of permanent members wielding a veto on vital matters. The circumstances under which UNEF was set up taught the lesson that, even with a paralysed SC, the General Assembly and the Secretary-General might provide an alternative to run the operation nevertheless. With the 'Damocles sword'

---

[65] UN Doc SG/709, 24 July 1958, quoted in Urquhart, *Hammarskjöld*, 287.
[66] Unpublished note, quoted in ibid., 287.
[67] Ibid., 396.
[68] Article 99 of the UN Charter reads as follows: 'The Secretary-General may bring to the attention of the Security Council any matter which in his opinion may threaten the maintenance of international peace and security.'

of the Uniting-for-Peace procedure hanging over the heads of permanent members, this alternative especially affected the policy of the Soviet Union that had cast by far the most vetoes in the Council.[69] As Table 2 illustrates, between 1946 and 1965, the country took advantage of its privilege 101 times, with 109 vetoes cast in total during this period. John Stoessinger argues that this change in the prevailing conditions led the Soviet delegation 'to abstain on issues which it might have vetoed before, preferring to keep even an undesirable operation in the Council, where it could exercise more influence than it could if the General Assembly and the Secretary-General were in control'.[70]

The wording of the resolutions adopted by the SC defining a response to the crisis in Congo reflected a situation where the Soviet Union abstained even when it was obviously opposed to a certain course of action. At the same time, the price of gaining such abstention on Council resolutions was the agreement upon an ambiguous and vague diplomatic formula that left the interpretation to the Secretary-General who had to implement the unclear mandate. Those difficulties were already apparent in the early stages of crisis response when the SC called upon the Belgian government to withdraw its forces and authorized the Secretary-General

to take the necessary steps, in consultation with the Government of the Republic of Congo, to provide the Government with such military assistance as may be necessary until, through the efforts of the Congolese Government with the technical assistance of the UN, the national security forces may be able, in the opinion of the Government, to meet fully their tasks.[71]

The resolution did not entail a time limit for the Belgian withdrawal and a further definition of 'military assistance', which had been the diplomatic formula to paper over the differences among Council members. Securing compliance with the mandate, including the responsibility if anything went wrong, was left to the Secretary-General. A follow-up resolution adopted on 9 August somewhat specified the Council's request for withdrawal: Belgian troops should withdraw immediately from the province of Katanga 'under speedy modalities to be determined by the Secretary-General'.[72] Furthermore, operative paragraph 4 of SC Resolution 146 opened the way for the entry of UN forces into Katanga. They would

---

[69] See Table 2, Chapter 1.

[70] Stoessinger, *The United Nations and the Superpowers*, 18.

[71] UN Doc S/RES/143, 14 July 1960, op. 1 and 2.

[72] UN Doc S/RES/146, 9 August 1960, op. 2.

however neither be party to the conflict nor be used in any way to intervene or to influence the outcome of the internal conflict.[73] In this context, Hammarskjöld had written a special memorandum on how to implement this paragraph of this Resolution.

In general, Dag Hammarskjöld's performance in the Congo crisis must be understood against the background of his active role during the Suez crisis, which the Soviet Union had not actively opposed at this time. It had set the precedent that 'made it natural...to turn once again to the Secretary-General'.[74] However, the Soviet Union became increasingly uneasy with the Secretary-General's efforts to interpret the mandates adopted by the Council. The Soviet representative at the UN, Vasily V. Kuznetsov, even denied that the Secretary General had a mandate to interpret the Council's resolutions.[75] Basically, it was a desperate attempt to turn back the wheel by restricting the responsibility of the Secretary-General's office. The situation worsened after the assassination of Congo's Prime Minister Patrice Lumumba and two other Congolese leaders, Maurice Mpolo and Joseph Okito, in February 1961, culminating in the Soviet demand to dismiss Hammarskjöld. Even more, they no longer recognized him as an official of the UN, though the Soviet mission continued dealing with the Secretariat.[76] In response to the situation on the ground, the SC adopted resolution 161 on 21 February 1961, which considerably extended the framework for UN action on the ground, including the use of force in yet to be clarified circumstances.[77] The resolution had omitted any reference to the Secretary-General—the one who had to carry out the mandate—in order to gain Soviet abstention in that vote. Even though the Soviets doubtless opposed the resolution they did not cast the veto to keep the operation under the control of the SC. This may serve almost as a textbook example for the exposed stance the Secretary-General assumes when he has to implement resolutions serving as a fig leaf to hide the diverging positions of Council members. Hammarskjöld remarked accordingly in a statement before the Council:

Implementation obviously means interpretations in the first instance.... I have the right to expect guidance. That guidance could be given in many forms. But it

---

[73] Ibid., op. 3 and 4.
[74] Stoessinger, *The United Nations and the Superpowers*, 177.
[75] See United Nations, *Repertoire of the Practice of the Security Council: Supplement 1959–1963* (New York: United Nations; 1965), 105.
[76] See Urquhart, *Hammarskjöld*, 506.
[77] See UN Doc S/RES/161, 21 February 1961, op. A-1.

should be obvious that if the Security Council says nothing I have no other choice than to follow my conviction.[78]

In the Cold War context, convening a gathering of like-minded member states, adding weight to the Secretary-General's position, and thus serving as counterbalance to a divided SC, appeared therefore as the most promising strategy to share the burden (and the blame) growing out of the Secretary-General's responsibilities. However, Hammarskjöld clarified on various occasions that he did not want 'to unburden'[79] himself. The notion of sharing responsibilities did not refer to any explicit responsibility for decisions taken, though the individual advice given granted moral support to the efforts of the Secretary-General and strengthened his position. Furthermore, he gained additional leverage from the circumstance that some members of the Advisory Committee had been serving as non-permanent members of the SC, which had co-sponsored or participated in the drafting of key resolutions. These members had been able to serve as interlocutors between the Committee and the Council.

The Advisory Committee seemed to be therefore the 'natural solution' to increase the leverage of the Secretary-General against the SC, by advising and backing up his actions in the execution of SC's mandates. Hammarskjöld proposed 'a parallel to the Advisory Committee established in the case of the United Nations Emergency Force' which responded to a similar request by the Soviet delegation to convene such a group.[80] However, the Soviet Union obviously did not have a replication of the UNEF Advisory Committee in mind.[81] While the proposal of the Soviet delegation obviously reflected the aim to gain greater control over the actions of the Secretary-General, Hammarskjöld perceived the Advisory Committee at first instance as a means to decrease his vulnerability, increasing his room for manoeuvre in the Congo crisis. This problem of exposure and vulnerability has been, as noted earlier, a common pattern in the relationship between the Secretary-General and the SC. In this regard, the Congo conflict turned out to be the lens sharply focussing on the potential and limits of the office of the Secretary-General as a political organ of the UN. Dag Hammarskjöld elaborated further on these inherent tensions of his

---

[78] United Nations, *Repertoire of the Practice of the Security Council*, 105 *et seq.*

[79] Papers of the Secretaries-General, Advisory Committee on the Congo, Verbatim Records, twenty-sixth meeting, February 26, 1961.

[80] United Nations, *Repertoire of the Practice of the Security Council*, 117–8.

[81] On the night of 27 August, the Soviet representative, Vladimir V. Kuznetsov, heavily criticized Hammarskjöld for setting up an Advisory Committee on the Congo; see Urquhart, *Hammarskjöld*, 436.

office in summer 1961, delivering the Cyril-Foster Lecture in the Sheldonian Theatre at the University of Oxford:

This presents us with the crucial issue: Is it possible for the Secretary-General to resolve controversial issues on a truly inter-national basis without obtaining the formal decisions of the organs? In my opinion and on the basis of my experience, the answer is in the affirmative; it is possible for the Secretary-General to carry out his tasks in controversial political situations with full regard to his exclusively international obligation.... This is not to say that the Secretary-General is a kind of delphic oracle who alone speaks for the international community. He has available for his task varied means and resources.[82]

In the perception of the Secretary-General, the Advisory Committee on Congo constituted one of those various means at his disposal to assist him in dealing with this controversial political situation. The Committee, however, turned out to be a much larger and more unwieldy gathering than its predecessors, since it consisted of all eighteen countries contributing troops to the United Nations Operation in the Congo (ONUC).[83] Between August 1960 and April 1963, it held seventy-five meetings.[84] The composition of the Committee varied over time, since Hammarskjöld subsequently invited representatives of those countries contributing troops to ONUC at a later stage. Looking at the size of the Committee, Hammarskjöld disregarded one of his own lessons drawn out of the UNEF operation that the size of the Committee does matter: if the composition is too large, it might become ineffective.[85] The verbatim records show that meetings tended to be lengthy, producing much more red tape than the UNEF Advisory Committee.[86] Furthermore, the atmosphere was less informal due to the simultaneous English–French translations. The Secretariat had to distribute both English and French versions of the verbatim records, which were classified—parallel to the UNEF Advisory Committee—as confidential. Nevertheless, the closed meetings had been for the Secretary-General the 'best means of consulting, getting advice and rallying support for the UN operation in Congo'.[87]

---

[82] Andrew Cordier and Wilder Foote (eds.), *Papers of the Secretaries-General of the United Nations, Vol. V, Dag Hammarskjöld: 1958–1960* (New York: Columbia University Press, 1975), 487.

[83] Canada, Ethiopia, Ghana, Guinea, India, Indonesia, Ireland, Liberia, Malaysia, Mali, Morocco, Pakistan, Senegal, Sudan, Sweden, Tunisia, the United Arab Republic. Nigeria joined the Advisory Committee on 13 October 1960.

[84] See Papers of the Secretaries-General, Advisory Committee on the Congo, Verbatim Records, 1960–3.

[85] See UN Doc A/3943, 9 October 1958, para 181.

[86] Committee meetings often lasted three to four hours. Verbatim records used to be bulky documents of seventy to hundred pages.

[87] Urquhart, *Hammarskjöld*, 437.

However, such an assessment has to be seen in the wider context of the difficult relationship between the Secretary-General and some permanent members of the SC, notably the Soviet Union. The account reflects the desperate position of the Secretary-General at this time rather than the validity of the Committee as a means of supporting the Secretary-General in the interpretation of unclear SC mandates. Members on the Congo Advisory Committee were reluctant to commit themselves on controversial points. The Indian representative told Hammarskjöld during the second meeting quite bluntly that 'so far as the mandate of the Security Council is concerned, it is for you to interpret it in the light of the discussions and resolutions of the Security Council, and that interpretation is really a matter between you and the Security Council'.[88] The basic split in the SC over what the UN could or should do in Congo was merely mirrored within this group rather than discussed in a productive manner. The longer the crisis endured, the more members of the Committee tended to leave all contentious issues and related decisions to Hammarskjöld, who had actually hoped to get some advice.[89] Furthermore, Guinea, Indonesia, and the United Arab Republic would later leave the Advisory Committee because of their opposition to Congolese President Joseph Kasavubu, a strong rival of Prime Minister Lumumba.

Despite these difficulties, the Committee did take over some operational roles, such as appointing and defining the terms of reference of a Conciliation Committee that consisted of Asian and African member states to be sent into the Congo in order to assist the process of national reconciliation. Such action had been authorized by adopting General Assembly Resolution 1474 at the Emergency Special Session on 20 September 1960. Notably, the Advisory Committee discussed at some considerable length that the terms of reference had to observe strictly the principle of non-interference in the internal affairs of the Congo.[90] Kasavubu had stressed in an exchange of letters that such a Commission required the consent of the Congolese government.[91] Endless discussions around the timetable and the modalities of the departure of the Commission clearly showed the limited efficiency of this large Committee.

---

[88] Papers of the Secretaries-General, Advisory Committee on the Congo, Verbatim Records, second meeting, 26 August 1960.

[89] This became especially obvious after Lumumba's assassination; see Papers of the Secretaries-General, Advisory Committee on the Congo, Verbatim Records, twenty-third meeting, 21 February 1960.

[90] See Papers of the Secretaries-General, Advisory Committee on the Congo, Verbatim Records, seventh meeting, 21 October 1960.

[91] See A/4592, 24 November 1960, Annexes.

Furthermore, the leak of information to the press turned out to be a constant problem that spread considerable distrust among the members of the Advisory Committee. At the nineteenth meeting, Secretary-General Hammarskjöld remarked ironically that '[w]ith a group as large as this one, we have obviously already come to the point where the element of privacy is somewhat reduced'.[92] The greatest problem however arose through the complaints of the Soviet delegation that they had no access to the proceedings of the Advisory Committee. The work of the Committee was perceived in some quarters not as complementary, but standing in competition with the SC, potentially undermining its authority. From January 1961 onwards, SC members received a summary of the verbatim records dispatched by hand to the permanent representatives in a sealed envelope, marked 'confidential—by hand'. Such formalisation of a genuinely informal gathering of member states undermined even more the value of the Advisory Committee, a circumstance which did not remain unrecognized by the Secretary-General: 'The decision will have a certain impact on the character of our work and our deliberations',[93] he concluded at the nineteenth meeting of the Congo Advisory Committee on 29 December 1960.

Records reflect a growing disillusionment by the Secretary-General with the effectiveness of the Committee as the conflict progressed.[94] At a later stage, it became evident that at least some summary records of the meetings had been passed to Congolese leaders.[95] The frank exchange of views, which had been the special merit of the previous advisory committees, would no longer be possible if representatives, including the Secretary-General, did not want to run the danger of exposing themselves too much to the members of the SC. The tensions among Committee members rose considerably.[96]

Nevertheless, the verbatim records reveal that Hammarskjöld saw a great potential in the advisory committees, not only as an instrument to advise the Secretary-General in the implementation or interpretation of resolutions, but also in terms of executive functions, for example, in the

---

[92] Papers of the Secretaries-General, Advisory Committee on the Congo, Verbatim Records, nineteenth meeting, 29 December 1960.

[93] Ibid.

[94] Brian Urquhart, who attended both UNEF and Congo Advisory Committee meetings, confirms that view. Telephone interview with Brian Urquhart, 21 February 2001.

[95] See Papers of the Secretaries-General, Advisory Committee on the Congo, Verbatim Records, seventy-first meeting, 13 December 1962.

[96] See Papers of the Secretaries General, Advisory Committee on the Congo, Verbatim Records, thirty-fifth meeting, 13 March 1961. The Indian representative even threatened that one had to close down the Committee if the criticism by one member of the views of another continued.

longer-term implementation of resolutions or agreements. This requires a great deal of strategic coordination, which he would have liked to be delegated to those countries with a pre-existing level of commitment. Hammarskjöld assessed quite clearly the burden operations such as ONUC put on the Secretariat, encroaching heavily on other tasks.[97] In the discussions with the Advisory Committee he therefore sketched out some potential further developments of the Committee, drawing on the precedent of United Nations Relief & Works Agency (UNRWA), the administration of the Palestinian refugee assistance. The administration, headed by the Director-General, had been assisted by a small advisory committee on the ground, representing the countries most concerned, a mechanism that functioned exceptionally well: 'It has the advantage of current advice by people who live with the problem, with an administrative responsibility. It has the further advantage of not putting within the Secretariat tasks which, through their sheer mass, and also due to their quality, tend to swell like a kind of cancer and eat out all other necessary functions.'[98]

Furthermore, the Secretary-General himself favoured a certain detachment from the day-to-day business on the ground avoiding 'all sorts of rather unnecessary deep waters'.[99] Hammarskjöld's assessment would become especially applicable to the post-Cold War era when the UN had to take over more and more complex operations, deployed in countries emerging from long and bitter civil wars. Such analysis has become even more relevant from today's perspective with the growing shift of the typical mission of UN operations from peacekeeping to peace-building.

In conclusion, the Advisory Committee on the Congo operated under different structural conditions than at the time of the Suez crisis. While the UNEF Advisory Committee had advised the Secretary-General against the background of a paralysed SC that was overridden by the General Assembly's Uniting-for-Peace resolution, on the Congo crisis, the Council proved to be unable to produce clear mandates to take charge of the situation on the ground. Given the conflicting interests of the great powers, SC mandates tended to reflect a compromise on the basis of the lowest common denominator. In fact, Council members passed the buck to the Secretary-General, imposing upon him the burden of interpreting the resolutions that needed to be translated into action. By establishing

---

[97] See Papers of the Secretaries-General, Advisory Committee on the Congo, Verbatim Records, twenty-third meeting, 21 February 1961.
[98] Ibid.
[99] Ibid.

the Advisory Committee on the Congo, the Secretary-General aimed at sharing the burden and the blame to reduce his vulnerability against the great power tensions in the Council. However, the longer the crisis endured the more the Advisory Committee was perceived especially by the Soviet Union not as complementary to but in competition with the activities of the UN Security Council, as the Soviet request to receive summaries of the Committee's verbatim records made abundantly clear. Furthermore, discussions in the Advisory Committee merely reflected the tensions within the Council, which severely limited the usefulness of this *ad hoc* grouping.

Overall, advisory committees strengthened the role of the UN Secretary-General vis-à-vis the SC in crisis settings that were heavily affected by the structural conditions of bipolarity. The case study of Namibia will illustrate the difficulties of the UN in the early 1970s to adapt to the systemic change of decolonization. With the balance of power in the General Assembly and the SC shifting, the exit option, in terms of conducting conflict management outside the UN framework but within the objectives of the Organization, gained greater currency. Nevertheless, advisory committees would re-emerge under the label of groups of friends of the Secretary-General during and after the breakdown of the bipolar system.

3

Proliferation of Informal Groups in the Post-Bipolar Era

The breakdown of the bipolar system provided the permissive political context to engage the UN conflict resolution machinery in a plethora of conflicts. The quantity and quality of crisis settings widened and, for a certain time, overstrained the role of the UN Security Council (SC) leading to a problem of overload. This has often been accompanied by a sheer lack of interest in, or disagreement on the part of the Five permanent members of the SC (P-5) with respect to what action should be taken. The UN and its member states have been constantly facing hard choices regarding which conflicts to address. In addition to problems of overload and reluctance by the P-5 to become engaged, the structural conditions of the Council constitute a serious constraint in the development of consistent policies and standards, as Chapter 4 will elaborate.

The proliferation of informal groups of states in the post-bipolar era may be analysed against the background that they have been instrumental in adapting to systemic change and in alleviating its unanticipated consequences.[1] They provide the possibility of exit from the institutional and structural constraints of the SC by granting voice to those states being stakeholders in the conflict or like-minded supporters of peacemaking initiatives. This chapter argues, firstly, that informal groups of states may serve as agents of incremental change. Furthermore, they may enhance SC governance by bridging the gap between the substance of conflict management and the process of its legitimation.

---

[1] On the problem of unanticipated effects of international institutions, see Gallarotti, 'The Limits of International Organization', 183–220.

3.1 Systemic Changes and the Challenge to Adapt

Underlying the following section is the assumption that the UN Security Council is a *Janus*-faced structure of both an open system and a closed shop, which captures its sensitivity towards systemic changes while facing considerable constraints to adapt accordingly. Firstly, it sheds light on the crisis settings the SC has been increasingly confronted with in the post-bipolar era. Secondly, it examines the structural constraints of this institution that prevent it from formulating an effective crisis response.

3.1.1 *The Complexity of Crisis Settings*

The pattern of UN involvement in the post-bipolar era is characterized by conflict settings on an intrastate rather than an interstate level. One can observe a shift away from border conflicts between states to conditions of internal violence that often spill over into neighbouring countries in the region. Conflict scenarios involve a different mix of actors, ranging from regular armies over militias to armed civilians. They may include the collapse of state authority, with an absence of governance, accompanied by the breakdown of law and order. Furthermore, civil strife affects the economies of neighbouring countries, with economic growth rates shrinking and diseases such as malaria and HIV/AIDS spreading.[2] Complex crisis settings require differentiated responses from the international community, a varying mix of policies and flexible sequencing of different kinds of interventions such as peace enforcement with aid and reform.[3] Negotiated settlements that end conflicts are usually not only military arrangements to cease armed violence; they also include a variety of other tasks. These address both military and civilian issues, such as the supervision of ceasefires, (regional) disarmament, the demobilization of armed forces, the integration of former combatants into civilian life, humanitarian relief, the establishment and training of police forces, the reform of institutions, and the organization and supervision of elections. UN operations have increasingly had to combine peacekeeping with peace-building functions, reflecting the complex arrangements that ended the armed conflict. The international administration of war-torn territories like Bosnia, Eastern Slavonia, Kosovo, and East Timor—indeed, a kind of trusteeship—appears as a direct

---

[2] See Paul Collier, Lani Elliott, Håvard Hegre, Anke Hoeffler, Marta Reynal-Querol, and Nicholas Sambanis, *Breaking the Conflict Trap: Civil War and Development Policy* (Washington, DC: World Bank, 2003), 33–9 (hereinafter *Breaking the Conflict Trap*).

[3] Ibid., 185.

application consistent with the trend towards complex peacekeeping operations, though 'the challenges are unique'.[4]

The increasing demands of the changing security environment affected both the SC and the Office of the Secretary-General. The SC responded by extending the scope of Article 39, adopting far-reaching mandates to deal with the complexity of crisis situations.[5] The Secretary-General was pushed into a position where 'the management aspects ... have become more demanding and more politically charged'.[6] He had to oversee multifunctional operations involving the complete spectrum of preventive diplomacy, peacekeeping, peace enforcement, peace-building, including humanitarian aid, refugee assistance, and electoral campaigns which he increasingly entrusted to special representatives acting on his behalf. The complexity of tasks required the UN Secretariat to integrate all elements of this wide spectrum under the umbrella of a single peace-support operation deployed into settings of intrastate conflict. While the UN had established only thirteen peacekeeping operations in the thirty years between 1948 and 1978, the fading bipolar international system created the permissive political context in which to establish twenty-six operations in the short, seven-year period between 1988 and 1995, as Table 3 illustrates. The quality and quantity of crisis settings called for flexible mechanisms that would allow the UN to deal with these complex and sensitive operations in an effective way.

In conclusion, informal groups of states proliferated out of the demands the UN faced at various levels. They constitute a flexible diplomatic device for increased cooperation. While the Groups of Friends originally developed as an informal arrangement to complement peacemaking efforts of the Secretary-General, contact groups tended to choose the exit option by conducting conflict management outside the UN framework, acting either within the objectives of the UN or on their own accord. The sheer number and complexity of crisis settings in the post-bipolar era exacerbated the structural constraints that are inherent in the UN conflict resolution machinery, as the following section will elaborate.

---

[4] Richard Caplan, *A New Trusteeship? The International Administration of War-torn Territories*, Adelphi Paper 341, International Institute for Strategic Studies (Oxford: Oxford University Press, 2002), 9; see also Richard Caplan, *International Governance of War-Torn Territories: Rule and Reconstruction* (Oxford: Oxford University Press, 2005).

[5] See Helmut Freudenschuß, 'Article 39 of the UN Charter Revisited: Threats to Peace and Recent Practice of the UN Security Council', *Austrian Journal of International Law*, 46/1 (1993), 1–39.

[6] James S. Sutterlin, *The United Nations and the Maintenance of International Peace and Security: A Challenge To Be Met* (Westport, CT: Praeger, 1995), 116.

Table 3. UN Peacekeeping Operations (PKOs), 1948–2004

Period	PKOs established
1948–87	Middle East—UNTSO (1948–); India and Pakistan—UNMOGIP (1949–); Middle East—UNEF I (1956–67); Lebanon—UNOGIL (1958); Congo—ONUC (1960–4); West New Guinea—UNSF (1962–3); Yemen—UNYOM (1963–4); Cyprus—UNFICYP (1964–); Dominican Republic—DOMREP (1965–6); India and Pakistan—UNIPOM (1965–6); Middle East—UNEF II (1973–9); Golan Heights—UNDOF (1974–); Lebanon—UNIFIL (1978–)
1988–95	Iran and Iraq—UNIIMOG (1988–91); Angola—UNAVEM I (1988–91); Afghanistan and Pakistan—UNGOMAP (1988–90); Namibia—UNTAG (1989–90); Central America—ONUCA (1989–92); Iraq and Kuwait—UNIKOM (1991–2003); Western Sahara—MINURSO (1991–); Angola—UNAVEM II (1991–5); El Salvador—ONUSAL (1991–5); Cambodia—UNAMIC (1991–2); Former Yugoslavia—UNPROFOR (1992–5); Cambodia - UNTAC (1992–3); Somalia—UNOSOM I (1992–3); Mozambique—ONUMOZ (1992–4); Somalia—UNOSOM II (1993–5); Georgia—UNOMIG (1993–); Haiti—UNMIH (1993–6); Liberia—UNOMIL (1993–7); Rwanda and Uganda—UNOMUR (1993–4); Rwanda—UNAMIR (1993–6); Chad and Libya—UNASOG (1994); Tajikistan—UNMOT (1994–2000); Angola – UNAVEM III (1995–7); Croatia—UNCRO (1995–6); FYROM—UNPREDEP (1995–9); Bosnia and Herzegovina—UNMIBH (1995–2002)
1996–98	Croatia—UNTAES (1996–8); Prevlaka Peninsula—UNMOP (1996–2002); Guatemala—MINUGUA (1997); Haiti—UNSMIH (1996–7); Angola—MONUA (1997–9); Haiti—UNTMIH (1997); Haiti—MIPONUH (1997–2000); Croatia—UNPSG (1998); Central African Republic—MINURCA (1998–2000); Sierra Leone—UNOMSIL (1998–9)
1999–2004	Kosovo—UNMIK (1999–); East Timor—UNTAET (1999–2002); Sierra Leone—UNAMSIL (1999–); Democratic Republic of Congo—MONUC (1999–); Ethiopia and Eritrea—UNMEE (2000–); East Timor—UNMISET (2002–); Liberia—UNMIL (2003–); Côte d'Ivoire—UNOCI (2004–); Haiti—MINUSTAH (2004–); Burundi—ONUB (2004–)

Source: UN Department of Peacekeeping Operations. Available at:
www.un.org/Depts/dpko/dpko/ index.asp.

3.1.2 *Structural Constraints of the UN Security Council*

The UN presents, as Michael Doyle has rightly observed, 'an almost textbook case of multiple strategic incapacities produced by both institutional incapacity and lack of support from its member countries'.[7] Looking through the prism of the SC, the body lacks an external federator that may serve as the uniting moment to develop a 'commonality of interests'.[8] It is first and foremost a political body, with its resolutions and statements reflecting the bargaining and trade-off of the various interests involved in the decision-making process. Another factor to be taken into account is

[7] Michael Doyle, 'War Making and Peace Making', 539.
[8] Ibid.

the lack of a 'cultural consensus'[9] which constitutes an impediment to the application of consistent policies towards crisis situations. While it certainly appears as a truism that the workings of the SC are to a great deal dependent on the prevailing structural conditions of the international system, any analysis of the potential and limits of this body should go beyond the focus on external constraints and also include a deeper examination of its internal constraints. The following section concentrates therefore on three crucial factors: firstly, the varying capacity of UN member states to contribute to the Council's work; secondly, the biannual rotation of elected members as an impediment to formulate long-term policies; and thirdly, structural constraints of the Council, resulting from adaptations to systemic changes.

As far as the capacities of UN member states are concerned, only a few delegations serving on the Council have the necessary (human) resources—taking into account, for example, the size of their permanent missions—to deal in depth with the plethora of conflicts placed on its daily agenda. Table 4 shows the number of professionals on staff of member states serving on the SC in the period of 1995 to 2002. The size of permanent missions such as Bangladesh, Jamaica, Mauritius, or Mali ranged, for example, in the year 2001 between six and eight professionals. Those numbers may illustrate the extremely limited resources of some UN member states to bear the additional burden of a two-year term on the Council. At the same time, they demonstrate the dominance of the five permanent members to set the Council's agenda and to define the chain of action.[10] Although the focus on the number of professionals on staff is just one indicator among others to assess the potential influence of a delegation in defining the chain of SC action, it is nevertheless an obvious one. The question of resources becomes especially relevant at times when the number of conflicts on the Council's agenda and the frequency of its meetings tend to be high. However, a certain degree of accumulated expertise and experience, based on special skills or knowledge, or privileged access to information, may compensate to some extent for the sheer lack of resources. The size and effectiveness of foreign ministries to back up permanent missions with information is another point of consideration. Notably, some delegations are punching above their actual weight due to the skilful work of their permanent representatives, including their dele-

---

[9] Ibid.
[10] See David D. Caron, 'The Legitimacy of the Collective Authority of the Security Council', *American Journal of International Law*, 87/4 (1993), 564.

Table 4. Size of Permanent Missions—Number of Professionals on Staff, 2000–04

	2004	2003	2002	2001	2000
Permanent Five					
China	65	61	70	59	67
France	29	28	28	30	30
Russia	83	83	78	75	81
United Kingdom	38	42	40	36	34
United States	128	124	123	112	115
Elected members 2004–05					
Algeria	16				
Benin	10				
Brazil	34				
Philippines	24				
Romania	17				
Elected members 2003–04					
Angola	17	18			
Chile	18	17			
Germany	63	62			
Pakistan	15	15			
Spain	21	20			
Elected members 2002–03					
Bulgaria		12	11		
Cameroon		18	17		
Guinea		12	11		
Mexico		25	23		
Syria		15	17		
Elected members 2001–02					
Colombia			16	14	
Ireland			21	20	
Mauritius			7	6	
Norway			18	19	
Singapore			13	13	
Elected members 2000–01					
Bangladesh				8	8
Jamaica				7	10
Mali				6	5
Tunisia				13	12
Ukraine				18	13

Source: www.globalpolicy.org/security/data/tabsec.htm.

gates, at UN Headquarters in New York. Individuals do matter, and they are able to make a difference.

Secondly, the biannual rotation of non-permanent members constitutes another structural constraint, which prevents the formulation of comprehensive approaches to crisis settings. Consequently, much of the crisis response occurs *ad hoc* and in a rather incremental way. The very concept of non-permanent membership is an impediment to any long-term commitment towards a conflict, especially civil wars. Given the fact that the average civil conflict goes on for about seven years, with a need for continued commitment lasting well into the decade of post-conflict peace, the development and pursuance of long-term policy goals within the framework of the SC remains a difficult task.[11] At the same time, these structural conditions add to the preponderance of the P-5 on the Council, in addition to their prerogative to cast a veto on SC action.

The third internal constraint relates to adaptations in the Council's working methods and procedures as a response to systemic changes. In essence, the breakdown of the bipolar system exacerbated structural limitations of the SC that had originated in the 1970s.[12] The proliferation of informal consultations of the SC, the so-called consultations of the whole, from the mid-1970s onwards has to be analysed in particular against this background.[13] It is important to understand that the rise of informal consultations constituted an incremental adaptation of SC working methods and practices. In essence, it was a partial exit from the constraints of formal meetings in order to cope with systemic changes that had seriously affected the efficient working of the body. The breakdown of the bipolar system resulted in a similar pattern of adapting SC working methods and procedures in response to systemic change. In the 1990s, the post-bipolar international context had been permissive for a greater use of the UN's conflict resolution machinery. The frequency of the formal meetings and informal consultations resembles the trend of the 1970s, albeit on a much higher scale, given the large number of conflicts on the Council's agenda. As Figure 1 shows, the number of informal consultations rose much faster than the number of formal meetings, culminating in 1994, when the SC convened 165 formal meetings but closed the door 273 times for informal consultations. The number of informal consultations clearly outweighed the formal meetings prior to the year 2000, with the trend reversing in the following years.[14] In 2002, the Council held 273 formal meetings and 259 informal consultations, which reflected an increasing number of public debates and open meetings that allowed non-members to participate in the discussions of the SC. This trend illustrates

---

[11] See *Breaking the Conflict Trap*, 3 and 7.

[12] This will be further elaborated in the case study on Namibia.

[13] See Chapter 5.

[14] On recent procedural developments to promote greater transparency in the procedure and working methods of the Security Council, see UN Doc S/2002/603, 6 June 2002.

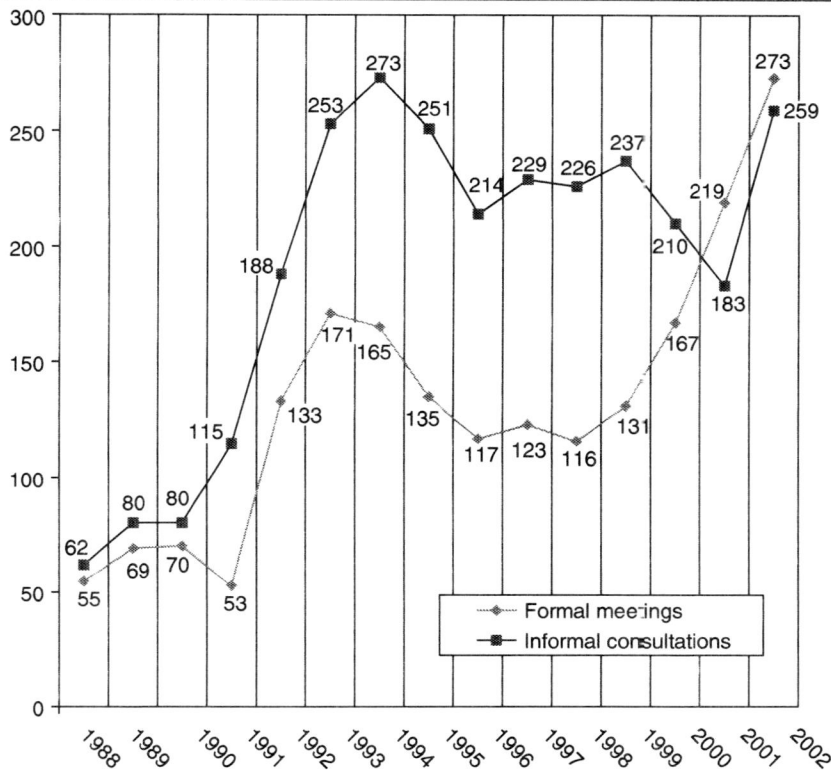

Figure 1 Formal meetings and informal consultations of the Security Council, 1988–2002

Source: Data as provided by the Global Policy Forum, New York;
http://www.globalpolicy.org/security/data/secmgtab.htm, accessed on 21 April 2005.

the synchronization of partial exit and voice as mutually reinforcing factors to secure loyalty towards the organization. Granting voice to non-members has become to some degree a compensation for the lack of formal adaptation of the Council. Voice channels the growing pressure resulting from demands for greater transparency of SC working methods and procedures and expansion of its membership, which could only be partially supplied by opening the doors of the Council.[15] Furthermore, analysis of the SC enlargement in 1965 suggests that those demands are

---

[15] Especially since 1993, the SC has been adopting a plethora of working methods in response to demands for more transparency. Most of them originated in the so-called 'Informal Working Group of the Security Council concerning the Council's documentation and other procedural questions'; see Bailey and Daws, *The Procedure of the UN Security Council*, 50–75 and 377–8.

unlikely to fade, even if UN member states should agree upon a formula to adapt its current composition.

In conclusion, systemic changes in the 1960s and at the end of the 1980s generated adaptations in the SC working methods and procedures resulting in the retreat to informal consultations that constituted a partial exit from the UN's constitutional framework. The proliferation of informal consultations of the SC in the mid-1970s and again from the early 1990s onwards has to be analysed against the background of the devaluation of the Council's formal meetings as the institutional setting for the agreement on substantive action. Formal meetings have become first and foremost a platform for the articulation of voice. However, various diplomats of permanent missions and officials of the UN Secretariat pointed already in the early 1980s to the downside of informal consultations that had been inherent in the process, that is, 'deliberate stalling, inaction, watered-down resolutions, secrecy, over-formalization of an informal process, and lack of outside input'.[16] The maximum retreat to informal consultations has not been able to overcome the structural constraints of the Council. For this reason, informal groups of states basically continued and deepened the trend towards exit. In the 1990s, this trend developed in parallel with the proliferation of informal consultations as well as the continuing calls for greater transparency of SC working methods and procedures. In this regard, exit and voice may have complementary and substitutional effects at the same time. They have been complementary in terms of answering parallel calls for transparency and increased effectiveness. Equally, overemphasizing transparency may lead to further constraints in the effectiveness of the SC and result in greater recourse to the exit option.

3.2 Agents of Incremental Change

This section elaborates on the argument that informal groups of states have taken on certain functions as agents of incremental change, without formally changing the UN Charter. From the early 1990s onwards, key reports of the UN Secretariat to adapt the organization to the post-bipolar security environment have been repeatedly referring to Groups of Friends and Contact Groups as—at least potentially—a useful tool for complementing the work of the UN in various regards. In 1992, the Secretary-General's

---

[16] Cited in Loie Feuerle, 'Informal Consultation: A Mechanism in Security Council Decision-Making', *New York University Journal of International Law and Politics*, 18/1 (1985), 294.

report on An Agenda for Peace encouraged the wider use of Groups of Friends especially as a means of cooperation with regional arrangements and organizations:

In this regard, the United Nations has recently encouraged a rich variety of complementary efforts. Just as no two regions or situations are the same, so the design of cooperative work and its division of labour must adapt to the realities of each case with flexibility and creativity.... For El Salvador, a unique arrangement—the 'Friends of the Secretary General'—contributed to agreements reached through the mediation of the Secretary General.[17]

The rather promising performance of the Group of Friends of the Secretary-General on El Salvador in the period between 1989 and 1991 facilitated the subsequent formation of informal groups of states. The informal arrangement became a model applied to other crisis situations such as in Guatemala and Haiti.[18] By 1995, the Group of Friends had become an established instrument 'to support the Secretary-General in the discharge of peacemaking and peacekeeping mandates entrusted to him,' as the Supplement to An Agenda for Peace suggested.[19] Inside the Secretariat, their role has been perceived as mostly positive. In addition to granting leverage to the Secretary-General's peacemaking efforts, the Groups have been appreciated as a buffer to decrease his vulnerability in the discharge of politically sensitive mandates.[20] At the same time, the flexibility of the mechanism may easily accommodate divergent concepts on the side of UN member states and the UN Secretariat of how the informal setting should actually work. The strength of the groups is based upon their constructive ambiguity.

At the end of the 1990s, after the stocktaking of the successes and failures of UN peacemaking efforts in the first post-bipolar decade, the perceived added value of informal groups of states had shifted somewhat towards a device for mobilizing international support, as a report by the UN's Lessons Learned Unit underlined: 'The mechanism of a 'Group of Friends' ... which would include concerned regional and extra-regional Powers that command influence over parties to the conflict, can be another effective tool for mobilising support for the peace process.'[21] The

---

[17] UN Doc A/47/ 277–S/24111, 17 June 1992, para 62.
[18] Prantl and Krasno, 'Informal Groups of Member States', 335–51.
[19] UN Doc A/50/ 60–S/1995/1, 3 January 1995, para 83.
[20] Author interview with a senior official in the UN Secretariat, New York, 24 October 2002.
[21] Lessons Learned Unit, *Cooperation between the United Nations and Regional Organizations/ Arrangements in a Peacekeeping Environment: Suggested Principles and Mechanisms* (New York: United Nations, 1999), para B–XII. Available at: http://pbpu.unlb.org/ pbpu/library/ Regional%20Organizations%201999.pdf.

reluctance of UN member states to engage in crisis situations in Africa after the traumatic experiences of Somalia and Rwanda has fostered initiatives to consider concerted international efforts to promote peace and security in the region. In order to generate the critical mass of leverage, the Secretary-General encouraged the formation of groups of friends and especially contact groups as a way of mobilizing support for the promotion of peace and sustainable development in Africa.[22] And indeed, with the limitation of objectives, the possibility of maintaining flexible options, and the close perception of the adversary, informal groups of states tend to combine key principles for the successful performance of crisis diplomacy.[23]

Another key function is the coordination and bundling of peacemaking and peace-implementation efforts vis-à-vis crisis settings and parties to a conflict. While the Secretariat has acknowledged the great potential of informal groups of states, the 'risk of duplication or overlapping of efforts, which can be exploited by recalcitrant parties',[24] clearly define their limits. The Agenda for Democratization pointed again to that risk specifically in those areas where the support of democratization had led to a proliferation of actors and activities. Informal groups of states may serve in this context as an instrument 'to harmonize diplomatic initiatives and to achieve ... a coordinated approach'.[25] Furthermore, the Secretary-General's report on the prevention of armed conflict identified strategic coordination as the great potential strength of a Group of Friends, not only in the field of UN crisis response but also conflict prevention.[26]

As recent studies have underlined, strategic coordination is also a key element in the implementation of peace agreements. Here, a Group of Friends may take on the role of a coordinating hub to bundle the various efforts taken by governmental and non-governmental implementation agencies.[27] Finally, the report of the Panel on United Nations Peace Operations,[28] the so-called Brahimi Report, suggested a greater institutional-

---

[22] See UN Doc S/1998/318, 13 April 1998, para 24; UN Doc S/1999/1008, 25 September 1999, paras 9–11; UN Doc A/56/371, 18 September 2001, para 9.
[23] See James L. Richardson, *Crisis Diplomacy: The Great Powers since the Mid-Nineteenth Century* (Cambridge: Cambridge University Press, 1994), 363.
[24] UN Doc A/50/ 60–S/1995/1, 3 January 1995, para 84.
[25] UN Doc A/51/761, 20 December 1996, para 48.
[26] UN Doc S/2001/574, 7 June 2001, para 76.
[27] Bruce D. Jones, *The Challenges of Strategic Coordination: Containing Opposition and Sustaining Implementation of Peace Agreements in Civil Wars*, IPA Policy Paper Series on Peace Implementation (New York: International Peace Academy, June 2001), 2 and 13; Stephen John Stedman, *Implementing Peace Agreements in Civil Wars: Lessons and Recommendations for Policymakers*, IPA Policy Paper Series on Peace Implementation (New York: International Peace Academy, May 2001).
[28] See UN Doc S/2000/809, 21 August 2000.

ization of the relationship between troop-contributing countries on the one side and the Secretariat and the SC on the other. Although the Brahimi panel did not explicitly discuss the role of informal groups of states, given its limited time frame, the resources available, and the mandate to focus on the most urgent needs,[29] in the debate on the implementation of the report, the SC stressed the importance of Groups of Friends as a useful tool to increase the coherence and effectiveness of UN action in the peacekeeping realm, provided that they maintain close cooperation with the Council.[30]

However, the perception of their role has not been uncontroversial among UN member states. Permanent members of the SC such as France like to stress the point that 'groups of friends do not exist to do the work of the Council'.[31] Their work is appreciated as long as 'such groups are open and when they bring together the members of the Council, the main troop contributors, the countries of the region and possibly foreign donors as well'.[32] For example, the delegation of Bangladesh has been at times a particularly outspoken advocate of greater transparency of the workings of informal arrangements, such as the Group of Friends, during its non-permanent membership on the Council in the period of 2000–1:

It has been a convenient practice to have a group of friends for each conflict area. We recognize the extremely valuable contribution made by these groups in drafting Council resolutions, but we join others in calling for greater transparency in the working methods of these groups to prevent those Council members that are not represented in any of these groups from being virtually excluded from the decision-making process.[33]

On the other hand, SC resolutions tend to reflect consensus and unanimity between its members to the greatest possible extent. Opposite views held by non-permanent members are not just overridden, as a closer look at the voting pattern reveals. As the Permanent Representative of the United Kingdom has reminded during a recent discussion on the work of the Council: '[T]he Security Council actually likes to show that it is unanimous on a subject because its authority is greater if we are unanimous.... I think we are beginning to understand each other better on that.'[34] Furthermore, calls for greater transparency of informal settings are likely to diminish as soon as the states concerned participate in *ad hoc* groupings. In addition, the maximum application of

[29] Interview with William B. Durch, Washington, DC, 11 September 2001.
[30] See UN Doc S/RES/1353 (2001), 13 June 2001, Annex II and op. C-2.
[31] UN Doc S/PV.4432, 30 November 2001, 11.
[32] UN Doc S/PV.4257, 16 January 2001, 17.
[33] UN Doc A/56/PV.27, 16 October 2001, 17.
[34] UN Doc S/PV.4432, 30 November 2001, 5.

transparency is detrimental to the informality of *ad hoc* mechanisms and may ultimately limit their potential and impact, as the US representative remarked during a debate of the SC in 2001: '[T]he less formal the setting ... the more genuine the discussion and interaction we have.'[35] The composition and proceedings of *ad hoc* groupings therefore have to reflect a trade-off serving these diverging demands.

In conclusion, informal groups of states have been part and parcel of key UN reports dealing with the adaptation of the organization to the post-bipolar security environment. They reflected the actual performance of informal groups in the past and, at the same time, projected the perception of their potential into the future. Analysis of UN documents suggests the allocation of four different, coexisting functions to informal groups of states: firstly, to assist the UN Secretary-General in discharging his mandates; secondly, to mobilize international support; thirdly, to coordinate and bundle peacemaking and peace-implementation efforts vis-à-vis crisis settings and parties to a conflict; and fourthly, to institutionalize the relationship between troop-contributing countries and the SC as well as the Secretariat respectively.

However, it seems to be the prevailing understanding in the UN Secretariat that overconceptualizing informal settings would already restrain their flexibility and limit their usefulness.[36] The allocated functions should be understood therefore as a rough indicator of areas where informal groups of states are perceived to be especially useful. In that sense, they may serve as flexible agents of incremental change. Change is incremental, since the constitutional foundation of the organization, that is, the Charter of the UN, remains unaltered. While these indicators may suggest a complementary role of informal settings in the field of UN crisis response, the following section extends the analysis to crisis situations where informal groups of states take over the substance of conflict management, often operating outside the UN framework. It elaborates on the function of loyalty towards the organization, which reflects an interest-based pattern of UN member states to seek legitimation for their action by the UN Security Council.

3.3 Mediator between Process and Substance

The structural conditions of the post-bipolar era pushed the devolution of the substance of crisis management to *ad hoc* coalitions of able and willing

---

[35] Ibid., 17.
[36] Interview with a senior official in the UN Secretariat, UN, New York, 29 October 2002.

countries or informal arrangements, whereas the SC still remains a pull factor by providing the platform—at least in most cases—for the 'right process', namely the legitimation for state action.[37] While the detachment of the process of legitimation and the substance of crisis response is far from being new,[38] it has been a significant pattern from the mid-1990s onwards. This pattern was most visible when North Atlantic Treaty Organization (NATO) member states intervened in Kosovo without the explicit authorization of the SC. Similar lessons apply to the more recent US intervention in Iraq. Even if the exit option is pushed to its extreme, loyalty prevents the long-term marginalization of the organization. The further states push for exit, the greater the pull of loyalty.[39]

Legitimacy shall be defined in this context as 'a property of a rule or rule-making institution which itself exerts a pull towards compliance on those addressed normatively because those addressed believe that the rule or institution has come into being and operates in accordance with generally accepted principles of right process'.[40] This pull towards compliance or, in other words, loyalty towards the organization, is still one of the most important functions of the SC. The body carries a large degree of symbolic power that helps to create a perception of legitimacy, as Ian Hurd has convincingly argued: 'The symbolic power of the Security Council is evident in the energy states expend on having the Council pay attention to issues of concern to them.'[41]

The most visible symbolic recognition may be observed when analysing the electoral campaigns of UN member states to gain a non-permanent seat on the Council. In the late 1990s, those efforts stood higher than ever on UN member states' policy agenda.[42] Campaigning for a non-permanent seat mattered despite the fact that the composition of the SC is unrepresentative and the open-ended discussions on its reform are still continuing. Recognizing its symbolic power together with the under-

---

[37] On the supposed failure of the democratic process to produce substantive outcomes, see Robert A. Dahl, *Democracy and its Critics* (New Haven, CT: Yale University Press, 1989), 163–75.

[38] In 1977, the Western Contact Group on Namibia negotiated a settlement plan outside the UN framework but within its objectives that eventually led to the independence of the country in 1990; see Chapter 5.

[39] This argument is not to be understood as entirely sequential. The US invasion in Iraq illustrates that the pull for UN reinvolvement did not follow immediately but subsequently with the invasion forces facing growing resistance on the ground and the political (and financial) costs of the operation rising. I have to thank Joseph Nye for raising this caveat.

[40] Thomas M. Franck, *The Power of Legitimacy Among Nations* (Oxford: Oxford University Press, 1990), 24.

[41] Ian Hurd, 'Legitimacy, Power, and the Symbolic Life of the UN Security Council', *Global Governance*, 8/1 (2002), 39.

[42] See David Malone, 'Eyes on the Prize: The Quest for Nonpermanent Seats on the UN Security Council', *Global Governance*, 6/1 (2000), 3–23.

standing of this body as a rule-making institution, which exerts a pull towards compliance upon UN member states, contributes to a better understanding of the dynamics between informal groups of states and the Council. Even in those cases where informal groups decide to solve conflicts outside the framework of the UN, it is the mandate of the SC that provides legitimacy for state action and acceptance among the wider UN membership.

Decentralization of substance while maintaining the process turned out to be one of the most important changes in SC governance. While informal groups may deliver substantial outcomes, the Council produces legitimacy through its formal decisions. Legitimacy is the common good, which merges substance and process. The common good, according to Robert Dahl, 'consists of the practices, arrangements, institutions, and processes that ... promote the well-being of ourselves and others—not, to be sure, of "everyone" but of enough persons to make the practices, arrangements, etc. acceptable and perhaps even cherished'.[43] The right process remains of crucial importance to achieve double-edged legitimacy in terms of procedure and output. It is both the decision-making process and the final result that have to pass the litmus test of perceived legitimacy that creates acceptance among UN member states. Procedural legitimation by the SC may well be seen as the embodiment of a normative constitutional bargain that enables the 'international community', that is, the actors of the international system, to tolerate policies without having necessarily reached full agreement on the substance of the matter and without having necessarily direct participation in the decision-making process. This primacy of procedure helps to create the broadest possible acceptance and ultimately contributes to the stability of international order.[44] Looked at from this perspective, the relationship between informal groups of states and the SC bears the potential of being mutually reinforcing, as will be further elaborated in the following.

Legitimacy equally demands, as Henry Kissinger has argued, 'the acceptance of the framework of the international order by all major powers, at least to the extent that no state is so dissatisfied that ... it expresses its dissatisfaction in a revolutionary foreign policy'.[45] While Thomas Franck's

---

[43] Dahl, *Democracy and its Critics*, 307.

[44] Talcott Parsons underlines the importance of 'procedural primacy' to explain the workings of domestic institutions; see Talcott Parsons, *The Evolution of Societies*, edited and with an introduction by Jackson Toby (Englewood Cliff, NJ: Prentice-Hall, 1977).

[45] Henry A. Kissinger, *A World Restored—Metternich, Castlereagh and the Problems of Peace 1812–22* (Boston, MA: Houghton Mifflin, 1957), 1.

understanding of legitimacy helps to understand the SC as a rule-making institution, Kissinger's definition opens the gate to grasping the relationship between legitimacy and institutional change. The legitimacy of the Council, in terms of acceptance by major powers, may fade if the institution is not able to adapt itself according to changes in the international system, especially with regard to its representativeness.

Informal groups may therefore alleviate tensions resulting from the structural deficiencies of the SC, including its lack of representativeness, by providing a flexible mechanism for stakeholders to conduct crisis management outside the UN framework. In this context, the relationship between informal groups of states and the SC seems to be mutually dependent. In those cases where informal groups are able to formulate an effective crisis response outside the UN framework but within the objectives of the organization while, at the same time, achieving SC legitimation for their action, output, and procedural legitimacy of the Council may ultimately be enhanced. However, this argument heavily depends on two caveats: firstly, whether the informal group is complementing rather than competing with SC governance; and secondly, the extent to which the grouping is accepted and perceived as legitimate by third parties. Informal groups may achieve wider acceptance through a combination of successful performance and legitimation by the Council. Under these circumstances, the role of informal groups of states and the SC may be mutually reinforcing.

The perception of legitimacy, including the question of whether state action should be legitimized by a SC mandate or not, may differ significantly from one country to another. Legitimacy ultimately depends on who is gaining the monopoly of interpreting a given action as just and procedurally fair.[46] Based upon previous analysis, it is argued in the following that, despite its structural deficiencies, it is still the SC that bears the largest degree of symbolic power to create wider acceptance on the side of UN member states. Informal groups of states may act as a platform to facilitate cooperation between (like-minded) stakeholders outside the UN framework, but they do not bear any legitimacy on their own. The Council remains the ultimate rule-making institution in the maintenance of international peace and security. In those cases where informal groups compete with SC governance, the political cost of action for those states acting outside the UN framework may increase significantly.

---

[46] See Inis L. Claude, 'Collective Legitimization as a Political Function of the United Nations', *International Organization*, 20/ 3 (1966), 369.

The exceptionalist role of the United States may serve as the most prominent example to elaborate on different perceptions of legitimacy. 'US ambivalence toward rules and organization reflects a distinctive conception of political legitimacy',[47] argues Edward Luck, hinting, *inter alia*, at a certain US exceptionalism given both its domestic political culture and its preponderant power position in the international system (in terms of military and economic power, including cultural attraction). A closer look at US interventions in Iraq, Grenada, Panama, and Haiti clearly illustrates 'that the power of international legitimation as a factor in shaping US public and congressional attitudes toward the use of force is decidedly modest'.[48] While senior officials in the administration consider UN blessing desirable, it is not perceived as sine qua non of state action.[49] The picture may change when expanding the initial question of UN legitimization with the choice of acting unilaterally or in a multilateral concert. Overreliance upon unilateral action may ultimately weaken the United States, since this may invite the building of counter-coalitions to balance US power.[50] Acting in a multilateral concert may eventually enhance the perceived legitimacy of action. In fact, 'power and legitimacy are not antithetical, but complementary',[51] as Inis Claude has observed. It is for this reason that 'rulers seek legitimation not only to satisfy their consciences but also to buttress their positions'.[52] Paradoxically, the higher the asymmetry of power between the units of an international system, the stronger the incentive for the hegemon to seek what Ian Clark has called, a 'just disequilibrium'.[53] The just disequilibrium reflects a bargain between the hegemon and those affected by its preponderance: while the former agrees to stay within the constitutional boundaries of the international system, the latter acknowledge the leading role of the hegemon in maintaining international peace and security. Consequently, participation in informal settings may constitute both a sheer necessity and a convenient forum for sanctioning the exercise of US leadership that might be criticized as unilateral otherwise.

[47] Edward Luck, 'The United States, International Organization, and the Quest for Legitimacy', in Stewart Patrick and Shepard Forman (eds.) *Multilateralism and US Foreign Policy: Ambivalent Engagement* (London: Lynne Rienner, 2002), 51.

[48] Ibid., 66.

[49] Author interview.

[50] See Joseph S. Nye, *The Paradox of American Power: Why the World's Only Superpower Can't Go It Alone* (Oxford: Oxford University Press, 2002), 39.

[51] Claude, 'Collective Legitimization as a Political Function of the United Nations', 368.

[52] Ibid.

[53] Ian Clark, *Legitimacy in International Society* (Oxford: Oxford University Press), 239.

4

Conclusion: Exit, Voice, and Loyalty as Analytical Framework

The first part of the book aimed at establishing the importance of informal groups of states. They are useful instruments of conflict resolution since they may answer the call for 'creative combinations of sub-regional, regional and global organizational activities that maximize the advantages and minimize the disadvantages at each institutional level through a synergistic approach to local problems'.[1]

Systemic changes have affected the performance of the UN Security Council (SC) as an effective instrument of crisis response. The quantity and complexity of conflict settings in the post-bipolar era exacerbated structural constraints that are inherent in the UN conflict resolution machinery. As the restrictive provisions of the UN Charter constrain the possibilities of formal adaptation towards these changes, informal groups of states have taken on the role of agents of incremental change constituting a flexible mechanism to exit from structural deficiencies of the Council. While the lack of SC performance might generate a push to conduct conflict management outside the UN framework, the SC exerts a strong pull on UN member states to remain loyal towards the organization.

Exit and voice operate in response to these push and pull factors. In essence, they constitute a means of generating an (incremental) adaptation process to systemic changes. Exit and voice are the 'cheaper option'

---

[1] S. Neil MacFarlane, 'On the Front Lines in the Near Abroad: the CIS and the OSCE in Georgia's Civil Wars', in Thomas G. Weiss (ed.), *Beyond UN Subcontracting. Task-Sharing with Regional Security Arrangements and Service-Providing NGOs* (London/New York: St Martin's Press, 1998), 115 *et sequ.*

than a complete overhaul of the organization's foundations, that is, the revision of the UN Charter. They are a 'safety valve'[2] to both divert and alleviate the pressure for substantial reform. The optimal mix of exit and voice may help to maintain the loyalty of member states towards the UN. The flexibility of the diplomatic device may accommodate different perceptions of how the informal setting should work in a specific crisis situation.

Thus, informal groups of states may accommodate the potential to serve as a stabilizing element for international institutions in transition.[3] This proposition challenges the causal link established by certain scholars that the UN SC is an unstable system because it has no mechanisms to adapt its hierarchy of influence according to the shifts of relative power in the international system.[4] The growing recourse to informal procedures, reshaping the SC's balance between power (in terms of effectiveness or order) and legitimacy (in terms of justice), may temper the pressure towards formal change.[5] At the same time, the preponderant position of the five permanent members of the SC (P-5) as gatekeepers of the Council remains largely unaffected.

States participating in informal groups of states (and not belonging to the P-5) may gain greater voice, enhancing their possibility to make a difference in the resolution of a conflict. Participation in informal groups of states may result in greater influence on the Council for non-permanent members, since decisions taken within informal groups are usually based upon consensus. Members of *ad hoc* groupings therefore tend to have a considerably higher potential of leverage at their disposal than non-permanent members of the Council. Ngaire Woods has pointed out that 'the longer-term considerations of effectiveness require a more active and participatory membership than the traditional hierarchical vision, and herein lies a powerful reason for applying lessons of good governance to

---

[2] Hirschman, *Exit, Voice, and Loyalty*, 124.

[3] It would be very useful to examine in greater detail how informal groups affect governance in other international institutions such as the International Monetary Fund (IMF), the World Bank (WB), the World Trade Organization (WTO), the European Union (EU), or the North Atlantic Treaty Organization (NATO).

[4] See Patrick A. McCarthy, *Hierarchy and Flexibility in World Politics: Adaptation to Shifting Power Distributions in the United Nations Security Council and the International Monetary Fund* (Aldershot: Ashgate, 1998), 159; also Mc Carthy, 'Positionality, Tension, and Instability in the UN Security Council', 147–69.

[5] See Bruce Russett, 'Ten Balances For Weighing UN Reform Proposals', in *The Once And Future Security Council*, 18–21.

international institutions'.[6] Applying the three core principles of good governance, that is, participation, accountability, and fairness,[7] to the specific context of the UN SC, it can be argued that informal groups of states (provided they operate within the objectives of the UN) may increase the number of participants in SC decision-making. In a sense, they may help 'to link the Security Council with the General Assembly members'.[8] Enlargement of the ownership of SC decision-making may be perceived as more accountable and procedurally fair.

However, this brave new world of good governance based on the pillar of informal groups of states is far from being the Weberian ideal-type solution to meet longer-term considerations of effectiveness. Many of these groupings tend to be self-selected, with an exclusive participation and a virtually absent degree of accountability. In positive terms, informal groups may affect SC governance by narrowing the operational and participatory gap growing out of the multiple strategic incapacities that prevents the Council from formulating an effective response to crisis situations. The minilateral setting may be an attractive diplomatic device to accommodate US exceptionalism, since it locks US foreign policy into a cooperative framework, disguises its preponderance, and avoids the appearance of unilateral action. In negative terms, informal arrangements or *ad hoc* coalitions may enter into competition with the SC for governance, leading to a gap between the process and substance of crisis management. Enhancing governance of the SC ultimately depends on the successful merger of right process and substantive outcome. Good governance may be achieved if informal groups of states are able to reflect a precarious trade-off between inclusiveness, efficiency, informality, transparency, and accountability.

The second part of the book tests those assumptions within the context of the crisis settings of Namibia, El Salvador, and Kosovo. The cases provide rich data that allow a demonstration of the explanatory leverage of exit, voice, and loyalty in order to analyse the institutional effects of the UN SC under conditions of systemic change.

---

[6] Ngaire Woods, 'Good Governance in International Organizations , *Global Governance*, 5/1 (1999), 43.

[7] Ibid.

[8] So the statement by the representative of Singapore, UN Doc S/PV.4432, 30 November 2001, 14.

Part II

The Cases of Namibia, El Salvador, and Kosovo

[T]here is sometimes a tendency born perhaps more of hope than of experience, to think that as the Security Council we can wave a wand over certain problems and solve them; that as a body, if not as individuals, we are the repository of international wisdom, whereas in fact we are only the reflection of a confused and divided world.[1]

Sir Colin Crowe, Permanent Representative of the United Kingdom to the United Nations, New York, 1970–3.

[1] UN Doc S/PV.1635, 2 February 1972, para 6.

5

Namibia: Group of Three and Western Contact Group

This case study examines the role and performance of the Group of Three and the Western Contact Group in the process leading towards the independence of Namibia in 1990. Optimists may argue that Namibia 'stands as a model for the utilization of the disparate capacities of the Organization and of its members towards a commonly agreed goal'.[2] Informal arrangements of like-minded states may successfully conduct conflict management outside the UN framework, but within the objectives of the Organization. Pessimists may however interject that the case of Namibia also illustrates the sobering realities under which UN conflict resolution takes place. Firstly, it illustrates the problems of the UN in adapting to systemic change. At the level of the UN, decolonization resulted in a significant increase of membership that shifted governance in the General Assembly and the Security Council (SC). With the admission of postcolonial states, decolonization turned into an ideological issue that contributed to a situation where direct UN involvement had proven ineffective. It complicated the process towards the further dismantling of the colonial system and generated a push towards exit, as epitomized in the formation of the Contact Group. Secondly, the case sheds light on the factors that define success or failure of informal groups of states. While the Group of Three could not produce any significant progress, the Contact Group turned out to be more successful by negotiating a settlement proposal that found the acceptance of the SC. And thirdly, the case of Namibia illustrates the potential and limits of engaging the United States in a

---

[2] Javier Pérez de Cuéllar, *Pilgrimage for Peace* (New York: St Martin's Press, 1997), 321.

cooperative framework. This chapter analyses, in a first step, the setting of the conflict by focusing on four factors that examine both the root causes of the conflict as well as the set of parameters that generated a push towards the emergence of the Group of Three and the Western Contact Group respectively. In a second step, the case study sheds light on the contribution of these informal arrangements to the resolution of conflict. The concluding part summarizes key findings from the perspective of exit, voice, and loyalty.

5.1 Conflict Setting

This section defines the setting of the conflict by concentrating on four levels of analysis: firstly, it reviews the development of the legal dimension of the dispute over South West Africa/Namibia until 1971 when the advisory opinion of the International Court of Justice (ICJ) effectively ended the legal dispute and transferred the question back to the political arena; secondly, it sheds some light on the extent to which the Cold War affected the setting of the conflict; thirdly, the section elaborates on the economic agendas of the conflict, especially from the perspective of Western powers; and fourthly, it concentrates on systemic changes such as decolonization and their effects on the workings of the General Assembly and the SC.

5.1.1 South West Africa/Namibia and Decolonization: Legal Dimension

Namibia, formerly known as South West Africa,[3] had been a colony of Germany since 1883. German forces had to withdraw when South African troops under the command of Generals Botha and Smuts conquered the territory in 1915 and occupied it. After World War I, the peace conference in Paris decided to grant South Africa a Class 'C' mandate over South West Africa that placed the territory under the administration of South Africa in accordance with Article 22.6 of the League of Nations Covenant.

The San Francisco Conference in 1945, with the adoption of the UN Charter, created an International Trusteeship System that resulted in the conclusion of various agreements with former mandatory powers in Africa, leading to the independence of territories such as the

---

[3] In 1968, the General Assembly adopted a decision to change the name of the territory, see UN Doc A/RES/2372 (XXII), 12 June 1968.

British-administered Togoland, Cameroons, and Tanganyika, and the for-mer Belgian colony Ruanda-Urundi. The conflict over Namibia in the UN went far back to 1946, when South Africa refused to place the territory under a UN trusteeship.[4] Originally, the International Trusteeship System was designed, according to Article 76 of the UN Charter, 'to promote the political, economic, social, and educational advancement of the inhabitants of the trust territories, and their progressive development towards self-gov-ernment or independence'. The provisions reflected 'the very limited will-ingness of the colonial powers to superimpose a formal trusteeship structure upon their administration of dependent areas'.[5] Article 77 therefore did not entail any legally binding obligation for mandatory powers to transfer their mandates over territories to the UN trusteeship system. It was a voluntary act, as the ICJ confirmed in its advisory opinion on Namibia in 1950.[6] The ruling suggested that any solution to the conflict had to be found via political negotiations, not legal claims. The period between 1948 and 1960 saw a legal contest between the South African government and the UN General Assembly as protagonists that subsequently tried to settle a political question by legal means via reference to the ICJ.

The adoption of the Declaration on the Granting of Independence to Colonial Countries and Peoples by the General Assembly in December 1960 marked a significant shift from the original provisions of the Char-ter.[7] As Inis Claude has observed, the declaration 'undermined the legal claim of sovereignty over dependent countries'.[8] This ideological sea change that had been gradually developing in the aftermath of World War II illustrated serious tensions between the legality and legitimacy of the trusteeship system. Those tensions became abundantly clear in 1961, when India invaded and incorporated the Portuguese territory of Goa, justifying its intervention on the grounds of Resolution 1514.[9] The in-creasing militancy within the Organization prevented any serious efforts to deal with the problem of Namibia in an impartial manner.

In July 1966, the ICJ decided after six years of consultations by eight votes to seven not to rule on the substance of the case, arguing that Ethiopia and Liberia, the two plaintiffs, had not established any legal

---

[4] See Anthony Parsons, *From Cold War to Hot Peace. UN Interventions 1947–1995* (London: Penguin Books, 1995), 107.

[5] Claude, *Swords into Ploughshares*, 327.

[6] See United Nations, *Yearbook of the United Nations 1950* (New York: Department of Public Information, 1951), 807.

[7] See UN Doc A/RES/1514 (XV), 14 December 1960.

[8] Claude, *Swords into Ploughshares*, 334.

[9] See Hiscocks, *The Security Council*, 182–3.

right or interest that provided the basis to act against South Africa.[10] The decision made clear that the question of Namibia did not constitute a legal dispute but a political matter. The General Assembly reacted accordingly and adopted a resolution that claimed the termination of South Africa's mandate in October of the same year, placing the territory under the direct responsibility of the UN.[11] Furthermore, the General Assembly authorized the constitution of a so-called UN Council for Namibia that should provide for the transfer of authority over the territory to the people of the former colony until June 1968.[12] By revoking South Africa's mandate, the UN had taken direct responsibility for Namibia. The South African government refused to accept the UN as the legal successor of the League of Nations and rejected on these grounds the legally not binding resolutions of the General Assembly.

In late 1967, the SC for the first time dealt with the matter when the South African government had arrested thirty-seven Namibians under a terrorism law and deported them to Pretoria.[13] In response, the Council adopted two resolutions calling on South Africa to release and repatriate the prisoners. Following a debate on the future of Namibia in March 1969, the SC adopted a series of resolutions that declared the South African presence in Namibia illegal, demanding its withdrawal, and urging the government to comply with previous resolutions that called for the immediate release of the thirty-seven prisoners. With South Africa's continuous disregard of any responsibility of the UN, in 1970 the Council adopted another resolution in which it asked the ICJ to deliver an advisory opinion on the question of the legal consequences of the continued presence of South Africa in Namibia. By thirteen votes to two, the Court advised the Council that South Africa was considered an occupying power, its presence illegal, and it should therefore withdraw from the territory.[14] The legal backing of the political decisions taken by the Council also constituted an implicit endorsement of the positions taken by the General Assembly and prepared the ground for the combined initiative of the Secretary-General and the Group of Three in the early 1970s, as will be examined later. The continued resistance on the side of the South African

[10] See International Court of Justice, *South–West Africa Cases (Ethiopia v. South Africa; Liberia v. South Africa), Judgment of 18 July 1966* (The Hague: International Court of Justice, 1966).

[11] See UN Doc A/RES/2145 (XXI), 27 October 1966.

[12] UN Doc A/RES/2248 (S-V), 19 May 1967.

[13] See Parsons, *From Cold War to Hot Peace*, 108.

[14] See John Dugard (ed.), *The South West Africa/Namibia dispute: Documents and Scholarly Writings on the Controversy between South Africa and the United Nations* (Berkeley, CA: University of California Press, 1973), 447–52.

government led to increasing pressure by the African member states on the Western powers of the SC to exert their leverage over South Africa and to become more actively involved in the solution of the conflict.

5.1.2 Cold War Dimension

The Cold War dimension constituted less a constant rather than a variant that impacted on the conflict setting. While the conflict was originally rooted in the larger process of dismantling the colonial empires, the year of 1974 turned out to be the watershed that prepared the ground for 'the long-delayed advent of the Cold War into southern Africa'.[15] The *coup d'état* in Portugal establishing a socialist regime in the country resulted in the demise of the Portuguese colonial empire in Africa the following year.[16] Although the Portuguese government had secured an agreement between the three contesting factions, that is, the National Front for the Liberation of Angola (FNLA), the National Union for the Total Independence of Angola (UNITA), and the Popular Movement for the Liberation of Angola (MPLA), the implementation failed primarily due to Portugal's drive for early exit without an accompanying strategy. The country's withdrawal from Angola changed also the parameters of the Namibian conflict, as it became the place for military confrontations between Cuban and South African forces.[17] The three liberation movements operating on Angolan soil attracted support from different quarters. While the United States and South Africa supported the FNLA and later UNITA, the MPLA secured military assistance from the Soviet Union, with a maximum of 50,000 Cuban troops backing the government in Luanda.[18] As Maurice Halperin has observed, 'Cuba's massive—and decisive—intervention in the Angolan civil war resulted in a victory for the Soviet Union and a sharp setback for the United States and China.'[19] However, this victory displayed at the political–diplomatic rather than military–strategic level: 'increasing . . . prestige and increasing Western discomfort' were the primary motives of the Soviet involvement.[20] Following the collapse of the Portuguese colonial empire with the subsequent outbreak of civil strife

---

[15] See Parsons, *From Cold War to Hot Peace*, 111.

[16] For an analysis of the regional implications, see John Seiler (ed.), *Southern Africa since the Portuguese Coup* (Boulder, CO: Westview Press, 1980).

[17] Parsons, *From Cold War to Hot Peace*, 111.

[18] Ibid., 112.

[19] Maurice Halperin, 'The Cuban Role in Southern Africa', in *Southern Africa since the Portuguese Coup*, 25.

[20] Christopher Stevens, 'The Soviet Role in Southern Africa', in *Southern Africa since the Portuguese Coup*, 57.

in Angola and Mozambique, the United States started to review its policy that had been based upon the principles of strengthening trade and economic relations with South Africa in order to induce change and undermine the structures of apartheid.[21] In consequence, to the conflict over Namibia was added another dimension that should complicate efforts for conflict resolution. It is important to note that succeeding administrations in Washington drew different conclusions from the conflict setting, especially regarding the means of coping with the situation in southern Africa. As will be further elaborated later, differences between the Carter and Reagan administrations displayed less in substance than style. The cooperative approach of the former, as epitomized in the Western Contact Group, significantly differed from the assertive leadership approach of the latter. While the policy end of regional stability and containing Soviet influence had not been contentious issues, the question of how to achieve these goals became a matter of intense dispute.

5.1.3 *Economic Dimension*

The economic agendas of Western powers and South Africa constituted a third important parameter that defined the setting of the conflict. Examination of the Namibian case exclusively through the lens of decolonization obscures the fundamental reasons behind South Africa's lack of cooperation and the reluctance of Western powers to adopt mandatory sanctions against the country. It sheds light on the reasons why previous efforts made by the General Assembly or the Secretary-General to achieve progress in the solution of the conflict were doomed to fail and why the Western Five had the critical mass of both political and economic clout at their disposal to make a difference.

The European Community (EC) constituted by far the most important trading market for the South African economy. In 1983, it accounted for 43.9 per cent of South Africa's imports and 31.2 per cent of its exports, with the United Kingdom and the Federal Republic of Germany as the dominating trading partners.[22] In comparison, the United States accounted for only 18.8 per cent of the imports and 15.4 per cent of the exports of the South African economy. Looking at South Africa's stock of

---

[21] See Paul Rich, 'The United States, its history of mediation and the Chester Crocker round of negotiations over Namibia in 1988', in Stephen Chan and Vivienne Jabri, (eds.), *Mediation in Southern Africa* (London: Macmillan, 1993), 76.

[22] See Martin Holland, 'Three Approaches for Understanding European Political Co-operation: A Case Study of EC–South African Policy', *Journal of Common Market Studies*, 25/4 (1987), 304.

foreign direct investment (FDI) reveals both its dependency on transfers from European and American countries as well as the economic stakes of these countries. The total stock of direct investments tripled between 1956 and 1972.[23] In 1974, the EC accounted for two-thirds (66.7 per cent) of the total FDI, with the North and South American region as the second largest source of investment (22.8 per cent).[24] The African continent accounted for just 1.6 per cent of FDI.

The single most important country for the South African economy was the United Kingdom. About half of the stocks of total FDI originated from UK-based transnational corporations (TNCs).[25] In the period from 1965 to 1974, their investment increased by over 250 per cent. US-based corporations represented the second largest source of FDI. Between 1960 and 1975, direct investment by US TNCs increased by over 300 per cent, which amounted to about one-sixth of the total FDI in South Africa.[26]

Another factor that contributed to South Africa's dependency on the EC was the extent to which European banks serviced the economy with private bank loans. For 1985, it was estimated that British, German, and French banks serviced US$8.6 billion out of South Africa's total foreign debt of US$18.5 billion.[27] Furthermore, affiliations of the United Kingdom and the United States-based TNCs had established close links with several mining finance houses. French and German corporations were also active in South Africa, although to a lesser extent.

Figures relating specifically to Namibia's economy are harder to obtain and have to be extracted from the trade statistics of trading partners. As the South African government prohibited the release of comprehensive data in 1967, the collection of reliable information for that period has been somewhat problematic. TNCs controlled large parts of the Namibian economy, especially in the mining sector that accounted for almost fifty per cent of its gross domestic product (GDP).[28] Namibia's mining sector was defined by its oligopolistic structure. Only three companies—Consolidated Diamond Mines (CDM), Tsumeb Corporation, and Rössing Uranium—accounted for ninety per cent of the total output in terms of value.[29] While Tsumeb's parent corporation was a conglomerate of US, UK, and

[23] See UN Doc E/C.10/26, 6 April 1977, 10 (Table 1).
[24] Ibid., 11.
[25] Ibid., 15.
[26] Ibid.
[27] See Martin Holland, 'Three Approaches for Understanding European Political Cooperation', 306.
[28] United Nations Institute for Namibia, *Namibia: Perspectives for National Reconstruction and Development* (Lusaka: United Nations Institute for Namibia, 1986), 292.
[29] Ibid.

South African companies, Rössing comprised an international consortium of, *inter alia*, Canadian, French, South African, and UK enterprises, each holding different shares.[30]

Some scholars argue that the Namibian territory had assumed a certain kind of 'bail-out' function for the South African economy that suffered under a notorious deficit of the balance of payments. In 1980, a report of the German Development Institute on perspectives of Namibia's independent economic development concluded that 'over the last few years, the positive balance has made a considerable contribution towards improving the South African balance of payments situation'.[31] According to the study, in 1977, the Namibian balance of payments totalled 165 million Rands. Those accounts underline the economic importance of Namibia for the South African economy.

As the Economist Intelligence Unit reported in its country profile, exports of the Namibian economy quadrupled between 1970 and 1980.[32] This boom can be largely explained with the start of the production of the world's largest uranium mine, Rössing Uranium Ltd, in 1976, as well as high prevailing prices for diamonds. In 1987, the Department of Finance in Windhoek released for the first time official data that confirmed the preponderance of the mining sector: in the period 1980–6, it contributed seventy-seven per cent of total exports by value on average, with diamonds and uranium as the most important export commodities.[33] Until 1980, diamonds had been the largest single export by value, and they was exceeded by uranium in subsequent years. Main export markets were the United Kingdom, which accounted for about ten per cent of the total exports, Japan, the Federal Republic of Germany, France, and the United States.[34] Except for the United States, all of these trading partners had contracted for uranium from Namibia.[35]

---

[30] Rio Algom Mines Ltd (Canada) and the French firm Total-Compagnie minière et nucléaire (CMN) each held ten per cent of Rössing. The Industrial Development Corporation of South Africa accounted for a share of 13.2 per cent, General Mining and Finance Company, South Africa, 8 per cent, the British Rio Tinto Zinc Corporation Ltd (RTZ) 46.5 per cent and others 13.5 per cent; ibid., 303.

[31] Wolfgang Zehender, 'Namibia's Dependency in External Economic Affairs', in Hartmut Brandt et al. (eds.), *Perspectives of Independent Development in Southern Africa: The Cases of Zimbabwe and Namibia* (Berlin: German Development Institute, 1980), 167.

[32] See Economist Intelligence Unit, *Country Profile: Namibia, 1986–87* (London: The Economist Publications, 1986), 34.

[33] See Economist Intelligence Unit, *Country Profile: Namibia, 1987–88* (London: The Economist Publications, 1987), 37

[34] Ibid., 35.

[35] See United Nations Institute for Namibia, 304.

In conclusion, the economic significance of the Namibian territory contributed to the reluctance of the South African government to enter into serious negotiations over Namibia's transitions towards independence. Instead, it preferred a strategy of constant delay and tactical bargaining in order to gain time. At the same time, the economic agendas of the Western powers prevented a deeper engagement since it would have brought them in direct opposition to South Africa. However, this situation had been slowly changing since 1976, with the economic importance of Black African countries such as Nigeria steadily on the rise. In the case of the United Kingdom, the exchange of goods and services with Black Africa doubled the exports to and imports from South Africa.[36] In consequence, the changing economic balance of power on the ground became another factor that affected Western strategies towards the region.[37] Western powers had to redefine the trade-off between the political costs and the economic gains becoming engaged in the settlement of the conflict.

5.1.4 Systemic Change and UN Conflict Resolution Machinery

The following section examines the effects of decolorization on the UN conflict resolution machinery, particularly its impact on governance in the General Assembly and the SC. This section argues that the emergence of informal arrangements such as the Group of Three and the Western Contact Group constituted an exit from the structural deficiencies of the UN conflict resolution machinery that had been worsening in response to systemic change resulting from the process of decolonization.

GENERAL ASSEMBLY

Politics in the UN of the 1970s has to be analysed through the lens of the growing dominance of a North–South division within the UN system.[38] From the 1950s onwards, decolonization had brought an enlargement of

---

[36] See Colin Legum, *The Western Crisis Over Southern Africa. South Africa, Rhodesia, Namibia* (New York and London: Africana Publishing Co., 1979), 26.

[37] See Helmut Bley, 'Die Namibia-Initiative der westlichen Mitglieder des Sicherheitsrates', *Vereinte Nationen*, 26/2 (1978), 55.

[38] Although the general distinction between 'North' and 'South' is vague and appears as oversimplification, it is a useful description when being applied to the specific political context at UN Headquarters, where many of the consultations outside the SC chamber are conducted along these lines. While the southern countries articulate and coordinate their interests through the G-77 or the NAM, 'the North' tends to be more fragmented, with the EU as one important player.

UN membership, which significantly transformed the character of the UN. Between 1945 and 1965, UN membership rose from fifty-one to 117 member states, with the proportion of Asian, African, and Caribbean states increasing from twenty-five per cent to roughly fifty per cent.[39] The Organization achieved almost universal membership, with the balance of power in the Western-dominated General Assembly gradually shifting in favour of the post-colonial states. While the number of seats and the influence of African states in the Assembly increased, their actual influence on the course of international relations 'progressively diminished'.[40]

Especially for the United States, the Assembly had been at times a convenient instrument at its disposal that could be mobilized—for example, during the Korean crisis in 1950—when the SC was deadlocked. The Non-Aligned Movement (NAM) and the Group of 77 (G-77) became an important hub of coordination between the so-called Third World countries. They achieved a predominant status in the Assembly and tried to exert their influence on SC decision-making as well. Representing roughly two-thirds of the membership, the movement perceived itself as the 'replica' of a community of peacefully coexisting states.[41]

Viewed from that perspective, the non-aligned constituted a kind of second UN that tried to play an independent role beyond the East–West antagonism of the Cold War. However, efforts to reshape the Organization by placing development and anti-colonial issues higher on the agenda made a clash of interests with countries from the North almost unavoidable. The divide gained particular visibility in the framework of the debate on the New International Economic Order. It also affected the management of conflicts in southern Africa. The former colonial powers were often confronted with allegations of post-colonial ambitions raised by representatives of the South that formed an anti-colonial bloc. With the UN General Assembly becoming the international forum to deal with the colonial heritage, the question of colonialism was discussed within a political arena comprising post-colonial states that were vociferous advocates of anti-colonialism. However, the anti-colonial bloc tended to be much more heterogeneous than may appear at first sight. Although the Afro-Asian group constituted the core, it was widely supported (for different reasons) by countries from the Communist bloc, Latin American

---

[39] For the growth in UN membership, see Figure 2.

[40] See James Mayall, *Africa: The Cold War and After* (London: Elek Books, 1971), 9.

[41] M. S. Rajan, 'The Role of the Nonaligned States in the United Nations', in M. S. Rajan, V. S. Mani, and C. S. R. Murthy, (eds.), *The Nonaligned and the United Nations* (New Delhi: South Asian Publishers, 1987), 309.

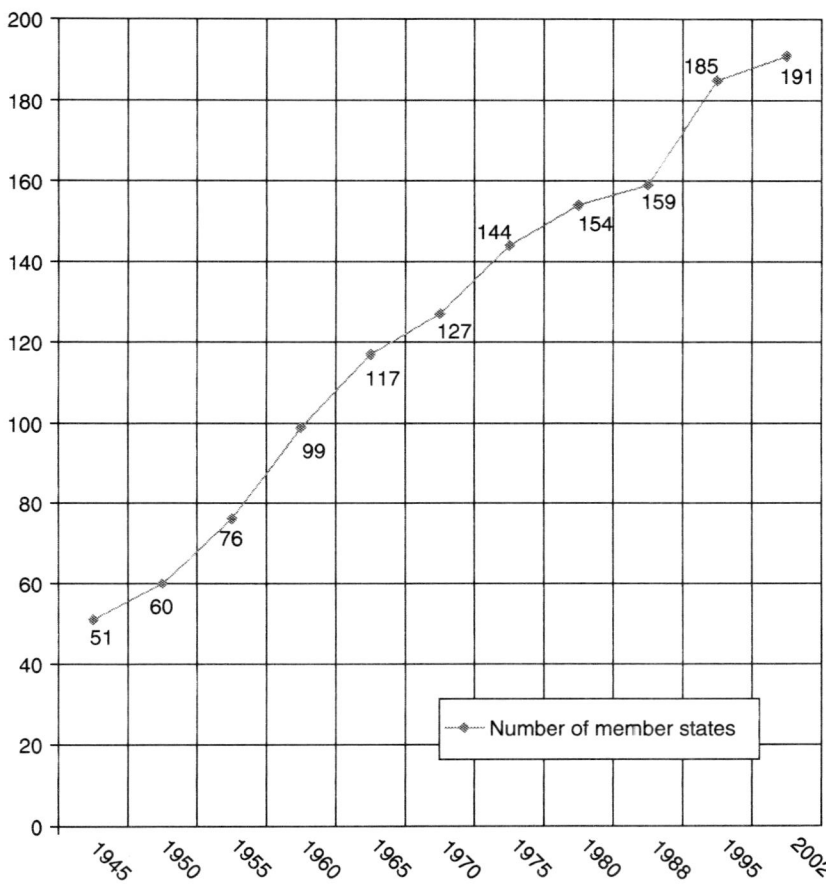

Figure 2 Growth in United Nations membership, 1945–2002
Source: www.un.org/Overview/growth.htm.

states, and members from the Western community that sympathized with the anti-colonial cause.[42]

Despite these shifting alignments, decolonization fostered the emergence of two poles whose interaction started to define politics in the General Assembly with certain effects on the workings of the SC. Those battles often resulted in the adoption of resolutions that, although enjoying the broad support of the non-aligned majority, did not have a great effect on the issue under consideration since key Western states opposed

---

[42] Ibid., 332.

them from the start. In September 1971, then Secretary-General U Thant stated soberly in his annual report to the UN that such pattern would ultimately erode the authority of the Assembly.[43]

In conclusion, in order to understand the dealings of the UN with the conflict over Namibia, it is crucial to take into account the systemic change that had taken place since its foundation. The General Assembly converted into the platform that dealt with all aspects of colonization. This resulted in bitter clashes between the colonial and anti-colonial forces in the Organization. Systemic change also affected the workings of the SC, especially after the enlargement of the body in 1965, as the following subsection argues.

SECURITY COUNCIL

Decolonization and the subsequent accession of new members to the Organization had a long-term impact on SC governance. The most immediate impact was the increasing pressure to enlarge the membership of the body in order to enhance the equitable geographical distribution of countries serving as non-permanent members. It became an issue raised in particular by the new post-colonial members of the Organization. In December 1963, on the initiative of forty-four African and Asian countries, the General Assembly adopted Resolution 1991, which provided for an enlargement of the number of elected members from six to ten, with five seats being allocated to African and Asian, one to Eastern European, two to Latin American, and two to Western European states.[44] As the number of African member states exceeded those of the Asian ones, it was agreed that the former gained three and the latter two seats on the Council. The quorum to reach a decision, that is, the action threshold, increased from seven to nine affirmative votes. With the exception of Nationalist China (Taiwan), which supported enlargement, the permanent members of the SC only reluctantly went along with the new formula, as their voting pattern demonstrates: France and the Soviet Union voted against the resolution, while the United Kingdom and the United States abstained.[45]

---

[43] UN Doc GAOR, Twenty-Sixth Session, Supplement No. I A (A/8401/Add. 1), para. 143.

[44] See UN Doc A/RES/1991 (XVIII), 17 December 1963.

[45] See Ingo Winkelmann, 'Bringing the Security Council into a New Era: Recent Developments in the Discussion on the Reform of the Security Council', in Jochen A. Frowein and Rüdiger Wolfrum (eds.), *Max Planck Yearbook of United Nations Law*, 1 (1997) (The Hague: Kluwer Law International, 1998), 40.

Despite their reservations all permanent members ratified the amendments later.[46] The enlargement came into effect on 31 August 1965.

The change in the composition of the SC, including the new quorum, had the immediate effect that it altered the body's inner-institutional balance of power and diplomacy, with the dominance of Western countries waning. Provided there was a convergence of interests, the Afro-Asian group, together with the Soviet Union and the Eastern European members, could display a blocking majority of seven votes that would prevent any Council decision from being taken. Enlargement affected therefore the process of coalition building, which in turn impacted on the pattern in the use of the veto by the permanent members. Prior to this the Western powers and the United States in particular had been in the comfortable position to build voting alliances in the Council that facilitated the pursuance of their interests and made the casting of vetoes unnecessary. Since 1966, this pattern reversed almost completely: while the Soviet Union had cast ninety-two per cent of the vetoes before the enlargement of the Council, the P-3 accounted for eighty-six per cent of the vetoes thereafter.[47] It also affected the diplomacy within that body, as Richard Hiscocks observed:

Up to 1965, apart from the Chinese and Middle East representatives and an occasional Asian member replacing an East European state or representing the Commonwealth, all members of the Council were either European or strongly influenced by the European cultural tradition. Now the UN had given the new African and Asian states, nearly all of them developing countries, the opportunity for the first time to play an important role in international affairs. They took advantage of it to air their problems and their racial anxieties, and to develop the diplomatic contacts which UN Headquarters offered on a, for them, unprecedented scale.[48]

In effect, the ideological battles taking place between 'North' and 'South' in the General Assembly were transferred into the SC. This situation was exacerbated through the increased recourse to Article 31 of the Charter (in combination with Rules 37 and 39 of the SC's Provisional Rules of Procedure) that allowed delegations, not being members of the Council but specially affected in their interests, to participate in the discussions of

---

[46] The enlargement of the SC had to be adopted according to Article 108 of the UN Charter which includes the following provisions: 'Amendments to the present Charter shall come into force for all Members of the United Nations when they have been adopted by a vote of two thirds of the members of the General Assembly and ratified in accordance with their respective constitutional processes by two thirds of the Members of the United Nations, including all the permanent members of the Security Council.'

[47] See Table 2.

[48] See Hiscocks, *The Security Council*, 99.

its formal meetings. Originally, during the negotiations at the San Francisco Conference in 1945, Article 31 emerged as compensation for non-members of the SC. Since Article 23 of the Charter initially limited the composition of the UN Security Council to six elected and five non-elected member states, this provision should ameliorate its effects, which restricted the principle of the sovereign equality of UN member states, as embodied in Article 2.1.[49] It became general practice that non-members requesting participation in the Council's debate were granted access to the meetings without any further discussion.

Especially after the enlargement of the SC, this practice became a great impediment to the effective working of the body. Representatives of post-colonial countries asking for participation in the debates of the Council acknowledged that very often this was, indeed, 'a public relations exercise' to signal to the domestic audience that the government's position was being heard at the UN Headquarters.[50] Consequently, the body had often been used as machinery for the creation of international public opinion and the delivery of invectives.[51] Related requests to participate in the discussions of the Council increased from the 1960s onwards.[52] At peak times, as much as 50 per cent of the total UN membership participated in its formal meetings discussing issues related to South Africa and Namibia respectively.[53]

Enlargement increased the (mis)use of the SC as a forum for exercising propaganda, which undermined the effectiveness to display its responsibility for the maintenance of international peace and security, as Article 24 of the Charter suggests. This became particularly apparent when the SC discussed matters related to decolonization and apartheid. The proliferation of informal consultations of the SC from the mid-1970s onwards has to be analysed against the background of the devaluation of the SC's formal meetings as the institutional setting for the approval on substantive actions. Figure 3 shows the number of formal meetings and informal consultations between 1972 and 1982.[54] The year 1978 appears as a watershed, with the

---

[49] See Bruno Simma (ed.), *Charter of the United Nations*, 2nd edn., (Oxford: Oxford University Press, 2002), 573–80.

[50] See Davidson Nicol, *The United Nations Security Council: Towards Greater Effectiveness* (New York: UNITAR, 1982), 91.

[51] Ibid.

[52] Bailey and Daws, 155.

[53] See UN Doc S/PV.2451, 1 June 1983. A total number of sixty-four delegations not being members on the Council participated in this meeting under Article 31 of the UN Charter. Further participants included representatives of the UN Council for Namibia, SWAPO, the African National Congress (ANC), and Pan African Congress (PAC).

[54] See Figure 3.

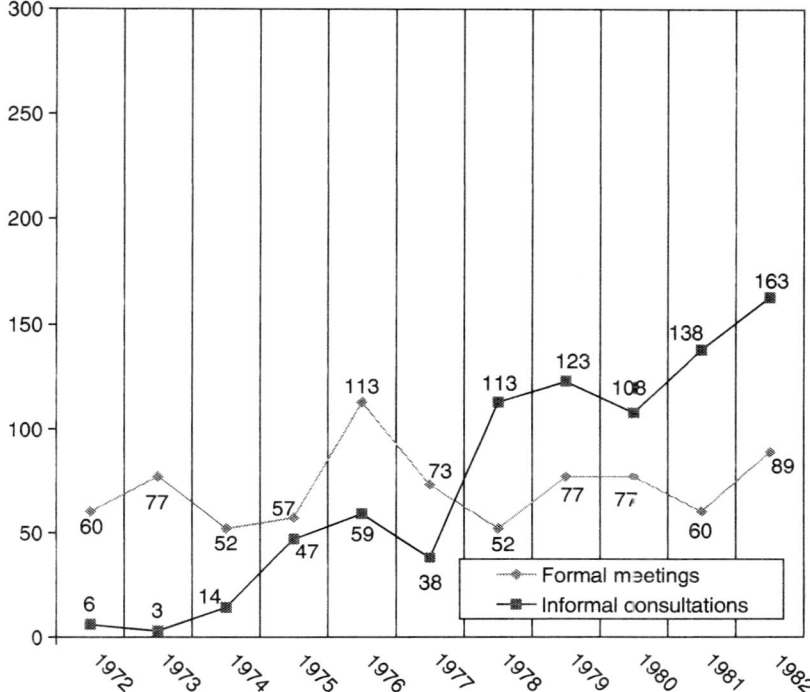

Figure 3 Formal meetings and informal consultations of the UN Security Council, 1972–82

Source: Index to Proceedings of the Security Council (New York: United Nations, 1973–83); Loie Feuerle, 'Informal Consultation: A Mechanism in Security Council Decision-Making', *New York University Journal of International Law and Politics*, 18/1 (1985), 288.

number of informal consultations tripling from thirty-eight meetings in 1977 to 113 the following year.[55] At the same time, the number of formal meetings declined in the same period from seventy-three to fifty-two. In 1978, members of the SC had started meeting in a new consultation room, which had been built in addition to the SC chamber for the exclusive purpose of holding informal meetings.[56] This was the most visible sign that these consultations had become increasingly formalized.

[55] This increase was however no result of détente. In 1978, the new consultation room, established for the single purpose of holding informal meetings of the Council, was completed. The de facto formalization contributed to a significant increase of informal meetings.
[56] See Bailey and Daws, *The Procedure of the UN Security Council*, 62.

The greater recourse to informal consultations that remained restricted to the fifteen member states of the Council limited options for non-members to express voice. In essence, this constituted an exit strategy in order to cope with systemic change that seriously affected the efficient working of the body. Informal consultations became the forum where the substantial work took place, for example, negotiations on SC resolutions and statements, while formal meetings transformed into settings where the members of the Council adopted resolutions or Presidential statements. Although informal consultations became gradually formalized without being formal, they did not necessarily increase the efficiency of the workings of the Council. Various diplomats of permanent missions and officials of the UN Secretariat at that stage referred to the downside of informal consultations. 'Deliberate stalling, inaction, watered-down resolutions, secrecy, overformalization of an informal process, and lack of outside input,' were certain dangers inherent in this process.[57]

Another factor that has to be considered is the question of resources. Permanent missions of the post-colonial countries tended to be understaffed, and most of the personnel did not enjoy adequate professional training. In addition, they did not receive the necessary resources as well as the support from their capitals to conduct more subtle and substantive policies. For example, permanent missions such as Côte d'Ivoire serving on the Council in the period of 1964–5, Mali (1966–7), Senegal (1968–9), and Burundi (1970–1) operated with a total number of six professionals on staff or less.[58] The relative capacity of those states and others to contribute to the maintenance of international peace and security, which is according to Article 23.1 the key qualification criterion for being elected a non-permanent member of the Council, therefore remained rather limited. In fact, the Organization of African Unity (OAU) had been always keen to support the candidacy of those member states that supported the common positions of the regional organization rather than focusing on criteria such as size of the country or diplomatic experience.[59]

In conclusion, the systemic change of the 1960s had a profound impact on SC governance. The retreat to informal consultations constituted a partial exit from the structural deficiencies of the Council. The proliferation of informal consultations of the SC in the mid-1970s has to be

---

[57] Cited in Loie Feuerle, 'Informal Consultation: A Mechanism in Security Council Decision-Making', *New York University Journal of International Law and Politics*, 18/1 (1985), 294.

[58] United Nations, *Permanent Missions to the United Nations* (New York: United Nations, 1954–), Vols. 185, 197, 219, and 228.

[59] See Hiscocks, *The Security Council*, 100.

analysed against the background of the devaluation of the Council's formal meetings as the institutional setting for the agreement on substantive action. Formal meetings became primarily a platform for the articulation of voice. However, the maximum retreat to informal consultations had not been able to overcome the structural constraints of the Council. For this reason, the establishment of informal groups of states continued and deepened the trend towards exit.

5.2 Conflict Resolution

This section examines the role and performance of the Group of Three and the Western Contact Group, which were two different attempts to exit from the structural deficiencies of the UN. While the SC had mandated the former initiative, with the Group of Three supporting and supervising the efforts taken by the Secretary-General, the Western Contact Group operated outside the UN framework but within the objective of SC Resolution 385.

5.2.1 *Group of Three, 1972–3*

The 1971 ruling of the ICJ, which had declared the South African presence in Namibia illegal, increased the pressure on the SC members to develop a viable political strategy in order to achieve some progress on the question of Namibian independence. With the adoption of Resolution 301 on 20 October 1971, the Council had accepted the Court's opinion, even though France and the United Kingdom abstained in the vote due to the dissenting voices of their national judges in the ICJ ruling.[60]

However, it was clear that all legal possibilities had been exhausted by then, and any solution to the conflict had to be found in the political arena. From 28 January to 4 February 1972, on invitation of the OAU, the Council held a series of meetings away from Headquarters in Addis Ababa to discuss strategies on how to force the South African government to comply with the advisory opinion of the ICJ. The meeting reflected a growing frustration on the side of African states. Despite the 128 resolutions on decolonization and apartheid, adopted by the General Assembly and the SC since 1960, the situation of the people on the ground had not

---

[60] See UN Doc S/RES/301, 20 October 1971.

been improved so far.[61] The 'verbal escalation' had not produced any significant impact on the resolution of the conflict.[62] In effect, the growing dichotomy between words and deeds undermined the credibility of the UN. Reflecting those concerns, the Lusaka Manifesto on southern Africa, adopted on 16 April 1969 at the Fifth Summit Conference of East and Central African States, invited especially a greater commitment of Western powers in the solution of regional crises.[63] Western members of the SC became the subject of intense criticism for their lack of commitment. As the representative of Ghana stated:

The Western members of this Council, particularly the permanent members, have often been the ones which have done their best to prevent positive action by the Council.... Considerations of kith and kin, unjustifiable economic, trade and military interests have prevented these members of the Council from living up to their membership obligations.... By this policy of indifference and obstruction the West is creating in the minds of responsible Africans the idea that it is the enemy of African freedom. Africa can never forget such betrayal.[64]

At the same time, there was however a clear understanding that any solution could not be accomplished against the will of the Council's key members. One could observe a growing sense of sober realism and pragmatism among African states that furthered the thinking about how conflict resolution might be achieved by unconventional means in order to restore the credibility of the UN. This included ideas of pursuing 'practical and concrete measures, *in* or *out* of the United Nations'.[65] Such practical measures included the suggestion to form a group of UN member states that may use their leverage on respective countries.[66] Exit from the principal organs of the Organization in order to achieve progress towards the settlement of the conflict outside the UN framework was considered a pragmatic policy option that eventually should restore the credibility of the UN. This aspect is of paramount importance for understanding the dynamics between informal groups of states and the SC. The exit option appeared as a viable political strategy grown out of a general sense of loyalty towards the Organization.

---

[61] See, for example, the statement by the Chairman of the OAU at the SC meeting on 28 January 1972, UN Doc S/PV.1627, 28 January 1972, para 28.

[62] Statement by the representative of Argentina, UN Doc S/PV.1630, 31 January 1972, para 172.

[63] See Legum, *The Western Crisis Over Southern Africa*, 3.

[64] UN Doc S/PV.1631, 31 January 1972, para 161.

[65] Ibid., para 162.

[66] So, for example, the request by the representative of Ghana; ibid., para 163.

On 9 February 1972, the SC adopted Resolution 309, which invited the Secretary-General, 'in consultation and close co-operation with a group of the SC, composed of the representatives of Argentina, Somalia and Yugoslavia, to initiate as soon as possible contacts with all parties concerned, with a view to establishing the necessary conditions so as to enable the people of Namibia...to exercise their right of self-determination and independence'.[67] The Secretary-General and the Group of Three were expected to act as 'a single entity' in the implementation of Resolution 309.[68] Argentina as the initiator of the resolution, Somalia, having the presidency of the Council in the month of February, and Yugoslavia had been finally appointed as members of the mechanism in close cooperation with the African Group that was apparently keen to keep control over the process.[69] This gathering may be seen as another precedent of the later-emerging Groups of Friends of the Secretary-General at the end of the 1980s. It should basically assist the Secretary-General in his efforts to contact the parties to the conflict.

The Soviet Union had voted in favour of the resolution despite its deep scepticism that the initiative would eventually succeed.[70] On the same day, the Council adopted another resolution that, *inter alia*, strongly condemned South Africa's intransigent behaviour and the repressions of African labourers in Namibia.[71] With France and the United Kingdom abstaining, this resolution sent a strong signal to the South African government that the Secretary-General's initiative would not have the full backing of two key members of the SC. This turned out to be almost an invitation for further South African intransigence.[72] Originally, France had suggested a close consultation with the Five permanent members (P-5), which signalled that it wanted the SC to remain in charge of the entire process.[73] Reactions to this proposal were rather mixed given the lack of unity among the P-5. As the representative of Argentina stressed somewhat ironically in the discussions, the permanent members were not even

---

[67] UN Doc S/RES/309 (1972), 9 February 1972, op. 1; the resolution was adopted by fourteen votes in favour, with China not participating in the vote.

[68] Statement by Argentina when introducing the draft that later became Resolution 309; UN Doc S/PV.1637, 3 February 1972, para 40.

[69] Ibid., para 170.

[70] Statement by the Soviet Permanent Representative Jakob Malik, UN Doc S/PV.1638, 4 February 1972, para 92.

[71] See UN Doc S/RES/310, 4 February 1972, op. 1 and 4.

[72] See Helmut Bley, 'Die Bundesrepublik, der Westen und die internationale Lage um Namibia', in Helmut Bley and Rainer Tetzlaff (eds.), *Afrika und Bonn* (Reinbek bei Hamburg: Rowohlt, 1978), 152.

[73] UN Doc S/PV.1635, 2 February 1972, para 129. France showed a similar pattern during discussions on the establishment of UNEF II in October 1973 (see Chapter 2).

able 'to agree on where they should install a traffic light' if they had to administer Namibia one day.[74] On the surface, the Group of Three constituted a 'safeguard' for the new Secretary-General Waldheim taking over some burden—as well as blame-sharing functions.[75] It reflected a compromise solution that bridged these different schools of thought. One important function of the group would include supervising the contacts of the Secretary-General with the South African authorities. Any proactive role of the Group seemed to be doubtful from the outset when looking at the human resources of the permanent missions of these countries. Especially in the case of Somalia, with the number of professionals on staff totalling four people,[76] it was obvious that any significant input would originate less in the permanent mission proper rather than the African Group or the OAU respectively.

The direct talks of the Secretary-General with the South African authorities that followed in March 1972 constituted a shift away from the legal battle to the political substance of the question of Namibian independence. Discussions resulted in a memorandum of the government by which it formally committed itself to self-determination and independence for Namibia, without however clarifying the terms of this policy.[77] The Secretary-General kept the Group of Three fully informed about the contacts with the South African government. Following these talks, the Group presented to the Secretary-General a formal *aide-mémoire* that sketched out the lines within which subsequent negotiations should proceed.[78] The contents of the paper and the related comments by the Secretary-General suggest that the Group of Three has to be understood much more as a device to control his discussions with South African authorities than a means to provide additional leverage for the chief administrative officer of the Organization. An internal note of the UN Secretariat on the *aide-mémoire* suggests that he was in the hands of its members when deciding whether his mission to South Africa should be advertised as success or failure: 'The Group has to make a choice as to whether it wants to take the responsibility for ending the contact at this stage or whether the Secretary-General should continue with his mandate.'[79]

---

[74] UN Doc S/PV.1637, 3 February 1972, para 169.

[75] Statement by Ambassador Jakob Malik, UN Doc SCOR, twenty-seventh year, 1637th meeting, 3 February 1972, para 114.

[76] United Nations, *Permanent Missions to the United Nations*, Vol. 228 (New York: United Nations).

[77] UN Doc S/10738, 17 July 1972, para 16.

[78] Ibid., Annex I.

[79] Kurt Waldheim Papers, *Note on the Aide Memoire of the Group of Three*, 24 April 1972.

The *aide-mémoire* put particular emphasis on the notions of self-determination and independence, which 'should be exercised by the people of Namibia in a manner agreed upon and approved by the United Nations'.[80] Furthermore, all steps were to be taken in close consultation and cooperation with the Group of Three, another indicator that limiting the Secretary-General's room for manoeuvre instead of increasing his leverage constituted the rationale of this informal group.[81] The SC finally endorsed the limited progress of the talks in its Resolution 323 and invited the Secretary-General to continue discussions with the South African authorities.[82] In addition, it changed the composition of the Group of Three, since Argentina and Somalia terminated the terms of office of their non-permanent membership of the SC on 31 December 1972. The Council decided to replace the countries by Peru that started its two-year term the following month, and Sudan, a non-permanent member in the second year of office.[83] In close consultation with the Group of Three, Waldheim and his personal representative held another series of meetings in early 1973 that were primarily devoted to seeking clarification regarding the South African policy on self-determination and independence for Namibia.[84]

However, it became increasingly clear that the government of South Africa's definition of self-determination and independence implied a de facto fragmentation of the territory into homelands, which was diametrically opposed to the UN concept of Namibia as a multi-ethnic entity. Parallel to the ongoing discussions, the government declared that the Ovambo and Eastern Caprivi territories would be granted self-government 'in the immediate future'.[85] Establishing ethnically divided homelands was seen as a promising strategy to achieve a fait accompli that would be hard to reverse at a later stage. The ambiguous pattern of the South African government became the subject of much criticism in the fourth Committee of the UN General Assembly. For example, the Permanent Observer of the South West Africa People's Organization (SWAPO)[86] to the UN, Theo-

---

[80] UN Doc S/10738, 17 July 1972, Annex, para 3.

[81] Ibid., para 6.

[82] UN Doc S/RES/323, 6 December 1972.

[83] See UN Doc S/RES/323 (1972), 6 December 1972, op. 8 and UN Doc S/PV.1684, 16 January 1973, para 10.

[84] See Report by the Secretary-General on the implementation of SC Resolution 323 (1972) concerning the question of Namibia, UN Doc S/10921, 30 April 1973, para 6.

[85] Geisa Maria Rocha, *In Search of Namibian Independence: The Limitations of the United Nations* (Boulder, CO: Westview Press, 1984), 84.

[86] SWAPO was founded in 1960. In 1966, the liberation movement began its armed struggle for Namibian independence.

Ben Gurirab, referred in a statement before the Committee to the 'insidious design' of the talks held 'to legitimize the illegal occupation of the country and to enable the racist rulers of South Africa to overcome their isolation'.[87] For this reason, he demanded the immediate termination of the talks.

In April 1973, Secretary-General Waldheim concluded in his report on the implementation of SC Resolution 323 that SC members were now confronted with the question whether the initiative should be continued given the limited progress achieved so far.[88] At the same time, the UN Council for Namibia declared that it opposed the continuation of any talks as the UN would implicitly accept South African policy through maintaining those contacts.[89] In consequence, the SC decided to discontinue further activities in December 1973.[90] The Troika terminated its efforts. The statement by the representative of Nigeria who had been invited to participate in the discussions of the Council reflected a widespread feeling among members of the African Group that Western members of the Council had to share the blame for the lack of progress in the question of Namibia's independence:

Namibia is today, for all practical purposes, the exclusive colonial preserve of the United States of America, the United Kingdom, France, the Federal Republic of Germany and Japan, with their two colonial representatives - South Africa and Portugal. . . . Since the start of these contacts, a large number of mining companies from the United States of America have started new prospecting activities in Namibia. The United Kingdom has never accepted the termination of South Africa's Mandate over Namibia. It therefore continues to deal with South Africa over Namibia. France supplies sophisticated weapons which are far beyond the normal needs of a State enjoying internal peace and willing to live in peace with its neighbours.[91]

The frontlines became even harder when the General Assembly adopted a resolution the following day stating that SWAPO was 'the sole and authentic representative of the Namibian people'.[92] At the end of 1973, the mounting pressure on South Africa within the UN also generated much

---

[87] UN Doc GAOR, twenty-seventh session, fourth Committee, 2018th meeting, 11 December 1972, para 12.

[88] See UN Doc S/10921, 30 April 1973, para 19.

[89] See the position of the UN Council for Namibia, adopted on 27 March 1973, contained in UN Doc S/10921/Corr. 1, Annex II.

[90] See UN Doc S/RES/342 (1973), 11 December 1973, op. 2.

[91] UN Doc SCOR, twenty-eighth year, 1758th meeting, 11 December 1973, paras 15–7.

[92] UN Doc A/RES/3111 (XXVIII), 12 December 1973.

criticism at the domestic level, reflecting a growing concern that the South African government stood 'publicly accused of dishonesty in the conduct of its negotiations'.[93]

In conclusion, the Waldheim initiative supported by the Group of Three was not able to produce the critical mass of leverage, which had granted the Secretary-General additional weight in his discussions with the South African government. By abstaining in the vote to SC Resolution 310, France and the United Kingdom had signalled from the start that they would not support a more assertive policy line of the SC vis-à-vis South Africa. The Group of Three had served primarily the interests of the P-3 since the Council demonstrated some initiative and activism, without forcing France, the United Kingdom, and the United States to become too deeply involved in the conflict.

However, the Western politics of limited action and averting mandatory sanctions in the Council became costlier with every day of South African intransigence. In December 1974, the Council unanimously adopted Resolution 366 that condemned the illegal occupation of Namibia and demanded South Africa's compliance with the ICJ advisory opinion of June 1971.[94] Although the wording reflected the least common denominator between African and Western demands, for the first time, the Council explicitly threatened to consider 'appropriate measures' such as the imposition of mandatory sanctions, if South Africa maintained its policy of non-compliance.[95]

5.2.2 Western Contact Group, 1977–83

Mounting pressure by the Western countries that were keen to avoid 'veto embarrassment at the United Nations',[96] including the demise of the Portuguese colonial empire, led to a further reassessment of South Africa's policy and resulted in the launch of constitutional talks in 1975 (the so-called Turnhalle Conference), which should seek an internal solution regarding Namibia's transition towards independence. In the first instance, this initiative constituted an attempt by the South African government to buy time and another manoeuvre to keep Western powers in a

---

[93] This position was stated by a member of the South African Parliament during a debate in August 1974; J. H. P. Serfontein, *Namibia?* (London: Fokus Suid Publishers, 1976), 94.

[94] UN Doc S/RES/366 (1974), 17 December 1974.

[95] Ibid., op. 6.

[96] Rocha, *In Search of Namibian Independence*, 88.

cooperative mood. Most importantly, the government calculated that the 'cautious support given to the plan by Western States will prevent any drastic decision by the Security Council at this stage'.[97] However, Western powers on the Council had become increasingly isolated and their positions untenable, since it was only the triple vetoes that could prevent the imposition of mandatory sanctions.[98] Explaining its reluctance to agree to mandatory sanctions, the Permanent Representative of the United Kingdom stated that the resolution was 'inappropriate both in timing and substance'. He maintained that 'a great deal could still be advised by quiet diplomacy'.[99] At the level of the General Assembly, Western countries faced public trials leading to resolutions that criticized their policies towards southern Africa in general and their support of the South African government with military equipment in particular.[100]

Besides those public condemnations, resolutions reflected the belief within the OAU that Western powers were holding the key to achieving progress in the process towards Namibian independence.[101] In December 1976, the General Assembly maintained the pressure by adopting further resolutions on that issue. The Assembly, *inter alia*, condemned the Turnhalle Conference as a continuation of South Africa's apartheid policy, declared that the situation in Namibia constituted a threat to international peace and security, and called upon the SC to impose mandatory sanctions on South Africa.[102] Furthermore, the Assembly asked the Secretary-General to report on the activities of foreign companies in Namibia and authorized the UN Council for Namibia to convene hearings on the exploitation and purchase of Namibian uranium.[103] By the end of 1976, Western countries intensified their consultations on how to deal with the increasingly hostile atmosphere at the UN. The election of Canada and Germany as non-permanent members on the Council for the period 1977–8 opened a window of opportunity to launch a joint Western

---

[97] John Barratt, 'Southern Africa: A South African View', *Foreign Affairs*, 55/1 (1976), 162.

[98] See, for example, the draft resolution that provided for a mandatory arms embargo against South Africa, as contained in UN Doc S/11713, 6 June 1975, which received ten affirmative votes, a triple veto by the western permanent members, and two abstentions by Italy and Japan; a similar draft resolution was tabled in October 1976, see UN Doc S/12211, 15 October 1976, also vetoed by the P-3.

[99] UN Doc S/PV.1963, 19 October 1976, paras 107 and 108.

[100] See, for example, UN Doc A/RES/7 (XXXI), 5 November 1976, op. 6.

[101] Bley, 'Die Bundesrepublik, der Westen und die internationale Lage um Namibia', 146.

[102] See UN Doc A/RES/146 (XXXI), 20 December 1976, adopted by 107 votes in favour, six against, and twelve abstentions.

[103] See UN Doc A/RES/148 (XXXI), 20 December 1976, adopted by 118 votes in favour, none opposed, and seven abstentions.

initiative to contain the fallout of anti-apartheid policies at the UN by entering into substantive talks with the South African authorities.[104]

Against this background, the formation of the Western Contact Group in 1977 constituted therefore not the least a damage limitation exercise, as will be further elaborated in the following section. The joint activities of the five Western members of the Council—Canada, France, Germany, the United Kingdom, and the United States—constituted an exit strategy to develop a constructive response to (and to escape from) that pressure. Following a closer examination of the rationale of the Western Contact Group the next section analyses key events of the initiative in the period between 1977 and 1981 with special consideration of the dynamics between Contact Group and SC. It proceeds with an analysis of the impact of US policy change in 1981 for conflict resolution, including the effects on the workings of the Contact Group and the SC.

RATIONALE OF THE CONTACT GROUP: EXIT

The formation of the Contact Group has to be understood against the background of the combination of factors as outlined in the previous section. It originated as a product of systemic change that affected governance in the General Assembly and the SC. The establishment of the Contact Group in 1977 therefore constituted both a response to the pressure imposed on Western powers as well as a damage limitation exercise in order to gain control over the increasingly hostile atmosphere towards South Africa that had taken over the General Assembly and, to a lesser extent, the SC. As then US Secretary of State Cyrus Vance recalls:

Without a strategy for achieving Namibian independence, the Western nations would soon be faced with the dilemma of how to respond to African demands for mandatory sanctions against South Africa. If there were no credible negotiation initiative, the Africans would be able to force a Security Council vote. We would then either damage our relations with black Africa by vetoing the resolution, which would be at odds with the Carter administration's Africa policy, or by approving it, destroy the negotiation process and harm important Western economic interests in South Africa, as well as set an undesirable precedent that might be used against our friends, such as Israel, in the future.[105]

Such a strategy included preventing the SC from adopting resolutions that might have compromised the workings of the Western Contact Group.

---

[104] The General Assembly elected Canada and Germany on 21 October 1976, see UN Doc A/31/PV.40, 21 October 1976.

[105] Cyrus R. Vance, *Hard Choices. Critical Years In America's Foreign Policy* (New York: Simon and Schuster, 1983), 275.

According to an internal paper of the German Foreign Office, drafted in 1977, Contact Group members sought to restrain the frequency of SC meetings on that matter in order to gain sufficient room for manoeuvre.[106] For example, when the Western Five set the framework for negotiations in 1977, the Council held not a single session on the question of Namibia proper.[107] Related resolutions, adopted in that period, constituted a collective response to South Africa's policy of apartheid rather than specific action on the question of Namibia.[108]

The Contact Group should operate '*alongside* and *not in* the Security Council simply to avoid obstruction from the Soviets'.[109] Launching the initiative inside the Council might also have resulted in resistance on the side of African countries. In consequence, the Contact Group developed its own terms of reference without having an explicit mandate of the Assembly or the Council.[110] Nevertheless, the SC should provide the platform for legitimizing the Western initiative. The Contact Group established a negotiation process that differed to a considerable extent from the previous ones as it involved key states that were able to exert a high degree of influence over the parties to the conflict. The minilateral approach, as epitomized in the Contact Group, should secure the exercise of influence especially over South Africa, while sharing the risks and the potential costs of failure.[111] Targeting South Africa was not unproblematic since the Western strategy was geared towards change within a sovereign state and not a colonial territory. The Contact Group operated on the understanding that it would secure compliance by the South African government while the front-line states would exert their influence on SWAPO.[112] The lack of trust on the side of SWAPO virtually excluded a role for the Contact Group as an impartial mediator. For this reason, it had not been possible to enter into direct negotiations with the SWAPO leadership. SWAPO

[106] Quoted in Christian Freuding, *Deutschland in der Weltpolitik: Die Bundesrepublik Deutschland als nicht-ständiges Mitglied im Sicherheitsrat der Vereinten Nationen in den Jahren 1977/78, 1987/88 und 1995/96* (Baden Baden: Nomos, 2000), 174.

[107] United Nations, *Index to Proceedings of the Security Council, Thirty-second year* (New York: United Nations, 1978).

[108] See UN Doc S/RES/417, 31 October 1977, UN Doc S/RES/418, 4 November 1977, and UN Doc S/RES/421, 9 December 1977.

[109] Donald McHenry, 'Statement', in Heribert Weiland and Mathew Braham (eds.), *The Namibian Peace Process: Implications and Lessons for the Future* (Freiburg: Arnold Bergstraesser Institut, 1994), 13.

[110] Donald McHenry recalls that he had received some explicit warning by an African representative that if the African Group had to set the terms of reference, the initiative would not succeed; ibid.

[111] See Margaret P. Karns, 'Ad Hoc Multilateral Diplomacy: The United States, the Contact Group, and Namibia', *International Organization*, 41/1 (1987), 94.

[112] The front-line states included Angola, Botswana, Mozambique, Tanzania, and Zambia.

originally did not prefer negotiations since the General Assembly had explicitly legitimized their armed struggle. At the same time, developments in Mozambique and Angola furthered SWAPO's perception that armed conflict may ultimately pay off. The front-line states as well as Nigeria therefore became important elements of the regional strategy. As Hans-Joachim Vergau has put it, 'they should deliver SWAPO to the negotiation table'.[113] Engaging the stakeholders and integrating them into a negotiation framework turned out to be a key concern. Looked at from this perspective, the Contact Group served not only as the coordinating hub for the Western Five but also as a means to secure the cooperation of other key players such as the front-line states. The joint presentation of a Western position provided an incentive for the front-line states, including SWAPO, to come up with a similarly coherent stance.[114] In many respects, the front-line states and Nigeria constituted 'an extended SWAPO delegation in the negotiations'.[115] However, this implied less the conduct of negotiations on behalf of SWAPO rather than to interpret their aims and to translate them into positions articulated in the negotiation process.[116] Engaging the front-line states was also crucial since this would reduce the probability of a Soviet veto in the Council, given its rhetoric that the Soviet Union strongly supported the course of decolonization and anti-apartheid in southern Africa.

In conclusion, the Contact Group provided a platform away from the ideological battle-place at the UN to tackle problems in a pragmatic way and in an informal atmosphere. The informal device assumed a triple role: it would act as strategic policy-planning unit, negotiation team, and drafting group. The initiative was characterized by six elements:

1. it constituted a pragmatic approach that deliberately excluded the legal dimension of the conflict;

2. the Contact Group established close contacts with the front-line states (Angola, Botswana, Mozambique, Tanzania, and Zambia), including Nigeria;

3. the leading liberation movement (SWAPO) participated in the negotiation process;

---

[113] Hans-Joachim Vergau, 'Statement', in *The Namibian Peace Process*, 20.
[114] Interview with Chester Crocker, Washington, DC, 21 November 2000.
[115] Theo-Ben Gurirab, 'Statement', in *The Namibian Peace Process*, 45.
[116] Comment by Paul Rupia, former Permanent Representative of Tanzania to the UN, in *The Namibian Peace Process*, 46 *et sequ.*, footnote 9.

4. independence, including the establishment of majority rule in the country constituted the declared aim of the initiative;
5. the process formed part of a broader regional strategy to deal with conflicts in Namibia, Zimbabwe/Rhodesia, including South Africa;
6. diplomacy was being offered as an alternative to the armed struggle towards independence.

DYNAMICS BETWEEN CONTACT GROUP AND SECURITY COUNCIL

The election of Canada and Germany as non-permanent members of the UN Security Council for the period 1977–8 fostered consultations with the P-3 on ways and means of becoming actively engaged in the resolution of the Namibian conflict. In January 1977, Germany had explored such a possibility in the Foreign Office among experts, and consultations with the US State Department in late February had led to the conclusion that the United States had been working in a similar direction.[117] Furthermore, informal working-level contacts among the five Western countries on 4 March in New York had shown a high convergence of policy agendas, which resulted in a first consultation on the level of Permanent Representatives (including experts) on 9 March 1977. However, at that stage the US mission was still waiting for the final decision of the White House to go ahead with this initiative. The next consultation took place a few days later, on 16 March, at the Canadian mission, which may be seen as the first official meeting of the Contact Group on Namibia.[118] The Western Five expected at this stage that the question could be solved during Canada's and Germany's term of office.[119]

The Western Contact Group worked primarily on the level of high-ranking members of the five UN missions. On several key occasions, meetings took place at foreign minister level along with their ambassadors in New York, Pretoria, Lusaka, and other capitals.[120] Until the presentation of the settlement proposal in April 1978, the Contact Group met daily for consultations.[121] Although the Western Five did not have a rotating chairmanship, they always appointed a speaker who delivered statements on behalf of the Contact Group to the public.

---

[117] See Hans-Joachim Vergau, 'Genscher und das südliche Afrika', in Hans-Dieter Lucas (ed.), *Genscher, Deutschland und Europa* (Baden-Baden: Nomos 2002), 228.
[118] Ibid., 229.
[119] Interview with Hans-Joachim Vergau, Berlin, 9 January 2001.
[120] Karns, 'Ad hoc Multilateral Diplomacy', 101.
[121] Ibid.

The announcement of the Western initiative showed some immediate effects during a series of SC meetings on Namibia from 21 to 31 March 1977, convened in response to a request by the African Group.[122] African members of the Council had introduced four draft resolutions to impose mandatory sanctions on South Africa.[123] Although the P-3 could have cast their veto on any of the drafts, such obstruction would have weakened the Western initiative right from the start, since it was dependent on the cooperation of front-line states. Furthermore, with the United States holding the Presidency of the SC for the month of March, casting a veto would have been in particular an embarrassment for the new Carter administration. The participation of thirty-one non-members in the formal meeting illustrated the growing impatience of African countries with South Africa's intransigence and Western reluctance to show some initiative. As a counter-initiative, the Western Five presented an eighteen-point draft declaration of principles in order to achieve a unified position of the Council towards the conflict.[124] Such a reference document would have granted greater leverage to the Contact Group in its negotiations with the parties. In essence, this constituted 'an attempt to forestall drastic African demands for mandatory sanctions against South Africa'.[125] The declaration called upon the South African government to 'bring its illegal occupation of Namibia to a speedy conclusion' and to 'facilitate the holding ... of free elections under the aegis of the UN and refrain from any steps inconsistent therewith'.[126] Especially the support of the African Group would have been crucial to strengthen the Contact Group's stance vis-à-vis SWAPO.

After intensive consultations with the Western Five, the African Group ultimately refrained from putting their four draft resolutions to a vote, which was, in effect, a tacit approval of the Western initiative. As for the declaration of principles, the Council did not take any decision either due to opposition from African states or pressure from the Soviet bloc.[127] Such opposition clearly indicated that the support of African states was limited and contingent upon the performance of the Contact Group in the negotiations with the South African government.

---

[122] See UN Doc S/PV.1988–99, 21–31 March 1977.

[123] See UN Doc S/12309–12, 30 March 1977.

[124] See André du Pisani, *SWA/Namibia: The Politics of Continuity and Change* (Johannesburg: Jonathan Ball Publishers, 1985), 336.

[125] D. S. Prinsloo, *SWA/Namibia: Towards A Negotiated Settlement* (Pretoria: Foreign Affairs Association, 1977), 20.

[126] Ibid.

[127] Ibid.

The South African government was forced to the negotiation table in April 1977 after the Ambassadors of the Western Five in Pretoria had presented a *démarche* to Prime Minister John Balthazar Vorster. It demanded, *inter alia*, the release of political prisoners, the withdrawal of South African forces, and the end of the territorial administration.[128] Furthermore, South Africa should abandon its efforts to set up an interim government in Namibia in accordance with the draft constitution of the Turnhalle Conference. The *démarche* underlined that the Western initiative was based upon SC Resolution 385.[129] The explicit reference to the resolution signalled that the initiative rested within the objectives of the UN, despite the fact that the Contact Group acted outside the UN framework. Resolution 385 had already provided a framework of objectives for a negotiated settlement. Key principles included the holding of free elections 'under the supervision and control of the United Nations'; furthermore, the resolution entitled the UN 'to establish the necessary machinery within Namibia to supervise and control such elections', and it called upon South Africa to withdraw 'its illegal administration maintained in Namibia and to transfer power to the people of Namibia with the assistance of the United Nations'.[130]

The presentation of the *démarche* reflected a different approach taken by the Western Five since it included the threat that the South African government might face 'stern action' by the UN Security Council if it did not comply with the demands.[131] Such an approach constituted at first sight a shift away from 'the artificial but nonetheless rigorous separation between commercial and political policies' of Western countries.[132] It elevated the conflict from a regional to an international level. Diplomacy backed by the implicit threat of mandatory sanctions forced the South African government to employ a more cooperative approach that resulted in the launch of negotiations on the question of Namibia with the Western Five.

Subsequent negotiations between Contact Group members and the South African government led to agreement on several points the Western Five had demanded in the *démarche*. On 27 April, during a meeting of Contact Group experts with the South African government, Vorster accepted the holding of free and fair elections and agreed not to implement the draft

---

[128] D. S. Prinsloo, *SWA/Namibia: Towards A Negotiated Settlement* (Pretoria: Foreign Affairs Association, 1977), 21

[129] See du Pisani, *SWA/Namibia*, 337.

[130] UN Doc S/RES/385 (1976), 30 January 1976, op. 7, 8, and 10.

[131] See Vergau, 'Genscher und das südliche Afrika', 229.

[132] Mayall, *Africa: The Cold War and After*, 189.

constitution of the Turnhalle Conference. Furthermore, he agreed in principle that the Secretary-General could appoint a special representative to secure the involvement of the UN in that process.[133] However, the withdrawal of South African forces, the nature of the UN presence in Namibia, the status of Walvis Bay,[134] and the release of political prisoners remained contentious issues. The decision of the South African government to place Walvis Bay under its direct administration by 1 September 1977 illustrated South Africa's reluctance to commit itself fully to the diplomatic initiative of the Western Five. The government continued with its efforts to create facts on the ground for an internal settlement, while keeping engaged in negotiations on the independence of Namibia. The distrust towards the Western effort reflected a growing fear that South Africa might lose control over the diplomatic process leading to Namibia's independence, with potential repercussions for South Africa's internal sovereignty. It was a defining moment of the process that 'both South Africa and SWAPO appeared to be pursuing two-track strategies, negotiating but drawing out the negotiations while they attempted to maneuver in search of more favourable outcomes'.[135]

SWAPO had articulated its doubts right from the start when it delivered a press statement in May 1977 that, on the one hand, acknowledged the position of Western powers 'to compel South Africa to comply with the resolutions and decisions of the United Nations on Namibia'; on the other hand, SWAPO expressed concerns that the Western initiative 'aimed at bailing South Africa out of her political predicament in Namibia'.[136] Furthermore, the steering committee of the UN Council for Namibia asserted in a meeting with the Secretary-General that informal discussions between the Contact Group and the South African government could only become binding if the Contact Group sought formal legitimation by the SC.[137]

This illustrated that the Western Five would have to strike a balance between competing demands of flexibility and accountability. On the one hand, choosing the exit option provided the Western Five with flexibility to conduct negotiations outside the constraints of the UN framework.

---

[133] See Vance, *Hard Choices*, 277 *et sequ.*

[134] Walvis Bay is the only deep-sea harbour in Namibia. Given its strategic importance, it remained a contentious issue throughout the negotiations. While South Africa claimed that Walvis Bay had been integral part of its territory since 1910 and therefore non-negotiable, SWAPO categorically declared that it must become part of independent Namibia.

[135] Study Commission on U.S. Policy Toward Southern Africa, *Southern Africa: Time running out* (Berkeley, CA: University of California Press, 1981), 364.

[136] Kurt Waldheim Papers, SWAPO Press Statement, 17 May 1977.

[137] See Kurt Waldheim Papers, Confidential note of meeting, 24 June 1977.

On the other hand, achieving legitimation inside the Organization was key for the wider acceptance of any settlement. Secretary-General Waldheim advised the Western Five that member states of the OAU would go along with the negotiations 'if they could result in the full implementation of Security Council Resolution 385'.[138] Although the new initiative would be conducted outside the UN framework, Contact Group members urged the Secretary-General right from the beginning 'that they needed to have, not formally but informally, a firm idea of the requirements for the U.N. involvement'.[139] As Martti Ahtisaari has confirmed, the Western Five sought to maintain an 'extremely close' cooperation with the UN Secretariat.[140]

With the South African government increasing its repressions against several individuals, organizations, and the media in Fall 1977, the Western Five felt compelled to support a more forceful response by the SC if they did not want to loose their credibility vis-à-vis the NAM and the African Group.[141] Consequently, SC Resolution 418 unanimously imposed a mandatory arms embargo on South Africa determining that 'the acquisition...of arms and related matériel constitutes a threat to the maintenance of international peace and security'.[142] Invoking Article 39 regarding the situation in southern Africa demonstrated the tension under which the Contact Group had to operate in the search for a settlement plan. On the one hand, it had to channel (and to deflect) the pressure in the Council for more forceful action by keeping especially the members of the African Group at bay, while, on the other hand, keeping the South African government in a cooperative mood. The voting pattern of the Western Five illustrates the dynamics between SC and Contact Group at that stage. By accommodating the claims of the African Group, the Council served as a safety valve for the expression of voice to release the pressure for a more confrontational policy vis-à-vis South Africa. In exchange, the Contact Group gained additional room for manoeuvre.

In order to create new momentum the Contact Group invited South African and SWAPO representatives for proximity talks at UN Headquarters in New York from 10 to 11 February 1978, with the foreign secretaries of the Western Five attending.[143] The setting of the talks allowed for

---

[138] Kurt Waldheim Papers, Confidential note of meeting, 21 July 1977.
[139] Ibid.
[140] Interview with Martti Ahtisaari, Helsinki, 9 May 2000.
[141] In this context, the brutal circumstances of the death of black activist Steve Biko gained particular prominence and increased the pressure to act.
[142] UN Doc S/RES/418, 4 November 1977, op. 1.
[143] See Vance, *Hard Choices*, 302.

parallel negotiations with the parties to the conflict and limited in particular South Africa's ability to raise obstacles by introducing new items on the agenda. At that stage, African states had tabled once again two draft resolutions in the Council that, *inter alia*, called for the adoption of mandatory sanctions against the South African government.[144] After intense consultations with the Western Five, the resolutions were not put to vote in the Council. Seen from that perspective, the high-level talks sent a signal to the African Group that the Western initiative was still in full swing, and any action by the SC would be counterproductive. However, the proximity talks ended abruptly on 11 February after German Foreign Minister Hans-Dietrich Genscher had outlined two central features of the Western proposal: firstly, South Africa should reduce its forces to 1,500 men that would be allowed to remain in Namibia through the elections; secondly, the Western Five would not agree with the South African position that Walvis Bay was part of its territory.[145]

With the special session of the General Assembly looming, to be held from 24 April to 3 May 1978, the pressure on the Western Five increased to present at least some preliminary results in order to prevent drastic action by the South. After intensified negotiations, on 10 April 1978, Contact Group members presented a refined settlement proposal that met several concerns of the South African government.[146] Firstly, South Africa's Administrator-General in Namibia would be in command of the police forces during the transition period; secondly, decisions regarding the size of the UN operation—the United Nations Transition Assistance Group (UNTAG)—would be taken by the UN Special Representative; and thirdly, the question of Walvis Bay would be deferred for settlement at a later stage. The proposal included the holding of free and fair elections to select a constituent assembly under the supervision and control of the UN by 31 December 1978.[147] All but 1,500 South African forces would withdraw from Namibia within twelve weeks, while 'SWAPO personnel outside of the territory [had] to return peacefully to Namibia through designated entry points to participate freely in the political process'.[148] Given the diverging positions of two members of the Contact Group, the Western proposal had remained especially vague regarding the demobilization of SWAPO forces. While the US administration claimed the existence of

---

[144] du Pisani, *SWA/Namibia*, 389.
[145] See Vergau, 'Genscher und das südliche Afrika', 231.
[146] See Vance, *Hard Choices*, 303 *et seq.*
[147] UN Doc S/12636, 10 April 1978, paras 5, 6, and Annex.
[148] Ibid., para 8 D.

SWAPO bases on the Namibian territory, the United Kingdom expressed doubt on that account.[149] The clarification of the matter would be the task of the Secretary-General and his Special Representative.

By presenting the settlement proposal to the SC, Contact Group members brought the process back into the framework of the UN. Although the UN had not been directly involved in the negotiations, Council and Secretariat were of crucial importance for the legitimation and implementation of the Contact Group proposal. In fact, the Secretariat would be in charge of elaborating the settlement plan, based on the proposal of the Western Five. The declaratory policy of the Contact Group strongly advertised that the Western proposal remained embedded in the context of previous UN efforts to reach a settlement of the conflict. By emphasizing that the proposal was 'an effective basis for implementing Resolution 385 (1976) while taking adequate account of the interests of all parties involved',[150] the Western Five sought to gain acceptance by the African Group, which would be necessary to achieve approval by the Council and subsequent support for the implementation of the proposal.

Prime Minister Vorster used the forum of the special session of the General Assembly on 25 April to accept the Contact Group proposals on the condition that the Secretary-General's report on the implementation of the proposal would meet the demands of the South African government. At the same meeting, SWAPO leader Sam Nuoma still rejected the proposal on the ground that they did not deal with the status of Walvis Bay and did not meet SWAPO's position regarding the location of South African security forces. The special session of the General Assembly failed to support the proposal of the Contact Group.[151] Instead, the Assembly asserted that:

[U]nless effective political, economic and diplomatic pressures are demonstrably brought to bear on South Africa, no negotiation will succeed. Moreover, any genuine attempt to resolve the problem of Namibia by negotiation must not undermine the position of the South West Africa People's Organization or diminish the role of the United Nations or the United Nations Council for Namibia as the legal Administering Authority for the Territory until its independence. It is imperative that any negotiated settlement be arrived at with the agreement of SWAPO and within the framework of the resolutions of the United Nations.[152]

---

[149] Vivienne Jabri's account is based on interviews with Henry Miller, who was assistant to Donald McHenry, and Sir James Murray, Permanent Representative of the United Kingdom to the United Nations; see Jabri, *Mediating Conflict*, 98.

[150] UN Doc S/12636, 10 April 1978, para 4.

[151] See UN Doc A/RES/S-9/2, 3 May 1978. The resolution was adopted by 119 votes in favour, none against, and twenty-one abstentions, including the members of the Contact Group.

[152] See UN Doc A/RES/S-9/2, 3 May 1978, para 19.

SWAPO ultimately accepted the Western proposal in July after the Contact Group suggested a further increase in the strength of the UN presence and some concessions on the question of Walvis Bay. On 27 July 1978, the SC endorsed the proposal of the Contact Group, with Czechoslovakia and the Soviet Union abstaining. Resolution 431 requested the Secretary-General, firstly, 'to appoint a Special Representative for Namibia in order to ensure the early independence of Namibia through free elections under the supervision and control of the United Nations', and secondly, 'to submit at the earliest possible date a report containing his recommendations for the implementation of the proposal for a settlement of the Namibian situation in accordance with resolution 385 (1976)'.[153]

As the Soviet Union had advertised itself as a strong proponent of decolonization in previous years, casting a veto in light of African support of the Western proposal would have severely damaged Soviet relations with African countries and limited its influence in the region. The Western strategy of co-opting the front-line states from the very beginning therefore constituted a safeguard to prevent direct Soviet opposition in the SC. Both the Soviet and the Chinese delegations seemed to feel a growing uneasiness about the Western initiative that was being conducted outside the UN framework beyond their direct control. Furthermore, Contact Group members objected when the Permanent Representative of the Soviet Union and his Chinese colleague had sought participation in the negotiations of the Western Five on the grounds that they were permanent members of the SC.[154] This illustrated the problems of the Contact Group to trade off competing demands of informality and inclusiveness.

In a separate resolution, the Council declared unanimously 'that the territorial integrity and unity of Namibia must be assured through the reintegration of Walvis Bay within its territory'.[155] The declaration provoked much protest on the side of the South African government since it was in contradiction to the agreement with the Western Contact Group that had provided for the postponement of the issue after Namibia's independence.[156] A closer analysis of the circumstances under which SC Resolutions 431 and 432 had been adopted reveals that they constituted a comprehensive package with considerable concessions to the NAM and

---

[153] UN Doc S/RES/431, 27 July 1978, op. 1 and 2.

[154] Christian Freuding quotes an interview with Rüdiger von Wechmar, Permanent Representative of Germany to the United Nations in 1978, who participated in the negotiations; see Freuding, *Deutschland in der Weltpolitik*, 162.

[155] UN Doc S/RES/432, 27 July 1978, op. 1.

[156] As South African Foreign Minister Botha stated during the Council meeting: 'We categorically reject the resolution on Walvis Bay.' See UN Doc S/PV.2082, 27 July 1978, para 274.

the African Group. Resolution 432 mirrored the central demands of the NAM, as contained in a telegram addressed to the President of the SC on 25 July 1978.[157] The fact that Contact Group members did not co-sponsor any of the draft resolutions strongly suggests that they contained compromises the Five did not welcome. Concessions on the question of Walvis Bay were the price for securing agreement of the African Group and achieving legitimation by the Council as a whole. The difficulties of the Contact Group to legitimize the proposal in the Council were further illustrated by the fact that Resolution 431 merely took note of the proposal in the preambular paragraph, without mentioning it in the operative part of the resolution.[158]

Secretary-General Kurt Waldheim and his Special Representative Martti Ahtisaari presented the settlement plan on 29 August 1978, based upon the proposal of the Western Contact Group. The plan provided for a four-phased process towards independence, *inter alia*, requiring 1,500 personnel for the civilian leg and 7,500 troops for the military leg of UNTAG. The South African government criticized in a letter to the Secretary-General that the report deviated in significant parts from the Western proposal, especially regarding the size of the UN force, the introduction of a UN civil police component, and the election date that had been postponed to May/June 1979.[159] In a parallel move, the government openly undermined the plan by announcing early elections in Namibia on 4 December. South African Foreign Minister Botha however left the door open for further consultations with the Western Five, as he underlined in a second letter to Waldheim.[160] South Africa apparently followed a diplomatic strategy that granted enough concessions to prevent the entire breakdown of negotiations and to avoid mandatory sanctions by the SC.

Despite South African concerns, the Council approved the plan by adopting Resolution 435 on 29 September 1978.[161] In close cooperation with African members of the Council, Contact Group members had tabled the draft resolution without any further debate. Cooperation with, and agreement by, African members again turned out to be key since this was a gate-opener to Soviet acquiescence on that matter. The resolution

---

[157] See UN Doc S/12791, 27 July 1978.
[158] See UN Doc S/RES/431, 27 July 1978, preambula paragraph 2; the resolution contains no explicit reference to the Contact Group.
[159] See UN Doc S/12853, 20 September 1978.
[160] See UN Doc S/12868, 27 September 1978.
[161] See UN Doc S/RES/435, 29 September 1978, with twelve Council members voting in favour, Czechoslovakia and the Soviet Union abstaining, and China not participating in the vote.

approved the report of the Secretary-General on the implementation of the Western proposal, without referring to the two dissenting letters of the South African government. Instead, the Council called upon South Africa 'to cooperate with the Secretary-General in the implementation of the present resolution'.

When the Council adopted SC Resolution 435, the representative of the United Kingdom expressed therefore his hope that the South African government could be persuaded 'over the next few weeks in a constructive spirit'.[162] The statement by the Indian representative reflected that the further support of non-aligned states would be contingent upon the short-term progress the Western Five would achieve in persuading South Africa to comply with SC Resolution 435.[163]

The subsequent mission by the foreign ministers of the Western Five to Pretoria in October 1978 that aimed at pressing the South African government to revise its decision is central to the understanding of the role and function of the Contact Group. In fact, it may be well argued that it turned out to be the turning point of the Contact Group initiative. At this stage, the Western Five were confronted with the decision whether or not to deliver on the threat of stern action. The problem with the threat of stern action was that it constituted a stick that should actually never be used.[164] The leverage over South Africa rested upon the perception that the Contact Group would be willing and able to impose mandatory sanctions in case of continued intransigence by the South African government. The high-level composition of the mission to Pretoria raised expectations that the Western Five could persuade the government to abandon its plan.

However, several indicators suggested that the Contact Group would not deliver. Firstly, it appeared as if South Africa had been informed before the meeting through back channels between London and Pretoria that the high-level mission Contact Group would not carry any stick.[165] The threat of stern action was not backed up at the highest political levels. Secondly, experts of the Contact Group remained excluded from the talks. They had advised their foreign ministers to reconsider their plans for the meeting.[166]

---

[162] UN Doc S/PV.2087, 29 September 1978, para 80.

[163] The Indian representative stated that in case of further non-compliance within the next fortnight, 'the Council will be obliged to apply such measures as may be necessary under Chapter VII of the Charter to help South Africa see the wisdom of cooperating with the Council in the implementation of resolution 385 (1976)', ibid., para 94. Nigeria expressed similar expectations, without however directly threatening with mandatory sanctions, ibid., para 115.

[164] See Comment by Hans-Joachim Vergau, *The Namibian Peace Process*, 30.

[165] See Comment by Winrich Kühne, *The Namibian Peace Process*, 35.

[166] Comment by Hans-Joachim Vergau, *The Namibian Peace Process*, 36.

In preparation of the mission, Contact Group experts had drawn up a list of carefully selected targeted sanctions, including an assessment of the likely impact. Proposed sanctions involved 'restrictions on landing rights for South African civil aircraft and Pretoria's access to export financing from Western sources', which would have backed up the diplomacy of foreign ministers with a credible threat.[167] Thirdly, the French government that had always been very reluctant to support such a course of action down-graded its participation by sending the state secretary instead of the foreign minister. British Secretary of State David Owen told his colleagues on the plane to Pretoria that he also did not have a mandate to impose mandatory sanctions.[168]

The Pretoria meeting had detrimental effects on the credibility of the Western powers. Viewed from the perspective of the front-line states, the Western powers had broken the unarticulated agreement that they would force South Africa to compliance. The subsequent meeting of the SC on Namibia exposed divisions between the front-line states and the Contact Group. The Western Five jointly abstained in the vote on SC Resolution 439 that condemned South Africa's decision to proceed unilaterally with the holding of elections and threatened with the adoption of mandatory sanctions.[169] Mozambique articulated the discomfort on behalf of the front-line states when it concluded 'that the five Western countries are still very much the traditional allies of South Africa'.[170] As Contact Group experts had not been directly involved in the talks they even seemed to distance themselves from the performance of their foreign ministers. The UK Permanent Representative to the UN, Sir Ivor Richard, told Secretary-General Waldheim on behalf of the Western Five that '[o]nly the Foreign Ministers, who had conducted the talks themselves, could provide all the clarifications that might be required.'[171] In December 1978, at the end of Canada's and Germany's term of office as non-permanent members on the Council, it seemed that the Western Five had underestimated South Africa's obstructionist policy. The loss of momentum became especially visible in February 1979 when Secretary-General Waldheim presented an amended version of his report on the implementation of the Western proposal, after consultations between the

---

[167] See Vance, *Hard Choices*, 309.

[168] Winrich Kühne, 'Frieden im südwestlichen Afrika? Der Durchbruch bei den Verhand-lungen um die Unabhängigkeit Namibias', *Europa-Archiv*, 44/4 (1989), 107.

[169] See UN Doc S/RES/439, 13 November 1978.

[170] UN Doc S/PV.2095, 2 November 1978, para 40.

[171] Kurt Waldheim Papers, Confidential note of meeting, 19 October 1978.

UN Special Representative and the parties to the conflict, including the front-line states and Nigeria. South Africa rejected in particular new provisions of the implementation plan that granted a de facto military presence of SWAPO in Namibia during the transition period.[172] Martti Ahtisaari explains the rationale of the report as follows:

It was an attempt to deal with a practical problem. During the endless negotiations of 1978—particularly with the South African military—there was recognition that there was a continuous presence of SWAPO in the north of the territory. We ... wanted to find a safe solution to that problem. So it was suggested in our discussions that the best thing would be to gather the SWAPO people together and put them into inhabited areas—in camps and hold them there.[173]

Although the Contact Group publicly supported the Secretary-General's report, such support appeared to be conditional, as the Western Five did not intend to seek endorsement of the revised implementation plan by the SC. While Contact Group members claimed during a meeting with the Secretary-General that they did 'not have much clout' to enforce the provisions, Special Representative Martti Ahtisaari warned that 'if one were now afraid of reminding South Africa that it would be held responsible for a breakdown, then one might as well forget the whole exercise'.[174] At this stage, it became evident that the task sharing between Contact Group and UN Secretariat would generate additional problems unless both presented a unified position vis-à-vis the parties to the conflict. With two members of the Contact Group divided over the particulars of SWAPO demobilization, South African acceptance to any report by the Secretary-General was most unlikely.

At the end of 1979, the Western Five reconsidered their approach and engaged in further talks to complement negotiations with confidence-building measures such as the agreement on constitutional principles along the lines of the Lancaster House Conference on Rhodesia.[175] Discussions on the so-called 'Principles Concerning the Constituent Assembly and the Constitution for an Independent Namibia' constituted, firstly, an attempt to break the logjam of the negotiations and, secondly, a response to the growing pressure in the General Assembly and the SC. The principles aimed at providing a safeguard that the Namibian constitution would include provisions for protecting the rights of the white minority.

---

[172] See UN Doc S/13120, 26 February 1979, paras 11–3.
[173] Comment by Martti Ahtisaari, *The Namibian Peace Process*, 33.
[174] Kurt Waldheim Papers, Confidential note of Meeting, 3 April 1979.
[175] See Vergau, 'Statement', *The Namibian Peace Process*, 23.

Furthermore, in response to South African claims for equal treatment of the internal political parties,[176] the Contact Group negotiated on a so-called impartiality package that would terminate SWAPO's observer status at the UN, including all funding as soon as the implementation of SC Resolution 435 had started.

However, the election victory of Robert Mugabe in Rhodesia/Zimbabwe in March 1980 contributed further to South Africa's intransigence. The outcome of the elections illustrated that those who had struggled for the independence of their country were likely to win subsequent elections.[177] This development fostered the perception inside the South African government that holding free and fair elections in Namibia could produce a similar result, with SWAPO gaining power in Windhoek. In consequence, the South African government introduced additional issues on the agenda or changed the parameters of the negotiations in order to gain time.[178] These included calls for the termination of SWAPO's observer status at the UN as well as UN funding for the liberation movement.

In parallel, the South African government escalated its activities on the domestic and regional levels by intensifying the repression of domestic opposition against apartheid, and launching major armed incursions into Angola, such as the three-week enduring Operation Smokeshell in June 1980.[179] Those operations constituted part of a comprehensive strategy to destabilize the region through continued attacks against the front-line-states and SWAPO proper. Although the SC condemned these activities in Resolutions 473 and 475 respectively, the Western powers sought to prevent any further escalation.[180] While the former resolution reflected the well-known condemnation of South Africa's apartheid policy, the latter requested UN member states 'to extend all necessary assistance to the People's Republic of Angola and the other front-line States, in order to strengthen their defence capacities in the face of South Africa's acts of aggression against these countries'.[181] Western powers could hardly support such requests if they wanted to continue negotiations with Pretoria.

With the US elections approaching in November 1980, the South African government balked at any significant progress in the negotiations

---

[176] UN Doc S/13935, 12 May 1980, paras 6–9.

[177] See John Seiler, 'Which Way in Southern Africa?', *Africa Report*, 26/3 (1981), 17 *et sequ.*

[178] See Deon Geldenhuys, *The Diplomacy of Isolation: South African Foreign Policy Making* (Johannesburg: Macmillan for the South African Institute of International Affairs, 1984), 226.

[179] Jabri, *Mediating Conflict*, 100.

[180] See UN Doc S/RES/473, adopted unanimously on 13 June 1980; UN Doc S/RES/475, adopted on 27 June 1980 by twelve votes in favour, with France, the United Kingdom, and the United States abstaining.

[181] UN Doc S/RES/475, op. 5.

using new items on the agenda, such as the question of the impartiality of the UN or discussions about the establishment of a demilitarized zone, as a pretext for further delay. At the so-called Pre-Implementation Meeting, held under the auspices of the UN in Geneva from 7 to 15 January, the stalemate became abundantly clear. There seemed to be a common understanding between the Western Five and the Secretary-General that South Africa 'had no intention whatever of going ahead'.[182] Brian Urquhart, who chaired the Geneva meeting, confirms in his memoirs: 'the incoming Reagan administration deflated both United States support for the Pre-Implementation Meeting and its leadership of the Western Contact Group. It also signalled unmistakably to the South Africans that the future U.S. administration would not mind at all if South Africa wrecked the meeting'.[183]

In conclusion, the high-level mission of the Contact Group to Pretoria in October 1978, in combination with the outcome of elections in Zimbabwe in March 1980, and the prospect of a new US administration after the presidential elections of November 1980, constituted a set of factors that raised objections within the South African government. It did not agree with the implementation plan, as outlined in SC Resolution 435. Initially, the Contact Group had been successful in manipulating the expression of voice before the SC in order to gain maximum room for manoeuvre for their negotiations with the parties to the conflict. This strategy was however contingent on tangible results in the process towards Namibian independence.

WESTERN CONTACT GROUP AND US LINKAGE

The arrival of the Reagan administration in 1981 and the subsequent adoption of the policy of constructive engagement, including the so-called linkage approach, altered the functioning of the Contact Group. Constructive engagement rested upon the assumption that 'effective coercive influence is a rare commodity in foreign policy'.[184] In terms of operational policy, the US administration employed a genuinely cooperative approach towards South Africa based upon open dialogue, compromise, and mutual understanding, by virtually excluding the application of sticks such as mandatory economic sanctions. Those measures tended 'to

---

[182] Kurt Waldheim Papers, Confidential note of meeting, 20 January 1981.

[183] Brian Urquhart, *A Life in Peace and War* (London: Weidenfeld & Nicolson, 1987), 317 *et sequ.*

[184] Chester A. Crocker, 'South Africa: Strategy for Change', *Foreign Affairs*, 59/2 (1980), 326.

erode rather than strengthen future influence and flexibility'.[185] The linkage approach made progress in the question of Namibia's independence dependent on a prior withdrawal of Cuban troops from the neighbouring country of Angola. Linkage had never before been explicitly articulated by the South African government as a precondition for agreement to the settlement plan of the UN.[186] Looking from the angle of the United States, it accommodated the concerns of neoconservative critics within the administration and Congress that this new approach would result in the containment or even the rollback of Soviet influence in the region.[187] The US administration employed a 'triangular approach'[188] that involved negotiations between the United States, South Africa, and Angola. SWAPO was being excluded from these negotiations.

However, it remains doubtful whether it is an accurate assessment that 'linkage was not invented, but written into the history and geography of the region'.[189] The policy shift towards linkage appeared rather as a conscious decision of the new administration to distinguish itself from its predecessor in terms of 'rhetoric, tone, and tactics rather than the substance of diplomacy'.[190] In 1978, President Carter had already raised concerns that the military engagement of Cuba and the Soviet Union may pose a threat for the security of the southern African region.[191] The Carter administration therefore did not ignore the Cold War dimension of the conflict, but it employed a different approach to cope with the security situation. The removal of the threat would be the consequence of the successful multiparty management of Namibia's transition towards independence. The Reagan administration analysed the conflict primarily through the lens of the East–West conflict, concluding that the withdrawal of Cuban forces was the sine qua non for Namibia's independence. The policy of constructive engagement operated under assumptions that did not accurately reflect South African perceptions of the conflict. From the perspective of the South African government, the presence of Cuban troops in Angola constituted less a threat than an opportunity. It

---

[185] Ibid., 351.

[186] See Robert S. Jaster, *South Africa in Namibia: The Botha Strategy* (Lanham, MD.: University Press of America, 1985), 87.

[187] See Gunther Hellmann, 'The Collapse of "Constructive Engagement"': U.S. Foreign Policy in Southern Africa', in Helga Haftendorn and Jakob Schissler (eds.), *The Reagan Administration: A Reconstruction of American Strength?* (Berlin: Walter de Gruyter, 1988), 271.

[188] Jaster, *South Africa in Namibia*, 89.

[189] Chester Crocker, 'Statement', *The Namibian Peace Process*, 38.

[190] Robert E. Osgood, 'The Revitalization of Containment', *Foreign Affairs*, 60/3 (1981), 486.

[191] See Ernst-Otto Czempiel and Carl-Christoph Schweitzer (eds.), *Weltpolitik der USA* (Opladen: Leske & Budrich, 1984), 376.

ultimately served Pretoria's interests in various regards. The Soviet–Cuban presence in the region effectively raised the strategic importance of South Africa for the United States.[192] In consequence, the more US policy in southern Africa concentrated on the containment of the Soviet threat, the more dependent it became on South African cooperation, with Pretoria holding the key for the final settlement of the conflict.[193]

High-level negotiations between South Africa's Foreign Minister Roelof Botha, US Secretary of State Alexander Haig, and President Ronald Reagan in May 1981 marked the shift away from the multilateral approach of the Contact Group towards bilateral consultations. Permanent missions in New York would no longer be the hub of coordination and consultation.[194] In the US State Department, the focal point for the matter shifted from the Bureau of International Organization Affairs to the Africa Bureau, with Assistant Secretary of State, Chester Crocker, becoming the principal negotiator.[195] Furthermore, President Reagan appointed General Vernon A. Walters and Frank Wisner to assist Crocker in his efforts in order to ensure that linkage remained an issue.[196] The new policy had been outlined in various memoranda that reflected the sea change within the administration. The continuation of the process based on SC Resolution 435 also came under review, as it was no longer perceived as a sufficient framework for the settlement of the conflict.[197] While linkage clearly stood at the forefront of the US operational policy towards the settlement of the Namibian question, it did not do so in its public declarations. In fact, the administration tried 'to camouflage its origin'.[198] The official wording stressed that linkage had *emerged* as an issue during consultations between South Africa and the United States. Although restarting the process from zero had been an option under discussion in Washington, the US administration finally opted for building the initiative upon previous efforts. During the review process, Contact Group members had met in London with Chester Crocker, Assistant Secretary designate at that stage, and consulted on the continuation of the Western strategy. They

---

[192] Robert M. Price, 'Pretoria's Southern African Strategy', in Stephen Chan (ed.), *Exporting Apartheid. Foreign Policies in Southern Africa 1978–1988* (London: Macmillan Publishers, 1990), 162.

[193] See Winrich Kühne, *Südafrika und seine Nachbarn: Durchbruch zum Frieden?* (Baden Baden: Nomos, 1985), 121.

[194] See Karns, 'Ad Hoc Multilateral Diplomacy', 114.

[195] See Jabri, *Mediating Conflict*, 102.

[196] Ibid., 107.

[197] The documents are reprinted in Richard Leonhard, *South Africa at War: White Power and the Crisis in Southern Africa* (Westport, CT: Lawrence Hill & Co., 1983), Appendix C, 250.

[198] Ibid., 122.

concurred that Resolution 435 should form the basis for all further ef-forts.[199] While the four other Western members publicly rejected the linkage approach, in fact they supported the continuation of US negoti-ations at the operational level. This strategy reflected the sober assessment that any obstructionist attitude might provoke the US administration to abandon the settlement plan. With potential repercussions in southern Africa, this might have led to the breakdown of the entire process.

Viewed from the US perspective, continuing efforts based on SC Reso-lution 435 had several advantages. Firstly, the settlement plan was the result of intense coordination between the Western Five and the six front-line states, which enjoyed the broad support of the key players involved in the process. Secondly, it was legitimized by the formal approval of the UN Security Council, which was considered instrumental to raise the level of US credibility vis-à-vis Angola, Cuba, and the Soviet Union.[200] Thirdly, legitimation by the SC implied that the final agreements 'would have a form of international "guarantee" in the event of South African viola-tions'.[201] Fourthly, such a framework would limit the room for manoeuvre of the South African government.[202] Finally, advertising linkage as an effort to complement the settlement plan should ultimately legitimize the US policy shift towards the settlement of the Namibian conflict. This illustrates that choosing this cooperative framework constituted a con-scious decision of the US government that reflected a trade-off between the often tedious diplomatic process of the minilateral framework and unrestrained US leadership.[203] The close cooperation with Western part-ners, the front-line states, and the UN Secretariat served both the process and the substance of negotiations. All the parties involved associated themselves 'with the aura of legitimacy... that the UN represents'.[204] However, from the perspective of the other four Contact Group members, linkage became more and more a matter of concern, as the informal device started to transform itself into a sounding board and instrument of US foreign policy rather than a multiparty mediation effort. The maintenance of a cooperative framework was also key for the continued support in the UN Security Council to prevent the adoption of mandatory sanctions.

In April 1981, the African Group tabled five draft resolutions in the SC demanding once again the discontinuation of diplomatic and economic

---

[199] See Brenke, *Die Bundesrepublik Deutschland und der Namibia-Konflikt*, 85.

[200] Interview with Chester Crocker, Washington, DC, 21 November 2000.

[201] Crocker, 'Peacemaking South Africa', 226.

[202] Ibid.

[203] See Crocker, *High Noon In Southern Africa*, 118 *et sequ.*

[204] Yale–UN Oral History, Interview with Chester Crocker, 20 July 1998.

relations with South Africa, including an arms and oil embargo.[205] Repeated calls for an arms embargo originated in the growing frustration of African states over the lack of means and machinery to secure compliance with the sanction regime.[206] Most importantly, the call for broadening the scope of sanctions reflected less a viable political strategy than a reflex, generated by the current stalemate of the negotiations. Furthermore, the initiative grew out of expectations that the Council had already set some precedents with the adoption of similar resolutions, calling for sanctions against Iran during the hostage crisis or condemning the invasion of Afghanistan by the Soviet Union.[207] Although the Council has always been driven by a case-by-case approach, the lack of consistency would increase the political costs of the Western vetoes on mandatory sanctions against South Africa.

The African Group introduced the draft resolutions despite the fact that the implementation of a comprehensive package of sanctions would have resulted in 'economic suicide' for several southern African states.[208] Countries such as Botswana, Lesotho, Malawi, Mozambique, Swaziland, Zambia, and Zimbabwe were highly dependent on the South African economy. In the cases of Botswana, Lesotho, and Swaziland, more than eighty per cent of their total imports originated in South Africa.[209] This dependence effectively excluded that these states would ultimately deliver on the call for sanctions. Yet, the triple veto of France, the United Kingdom, and the United States prevented the adoption of the draft resolutions.[210] Canada and Germany participated in the series of meetings under Article 31 of the UN Charter to demonstrate the united stance of the Contact Group.[211] This formula secured the continuation of direct access to the formal debate of the Council on Namibia even after the termination of their non-permanent membership on 31 December 1978.

Within the South African government, the perception prevailed that the SC would not deliver on the threat of mandatory sanctions. In the view of South African Foreign Minister Roelof Botha, this formed part of the terms of reference of the working relationship with the United States

---

[205] See UN Doc S/14459, 27 April 1981; UN Doc S/14460/Rev. 1, 29 April 1981; UN Doc S/14461–63, 27 April 1981.
[206] SC Resolution 418, adopted in November 1977, had already imposed an arms embargo.
[207] Andrew Young, 'The United States and Africa: Victory for Diplomacy', *Foreign Affairs*, 59/3 (1980), 662.
[208] Brenke, *Die Bundesrepublik Deutschland und der Namibia-Konflikt*, 90.
[209] Ibid.
[210] See UN Doc S/PV.2277, 27 April 1981.
[211] The Canadian and German delegations participated in the meetings from 22–7 April 1981; see UN Doc S/PV.2268–77, 22–7 April 1981.

and constituted a matter of 'mutual trust'.[212] The cohesion of the Contact Group faced considerable strains with President François Mitterrand coming to power in May 1981. The priorities of France's policy in southern Africa shifted towards supporting sanctions against the South African government, granting development and security aid to the front-line states. The policy shift included political support for SWAPO, including economic assistance and training.[213]

Those strains became visible during the SC sessions on the renewed South African incursions in August 1981. Canada and Germany participated again in the meetings under Article 31 of the UN Charter in order to support the stance of the Western Five.[214] However, the rainbow vote of France, the United Kingdom, and the United States on the tabled draft resolution underlined the divisions within the Group at that stage.[215] While the United States cast its veto, France voted in favour of the draft resolution, and the United Kingdom abstained. In his explanation of the vote, the US representative criticized the one-sided nature of the draft resolution, claiming that 'the presence of foreign combat forces in Angola—particularly the large Cuban force—the provision of Soviet-originated arms to SWAPO and the presence of Soviet military advisers fuel the explosive atmosphere of confrontation and violence . . .'.[216]

With the SC being deadlocked, the centre of action shifted to the General Assembly that convened, on the initiative of Zimbabwe, its eighth emergency special session from 3 to 14 September 1981. Under the strong pressure of the NAM, the General Assembly called for comprehensive mandatory sanctions against South Africa.[217] Furthermore, the Assembly criticized the new approach by the US administration, strongly rejecting 'the latest manoeuvres by certain members of the Western contact group aimed at undermining the international consensus embodied in Security Council Resolution 435 (1978) and depriving the oppressed Namibian people of their hard-won victories in the struggle for national liberation'.[218] Despite the growing divisions among Contact Group members over linkage, they kept a united front regarding their opposition to imposing mandatory sanctions.[219]

---

[212] Yale–UN Oral History, Interview with Roelof Botha, 5 March 2001.
[213] See Jabri, *Mediating Conflict*, 155.
[214] See UN Doc S/PV.2298, 29 August 1981, para 1 *et seq*.
[215] See UN Doc S/14664/Rev. 2, 31 August 1981; UN Doc S/PV.2300, 31 August 1981, para 45.
[216] UN Doc S/PV.2300, 31 August 1981, para 48.
[217] See UN Doc ES-8/2, 14 September 1981, para 12.
[218] Ibid., para 10.
[219] The resolution was adopted by 117 votes in favour, none against, and twenty-five abstentions, including the Western Five and member states of the European Community;

In an effort to counter the pressure at UN Headquarters, in late September 1981, the Western Contact Group agreed to adapt its strategy by employing a three-phase approach that aimed at complementing SC Resolution 435. Firstly, the Western Five elaborated principles for the constitutional assembly and the constitution proper, based upon the negotiations launched at the end of 1979. Secondly, it addressed the question of UN impartiality as well as defining the strength and composition of UNTAG. Thirdly, the Contact Group negotiated the date of the ceasefire, the holding of elections, including the start of the UN operation. The three-phase approach was based upon the assumption that the completion of each phase would generate the necessary momentum for overcoming the contentious issues of subsequent phases.[220] In consultations with the Secretary-General, the Western Five underlined that, while the constitutional principles would be negotiated 'mostly outside the UN framework', during the second phase, 'consultations with the Secretary-General and his staff would be of the utmost importance'.[221]

Negotiations at that stage were therefore progressing on at least three tracks. While US negotiators concentrated on the issue of the Cuban troop withdrawal from Angola, the Contact Group as a whole together with the front-line states worked on aspects related to the implementation of SC Resolution 435, including the constitutional principles with the UN Secretariat negotiating the details of the UNTAG operation. As the US administration had already introduced the concept of linkage in bilateral talks with the South African government, the various tracks could hardly move separately from each other. The third phase of the new approach would therefore not start until the linkage issue had been solved.

Between late September 1981 and October 1982, Contact Group members negotiated with the parties on the first two phases. Analysis of the 'Démarche by Heads of Mission of the Five to Governments of the Front Line States and Nigeria' that formed the basis for negotiations with the parties suggests that the Contact Group implicitly seemed to legitimize the US initiative to negotiate the withdrawal of Cuban troops from Angola. The Western Five shared the common understanding that 'a valuable opportunity now exists to achieve a settlement which could resolve other long-standing problems of the region at present hindering

see UN Doc GAOR, Eighth Special Emergency Session, Verbatim Records of Meeting, twelfth meeting, 14 September 1981.

[220] Javier Pérez de Cuéllar Papers, Confidential notes of meeting with the Western Five, 18 January 1982.
[221] Ibid.

the development of the climate of security and mutual confidence necessary for a Namibia settlement'.[222] Such a statement implicitly sanctioned
the US policy on the Cuban troop withdrawal from Angola. During the
summer of 1982, parties met in New York at UN Headquarters for proximity talks, which illustrated the interdependence of Contact Group mediation and the UN as a kind of legitimizer and guarantor of the process.
Besides the input of key UN personnel with respect to the details of the
suggested UN operation, the setting of the negotiations demonstrated that
the initiative, although formally acting outside the UN framework, still
rested within the objectives of the Organization. This was considered
instrumental to secure the broadest possible acceptance of the agreements. The first phase was formally concluded in July, when Contact
Group members submitted a letter to the Secretary-General on the 'Principles concerning the Constituent Assembly and the Constitution for an
independent Namibia', which settled all related questions except the
choice of the electoral system.[223]

From July to September, the Contact Group proceeded with negotiations on issues related to the second phase. The South African government informally agreed to the Secretary-General's earlier proposal of a UN
force of 7,500 troops.[224] This number constituted however an upper limit,
and there was an understanding that the actual deployment should be
considerably lower. In late September 1982, the parties finally secured an
informal understanding on the so-called impartiality package containing
measures that should guarantee the impartiality of the UN and the South
African government vis-à-vis all internal parties during the transition
towards Namibian independence.[225] The package aimed primarily at accommodating South African concerns, geared in particular towards the
UN's one-sided support of SWAPO. It contained provisions that would
terminate SWAPO's observer status at the UN, including its funding,
once the implementation of SC Resolution 435 had started. There was
agreement that the resolution, enabling the transition process towards
Namibia's independence, would 'reaffirm the responsibility of all concerned to ensure the impartial implementation of the settlement
plan'.[226] Potential opposition from UN member states not directly in-

---

[222] Javier Pérez de Cuéllar Papers, Démarche by Heads of Mission, 4 June 1982.
[223] The constitutional principles were published as UN doc S/15287, 12 July 1982.
[224] Crocker, *High Noon in Southern Africa*, 130.
[225] Ibid, 131.
[226] Javier Pérez de Cuéllar Papers, Confidential notes of meeting with the Western Five, 24
September 1982.

volved in the process should be prevented by restricting the number of speakers at the SC meeting to authorize the implementation process.[227] The Western Five and the front-line states committed themselves 'to ensure that General Assembly consideration of the question of Namibia is suspended during the transition period'.[228] This provision constituted, in essence, a manipulation of voice to channel criticism inside the Council and limit the probability of obstructionist attitude of states being critical of the process. Contrary to the constitutional principles, the agreement was initially not released as an official UN document but contained in an informal checklist and a memorandum of a meeting between Contact Group members, front-line states, and the UN Secretary-General. It became an official document of the UN only in May 1939.[229] As Chester Crocker concedes:

It would have been preferable to register the 'impartiality package' then emerging by means of public letter to Pérez de Cuéllar so that it could form part of the U.N. official record. But this would have sent the signal that all issues related to the Namibian independence plan had been solved. Logically, negotiation would then begin on the text of a Security Council resolution naming a date for the start of Resolution 435.[230]

The agreement on constitutional principles and the impartiality package inevitably shifted the focus towards linkage that remained the central issue before the third stage of the negotiations could be concluded. By the end of 1982, it could be anticipated that the pressure at UN Headquarters would soon be on the rise again, if the United States was not able to show visible progress on that matter. At the same time, there were growing concerns that the Contact Group would break apart if the negotiations did not succeed.[231]

An internal note of the UN Secretariat, elaborating on developments concerning Namibia during October 1982, emphasized the negative impact of linkage on the negotiations and concluded that they 'have come dangerously close to a deadlock'.[232] The deterioration of US–Soviet relations at that stage was considered another factor that made an early settlement of the conflict unlikely. In February 1983, the Secretary-General outlined in a

---

[227] Ibid.
[228] Ibid.
[229] See UN Doc S/20635, 15 May 1989.
[230] Crocker, *High Noon in Southern Africa*, 132.
[231] UK Permanent Representative Sir John Thompson raised these concerns during a meeting with the Secreary-General; see Javier Pérez de Cuéllar Papers, Notes of meeting, 21 October 1982.
[232] Javier Pérez de Cuéllar Papers, Confidential internal note, 10 November 1982.

strictly confidential note his impressions from consultations with front-line states, pointing to the 'growing frustration and impatience...over the delays in reaching an agreement on the implementation of Security Council Resolution 435 (1978)'.[233] The Western Five should 'intensify their efforts to reach a negotiated settlement...without further delay', with the UN being involved in that process. There was widespread concern that the countries had been misused 'to give credibility to the Contact Group exercise'.[234] Although the note underlined the unified rejection of linkage by the front-line states, the Secretary-General expressed the feeling that 'everybody wants to have a situation created, where the need to have Cuban troops in Angola would disappear'.[235]

Pressure further increased in April 1983, when 138 governments and fifty-nine non-governmental organizations (NGOs) gathered in Paris for the international conference for the support of Namibia's struggle for independence, organized by the UN in cooperation with the OAU.[236] Besides the strong support for the SWAPO liberation struggle, the Paris Declaration rejected the Cold War dimension of the conflict, emphasizing that the Namibian question should be dealt with as a problem of decolonization beyond the East–West conflict. The growing difficulties of the French government to support the US approach became most visible when Foreign Minister Claude Cheysson openly criticized the withdrawal of Cuban troops from Angolan soil as a precondition for the start of the transition process towards Namibian independence.[237]

The Secretary-General raised similar concerns in preparation for an SC meeting on Namibia in May 1983, which the front-line states had called. In his report to the SC, reviewing the process after the Pre-Implementation Meeting in Geneva of January 1981, Pérez de Cuéllar raised a warning that the introduction of new elements in the negotiation process would endanger the successful implementation of SC Resolution 435.[238] Although the front-line states were 'aware of the limitations of the Security Council and of the possibilities of achieving something constructive in the Council',[239] they needed the body as a platform for the expression of voice. The large number of countries that were already designated to participate in the meeting put high pressure on the Contact Group to limit the potential

---

[233] Javier Pérez de Cuéllar Papers, Strictly confidential note, 17 February 1983.
[234] Ibid.
[235] Ibid.
[236] See UN Doc S/15757, 29 April 1983.
[237] See UN Doc A.CONF.120/13, para 42.
[238] See UN Doc S/15776, 19 May 1983, paras 15–20.
[239] Javier Pérez de Cuéllar Papers, Strictly confidential note, 17 February 1983.

damage of any action that might result from discussions in the Council.[240] The trilateral consultation of the Western Five, the front-line states, with the Secretary-General as the channel of communication, is indicative of the importance of the chief administrative officer of the Organization. His role was crucial to avoid misperceptions in advance of the meeting and to reassure both sides of their least common denominator, that is, 'the debate should be constructive so as not to undermine the ongoing efforts to implement Resolution 435'.[241] Pérez de Cuéllar advised the Western Five that the front-line states planned 'to present a reasonable resolution and to attempt to avoid the possibility of any veto'. He underlined that, at this stage, the countries 'needed to be encouraged in their positive approach'.[242] This was a clear signal to Contact Group members to support the front-line initiative in order to prevent any further drastic measures.

The meeting of the SC from 23 May to 1 June developed into a public trial over the Western approach. A total number of sixty-three countries, not being members of the Council, participated in the debate, including Canada and Germany.[243] SWAPO leader Sam Nujoma concluded that the role of the Western Five had 'ceased to be that of an honest broker in terms of the implementation of Council Resolution 435 (1978)'.[244] Resolution 532 unanimously requested the Secretary-General to conduct further consultations with the parties to the conflict in order to secure the speedy implementation of the settlement plan.[245] The request indicated that the African Group and the front-line states respectively preferred to move the process back into the UN framework. Chester Crocker advised the Secretary-General that 'preliminary US/South African discussions might help pave the way for a productive result, especially on the South African response to the remaining question on UNTAG and the electoral system'.[246] The success of Pérez de Cuéllar's consultations was clearly in the US interest, as it would help to deflect criticism that the process had reached a stalemate.

---

[240] At that stage, thirty-one countries, not being members of the Council, intended to participate in the SC meeting; see Javier Pérez de Cuéllar Papers, Talking points, 23 March 1983.

[241] Javier Pérez de Cuéllar Papers, Confidential notes of meeting, 18 May 1983.

[242] Ibid.

[243] Together with the fifteen members of the Council, a total of seventy-eight countries participated in the debate, roughly fifty per cent of the entire UN membership in 1983; see UN Doc S/PV.2439–2451, 23 May–1 June 1983.

[244] UN Doc S/PV.2439, 23 May 1983, para 146.

[245] See UN Doc S/RES/532, adopted by unanimous vote on 31 May 1983.

[246] Javier Pérez de Cuéllar Papers, Message from Dr Crocker to the Secretary-General, 3 June 1983.

The Secretary-General's mission to Angola, Namibia, and South Africa from 22 to 26 August removed remaining obstacles vis-à-vis the composition of UNTAG. It became clear that the withdrawal of Cuban troops from Angola had remained the only contentious issue. In his report to the SC, the Secretary-General concluded that 'we have never been before been so close to finality on the modalities of implementing Resolution 435 (1978)'.[247] At the same time, he defined the position of the South African government regarding linkage as the main obstacle to the implementation of the settlement plan, without mentioning the role of the United States in this regard.[248] The wording of the report strongly reflected the interest of Contact Group members that it should contain positive elements in order to counter, as the German representative put it, 'attempts by certain countries to represent the negotiating process as dead'.[249] Crocker emphasizes in hindsight that the Secretary-General's rejection of linkage ultimately served both the United States and the UN. While Pérez de Cuéllar had to remain critical vis-à-vis the issue, given the opposition of the vast majority of UN member states, the report 'shed a brilliant spotlight on the issue and also made clear that South Africa was prepared to implement the UN plan for Namibia if it could be resolved'.[250] Seen from the perspective of the UN Secretariat, such an attitude rather originated in sober pragmatism since there was an understanding that the US administration would proceed with linkage anyway.[251] In fact, officials in the Secretariat were deeply concerned about the administration's 'ideologically-based approach...to the very concept of international co-operation and its corollary-suspicion of the UN as a whole'.[252] It was their understanding that 'the notion of international co-operation and that of multilateral approaches to peace and the very concept of a collective security system presuppose a basic understanding that...solutions to problems are essentially pragmatic, free of ideological pollution, and basically colourless'.[253] By accepting linkage as another parameter of the conflict setting, the UN Secretariat aimed at limiting any further damage that might result from the US policy in order to secure the eventual implementation of SC Resolution 435.

---

[247] UN Doc S/15943, 29 August 1983, para 24.

[248] Ibid., para 25.

[249] Javier Pérez de Cuéllar Papers, Confidential notes of meeting, 10 August 1983.

[250] Crocker, *Peacemaking in South Africa*, 227.

[251] See Javier Pérez de Cuéllar Papers, Confidential internal note, 10 November 1982.

[252] Javier Pérez de Cuéllar Papers, Strictly confidential note for the Secretary-General, 22 December 1982.

[253] Ibid.

When the Council discussed the report in its debate from 21 to 28 October, the South African Ambassador re-emphasized that the Cuban troop withdrawal was the sine qua non for commencing the transition towards Namibia's independence. The French representative revived the criticism of linkage, joined by his German colleague who addressed similar concerns.[254] The adoption of SC Resolution 539, which considered the adoption of further measures in case of continued obstruction by the South African government, came as a surprise and was much to the dismay of the South African government, since the United States did not vote against the draft. Prior to the meeting of the Council, at a gathering of the Contact Group in London on 20 October, the United States had unsuccessfully tried to gain assurances from France and the United Kingdom to prevent a condemnation of South African policy.[255] Both countries preferred a more flexible approach as long as the draft resolution did not call for sanctions. The voting pattern of the United States suggests that the US administration had still been keen to maintain a minimum level of agreement between Contact Group members serving on the Council in order to avoid isolation on this issue. At the same time, the United States sought to counter criticism that its constructive engagement was biased towards the South African position. The resolution reflected a growing frustration of Council members over the issue of linkage. It underlined 'that the independence of Namibia cannot be held hostage to the resolution of issues that are alien to resolution 435 (1978)'.[256]

South Africa further escalated its armed incursions into Angola from early December to the beginning of 1984. Against the background of this escalation of violence and the continued stalemate in the negotiations, France suspended its Contact Group membership with effect from 7 December 1983, though it still supported Resolution 435. Canada followed the French move and also terminated its participation over the question of linkage. In an effort to save the Contact Group, Pérez de Cuéllar had urged President Mitterrand and Prime Minister Trudeau 'to maintain a common front'.[257] SC Resolutions 545 and 546, condemning the attacks, constituted the habitual reflex of the Council. It did not receive any follow-up that might have forced the South African government to change its policy.

---

[254] See statements by the French and German representatives, UN Doc S/PV. 2485, 25 October 1983, paras 48–64 and paras 22–35.

[255] Brenke, *Die Bundesrepublik Deutschland und der Namibia-Konflikt*, 100.

[256] UN Doc S/RES/539, 28 October 1983, adopted by fourteen votes in favour, with the United States abstaining.

[257] Javier Pérez de Cuéllar Papers, Confidential notes of meeting, 14 October 1983.

In a conciliatory gesture, South African Foreign Minister Botha stated in a letter to the Secretary-General that the choice of the electoral system was 'not of great importance'. He confirmed however that 'no settlement plan can be implemented unless a firm agreement is reached on Cuban withdrawal from Angola'.[258] By December 1983, the Western Five as a unitary actor had ceased to exist. Later attempts to revive the diplomatic device failed.[259] Nevertheless, Western powers jointly abstained when the Assembly adopted a comprehensive resolution on almost all aspects of the Namibian question that, *inter alia*, condemned linkage and called upon the SC to impose mandatory sanctions on the South African government.[260] The joint abstention in the vote on the annual Namibia resolution of the General Assembly would be the least common denominator even after the Contact Group had become defunct.[261] In the Council, however, France no longer felt bound to conduct a coordinated policy and reviewed its voting pattern accordingly. By then, only the vetoes subsequently cast by the United Kingdom and the United States prevented the further escalation of crisis response by the Council.[262]

5.2.3 *US Hegemony and Conflict Resolution, 1984–8*

By the mid-1980s, many observers had concluded that the policy of constructive engagement had eventually failed. South Africa continued its attacks throughout the year of 1985, while, at the same time, expanding the domestic repression under the apartheid system.[263] The Reagan administration eventually had to bow under the domestic pressure of

[258] UN Doc S/16237, 29 December 1983, paras 4 and 9.

[259] Foreign Minister Genscher tried to revive the group when Germany commenced its term of office as elected member of the SC for the period of 1987 to 1988. France rejected the initiative on the grounds that it would be prepared to cooperate only after the termination of US linkage; see Vergau, 'Die Vereinten Nationen und die Namibia-Frage', 113.

[260] See UN Doc A/RES/38/36, 2 December 1983.

[261] See UN Doc A/RES/39/50, 12 December 1984; UN Doc A/RES/40/56, 2 December 1985; UN Doc A/RES/41/39, 20 November 1986; UN Doc A/RES/42/14, 6 November 1987; and UN Doc A/RES/43/26, 17 November 1988.

[262] See UN Doc S/17354/Rev. 1, 26 July 1985 and UN Doc S/PV.2602; UN Doc S/17633, 15 November 1985 and UN Doc S/PV.2629; UN Doc S/18087/Rev. 1, 18 June 1986 and UN Doc S/PV.2693; UN Doc S/18705, 2 February 1987 and UN Doc S/PV.2738; UN Doc S/18785, 9 April 1987 and UN Doc S/PV.2747, 9 April 1987; in all instances, draft resolutions were prevented from being adopted by the double veto of the United Kingdom and the United States. In 1987, the Federal Republic of Germany, non-permanent member of the Council for the period of 1987 to 1988, joined the countries in their opposition towards mandatory sanctions.

[263] The Council condemned the military attacks in Resolutions 567, 571, 574, and 577; see UN Doc S/RES/567, 20 June 1985; UN Doc S/RES/571, 20 September 1985, UN Doc S/RES/574, 7 October 1985, UN Doc S/RES/577, 6 December 1985. On the question of *apartheid*, Resolution 569 strongly condemned once again the practices of the South African government, without however imposing mandatory sanctions; see UN Doc S/RES/569, 26 July 1985.

anti-apartheid protests and imposed targeted sanctions against the South African government.[264] Although these measures constituted a significant development, they hardly represented a sea change within the US administration. Despite these flaws negotiations continued under US leadership given the lack of alternatives. Keeping the channels open without any decisive movement towards a settlement constituted the lesser evil and was therefore supported by all parties. While Western powers would have faced a showdown in the SC and the General Assembly respectively in case of a complete breakdown of the talks, front-line states and SWAPO had been aware of the fact that there was no real alternative to this process.[265] As Robert Jaster rightly concludes:

Thus, all the states involved in the Namibian negotiations have been playing the same game, though for different reasons and with different objectives. All the players have continued to support the talks even while doubting that South Africa was negotiating in good faith, and even when it was apparent that the talks were making no progress.[266]

It was only in 1988 that the conflict became ripe for resolution. Five factors contributed to a change in the parameters of the conflict setting. Firstly, the changing military balance in late 1987 resulted in a review of Angola's, Cuba's, and South Africa's military and strategic position. The situation forced the South African government to consider seriously a diplomatic solution and to abandon its attempts to hold South African forces in Angola as a main bargaining chip in the negotiations.[267] Secondly, the bilateral relations between the United States and the Soviet Union had been dramatically improving since 1987.[268] Thirdly, the political costs of delaying Namibian independence outweighed the economic benefits of exploiting the territory further: 'it had become a total liability'.[269] The South African economy could no longer afford continued engagements in conflicts such as Namibia and Angola, given the low

---

[264] Sanctions included, *inter alia*, the prohibition of transferring nuclear technology, or the importation of South African Krugerrand gold coins into the United States; see Sanford J. Ungar and Peter Vale, 'South Africa: Why Constructive Engagement Failed', *Foreign Affairs*, 64/2 (1985), 234–58.

[265] See Jaster, *South Africa in Namibia*, 108.

[266] Ibid., 109.

[267] Geoffrey Berridge, 'Diplomacy and the Angola/Namibian accords', *International Affairs*, 65/3 (1989), 465.

[268] Chester Crocker informed the Secretary-General in March 1988 about US initiatives to cooperate with the Soviet Union in order 'to explore the outlines of a mutually acceptable settlement'; Javier Pérez de Cuéllar Papers, Confidential notes of meeting, 1 March 1988.

[269] Comment by Theodor Hanf, *The Namibian Peace Process*, 56.

currency reserves and the growing foreign debt.[270] In the period between 1980 and 1990, the South African government had to allocate considerable resources in order to sustain the administration in Namibia.[271] The room-for-manoeuvre was further narrowed in 1985 by the decision of foreign banks such as Chase Manhattan to freeze loans to the government, which became 'the most dramatic, and unexpected, foreign pressure on South Africa'.[272] Fourthly, the US Congress considered the adoption of a comprehensive sanctions package that would have further aggravated the economic crisis of the country.[273] And fifthly, President Reagan's term of office was coming to a closure.[274] Presidential candidates such as George Bush and Michael Dukakis had shown much more reluctance during their campaign to maintain the level of support for South Africa. Looking from the perspective of the South African government, protracted delay was no longer an option. As Jeffrey Herbst has noted somewhat ironically:

Just as a man holds on to an unfashionable tie in the belief that one day styles will change and the garment will be appreciated, so linkage was presented for so long that a series of events finally occurred which made it seem appealing to all sides. It was not ingenuity but sheer perseverance which made it possible for the US to be able to successfully negotiate the accords.[275]

In July 1988, the governments of Angola, Cuba, and South Africa reached agreement on a set of principles. Firstly, the parties were required to agree upon a final date for commencing the implementation of SC Resolution 435.[276] Secondly, Angola and South Africa committed themselves to cooperate with the Secretary-General in the process leading to Namibia's independence and to refrain from any activities that may prevent the implementation of the resolution. Thirdly, the principles provided for

---

[270] Winrich Kühne, 'Frieden im südwestlichen Afrika?', 109.

[271] The costs for balancing the central government's budget alone amounted to US$2.5 billion between 1980 and 1990; see Paul Rich, 'The United States, Its History Of Mediation And The Chester Crocker Round of Negotiations Over Namibia in 1988', in Stephen Chan and Vivienne Jabri (eds.), *Mediation in Southern Africa* (London: Macmillan, 1993), 90; Robert Jaster comes to a similar conclusion; see Jaster, *South Africa in Namibia*, 110.

[272] J. P. D. Dunbabin, *International Relations since 1945: A History in Two Volumes, Vol. 2: The Post-Imperial Age: The Great Powers and the Wider World* (Harlow: Longman, 1994), 80.

[273] Winrich Kühne, 'Frieden im südwestlichen Afrika?', 109.

[274] See Brenke, *Die Bundesrepublik Deutschland und der Namibia-Konflikt*, 106 *et sequ*.

[275] Jeffrey Herbst, 'The United States in Africa 1988–89. A Very Good Year for Constructive Engagement', in Marion E. Doro (ed.), *Africa Contemporary Record* (New York and London: Africana Publishing Company, 1969), A 137.

[276] See Principles for a Peaceful Settlement in Southwestern Africa, July 20, 1988, paras A, B, C, K, reprinted in Crocker, *High Noon in Southern Africa*, 499 *et seq*.

the phased and total withdrawal of Cuban troops from Angolan soil, to be verified by the UN Security Council.[277] Fourthly, they required the parties to recognize the P-5 as guarantors for the implementation of any future agreements.

These principles provided the framework for the Brazzaville Protocol on 13 December 1988 as well as the Bilateral Agreement between Angola and Cuba, and the Tripartite Agreement among Angola, Cuba, and South Africa, both signed on 22 December 1988 in New York.[278] Although SWAPO had not participated in the negotiations, Angola and Cuba urged the liberation movement to comply with the provisions of the agreements and the settlement plan.[279] Provision (1) of the Tripartite Agreement provided that the implementation of the plan would commence on 1 April 1989, subject to an enabling resolution by the SC.[280] SC Resolution 628 endorsed the agreements and brought the process back into the UN framework.[281] In a further resolution, the Council reaffirmed 'the legal responsibility of the United Nations over Namibia' and formally decided that the implementation of SC Resolution 435 would begin on 1 April 1989.[282] The substance of Resolution 629 had been drafted by the P-5, which illustrated the shift of governance in the SC at this stage.[283] With the breakdown of the bipolar system, permanent members had started to consult informally and outside the Council chambers on a wide range of issues, which impacted on decision-making in the SC.

The SWAPO incursions on 1 April 1989, with the subsequent intervention by South African Defence Forces to avert them, constituted the last major incident that endangered the start of the transition period towards Namibia's independence.[284] Special Representative Martti Ahtisaari sought to limit the damage by reluctantly tolerating the intervention of

---

[277] The United Nations Angola Verification Mission (UNAVEM), consisting of seventy military observers, was deployed on 10 January 1989 to verify the withdrawal of 50,000 Cuban troops over a period of thirty months; see Marrack Goulding, *Peacemonger* (London: John Murray, 2002), 146.

[278] See the Brazzaville Protocol of 13 December 1988 and the Bilateral Agreement between Cuba and Angola and the Tripartite Agreement among Angola, Cuba, and South Africa, both signed on 22 December 1988, reprinted in Crocker, *High Noon in Southern Africa*, 503–11.

[279] See Goulding, *Peacemonger*, 143.

[280] See 'Tripartite Agreement, 22 December 1988', in Crocker, *High Noon in Southern Africa*, 510.

[281] See UN Doc S/RES/628, adopted unanimously on 16 January 1989.

[282] See UN Doc S/RES/629, adopted unanimously on 16 January 1989.

[283] See Pérez de Cuéllar, *Pilgrimage for Peace*, 306.

[284] The causes of the SWAPO incursions are beyond the scope of this case study. The most useful account may be found in *The Namibian Peace Process*, 73–88, containing differing interpretations by various individuals involved.

South African Defence Forces. By then, he had set up a structure of the peace operation that was both united under his leadership and enjoyed the broad international support of key players involved in the process. Ahtisaari was therefore in the position to take this decision with all the risks involved. Although the Special Representative had brought himself into an extremely difficult situation, at the same time, the deployment of the defence forces robbed the South African government of any excuse later to step out of the implementation process of SC Resolution 435.[285] The crisis was eventually resolved by the meeting of the Joint Commission, comprising representatives of Angola, Cuba, and South Africa at Mount Etjo on 8–9 April 1989.[286] The Commission had been part and parcel of the Brazzaville Protocol of 13 December 1988 to deal with problems related to the interpretation and implementation of SC Resolution 435. The United States and the Soviet Union were invited as observers, with UNTAG representatives also attending. The parties adopted a declaration that aimed at recommitting themselves to all aspects of the peace process. On 21 March 1990, Namibia became independent.

5.3 Conclusion: Exit, Voice, and Loyalty

This case study has illustrated the role and performance of the Group of Three and the Western Contact Group in the process towards Namibian independence. Both informal settings formed part of an exit strategy to escape from the structural deficiencies of the UN, exacerbated through systemic change. The process of decolonization had had profound effects on governance in the General Assembly as well as the SC. The Organization became increasingly ideologized over decolonization, which effectively excluded any direct involvement of the UN. In this context, establishing the Group of Three, mandated by the SC, appeared as a pretext to demonstrate some activism. It aimed at accommodating pressure from the African Group, without forcing Western countries to become actively involved in the resolution of the conflict. In contrast, the Contact Group comprised key players with leverage that were able to make a difference. The Western Five operated without an explicit mandate of the SC and negotiated a settlement proposal outside the UN framework, though within the objectives of the Organization. This final section summarizes

---

[285] See Interview with Martti Ahtisaari, Helsinki, 9 May 2000.
[286] See Goulding, *Peacemonger*, 157.

the dynamics of exit, voice, and loyalty in the case of Namibia, especially taking into account the interaction between Contact Group and SC.

5.3.1 *Exit as a Response to Voice*

The case study of Namibia illustrates that the relationship between exit and voice is not limited to complementary or substitutive functions. The emergence of the Western Contact Group has to be understood against the background of the articulation of voice at UN Headquarters, as expressed in numerous resolutions of the General Assembly and, to a lesser extent, the SC that had brought Western powers under increasing public pressure to become seriously engaged in the resolution of the conflict. The growing recourse to Article 31 of the Charter that allowed non-members of the Council to participate in its formal meetings effectively transformed the body into a mini-Assembly and limited its abilities for effective crisis management. The increased institutionalization of the so-called informal consultations of the SC, in itself an exit strategy to deal with the effects of systemic change, did not necessarily solve the structural deficiencies. Seen from this perspective, exit occurred in response to strong voice at the level of the UN. The expression of voice by African states had a catalytic effect on the Western choice of exit.

The Contact Group provided a framework for informal cooperation beyond the East–West and North–South antagonism within the General Assembly and the SC. This informal setting locked the parties to the conflict into a process orchestrated by Contact Group members and front-line states. The Contact Group turned out to be most successful as long as it had been able to perform the role of a unitary actor and to maintain the perception that it would deliver on the threat of stern action.

5.3.2 *Exit and the Manipulation of Voice*

In the period 1977–8, the Western Five managed to control voice at the UN level in order to generate the room for manoeuvre they needed especially for negotiations with the South African government. With the support of the front-line states, the Contact Group effectively silenced deliberations of the Namibian question inside the Council. Such constructive silence prevented the adoption of further resolutions or statements that might have undermined ongoing negotiations or that might have forced Western permanent members to cast their veto in order to avoid any damage that could have resulted in the breakdown of the entire process. Opting for exit, while deliberately manipulating voice inside the Council, is the most important feature of that period. With the failure of the Western Contact Group, and later the United States, to deliver a breakthrough in the settlement of the conflict, both the General Assembly and the SC were transformed again into platforms for the articulation of voice to channel the widespread criticism of the process. This scenario escalated further when the Reagan administration adopted the linkage approach from 1981 onwards, as this policy did not have any public backing either from Contact Group members and front-line states or from the UN Secretariat. By the mid-1980s, it had effectively become impossible to manipulate voice effectively at UN Headquarters. Casting the veto was the only option left to prevent the escalation of measures against the South African government. The inclusion of provisions in the final agreements of December 1988 that effectively controlled the articulation of voice in the process of formal legitimation through the UN Security Council therefore constituted a safeguard to prevent potential damage that might have resulted from any further discussion of the matter within the UN framework.

5.3.3 Loyalty: The Western Contact Group and US Linkage

While the settlement plan for Namibia's independence had been negotiated outside the UN, it was embedded inside the framework of objectives as outlined in SC Resolution 385. The cooperation between the Western Contact Group and the UN turned out to be crucial since the Organization provided the seal of legitimacy to the Western initiative. The Western Contact Group and later the United States sought to legitimize the substance of negotiations via the process of SC decision-making. At the same time, the UN assumed responsibility for implementing and monitoring the settlement plan. At the end of 1988, the process enjoyed the broad cooperation of Contact Group members, front-line states, Cuba, the Soviet Union, South Africa, and the OAU. In effect, such a strategy was key to gaining wider acceptance of the implementation process by UN member states. Similar settings such as the Contadora Group, established in 1983 to reach a negotiated settlement of conflicts in Central America, failed as they lacked the same degree of wider acceptance by the parties concerned.[287] It would be a futile exercise to elaborate on the counterfactual question whether the settlement could have been achieved earlier without

---

[287] See Susan Kaufman Purcell, 'Demystifying Contadora', *Foreign Affairs*, 64/1 (1985), 74–95.

linkage. However, any analysis that concludes with some kind of resignation that US policy had gone 'unilateral', ignoring the positions of Contact Group partners and the resolutions of UN principal organs, misses some central points. Firstly, it misses the point of US exceptionalism, which is a fact that has to be taken into account in the analysis of any conflict resolution with US involvement. Once the Reagan administration had started to deal with the situation in southern Africa primarily from the perspective of East–West conflict, Western partners as well as the UN Secretariat could only try to limit the damage growing out of this policy change. Consequently, the preservation of SC Resolution 435 as the legitimate basis for the settlement of conflict became the primary concern for Contact Group members and the UN Secretary-General. Preventing the complete exit of the superpower was achieved by tacitly acknowledging the US policy of linkage without publicly approving it. At the same time, the wiser heads within the Reagan administration appreciated the benefits of being granted the seal of UN legitimacy. This reasoning exerted a strong pull factor on the way Chester Crocker handled the negotiations from 1981 onwards as chief negotiator of the United States. It illustrates a pattern of US foreign policy to seek, on the one hand, maximum flexibility and unrestricted freedom in the conduct of crisis resolution while, on the other hand, securing an aura of legitimacy, lent by the UN Secretary-General and the SC. This approach reflected the desire 'to have the best of both worlds'.[288] Finally, the Western Contact Group provided, until December 1983, a minilateral setting to accommodate US exceptionalism. The informal setting disguised hegemony of the United States and avoided the perception of unilateral action.

[288] Yale – UN Oral History, Interview with Chester Crocker, 20 July 1998.

Si j'ordonnais à un général de voler d'une fleur à l'autre à la façon d'un papillon, ou d'écrire une tragédie, ou de se changer en oiseau de mer, et si le général n'exécutait pas l'ordre reçu, qui de lui ou de moi serait dans son tort?

Ce serait vous, dit fermement le petit prince.

Exact. Il faut exiger de chacun ce que chacun peut donner, reprit le roi. L'autorité repose d'abord sur la raison.[1]

Antoine de Saint-Exupéry

[1] Antoine de Saint-Exupéry, *Le Petit Prince* (Paris: Gallimard, 1946), 39 *et seq.*

6

El Salvador: Group of Friends of the UN Secretary-General

The second case study focuses on the Group of Friends of the Secretary-General on El Salvador, which was the first group operating under this label.[2] In contrast to the first case study, where the Western Contact Group led the negotiation process *outside* the UN framework, in the case of El Salvador, the UN Secretariat took over the leading role as intermediary to reach a negotiated political solution to the conflict in El Salvador. The process rested firmly *inside* the UN framework. Established in December 1989, the informal group served as a means at the disposal of the Secretary-General and his representatives to support the UN's efforts to mediate an agreement between the conflicting parties, that is, the government of El Salvador (GOES) and the rebel forces, the *Frente Farabundo Martí para la Liberación Nacional* (FMLN).[3] The Group of Friends was considered an *ad hoc* gathering of like-minded states with an interest in the resolution of the conflict, which affected regional stability. Although the UN had assumed the leading role, it had been clear from the beginning that the Organization would be dependent on UN member states having influence on the parties to the conflict. The *ad hoc* group of like-minded countries was needed to provide the necessary leverage to the efforts made by the Secretariat. At the same time, the informal setting served as a kind of balancer against the might of the permanent

---

[2] Originally, the group comprised Colombia, Mexico, Spain, and Venezuela, later joined by the United States.
[3] The movement called itself in remembrance of Augustín Farabundo Martí who had led an insurrection in 1931 that was suppressed by military officers; see Elisabeth Jean Wood, *Insurgent Collective Action and Civil War in El Salvador* (Cambridge, MA: Cambridge University Press, 2003), 20–30.

members of the Security Council (SC), and the United States in particular. The Friends of the Secretary-General on El Salvador somewhat revived the concept of the advisory committees that had been established in the 1950s and 1960s.[4] The case study elaborates in detail the reasons why this concept re-emerged in 1989. The transformation of the bipolar system created the permissive political context for a leading role of the UN, with the United States and the Soviet Union as guardians of the process in the background.

Given the relative success of the Group of Friends of the Secretary-General on El Salvador, the concept became a model, which was applied—with mixed results—to crises such as Haiti, Guatemala, Western Sahara, and Georgia afterwards. The case study on El Salvador therefore includes the question of the extent to which Groups of Friends, including the related division of labour between SC, Secretariat, and stakeholders, is dependent on prevailing structural conditions. Ancillary to this aspect is the question—to what extent can such a concept be applied as a ready-made strategy to other conflict situations, that is, 'When do informal groups matter?'

This chapter argues that choosing the voice option is dependent on the specific conflict setting. The transformation of the bipolar system illustrated the parallelism of the exit and voice option in response to systemic change. In the case of El Salvador, forming the Group of Friends amplified the leverage of the UN intermediary in the negotiations with the parties to the conflict. The chapter examines, firstly, the conflict setting by concentrating on three levels of analysis: (*a*) it analyses the root causes of conflict by elaborating on the horizontal inequalities in the country; (*b*) it concentrates on the changing structural conditions of the conflict that provided the permissive political context for conflict resolution; (*c*) it sheds light on the implications of systemic change for governance in the SC. In a second step, the chapter focuses on the resolution of conflict, especially taking into account the dynamics between Group of Friends, Secretary-General, and SC within that process.

6.1 Conflict Setting

This section analyses the conflict setting in El Salvador. It argues that the civil war originated in horizontal inequalities that reflected, in essence, a class conflict with the FMLN and the GOES struggling at opposite sides.

---

[4] See Chapter 2.

The transformation of the bipolar system at the end of the 1980s created the permissive political environment for a negotiated peace. The UN-led process provided the platform for addressing the root causes of conflict in El Salvador. Negotiations aimed at transforming the Salvadoran society by achieving reform in the military, political, and socio-economic realm of the country. At the level of the UN, the Cold War thaw facilitated consultation, coordination, and cooperation between the five permanent members of the SC (P-5), with the United States assuming a prominent role within that body. In this context, voice, as epitomized in the formation of the Friends mechanism, constituted a dependent variable of the specific conflict setting. The Friends mechanism would recalibrate the balance of power between Council and Secretariat and amplify the voice of the Secretary-General in the peace process.

6.1.1 Civil Conflict: Horizontal Inequalities

Civil conflict in El Salvador originated in long-standing social and economic inequalities in the smallest and most densely populated country of Central America.[5] Systematic exclusion of the majority of the population, including the failure to modernize the Salvadoran society, generated a long-standing political crisis.[6] Huge disparities in income distribution and land-ownership together with the militarization of society constituted the root causes of conflict. According to Edelberto Torres-Rivas: 'Socio-economic polarization was extreme, based on the concentration of land in the hands of a very few, beginning in the nineteenth century with the creation of a primary-export economy. A small group of land-owners monopolized land, water, and financial resources, to the constant exclusion of four-fifths of the population'.[7]

Armed forces, special security forces, and national police dominated the country. Armed insurrection erupted in 1980 over the assassination of Archbishop Oscar Romero who had taken on a prominent role to criticize the social injustice in El Salvador. A gathering of five revolutionary groups

[5] For a good introduction to the conflict, see Wood, *Insurgent Collective Action*; also David Browning, *El Salvador: Landscape and Society* (Oxford: Clarendon Press, 1971); Héctor Lindo-Fuentes, *Weak Foundations: The Economy of El Salvador in the Nineteenth Century* (Berkeley, CA: University of California Press, 1990); William Stanley, *The Protection Racket State: Elite Politics, Military Extortion and Civil War in El Salvador* (Philadelphia, PA: Temple University Press, 1996).

[6] See Edelberto Torres-Rivas, 'Insurrection and Civil War in El Salvador', in Michael W. Doyle, Ian Johnstone, and Robert C. Orr (eds.) *Keeping the Peace: Multidimensional UN Operations in Cambodia and El Salvador* (Cambridge, MA: Cambridge University Press, 1997), 209.

[7] Ibid., 211 *et seq.*

formed a movement called the FMLN.[8] By 1992, an estimated 75,000 people would have lost their lives, with over one million becoming displaced persons or refugees. The conflict was spurred by external support. The armed forces of El Salvador received military aid, including training, from the United States, and the FMLN was supported by Cuba, Nicaragua, and to a lesser extent by the Soviet Union.[9] A primary feature of US relations with Latin America during the Cold War was that 'ideological considerations [had] acquired a primacy over US policy in the region that they lacked in earlier moments'.[10] With support from the Reagan administration, the GOES expanded the strength of the armed forces to about 70,000 troops.[11] The Reagan presidency continued the arms supply that had already increased at the end of the Carter administration, though the political message was slightly different: 'It posed El Salvador as a test case of U.S. determination to counter Soviet and Cuban aggression worldwide, thus demonstrating U.S. resolve to defend its global interests.'[12] Military aid peaked in 1984, totalling US\$ 196.6 million, and gradually decreased to US\$ 116 million in 1987.[13] In the period of intensified negotiations between 1989 and 1991, it would stagnate at the level of US\$ 81–5 million. However, by 1984 the civil war had reached a stalemate that originated in 'a set of mutually reinforcing vetoes'.[14] While the strong ideologization of the Reagan administration virtually excluded military victory for the FMLN, the US Congress was reluctant to grant support to the Salvadoran regime sufficient to achieve victory over the FMLN.[15] In the mid-1980s, many authors posited a failure of US policy in the region, given its mono-dimensional concentration on a perceived Soviet threat.[16] Then Secretary

[8] See Barbara Messings, 'El Salvador', in Melanie C. Greenberg, John H. Barton, and Margaret E. McGuiness (eds.), *Words over War: Mediation and Arbitration to Prevent Deadly Conflict* (Oxford: Rowman & Littlefield, 2000), 163.

[9] See Nicola Miller, *Soviet Relations with Latin America, 1959–1987* (Cambridge, MA: Cambridge University Press, 1989), 188–216.

[10] Jorge I. Domínguez, 'US–Latin American Relations during the Cold War and its Aftermath', in Victor Bulmer-Thomas and James Dunkerley (eds.), *The United States and Latin America: The New Agenda* (Cambridge, MA: Harvard University Press, 1999), 33.

[11] See Fen Osler Hampson, 'The Pursuit of Human Rights: The United Nations in El Salvador', in William J. Durch (ed.), *UN Peacekeeping, American Politics, and the Uncivil Wars of the 1990s* (London: Macmillan, 1997), 69.

[12] Cynthia J. Arnson, 'The Salvadoran Military and Regime Transformation', in Wolf Grabendorff, Heinrich-W. Krumwiede, and Jörg Todt (eds.), *Political Change in Central America: Internal and External Dimensions* (Boulder, CO: Westview Press, 1984), 105 *et seq.*

[13] See James Dunkerley, *The Pacification of Central America: Political Change in the Isthmus, 1987–1993* (London: Verso, 1994), 145.

[14] Terry Lynn Karl, 'El Salvador's Negotiated Revolution', *Foreign Affairs*, 71/2 (1992), 148.

[15] Ibid., 149.

[16] See for example the collection of articles in Kenneth M. Coleman and George C. Herring (eds.), *The Central American Crisis: Sources of Conflict and the Failure of U.S. Policy* (Wilmington,

of State Alexander Haig outlined the US policy in El Salvador at the beginning of President Reagan's term of office as follows:

This situation is global in character. The problem is worldwide Soviet interventionism that poses an unprecedented challenge to the free world. Anyone attempting to debate the prospects for a successful outcome in El Salvador who fails to consider the Soviet menace is dealing with the leg or the trunk of the elephant.[17]

In consequence, the stalemate could not generate a ripe moment for conflict resolution since the incoming Reagan considered El Salvador a test case to roll back Soviet influence. Such policy rested upon the assumption that the Soviet Union supplied the FMLN with a constant flow of arms. Such an assumption however virtually ignored Soviet reluctance, especially after the diplomatic backlash over its intervention in Afghanistan in 1979, to become too deeply involved in the region which the United States considered their *chasse gardée* and where the Soviet Union had no direct security interests involved.[18] With the US administration analysing the setting through the lens of East–West conflict, political negotiations with the FMLN were not an option. It was the prevailing view within the administration that the Salvadoran army, with the military assistance of the United States, would eventually win the war.[19] As Adolfo Aguilar Zinzer concluded in 1986, 'without a substantial change in US policy towards El Salvador, a negotiated solution seems impossible'.[20] Under the chairmanship of Henry Kissinger, in 1984, a rational bipartisan commission had called for the greater participation of the insurgents in the political arena of El Salvador.[21] Furthermore, the US President should 'reinstate the link between progress on human rights and US aid to that country'.[22] The commission left no doubt that the prospect of peace in El Salvador rested upon a well-coordinated multilateral effort in the

DE: SR Scholarly Resources, 1985); see also Adolfo Aguilar Zinzer, 'Obstacles to Dialogue and a Negotiated Solution in Latin America', in Jack Child (ed.), *Conflict in Central America* (London: C. Hurst & Company, 1986), 55–68.

[17] Quoted in Jonathan Steele, *World Power: Soviet Foreign Policy under Brezhnev and Andropov* (London: Michael Joseph, 1983), 222.

[18] In this regard, the relationship with Cuba is certainly exceptional; see Miller, *Soviet Relations with Latin America*, 189 *et seq.*

[19] Cynthia J. Arnson, 'The Salvadoran Military and Regime Transformation', in Wolf Grabendorff, Heinrich-W. Krumwiede, and Jörg Todt (eds.), *Political Change in Central America: Internal and External Dimensions* (Boulder, CO: Westview Press, 1984), 110.

[20] Zinzer, 'Obstacles to Dialogue', 67.

[21] See William D. Rogers, 'The United States and Latin America', *Foreign Affairs*, 63/3 (1985), 560.

[22] Ibid., 561.

socio-economic, political, and military realm. However, the report did not produce a policy shift of the Reagan administration.

The civil war had a devastating effect on the economy. By 1989, coffee production had fallen by thirty per cent, and the gross domestic product (GDP) per head had decreased to the level of 1975, which built up a momentum towards negotiations between the GOES and the FMLN.[23] The overwhelming majority of the Salvadoran population opted for a negotiated settlement to end the conflict.[24] Because of ongoing conflict and instability, transnational corporations (TNCs) left the country. Roughly fifty per cent of the annual budget had to be allocated for the costs of conflict, with the armed forces consuming the lion's share.[25] It is important to see the different perceptions of the UN and the GOES regarding the substance and format of the peace process. For President Cristiani, the substance was about providing political space for the FMLN within the Salvadoran society. He was not willing to grant them a preferential status compared to other political parties in El Salvador working within the democratic framework.[26] However, the UN established a format of negotiations that treated the GOES and the FMLN as political equals, which was unavoidable if the peace process should produce some tangible results.

6.1.2 Transformation of the Bipolar System

Progress in the settlement of conflict in Central America was facilitated through the transformation of the bipolar system that removed the East–West dimension of civil wars. The UN assumed an instrumental role in the transformation of the bipolar system in the western hemisphere. The involvement of the UN in the Central American peace process took place at a time when the Organization had built a record of successes in Afghanistan and Namibia. Although this situation would change later with the perceived failures of the Organization in former Yugoslavia, Somalia, Rwanda, and Burundi, at this stage, the Secretary-General enjoyed a relatively high degree of acceptance to assume good-offices functions in the settlement of conflicts. Like in Afghanistan, the UN's involvement in Central America provided a face-saving device for the superpowers to

---

[23] See Hugh Byrne, *El Salvador's Civil War: A Study of Revolution* (Boulder, CO: Lynne Rienner, 1996), 173–6.

[24] According to Karl, by September 1987, 83.3 per cent of the population supported a negotiated peace; see Karl, 'El Salvador's Negotiated Revolution', 151.

[25] See Hampson, 'The Pursuit of Human Rights', 70.

[26] Yale–UN Oral History Interview Transcripts, Alfredo Cristiani, 25 July 1997.

engage in the controlled transition of conflicts within their spheres of influence.[27] Beyond the dimension of Cold War transition, the UN facilitated contacts between parties to the conflict, stakeholders, and like-minded countries by assuming an intermediary role.[28] Another factor that facilitated opening the window of opportunity for the settlement of armed conflicts in Central America was the breakdown of US strategic consensus over policy in the region. This sea change predated the Cold War thaw and was caused by the Iran-contra affair of 1986–7. The funding of the contra war in Nicaragua was blocked in the US Congress in 1984 and approved by only very thin majorities in 1985 and 1986, which illustrated the erosion of the bipartisan consensus at this early stage.[29]

In El Salvador, the year 1989 constituted a watershed in two different aspects. Firstly, with the economies of the Soviet Union and Cuba in deep crisis, continued support for the FMLN seemed to be uncertain at best. The Soviet Union stopped its transfer of arms to the Sandinista government of Nicaragua which eliminated the prospect of a 'revolutionary triumph'.[30] The transformation of communist regimes in Eastern Europe contributed to the perception that the establishment of a post-revolutionary government based on the Soviet or Cuban model appeared as a less attractive option. Pragmatism turned out to be more important than ideology.[31] At the same time, one could also observe a shift in support from Latin American and European governments. Secondly, the November offensive by the FMLN, the largest of its kind during this civil war, illustrated that the conflict had reached a military stalemate. The FMLN did not succeed in launching a major uprising in the capital, while the GOES did not seem to be in the position to contain the military operations of the liberation movement in the centre of power. In this context, Salvadoran President Cristiani asserts 'that the FMLN never had a sincere intention of negotiating politically until after the 1989 offensive'.[32]

The assassination of six Jesuit priests by members of the military of the Salvadoran army attracted great international public attention and

[27] See Thomas G. Weiss, David P. Forsythe, and Roger Coate (eds.), *The United Nations and Changing World Politics*, 4th edn. (Boulder, CO: Westview Press, 2004), 52.
[28] Blanca Antonini, 'Scenarios for Multilateral Approaches to Political Transitions in the Western Hemisphere', in Tommie Sue Montgomery (ed.), *Peacemaking and Democratization in the Western Hemisphere* (University of Miami, FL: North South Center Press, 2000), 304.
[29] See Cynthia J. Arnson, 'Introduction', in Cynthia J. Arnson (ed.), *Comparative Peace Processes in Latin America* (Stanford, CA: Stanford University Press, 1999), 12 *et seq.*
[30] Karl, 'El Salvador's Negotiated Revolution', 151.
[31] See Montgomery, *Revolution in El Salvador*, 216.
[32] Yale–UN Oral History Interview Transcripts, Alfredo Cristiani, 25 July 1997.

increased the pressure on the US administration to review its military aid for El Salvador.[33] In the United States, it was no longer possible to maintain 'a foreign policy consensus based on the twin premises that the army had successfully contained the FMLN and that democracy was being constructed'.[34] Consequently, the Bush administration sought to find a new bipartisan approach for US policy in Central America.[35] The perception of a military stalemate and the breakdown of the bipolar system, which shifted the strategic importance of the region, prepared the ground for a different role of the United States. The following year, US Congress adopted a fifty per cent cut in military aid to the armed forces of El Salvador, which helped to maintain the strategic equilibrium on the ground. Pressure increased on the Bush administration to support a negotiated settlement, especially after the US invasion of Panama in December 1989 and the victory of Violetta Barrios de Chamorro in Nicaragua that 'removed even the appearance of a regional threat'.[36] However, US policy shift was less substantive than it may appear from this perspective. What changed significantly with the Bush administration was the style of foreign policy decision-making rather than the substance. The willingness to broaden the process created a sense of ownership on the side of regional players that they were part and parcel of the peace process.[37]

The situation in late 1989 genuinely reflected the Zartman scenario of a perceived stalemate with a no-win situation for both sides and generated the ripe moment for the resolution of conflict.[38] At that stage, the gains of a negotiated settlement started to outweigh the costs imposed by the civil war. In consequence, since the military stalemate illustrated that the continuation of conflict by military means had produced a no-win situation, the prospect of a mutual agreement on a settlement would be 'the least-cost solution'.[39] The process would become 'a vehicle

[33] For a detailed study on the significance of this event, see Teresa Whitfield, *Paying the Price: Ignacio Ellacuría and the Murdered Jesuits of El Salvador* (Philadelphia, PA: Temple University Press, 1994).

[34] Karl, 'El Salvador's Negotiated Revolution', 153.

[35] See Byrne, *El Salvador's Civil War*, 174.

[36] Karl, 'El Salvador's Negotiated Revolution', 153.

[37] See Yale–UN Oral History Interview Transcripts, Beatrice Rangel, 16 September 1997.

[38] See I. William Zartman, 'Dynamics and Constraints in Negotiations in Internal Conflicts', in William Zartman (ed.), *Elusive Peace: Negotiation an End to Civil Wars* (Washington, DC: The Brookings Institution, 1995), 3–29.

[39] General Mauricio Vargas, member of the negotiation team, stated that claim. This was confirmed by FMLN commander Ana Guadalupe Martínez who underlined that military struggle as a means to achieve political outcomes was rejected by society; Cynthia J. Arnson, 'Introduction', 17

for addressing structural issues that previously had not or could not be addressed within the existing political system'.[40]

6.1.3 *Systemic Change and Governance in the Security Council*

The transformation of the bipolar system furthered cooperation between the P-5. P-5 consultation, coordination, and cooperation had become a prominent feature since the Iran–Iraq war. In 1987, on the initiative of the United Kingdom, the permanent members of the Council engaged in informal meetings for an exchange of views outside the Council chambers to coordinate their positions vis-à-vis the conflict.[41]

The coordination set a precedent that would define SC governance in the post-bipolar era, with the perception growing that the P-5 had become the gatekeeper of SC decision-making and procedures. The United States assumed a preponderant role within the body, especially after the demise of the Soviet empire. US dominance was especially apparent in the process of adopting SC Resolution 678 that delegated the use of force against the government of Iraq to a coalition of UN member states under the leadership of the United States.[42] The genesis of this resolution fostered the perception of outside observers that decision-making in the SC was actually driven by the one remaining superpower.[43] In parallel, as David Malone has observed, 'the ability of NAM members in the Council to play the superpowers off against each other vanished while, at the same time, differences in perspective and interests among the NAM countries were coming to the fore'.[44]

This new pattern of consultation, coordination, and cooperation between the permanent members was also welcomed by China and the Soviet Union. The strengthening of the P-5 was especially in the interest of the latter country as the declining Soviet empire sought to compensate for its weakness by upgrading the role of the SC in order to maintain its relative influence in world affairs. In addition, China and the Soviet Union had a strong interest in retaining control over the growing

---

[40] Ibid., 8.

[41] See the most informative account by Cameron Hume, *The United Nations, Iran, and Iraq: How Peacemaking Changed* (Bloomington, IN: Indiana University Press, 1994).

[42] See UN Doc S/RES/678, 29 November 1990, op. 2. The resolution was adopted in response to the Iraqi invasion of Kuwait.

[43] See Burns H. Weston, 'Security Council Resolution 678 and Persian Gulf Decision-Making: Precarious Legitimacy', *American Journal of International Law*, 85/3 (1991), 516–35.

[44] David M. Malone, 'The UN Security Council in the Post-Cold War World: 1987–97', *Security Dialogue*, 28/4 (1998), 396.

interventions of the Council in internal conflicts such as Cambodia and El Salvador. Given the expansion of the scope of Article 39 and the subsequent erosion of Article 2.7 of the UN Charter, the two permanent members were especially keen to keep in control of the process and to avoid any unwanted involvement of the UN especially in areas within their sphere of influence.[45] Furthermore, the plethora of items on the SC's agenda furthered the dominance of permanent members, as the factor of human resources became more important with the increasing workload of the Council.[46] The P-5 tended to have much more personnel at their disposal to cope with the multiple crisis settings.[47]

The process leading towards Namibia's independence at the end of the 1980s illustrated the difficult position of the Secretary-General towards conflicting forces on the side of UN member states. The debate over the strength of troops to be deployed for the United Nations Transition Assistance Group (UNTAG) suggested that the position of the P-5 could hardly be ignored without endangering the entire operation.[48] At the same time, the Iran–Iraq war had demonstrated that Pérez de Cuéllar actively promoted a strengthened cooperation between the P-5. In his view, the P-5 should assume 'a central role' in the maintenance of peace and international security of the post-bipolar era.[49] While this vision constituted the realistic assessment that the effective working of the SC depended on the cooperation of its five permanent members, it also entailed the danger to compromise the Secretary-General's aura of impartiality and legitimacy as he might tend to be more receptive to their positions than the stance of other UN member states. P-5 diplomacy vis-à-vis Cambodia underlined the key role permanent members of the SC were prepared to assume in the resolution of conflicts. The peace process that led to the conclusion of the Paris Agreements constituted an exercise under the leadership of the Council's permanent members in cooperation with like-minded countries such as Australia, Japan, and Indonesia.[50]

---

[45] For example, the limited involvement of the UN in the Georgian–Abkhazian conflict via the UN Observer Mission (UNOMIG) constituted a manifest interest of the Russian Federation since it legitimized the presence of Confederation of Independent States (CIS) forces in the region.

[46] See David Caron, 'The Legitimacy of the Collective Authority of the Security Council', *American Journal of International Law*, 87/4 (1993), 552–88.

[47] This becomes obvious when looking at the number of professionals on staff, see Table 4, Chapter 3.

[48] For the conflict of interests regarding the deployment and financing of UNTAG, see Goulding, *Peacemonger*, 146.

[49] Ibid.

[50] See Doyle, 'War Making and Peace Making', 540 *et seq.*

The UN Secretariat remained closely involved in this process by participating in many P-5 meetings and by receiving regular briefings by the permanent members of the SC.[51]

Cooperation between the P-5 had a lasting impact on the actual and perceived functioning of the SC.[52] The frequency of meetings especially between 1991 and 1993, the number of resolutions adopted, as well as the increasing reluctance of permanent members to cast the veto, illustrated the high expectations of UN member states vis-à-vis the potential of the Council to discharge its primary responsibility for the maintenance of international peace and security. At the same time, it demonstrated its limits, as the increasing workload exacerbated the structural deficiencies of the Council. In the period between 1987 and 1992, the list of matters under consideration by the SC rose from eleven to twenty-seven.[53] Besides dealing with the Central American peace process in general and the situation in El Salvador in particular, from 1991 to 1992, the SC had to consider a plethora of other agenda items such as the situation in Afghanistan, Cambodia, Cyprus, Liberia, the political conditions in Haiti and Yugoslavia, as well as the situation of Iraq–Iran and Iraq–Kuwait respectively.[54]

Looking from this perspective, the formation of informal groups of states constituted a mechanism to cope with the increasing workload of the Council. However, diplomatic devices such as the Extended P-5/Core Group on Cambodia and the Group of Friends of the Secretary-General on El Salvador were variations on the theme of informal settings. Although the formation and proliferation of informal groups of states occurred in response to systemic change, it is of crucial importance to understand the parallelism of exit and voice which provided a set of alternative options to deal with conflict settings. For example, it resulted in significantly different approaches to conflict resolution in the cases of Cambodia and

---

[51] See Pérez de Cuéllar, *Pilgrimage for Peace*, 465.

[52] It is important to make this distinction since the actual impact of P-5 cooperation is not a constant but a variable dependent on structural conditions and specific conflict settings. The predominance of the P-5 tends to be overemphasized and has developed into a certain kind of 'paranoia' of non-permanent members, according to a former senior official of the US Permanent Mission to the UN; see Author interview, New York, 24 November 2000. Even though one might suspect a certain degree of motivated bias by the interviewee, P-5 cooperation tends to be case-by-case and *ad hoc*; Neylan Bali considers the Group of Friends as a flexible response to the perceived predominance of the P-5; see Interview with Neylan Bali, former Director of the SC Affairs Division, UN, New York, 1 December 2000.

[53] See United Nations, *Index to Proceedings of the Security Council, Forty-second to Forty-seventh year, 1987–92* (New York: United Nations, 1988–93).

[54] Ibid.

El Salvador. While P-5 diplomacy dominated the later stages of the peace process in Cambodia, the UN Secretary-General and his personal representative orchestrated the negotiated peace in El Salvador as impartial intermediaries between the parties to the conflict. Activities of the Extended P-5/Core Group illustrated the willingness of the permanent members to manage conflicts outside the institutional constraints of the SC. The partiality of the General Assembly vis-à-vis the conflict setting in Cambodia significantly limited the Secretary-General's room for manoeuvre as an impartial mediator, together with the exceptional circumstance that all permanent members had a stake in the conflict.[55] In parallel, the Friends mechanism demonstrated that the breakdown of the bipolar system had affected the institutional balance of power of the UN's principal organs, with the SC and its permanent members assuming a dominant position. This shifting-power constellation increased the vulnerability of the Secretary-General to the P-5, and especially the United States as its most powerful member. In consequence, strengthening the voice of the Secretary-General by forming a group of like-minded states that lent leverage to his peacemaking efforts, recalibrated the inner institutional balance of power between Secretariat and Council. The Friends mechanism on El Salvador allowed him to exclude the Council to the greatest possible extent from the peace process. Providing the Secretary-General with greater voice while excluding the SC also accommodated the interests of the FMLN, which had raised related concerns from the very beginning.[56]

In conclusion, the parallelism of exit and voice constituted a significant pattern of the UN's adaptation process to cope with the old and new challenges of the post-bipolar world. While in the case of Cambodia permanent members chose exit to escape from the structural deficiencies of the UN's conflict resolution machinery, in the case of El Salvador, voice, as epitomized in the Group of Friends, emerged as a counterbalance to mitigate the preponderance of the SC and its permanent members. The Friends mechanism turned out to be key to protect the Secretary-General from any potential pressure exerted on him by Council members, which might have compromised the Secretary-General's aura of impartiality and legitimacy on which the peace process rested. While the breakdown of the bipolar system certainly facilitated an enhanced role for the SC, conflict settings such as in El Salvador required a device that would counterbalance the P-5, especially

---

[55] See Goulding, *Peacemonger*, 249 *et seq.*
[56] Interview with Alvaro de Soto, New York, 17 November 2000.

the United States, in order to gain the FMLN's acceptance of the UN's intermediary role in the peace process. The FMLN's insistence on the establishment of such a mechanism also reflected the widespread perception that the UN Secretariat was sometimes 'excessively compliant to the wishes of the Permanent Members'.[57] This circumstance suggests that the Friends' balancing role also encompassed—at least to some extent—a de facto supervisory role for the efforts made by the Secretary-General.

6.2 Conflict Resolution

This section analyses peacemaking efforts for conflict resolution in El Salvador by concentrating in particular on the role of informal arrangements such as the Contadora Group in the 1980s and the Friends of the Secretary-General in the early 1990s. The reference to earlier attempts is crucial to understand why the peace process succeeded when the UN Secretariat assumed the role of an intermediary between the parties, supported by the Group of Friends and other key states. The section, firstly, sheds light on the Contadora process from 1983 to 1988, followed by a closer examination of the role of the Friends mechanism between 1990 and 1992.

6.2.1 Contadora Group, 1983–8

The Contadora Group, comprising Colombia, Mexico, Panama, and Venezuela, constituted an informal arrangement of regional players that aimed at settling the conflict by Latin American means without actively involving key powers such as the United States.[58] Launched in 1983, it sought to find a negotiated solution to the conflicts in Central America as an alternative to limit the widely perceived risks of a US military intervention or regional war.[59] Looking from this perspective, this regional effort introduced 'the idea of dialogue as an instrument for solving conflict'.[60]

---

[57] See David Malone, 'The Security Council in the post-Cold War era', in Muthiah Alagappa and Takashi Inoguchi (eds.), *International Security Management and the United Nations* (Tokyo: United Nations University Press, 1999), 398.

[58] See Jack Child, *The Central American Peace Process, 1983–1991: Sheathing Swords, Building Confidence* (Boulder, CO: Lynne Rienner, 1992), 147.

[59] See Kaufman Purcell, 'Demystifying Contadora', 74; see also Yale–UN Oral History Interview Transcripts, David Escobar Galindo, 21 June 1997.

[60] See Yale–UN Oral History Interview Transcripts, Ruben Zamora, 24 July 1997.

The Contadora Group established and maintained such dialogue by subsequently approaching the five Central American governments of Costa Rica, El Salvador, Guatemala, Honduras, and Nicaragua. In this effort, it aimed at trying 'to isolate the Central American region from the East/West rivalry in order to tackle the problems of constitutional reform, the reform of the military... since they were of a domestic nature'.[61] The SC had commended the efforts of the group in its Resolution 530 and supported the call for strengthening the principles of self-determination and non-interference in the internal affairs of the Central American countries.[62] By September 1983, the informal arrangement had agreed upon a set of objectives that provided the framework for a negotiated settlement. Those objectives included, *inter alia*, democracy, national reconciliation, termination of support for cross-border activities of paramilitary forces, regional arms control, and the reduction of foreign military support to the region.[63] In mid-1984, the group tabled a draft treaty (*acta*) on peace and cooperation, to be signed and ratified by the Central American governments. However, without the support of the United States and the approval of the Central American countries the Contadora Group was not able to produce tangible results. While the process enjoyed broad support in Latin America, '[f]or the United States Contadora represented at best a well-meaning initiative that would eventually converge with U.S. goals in the region and at worst a serious challenge to U.S. influence and hegemony, not only in Central America but in the Western Hemisphere as a whole.'[64] Although the FMLN remained excluded from this inter-governmental process, it did not openly reject the initiative since they considered it crucial to prevent US interventions, especially against the Sandinista government in Nicaragua, which provided military and political support to the movement.[65]

It is important to understand that the formation of the Contadora Group originated in the common interest of regional powers 'to constrain the United States from its habitual unilateral actions and thereby enhance their own role'.[66] This included the shared goal of de-emphasizing the Cold War dimension of conflicts by dealing with their root causes rather than their symptoms. Looking from this perspective, while the process

---

[61] Yale–UN Oral History Interview Transcripts, Beatrice Rangel, 16 September 1997; see also Yale–UN Oral History Interview Transcripts, Manuel Tello and Gustavo Albin, 6 August 1997.

[62] See UN Doc S/RES/530, 19 May 1983, preambular paragraph 6.

[63] See Kaufman Purcell, 'Demystifying Contadora', 77.

[64] Child, *The Central American Peace Process*, 148.

[65] See Yale–UN Oral History Interview Transcripts, Ruben Zamora, 24 July 1997.

[66] Kaufman Purcell, 'Demystifying Contadora', 75.

constrained unilateral policies by the United States, it was still a victim of its own ambitions, as the group sought to deal with the root causes of conflicts in El Salvador, Guatemala, and Nicaragua within the same negotiation context. Given the overload of its agenda, 'the Contadora group overreached the limits of the possible'.[67] Despite the assistance of the so-called support group, comprising representatives from influential regional players such as Argentina, Brazil, Peru, and Uruguay from mid-1985 onwards, negotiations stalled. By late 1986, it had become clear 'that the Contadora process was running out of steam'.[68]

In February 1987, the peace plan of Costa Rican President Oscar Arias Sánchez restored the momentum of the peace process by providing a well-defined framework for conflict resolution. Although it was built upon the principles of the *acta*, the Arias plan went beyond by setting terms and time limits for verification and implementation. The plan paved the way for the signing of the Esquipulas II Agreements by the five Central American Presidents in August 1987. The Agreements set up a 'Procedure for the Establishment of a Firm and Lasting Peace in Central America', aiming at promoting democracy and the holding of free and fair elections. An International Verification and Follow-up Commission (CIVS) should monitor the process, comprising the foreign ministers of the Central American countries, the Contadora/Support Groups, and the Secretaries-General of the Organization of American States (OAS) and the UN.

The discussion about a stronger UN involvement emerged with the question of how to verify compliance in an impartial way with the Esquipulas II Agreements. They obliged the Central American governments to cease aid to irregular forces and insurrectionist movements in the region. Furthermore, none of the territories were allowed to be used for attacks on another country. The Acapulco Summit of the Heads of States composing the Contadora and Support Groups from 27 to 29 November 1987 discussed the limits of the OAS to deal effectively with the problems of the region.[69] Given the broad agenda of the summit that mirrored the questions under consideration within the framework of the OAS, diplomats and observers from the region expressed growing concerns that the

---

[67] Pérez de Cuéllar, *Pilgrimage for Peace*, 398. Alvaro de Soto also confirms the 'excessive ambition' of Contadora's comprehensive approach; de Soto, 'Ending Violent Conflict in El Salvador', 353.

[68] Yale–UN Oral History Interview Transcripts, Francesc Vendrell, 13 April 1996.

[69] See UN Doc A/42/844 and UN Doc S/19314, 1 December 1987.

Contadora/Support Groups might attempt 'to supersede' the regional organization.[70]

At the same time, the governments of El Salvador and Honduras stressed the need to maintain an equilibrium between the roles of the UN and the OAS.[71] Furthermore, Honduras and Mexico were keen to establish a framework of negotiations that included external players such as the United States and the Soviet Union. While Honduras aimed at finding an effective solution to remove the Contras from its territory, Mexico did not want to continue its prominent role in the Contadora Group, which had been a constant source of tensions between the Mexican and US administrations.[72] According to Jorge Montaño, during the Reagan Presidency, 'Central America became the excuse for the U.S. to establish the certification process on drugs, to start also the legislation against immigrants to the United States.'[73] At the end of 1988, Mexico therefore approached the UN Secretary-General to assume a more active role in the Central American peace process, while supporting the enhanced engagement of the UN 'from behind'.[74]

In conclusion, the Contadora process managed to prevent the unilateral engagement of the United States in the region, but failed to mobilize international support to generate the necessary momentum for setting up a negotiation process that included the insurgent movements. The UN constituted the mechanism of last resort to provide a framework for negotiations towards peace in El Salvador.

6.2.2 Group of Friends of the Secretary-General, 1989–92

At the beginning of 1989, the perception prevailed in the UN Secretariat that '[a] new opportunity is emerging in the search for peace in Central America, but a fresh approach is required.'[75] While the Esquipulas Agreements committed the five Central American governments to a new code of

---

[70] See Javier Pérez de Cuéllar Papers, Confidential note by the Department of Political and Security Council Affairs on 'The Acapulco Summit—A New Regional Approach to International Problems', 14 December 1987.

[71] See Javier Pérez de Cuéllar Papers, Nota confidencial para el Secretario General, 13 October 1987.

[72] The Presidents-elect of Mexico and the United States, Salinas and Bush, had met in late 1988 to cooperate more closely vis-à-vis the Central American peace process. See Yale–UN Oral History Interview Transcripts, Jorge Montaño, 1 October 1999.

[73] Ibid.

[74] Yale–UN Oral History Interview Transcripts, Francesc Vendrell, 18 April 1996.

[75] Javier Pérez de Cuéllar Papers, Strictly confidential note on Central America, January 1989.

conduct that aimed at promoting stability in the region, there would be no lasting peace without dealing effectively with the Contras and the FMLN. The Esquipulas peace process explicitly supported the GOES and strengthened both its international and domestic legitimacy, which eventually led to a sea change among the Salvadoran parties located on the left side of the spectrum, with close links to the FMLN to participate in the electoral process.[76]

At the same time, the new Bush administration undertook a review of its policy in Central America. Priorities shifted in favour of a greater emphasis on diplomacy to further the Central American peace process while de-emphasising the military aspects of US policy in the region. A series of meetings in late March 1989 with US representatives from various agencies such as the State Department, the Pentagon, Joint Chiefs of Staff, and the CIA illustrated the willingness to engage in close consultations and collaboration with the UN Secretariat.[77] In addition, the Soviet Union and Cuba signalled that they would appreciate any role of the UN Secretary-General as a facilitator of a settlement in Central America. The transformation of the bipolar system created the permissive political context for a greater involvement of the UN in the Central American peace process.

Resolution 637, unanimously adopted by the SC during a ten-minute formal session on 27 July 1989, opened the gate for an intensification of the good offices of the Secretary-General in support of the Central American peace process.[78] The resolution was sponsored by Colombia and Algeria.[79] Colombia especially had been extremely active in the SC for months to secure the approval of the draft.[80] The resolution constituted a watershed as it formally requested the UN to become more actively engaged in a region which the United States had always been considering their *chasse gardée* since US President James Monroe's seventh annual message to Congress in December 1823.[81] Interventions by external actors were perceived as unfriendly acts. In effect, SC Resolution 637 essentially provided the overall framework to broadly define the engagement of the UN in the peace process. While it supported an upgraded role for the

[76] See David Moreno, *The Struggle for Peace in Central America* (Gainesville, FL: University Press of Florida, 1994), 134 *et seq.*

[77] Javier Pérez de Cuéllar Papers, Strictly confidential note for the Secretary-General, 28 March 1989.

[78] See UN Doc S/RES/637, 27 July 1989.

[79] Yale–UN Oral History Interview Transcripts, Francesc Vendrell, 18 April 1996.

[80] Yale–UN Oral History Interview Transcripts, Alvaro de Soto, 9 April 1996.

[81] US President Monroe's address referred in particular to interventions by Russia and France. It later transformed into the so-called Monroe Doctrine; see Ernest R. May, *The Making of the Monroe Doctrine* (Cambridge, MA: Harvard University Press, 1975).

Secretary-General, it also requested him to keep the SC regularly informed about all those efforts he would undertake in this regard.[82] Furthermore, the resolution linked three crucial elements being part and parcel of agreements adopted by the five Central American countries between August 1987 and February 1989: firstly, democratization of the region; secondly, demobilization of insurrectional movements; and thirdly, repatriation of former combatants. This formal request by the SC, including subsequent specific requests by Alfredo Cristiani, who had assumed the Presidency of El Salvador in June 1989, and FMLN leaders prepared the ground for a peacemaking initiative of the Secretary-General on a consensual basis.

By the end of 1989, the UN Secretariat started considering various models on how to frame negotiations under the auspices of the UN. Combinations and permutations of models such as the United Nations Emergency Force (UNEF) Advisory Committee, the Jakarta Informal Meetings on Cambodia, and the Quadripartite talks on Cuban troop withdrawal from Angola were considered precedents that should allow for some flexibility to address complex crisis settings such as in El Salvador.[83] At that stage, there was not any preconceived scheme for the conduct of negotiations, neither in the Secretariat nor on the side of key players in the process. The US government expressed strong reservations regarding the inclusion of Cuba in the process, given the fact that the Cuban government had not yet publicly accepted the Esquipulas process. With reference to the Soviet Union, the United States appeared to prefer the use of bilateral relations rather than a framework that might 'confuse process over substance'.[84] This reflected concerns of the US government that the larger framework under the auspices of the UN might 'serve as an excuse for the Soviets to claim that our concerns are more effectively addressed merely by enlarging the discussion'.[85] However, relations with Latin America deteriorated and the credibility in the region eroded after the US intervention in Panama in December 1989, which effectively increased the demand for an impartial player in the Central American peace process. The Soviet government supported the flexible approach of the UN Secretariat and favoured in particular the framework of negotiations on Angola, held with participation of the United States, Cuba, and the Soviet Union.

---

[82] See UN Doc S/RES/637, 27 July 1989, op. 5 and 6.
[83] See Javier Pérez de Cuéllar Papers, Draft note on El Salvador, 14 December 1989.
[84] Javier Pérez de Cuéllar Papers, Confidential note to the file, 12 January 1990.
[85] Ibid.

The UN Secretariat received official requests from the FMLN and the GOES for the Secretary-General's good offices in December 1989 and January 1990 respectively. In both cases, the request for UN assistance constituted less a choice by preference than the lack of other options. President Cristiani requested the Secretary-General to facilitate the resumption of negotiations between the parties that should result in the elimination of the root causes of the conflict.[86] The involvement of the UN had also received the strong backing of the five Central American Presidents in their Declaration of San Isidro Coronado 'to request respectfully the Secretary-General of the United Nations to do everything within his power to take the necessary steps to ensure the resumption of the dialogue between the Government of El Salvador and FMLN, thereby facilitating its successful continuation'.[87] Furthermore, they underlined that demobilizing the FMLN constituted a key element to reach a settlement of the conflict.[88]

However, perceptions differed among the GOES and the FMLN regarding the degree to which the UN Secretary-General or his representative should become involved in the process. While the government would have preferred a facilitating function of the Secretary-General, the FMLN subscribed to the idea of the Secretary-General assuming the role of a mediator that would be fully in charge of conducting the negotiations between the two parties. Under the auspices of the UN, GOES and FMLN agreed on the format, mechanism, and pace of the negotiations, as became formalized in the Geneva Agreement of 4 April 1990.[89] The Agreement focussed the peace process on four objectives: firstly, the resolution of conflict by political means; secondly, the promotion of democracy; thirdly, the guarantee of the respect of human rights; and fourthly, the reunification of the Salvadoran society.[90] Within this process, the role of the UN Secretary-General or his representative would be limited to an intermediary between the parties, and not a mediator.[91]

The Caracas Agreement of 21 May 1990 further specified the general agenda and the timetable of the process. The UN would structure

---

[86] See 'Letter dated 29 January 1990 from President Alfredo Cristiani of El Salvador to the Secretary-General concerning the peace process and United Nations involvement', in United Nations, *The United Nations and El Salvador: 1990–1995* (New York: United Nations, 1995), 105–07.

[87] UN Doc A/44/872–S/21019, 12 December 1989, para 3.

[88] Ibid., para 6.

[89] See UN Doc A/45/706–S/21931, 8 November 1990, Annex I.

[90] Ibid., para 1.

[91] While a mediator would have been able to table proposals on its own initiative, the role of an intermediary would be refined to act as a facilitator between the contending parties.

negotiations in two phases that made the conclusion of the first phase, the adoption of a ceasefire, contingent upon the political agreement on a wide range of political issues such as the armed forces, human rights, the judicial system, the electoral system, constitutional reform, economic and social issues, as well as verification.[92] The second phase would establish guarantees and conditions for the reintegration of the FMLN into the Salvadoran society. The agreement also prepared the ground for the widest possible informal involvement of interested or like-minded parties being willing and able to 'contribute to the success of the process through their advice and support'.[93] This provision opened the gate for conducting consultations and seeking support on various levels, such as the Group of Friends, the United States, as well as the Soviet Union and Cuba. UN engagement in other conflicts such as Afghanistan, Southern Africa, and South-east Asia had already underlined the importance of 'including the key stakeholders in the negotiating effort rather than to seek to isolate them'.[94]

There seemed to be a clear understanding that framing an international consensus on the matter constituted the sine qua non for the successful settlement of the conflict. Officials in the UN Secretariat therefore believed that negotiations on El Salvador could be structured along a multi-tiered framework with flexible mechanisms, coordinated by a 'broadly acceptable focal point'.[95] Such a focal point would be the UN Secretary-General's personal representative for the Central American peace process, Alvaro de Soto, who had been appointed in September 1989. In order to insert momentum into the process, de Soto started with negotiations on the least contentious issues. The San José Agreement on Human Rights, signed by the parties on 26 July 1990, aimed at securing unrestricted respect for human rights in the country. The UN should monitor compliance with the provisions of the Agreement. The provision to establish a United Nations Observer Mission in El Salvador (ONUSAL), which would formally start by July 1991, constituted a crucial mechanism to build confidence between the parties prior to the conclusion of a formal ceasefire. Seen from this perspective, ONUSAL's mission contained elements of peace-building and conflict prevention at the same time.[96] For the peace process, stra-

[92] See UN Doc A/45/706–S/21931, 8 November 1990, Annex II.

[93] Ibid., Annex II, para 5.

[94] Javier Pérez de Cuéllar Papers, Strictly confidential note on Central America, January 1989.

[95] Ibid.

[96] See Teresa Whitfield, 'The UN's Role in Peace-Building in El Salvador', in Margarita S. Studemeister (ed.), *El Salvador: Implementation of the Peace Accords* (Washington, DC: United States Institute of Peace, 2001), 36.

tegically more important was the meeting of FMLN commanders and GOES representatives in October in which they agreed to upgrade the role of the Secretary-General's personal representative from a mere facilitator to a quasi-mediator who would be allowed to present proposals to both sides. However, the GOES would never accept the UN Secretariat as a formal mediator.

In conclusion, the transformation of the bipolar system facilitated the launch of the peace process with the UN Secretary-General assuming the role of an intermediary to the parties. However, after the conclusion of the San José Agreement, negotiations stalled over the reform of El Salvador's armed forces, which remained the most contentious issue on the agenda. Although the idea to gather a group of friends had been developed in the early stages of the process, it would gain greater currency only when the US administration increased its pressure on the UN negotiator.

RATIONALE OF THE GROUP OF FRIENDS: VOICE

The idea to establish an informal mechanism emerged during the meeting of FMLN representatives, Salvador Samayoa and Ana Guadalupe Martínez, with Alvaro de Soto and Francesc Vendrell at the International Civil Aviation Organization in Montreal on 8 December 1989. The semi-clandestine gathering had to be arranged in Canada as FMLN members were not allowed to enter the United States. At the meeting, the FMLN had raised concerns over the terms of reference of the UN involvement. International events at the end of the 1980s such as the settlement of the Namibian question or the handling of the Soviet troop withdrawal from Afghanistan had furthered the perception of US dominance within the Organization, especially in the SC, that might also affect the UN involvement in the context of the Central American peace process. As Alvaro de Soto recalls, FMLN commanders

were nervous about the prospect that the Security Council might play too preponderant a role and bring pressure on the Secretary-General. Obviously what they feared was that the U.S., which was at the time an ally of the El Salvadoran government, would take sides and put the Secretary-General in a position where he would have to take sides in favor of the government. What they wanted to ensure was the genuine impartiality of the Secretary-General.[97]

[97] Yale–UN Oral History Interview Transcripts, Alvaro de Soto, 9 April 1996; Francesc Vendrell argues in a similar vein, see Yale–UN Oral History Interview Transcripts, Francesc Vendrell, 18 April 1996.

As the Soviet Union was not considered 'an unconditional ally', the FMLN advocated the establishment of a group of like-minded states, serving at the disposal of the UN Secretary-General.[98] In effect, this mechanism would be designed to balance the power of the SC.

The Friends mechanism borrowed its label from the so-called 'Friends of the Chairman' or 'Friends of the President' which is frequently used in the General Assembly. In substance, the mechanism resembled the rationale of the Advisory Committees, as convened especially during the term of office of Secretary-General Dag Hammarskjöld. At the same time, the involvement of the Friends was crucial for the FMLN to ensure 'that they would not be trapped by bureaucracies or by international agents, that they would really participate'.[99] The composition of the informal setting emerged during talks of the UN Secretariat with parties to the conflict, stakeholders, and like-minded states. The Group of Friends would initially comprise three former members of the Contadora Group, that is, Colombia, Mexico, and Venezuela, as well as Spain.[100] The active engagement of the Contadora Group members in the Central American peace process and their intimate knowledge of the conflict setting strongly suggested their continued involvement in the process. Colombia had played an important role in securing the adoption of SC Resolution 637 that fully supported the good offices of the Secretary-General in the Central American peace process.[101] According to de Soto, it also served as a valuable source of intelligence for the UN Secretariat.[102] Mexico had established close ties with the FMLN as it hosted several of its commanders.[103] Venezuela maintained close contacts to Cuba that supported the FMLN.[104] The involvement of Spain, a European power with a Socialist government, was seen as beneficial to open a channel of communication with the Salvadoran opposition (via the International Socialist Movement). The later participation of other countries such as Canada, Costa Rica, France, Germany, Italy, Sweden,

---

[98] Alvaro de Soto, 'Ending Violent Conflict in El Salvador', 357; see also Teresa Whitfield, 'The Role of the United Nations in El Salvador and Guatemala: A Preliminary Comparison', in *Comparative Peace Processes in Latin America*, 267; see also Mark LeVine, 'Peacemaking in El Salvador', in Doyle, Johnston, and Orr (eds.), *Keeping The Peace*, 250.

[99] Yale–UN Oral History Interview Transcripts, Jorge Montaño, 1 October 1999.

[100] The participation of Panama remained de facto excluded given the US invasion of the country in December 1989.

[101] Colombia was elected member of the SC from 1989 to 1990.

[102] This is a significant factor, as the UN Secretariat does not have any intelligence sources at its own disposal. It is therefore dependent on external sources, though UN member states are usually quite reluctant to share them; see Interview with Alvaro de Soto, New York, 17 November 2000.

[103] See Prantl and Krasno, 'Informal Groups of Member States', 336–9.

[104] See Yale–UN Oral History Interview Transcripts, Diego Arria, 5 September 1997.

or the United Kingdom was considered an alternative option.[105] The Friends mechanism would comprise qualified observers on a standby basis to assist the diplomacy of the Secretary-General or his personal representative.

The Group of Friends involved countries with no direct stake in the conflict. The calculation was that those countries would exert their influence on the parties and use their contacts in order to prevent the conclusion of separate agreements between the FMLN and opposition parties, which might delay the cessation of conflict. The Secretariat considered the informal mechanism of greatest value as long as it would not become formalized.[106] Any formalization was perceived as potentially undermining the intermediary role of the UN. Alvaro de Soto initially rejected the establishment on the grounds that the Friends mechanism might eventually develop into 'a collectivization of the negotiating effort', which bore the potential to undermine the Secretary-General's good offices.[107] The GOES also expressed reservations, which not only reflected its own position but also concerns within the US administration. Given the strong concerns of the FMLN, the proposal to form a group of like-minded states stayed on the agenda and would be further developed in subsequent stages of negotiations.

The UN Secretariat was well aware of ongoing efforts of directly or indirectly interested parties that had not been involved in the process. Establishing an informal arrangement would provide the Secretariat with a mechanism to gain control over and coordination of the process in order to avoid parallel initiatives.[108] The stalemate of negotiations in the fall of 1990 furthered discussions about the potential benefits of the Friends mechanism to escape the deadlock. Internal documents of the Secretariat referred to the Soviet troop withdrawal from Afghanistan as a model that could be applied to frame negotiations between the parties. The permanent dialogue between Afghanistan's neighbouring countries and states with influence in the region, gathering as an informal *ad hoc* device, had facilitated a common strategy.[109] At the same time, the Secretariat and the US administration seemed to display a diametrically opposed interpretation on how to conduct negotiations. While the United States favoured

---

[105] Javier Pérez de Cuéllar Papers, Strictly confidential note, 24 September 1990.
[106] See Alvaro de Soto, 'Ending Violent Conflict in El Salvador', 367 *et seq.*
[107] Ibid., 357.
[108] See Javier Pérez de Cuéllar Papers, Strictly confidential note, 24 September 1990.
[109] See Javier Pérez de Cuéllar Papers, Estrictamente Confidencial: Nota sobre la reunión de Secretario General con el Presidente de El Salvador, 29 September 1990.

a process characterized by 'a pressure-cooker atmosphere', the Secretary-General and his personal representative perceived such an approach inconsistent with the role of the UN as an impartial intermediary in the peace process.[110] Alvaro de Soto became increasingly vulnerable to US concerns, especially against the background of the lacking progress in the negotiations. Assistant Secretary of State for Inter-American Affairs, Bernard Aronson, even demanded 'to see the shape of any deal before [it] is made'.[111]

Looked at from the perspective of the UN Secretariat, establishing a Group of Friends of the Secretary-General constituted therefore both a response to US pressure as well as a policy option to insert new momentum into the negotiations.[112] The Group of Friends constituted a mechanism to reduce the vulnerability of the UN intermediary and to strengthen his voice before the SC. With the United States attempting to alter the framework of the process that had been painstakingly negotiated by de Soto in a two-months' shuttling effort between the parties, the support of like-minded countries turned out to be crucial to maintain his impartiality. For the same reasons, the FMLN preferred a marginal role of the SC, given the predominance of the United States as a permanent member of this body. Furthermore, FMLN leaders sought to balance their comparative disadvantages vis-à-vis the government of El Salvador by engaging a group of like-minded countries with no direct stakes in the conflict. According to Ambassadors Tello and Albin of the Mexican mission to the UN, the Friends' function was to keep the process going through constant encouragement of both sides, without assuming any mediating role. They pressed both parties 'to accelerate, or to contemplate, or to study'.[113]

While the balancing of US preponderance constituted the primary function for forming the Group of Friends, it is of great importance to understand that the mechanism also accommodated a secondary one. The informal involvement of the US administration in the Friends mechanism turned out to be key for the successful conclusion of negotiations. According to the then Permanent Representative of Mexico to the UN, Jorge Montaño, the Friends and the United States held very substantial meetings with FMLN leaders and GOES representatives at the Mexican mission, without involvement of UN intermediaries.[114] As the primary rationale of

---

[110] See Javier Pérez de Cuéllar Papers, Strictly confidential note to the file, 1 October 1990.
[111] Ibid.
[112] See Javier Pérez de Cuéllar Papers, Estrictamente Confidencial: Acciones para desbloquear la negociación sobre El Salvador, 24 September 1990.
[113] Yale–UN Oral History Interview Transcripts, Manuel Tello and Gustavo Albin, 6 August 1997.
[114] See Yale–UN Oral History Interview Transcripts, Jorge Montaño, 1 October 1999.

the Group of Friends virtually excluded the direct participation of the United States, the device became informally extended to a 'four-plus-one' process. The Friends and the US administration therefore coordinated many of their activities within the informal four-plus-one framework. According to Bernard Aronson, such an approach was just a matter of 'good diplomacy', which reflected 'a triumph of form over substance'.[115]

Although those functions appeared at first sight mutually excluding, they had mutually reinforcing effects for the successful conclusion of the peace process. The informality of the process was able to accommodate opposing strands and diverging perceptions of the rationale of the Group of Friends. The importance of the four-plus-one mechanism originated in the circumstance that the Friends alone did not have the necessary leverage over the Salvadoran government. However, the de facto involvement of the United States in the negotiations was essential to secure leverage over the GOES and the command of El Salvador's armed forces. Viewed from the perspective of the UN Secretariat, a too prominent role of the four-plus-one countries bore the danger of parallel initiatives that might have undermined the good offices of the Secretary-General and his personal representative. At the same time, active US involvement in the process was considered a necessity.[116]

In conclusion, the Group of Friends mechanism accommodated four different interests and perceptions. Firstly, it accommodated the interest of FMLN leaders to have a diplomatic device that acted as a counterbalance to the United States and the US-dominated SC, thereby strengthening their position in the bargaining process. Secondly, it served the interest of the Secretary-General and his personal representative to prevent parallel initiatives by participating countries. At the same time, by engaging like-minded countries with leverage on the parties to the conflict, the Secretariat reduced its vulnerability vis-à-vis the Bush administration and prevented potential micro-management of the Council. Thirdly, countries comprising the Group of Friends amplified their influence on the peace process as they were constantly engaged by both the UN Secretariat and the US administration. And fourthly, the United States extended the Friends mechanism to an informal 'four-plus-one' formula to control the peace process without becoming the protagonist.

---

[115] Yale–UN Oral History Interview Transcripts, Bernard Aronson, 9 October 1997.
[116] See Javier Pérez de Cuéllar Papers, Nota confidencial para el Secretario General, 25 January 1990.

DYNAMICS BETWEEN FRIENDS, SECRETARY-GENERAL, AND SECURITY COUNCIL

The rationale of the Group of Friends translated into controlled dynamics between the informal device (plus the United States), the Secretary-General, and the SC. This section argues that opting for voice prevented potential micro-management by the Council by limiting its direct involvement to a minimum degree. Working together with a carefully selected group of like-minded UN member states reduced the Secretary-General's dependence on and vulnerability vis-à-vis the Council, including US dominance within that body. The United States sought to maintain its influence by effectively transforming the Friends mechanism into a four-plus-one process and by exerting pressure on the UN Secretariat to rely more on the assistance (and control) of the SC. In contrast to the process leading to the independence of Namibia, there was no substantive discussion on the subject of El Salvador within the framework of formal meetings of the Council.[117]

The litmus test indicating whether the UN Secretariat would be able to maintain control over the peace process was taken in the context of the stalemate of negotiations in late September 1990, when the Salvadoran government tried to undermine the good offices of the Secretary-General. It sought to persuade members of the SC to table a draft resolution that would comment on ongoing negotiations and criticize the FMLN. The initiative did not succeed after Cuba, the Soviet Union, and others had approached the Secretariat and received confirmation that any SC action at this stage would not contribute to the progress of the Secretary-General's good offices.[118] Active involvement of the SC in the peace process would have raised concerns among FMLN commanders about the Secretary-General's independence and impartiality. Any micro-management of the process by the SC therefore had to be avoided.[119]

The initiative of the Salvadoran government was a matter of concern as it had acted with the support of the United States. During a meeting with Alvaro de Soto, Assistant Secretary of State for Inter-American Affairs, Bernard Aronson, expressed his disappointment 'at the active interven-

---

[117] For example, Resolutions 637, 693, 714, and 729, adopted by the SC in the period between 27 July 1989 and 14 January 1992, did not generate any further discussion during formal meetings.

[118] See Alvaro de Soto, 'Ending Violent Conflict in El Salvador', 371. Cuba was elected member of the SC from 1990 to 1991.

[119] Alvaro de Soto had claimed in a meeting with the Salvadoran Minister of Justice, Santamaría, that this initiative by the GOES constituted a 'pretext' (*subterfugio*) to alter the negotiation framework as agreed upon in the Geneva agreement; Javier Pérez de Cuéllar Papers, Nota estrictamente confidencial para el Secretario General, 21 September 1990.

tion of the Secretariat to persuade Member States not to accept it [i.e. the initiative, J.P.]'.[120] In addition, the United States pushed for a stronger interaction between the Secretary-General and the SC. Firstly, they wanted to strengthen his mandate by adopting another SC resolution. Secondly, the more assertive approach of the Secretary-General would be subsequently backed up by strongly worded resolutions to be adopted by the Council. The US Permanent Representative to the UN, Thomas Pickering, stressed the point that the Council constituted 'an advantage and not a problem'.[121]

This circumstance raised the awareness within the Secretariat to the vulnerability of the mediator's role if the Salvadoran government would continue trying to set the SC against the Secretary-General. Even without formal agreement, Pérez de Cuéllar and Alvaro de Soto nevertheless used individually, not yet collectively, the services of like-minded states such as Mexico, Spain, and Venezuela. By fall 1990, the FMLN had established regular contacts with the Group of Friends.[122] At that stage, it was not yet a device acting at the disposal of the Secretary-General to assist his peacemaking efforts as the Salvadoran government still expressed reservations to establish such a grouping. De Soto sought to persuade Cristiani that the establishment of a Group of Friends of the Secretary-General would not only be beneficial for the FMLN but also for the GOES as the mechanism aimed at exerting pressure on both parties to the conflict.[123]

It is important to underline that the group of like-minded states, assisting the FMLN, predated the actual Friends mechanism. The countries would serve in their capacity as Group of Friends only from October 1990 onwards, after they had received a formal request by the UN Secretary-General.[124] This request legitimized the role of the Group of Friends in the peace process.[125] By its name, the informal setting signalled that it would support the impartial good offices of the Secretary-General

---

[120] See Javier Pérez de Cuéllar Papers, Strictly confidential note to the file, 1 October 1990.
[121] Ibid.
[122] See Javier Pérez de Cuéllar Papers, Nota sobre la reunión del Secretario General con representantes del FMLN, 20 September 1990.
[123] See Javier Pérez de Cuéllar Papers, Nota estrictamente confidencial al Secretario General, 19 September 1990.
[124] A joint letter from the Friends, including the United States, issued on the occasion of the ceremony to celebrate the cessation of the armed conflict in El Salvador on 15 December 1992, refers to October 1990 as the official date of the Secretary-General's request to Colombia, Mexico, Spain, and Venezuela to assist his good offices; see UN Doc A/47/842–S/25007, 23 December 1992.
[125] See Interview with Diego Arria, New York, 28 November 2000.

rather than leaning towards one party to the conflict. At the same time, it entailed the encrypted message that the GOES might use the Group of Friends as an alternative forum to the SC to exert influence on the FMLN. The informal arrangement would also serve as a sounding board (*tabla de resonancia*) during direct negotiations between the parties and provide diplomatic assistance.[126] The resistance of the Salvadoran government against the Group of Friends eventually faded with the stronger involvement of the US administration via the informal four-plus-one mechanism.

In order to break the logjam, Pérez de Cuéllar sought assistance in meetings with the Presidents of Mexico, Spain, and Venezuela: firstly, they should exert influence on President Cristiani to form a multiparty delegation for negotiations with the FMLN; secondly, they should help to convince President Bush to establish direct contacts with FMLN leaders; and thirdly, the US administration should enter into contacts with Cuba on the question of El Salvador.[127] However, the military offensive of the FMLN, launched in November 1990, further complicated the good offices. Repeated operations by the FMLN, especially in the capital of San Salvador, constituted a demonstration of the continuing ability to threaten the Salvadoran government at the centre of power.[128] Military offensives by the FMLN forced the army to maintain a strong presence in the capital and prevented further advances in the rural zones controlled by the FMLN. As neither the Geneva nor the Caracas Accords explicitly prohibited the continuation of military activities, any breakthrough in the negotiations was contingent upon the perception that military gains on the ground were unlikely to occur. As Hugh Byrne has observed:

During the last two years of the war the strategies of both sides were directed primarily toward the negotiating table. Whereas in the previous decade negotiations had played an ancillary or supporting role within the strategies of the opposing sides, during these two years military strategies were designed primarily to change the balance of forces at the bargaining table.[129]

While the perception of a military stalemate at the end of 1989 had facilitated the start of negotiations, military campaigns now constituted

[126] See Javier Pérez de Cuéllar Papers, Nota estrictamente confidencial al Secretario General, 19 September 1990.

[127] Javier Pérez de Cuéllar Papers, Estrictamente Confidencial: Reunion con Felipe González, 29 September 1990; and Javier Pérez de Cuéllar Papers, Estrictamente Confidencial: Reunión con el Presidente de Mexico y Venezuela, 1 October 1990.

[128] See Javier Pérez de Cuéllar Papers, Strictly confidential note to the Secretary-General, 27 February 1991.

[129] Byrne, *El Salvador's Civil War*, 178.

part and parcel of the bargaining between the parties to strengthen their respective positions at the negotiation table. Yet, the use of surface-to-air missiles by the FMLN threatened to shift the military balance in a way that would have endangered the continuation of the peace process that rested upon the perception of a mutual stalemate.[130] Although the attacks forced the GOES to compromise in the bargaining, the maintenance of the precarious balance was key to keep the FMLN inside the peace process. On 12 December 1990, the Secretary-General met with the Permanent Representatives of Colombia, Mexico, Spain, and Venezuela under the Group of Friends formula.[131] Pérez de Cuéllar sought the assistance of the countries, especially Mexico, to exert influence on the FMLN to terminate the offensive. Since the Mexican government hosted several of the FMLN commanders, it could use this circumstance as a lever in its talks with the FMLN command. Furthermore, they should convince the US administration to hold direct talks with the FMLN. In parallel, the Friends should approach the GOES to go along with that initiative. For example, Venezuela directly approached parties in El Salvador and expressed concern over the stalemate, while it urged representatives of the FMLN to engage in serious negotiations.[132] By the end of 1990, Pérez de Cuéllar noted in his report to the SC that 'considerable problems have been encountered in reaching agreement on armed forces, the most sensitive and complex issue on the agenda'.[133]

The setting of negotiations turned out to be extremely difficult since the primary concern of the Salvadoran government was the cessation of armed conflict while the FMLN aimed at achieving comprehensive political rights in El Salvador. Consequently, FMLN leaders had only a very limited number of bargaining chips at their disposal, namely the agreement upon a ceasefire with the government and the eventual demobilization of FMLN forces. The lack of progress resulted into the strengthening of the role of the Secretary-General's personal representative, though

---

[130] This constituted a repeated concern throughout the peace process; see, for example, Javier Pérez de Cuéllar Papers, Nota confidencial sobre la reunión de Secretario General con los Representantes Permanentes de Colombia, España, Mexico y Venezuela, 12 December 1990; see also Javier Pérez de Cuéllar Papers, Strictly confidential notes of the Secretary-General's meeting with the President of the United States, 9 May 1991.

[131] See Javier Pérez de Cuéllar Papers, Nota confidencial sobre la reunión de Secretario General con los Representantes Permanentes de Colombia, España, Mexico and Venezuela, 12 December 1990.

[132] See Tricia Juhn, *Negotiating Peace in El Salvador: Civil–Military Relations and the Conspiracy to End the War* (London: Macmillan, 1998), 79.

[133] UN Doc S/22031, 21 December 1990, para 4.

improvements on the process at that stage had only limited effects on the substance of negotiations. It had been clear from the beginning that the greatest obstacle to the successful conclusion of negotiations would be an agreement on El Salvador's armed forces, with the question of their 'purification' (*depuración*) as the most contentious issue. There seemed to prevail a clear understanding that this problem could only be solved with the support of the United States.[134] In this regard, the level of US military aid would be a defining pattern of the negotiations. It constituted the key lever that decided upon El Salvador's degree of cooperation at the negotiation table.

In early 1991, the US administration restored military aid after the FMLN had downed a helicopter with surface-to-air missiles, killing three US servicemen on board. The restoration of aid changed the calculus on the FMLN side.[135] In response to the altered strategic balance, FMLN commanders presented an initiative to accelerate negotiations.[136] In deviation from the Caracas Accords, they proposed to intensify efforts to reach agreement on armed forces, constitutional reforms, and a ceasefire by the end of April. Negotiations on the details of judicial and electoral reforms as well as economic and social reforms should be dealt with after the commencement of the ceasefire. Negotiations towards constitutional reform received additional momentum through the provisions of Article 248 for amending the Salvadoran Constitution. Any amendments had to be endorsed by two consecutive legislatures. Given the fact that the outgoing Legislative Assembly concluded its term on 30 April 1991 and the GOES did not want to change the provisions of Article 248, this date constituted a self-imposed deadline upon the negotiations.[137] As Alvaro de Soto observed in a note to the Secretary-General: 'The combination of the simplification of the agenda, together with simultaneous consideration of intricately linked issues, and the approach of the first real deadline of the negotiation...provide an opportunity for a major breakthrough.'[138]

At the same time, the US administration appeared to set another deadline by increasing public pressure on the Secretary-General's personal

---

[134] See Javier Pérez de Cuéllar Papers, Note for the Secretary-General, 6 September 1990.

[135] See Karl, 'El Salvador's Negotiated Revolution', 156.

[136] See Javier Pérez de Cuéllar Papers, Iniciativa del FMLN para accelerar las negociacón, 16 March 1991.

[137] Failure to reach agreement by that date would have postponed reforms until 1994, at the end of the legislature.

[138] Javier Pérez de Cuéllar Papers, Strictly confidential note to the Secretary-General, 22 March 1991.

representative. In February 1991, the *New York Times* published an article that quoted several anonymous sources within the US administration that expressed strong criticism at the UN's performance in the peacemaking process.[139] There seemed to exist a deliberate attempt from various quarters inside the US administration to question the impartiality of the Secretary-General's personal representative who allegedly tilted towards the FMLN.[140] In a parallel move, US Secretary of State James Baker had contacted the foreign ministers of countries comprising the Group of Friends and requested that they should approach the Secretary-General and his personal representative 'to urge them to redouble their efforts to achieve an immediate cease-fire'.[141] Such contacts were indicative of how the US administration sought to influence the good offices of the UN Secretariat via the Friends mechanism. As those calls stood diametrically opposed to the Geneva and Caracas Accords, de Soto concluded in his note to the Secretary-General on 13 February 1991 that '[w]e cannot rule out the hypothesis that the true target is not the mediator but rather the very idea of a negotiated political solution, or in any case a negotiated political solution at this time.'[142] It is however important to analyse and weigh de Soto's assessment in the wider perspective of the difficult US–UN relationship. At the heart of the problem was the fact that some quarters in the US administration considered the role of the UN representative much more instrumental for pursuing US foreign-policy objectives rather than leaving him the space to fulfil his role as impartial intermediary between the parties. The hypothesis of a deliberate attempt to undermine the peace process appears unlikely against the background of Washington's strong interest for 'a graceful exit from the region's wars'.[143] The UN personal representative therefore had to deal with incidents of 'robust US diplomacy' that aimed at dictating the terms of exit. In consequence, the more vulnerable de Soto became to US concerns, the more attractive the Group of Friends became to strengthen his role vis-à-vis the SC and the United States in particular.

In preparation of the new round of negotiations on constitutional amendments, the Secretary-General requested the Group of Friends, in particular Mexico and Spain, to approach the FMLN, the GOES, and the

---

[139] See *New York Times*, 1 February 1991, A3.

[140] See Javier Pérez de Cuéllar Papers, Strictly confidential note to the Secretary-General, 13 February 1991.

[141] The letter is quoted in ibid.

[142] Ibid.

[143] Arnson, 'Introduction', 12.

US administration. The special relations of the Mexican government to the FMLN and the GOES had made it to the 'preferred friend' (*amigo preferido*) of the Secretariat.[144] For this purpose, de Soto provided the Friends with detailed non-papers comprising key points they might discuss with the parties. Approaching the two sides was also crucial to avoid the perception of any bias on the side of the Secretary-General or the Group of Friends. As President Cristiani warned the Secretary-General in a letter concerning constitutional reforms: 'Any attitude of the intermediary which could be interpreted as an inclination in favour of one of the parties, particularly if it was transferred to the group of friends of the Secretary-General, would be an obstacle to progress towards the peace agreement we desire.'[145] The Friends were also asked to undertake *démarches* with the United States to encourage direct talks with the FMLN and to urge the government to suspend military aid to the Salvadoran armed forces in order to achieve concessions at the negotiation table.[146] In parallel, the Friends also received requests by the US Permanent Mission to the UN to discourage the FMLN from launching another military operation in the country.[147] The rounds of negotiations in Mexico illustrated the great value of the Friends mechanism to support the good offices of the Secretary-General and his personal representative. Throughout the meetings, the personal representative kept the Ambassadors of the three Friends and the representative from the Mexican Chancellery fully informed and requested their support on demand. Those representatives maintained contact and closely interacted with the respective missions at UN Headquarters in New York. The versatility of the Group of Friends constituted one of the significant assets of the Friends mechanism.

The Mexico Agreements, signed on 27 April 1991, provided for reforms of the judicial and electoral systems as well as the creation of a national civil police force under civilian control.[148] The US administration had assured the FMLN that 'it was prepared to provide training for a new civilian police force to assist with national reconstruction'.[149] At the

---

[144] Javier Pérez de Cuéllar Papers, Nota confidencial sobre la reunión de Secretario General con el Secretario de Relaciones Exteriores de Mexico, 28 March 1991.

[145] 'Letter dated 19 April 1991 from President Cristiani to the Secretary-General concerning constitutional reforms', in *The United Nations and El Salvador, 1990–1995*, 140.

[146] In December 1990, the FMLN envoy to the UN had formally requested the US Permanent Representative to engage in direct talks with the movement, see Juhn, *Negotiating Peace in El Salvador*, 79.

[147] See Javier Pérez de Cuéllar Papers, Confidential notes of the Secretary-General's meeting with the Permanent Representative of the United States of America, 24 April 1991, Annex C.

[148] See UN Doc A/46/553–S/23130, 9 October 1991, para I.1.

[149] Hampson, 'The Pursuit of Human Rights: The United Nations in El Salvador', 76.

same time, the FMLN demanded the inclusion of its former combatants in the new force. The agreement also established a Commission on the Truth 'to create confidence in the positive changes which the peace process is promoting and to assist the transition to national reconciliation'.[150] The question of armed forces could not be settled and became the 'Gordian knot' that had to be untied in subsequent negotiations. The agreement was badly received by the extreme right in El Salvador, a circumstance that effectively limited President Cristiani's room for manceuvre for further concessions without achieving a formula on the ceasefire and the demobilization of the FMLN forces. The National Assembly adopted the changes, which affected thirty-five of 274 articles, on 29 April 1991, confirmed by the subsequent Assembly. In retrospect, given the domestic opposition, the Salvadoran President himself considered the agreements as the 'most important' and 'most difficult' part of the process, with the remaining part being woodwork (*carpinteria*).[151] Representatives of the FMLN shared this perception.[152]

However, external support by the Friends would be crucial to strengthen the position of the Salvadoran president vis-à-vis the domestic opposition, as the UN Secretary-General stressed in a meeting with the Permanent Representatives of Colombia, Mexico, Spain, and Venezuela on 3 May 1991.[153] At this stage, emphasis should be put on the careful preparation of the upcoming negotiations rather than the quick fix of an agreement. Pérez de Cuéllar considered the establishment of direct and continuous contacts between the US administration and the FMLN of utmost importance. The very reason that the Secretary-General emphasized that he did not have the impression the Friends constituted 'a parallel channel or a separate instance' which might undermine the process, may hint at some reservations about the Secretariat's ability to control the group.[154] In an earlier note reviewing the state of the process before the agreement, de Soto had advised the Secretary-General that, besides Mexico and Spain, '[t]he role of the other 'friends' should be carefully considered.'[155] This reflected in particular the concern of the personal representative to keep in control of the peace process, and it illustrated his understanding that, in case of failure, it was

---

[150] See UN Doc A/46/553–S/23130, 9 October 1991, para IV.
[151] Yale–UN Oral History Project Transcripts, Alfredo Cristiani, 25 July 1997.
[152] See Karl, 'El Salvador's Negotiated Revolution', 157.
[153] See the Secretary-General's talking points, drafted by Alvaro de Soto; Javier Pérez de Cuéllar Papers, Estrictamente confidencial, 2 May 1991.
[154] Ibid.
[155] Javier Pérez de Cuéllar Papers, Strictly confidential note to the Secretary-General, 22 March 1991.

the UN that would be blamed. Furthermore, preparation talks for the upcoming round of negotiations revealed once again the concern of FMLN leaders vis-à-vis the SC. With regard to the question of the verification of agreements by the UN, the FMLN made clear that 'it will not simply give *carte blanche* to the Security Council to impose whatever provisions it might decide to make'.[156] The controlled dynamics between the Friends, Secretary-General/personal representative, and the SC remained therefore contingent upon the progress of the peace process.

The SC welcomed the Mexico Agreements in its Resolution 693.[157] While the resolution commended the good offices of the Secretary-General and his personal representative, it also reflected attempts by the United Kingdom and the United States to press the FMLN for the early conclusion of a ceasefire. The two permanent members had suggested the inclusion of a preambular paragraph that called upon both parties to exercise restraint in order to avoid any escalation of violence and to facilitate the conclusion of an agreement. As this provision would have run counter to the principles of the Geneva and Caracas Accords, the Secretariat together with the Group of Friends had sought to counterbalance those efforts by placing them into the wider context of ONUSAL's mandate.[158] The United States furthermore had intended to establish the mission for a period of six months, subject to review by the SC in order to retain maximum control. Instead, de Soto had suggested the establishment of ONUSAL for an initial period of one year, which eventually found the acceptance of the Council as a whole.[159] At the heart of the problem was the continued concern at the highest levels of the US administration about de Soto's alleged tilt towards the FMLN, as evolved during a meeting in the Oval Office between President Bush, Secretary of State Baker, National Security Adviser Scowcroft, and Secretary-General Pérez de Cuéllar.[160]

Despite the careful preparation of the three subsequent rounds of talks, negotiations on a political agreement on the armed forces in May and June

---

[156] Javier Pérez de Cuéllar Papers, Strictly confidential note to the Secretary-General, 20 May 1991.

[157] See UN Doc S/RES/693, 20 May 1991.

[158] See Javier Pérez de Cuéllar Papers, Confidential: Security Council Consultations—El Salvador, 3 May 1991; in its final version, preambular paragraph 7 of SC Resolution 693 points to the importance of restraining the use of force 'to ensure the security of all United Nations-employed personnel'.

[159] See UN Doc S/RES/693, 20 May 1991, op. 3.

[160] See Javier Pérez de Cuéllar Papers, Strictly confidential notes of the Secretary-General's meeting with the President of the United States, 9 May 1991.

1991 did not produce any tangible results, which the personal representative described as 'difficult and frustrating'.[161] FMLN representatives continuously expanded the agenda of salient points that needed to be further negotiated, whereby the GOES seemed to gamble that after President Cristiani's pending visit to Washington, the suspension of military aid would be terminated, which would have altered the strategic balance at the negotiation table again. However, Aronson had given assurance to de Soto that the question of military aid would remain in limbo in order to maintain the pressure on both sides.[162]

The stalemate of the process reflected the 'intrinsic difficulties' of the negotiation framework that was still based on two phases. The conclusion of the ceasefire remained the principal salient issue. The most sensitive problem constituted the claim by the FMLN to retain its military capability during the ceasefire as a safeguard to ensure that subsequent negotiations on core issues would address the main concerns. While there was a growing sense of uneasiness within the Salvadoran government to make concessions without achieving the primary goal, that is, the demobilization of the FMLN, the movement itself felt not to be in the position to accept a ceasefire unless there was agreement on military reform and guarantees related to the safety of FMLN members.[163] The parallel monthly talks that Under-Secretary-General for Special Political Affairs, Marrack Goulding, conducted on the conclusion of a ceasefire, did not therefore reflect the political reality of the peace process. It constituted an attempt 'to deflect Washington's pressure on the UN'.[164] As Goulding has underlined: 'My task was to maintain the pretence of a real cease-fire negotiation while de Soto strove to bring the parties to agreement on the issues which had caused the conflict—the role and size of the armed forces, the quality of policing and justice, the electoral system, access to land.'[165]

In an attempt to break the logjam and to take over the negotiations, on 7 July, Venezuelan President Carlos Andrés Pérez held a meeting in Caracas on behalf of the Friends of the Secretary-General with two members of the FMLN and three representatives of the GOES to finalize an agreement between the parties. According to then Venezuelan Permanent Representative to the UN, Diego Arria, the intervention originated in the perception that the UN-led effort lacked impartiality, tilting towards the

---

[161] Javier Pérez de Cuéllar Papers, Strictly confidential, 8 June 1991.
[162] Ibid.
[163] See Javier Pérez de Cuéllar Papers, Estrictamente confidencial: memorandum al Secretario General, 26 June 1991.
[164] Goulding, *Peacemonger*, 229.
[165] Ibid.

FMLN position. The one-sided pushing of the GOES might eventually 'derail the process'.[166] Neither the representatives of Colombia, Mexico, and Spain nor the UN Secretariat had been informed about this initiative, which had apparently been encouraged by President Cristiani, with the support of the US administration. Both had frequently expressed impatience about the inability of the UN to impose a ceasefire upon the FMLN by using the Friends mechanism. The attempt failed as the FMLN declined to leave the framework as set out in the Geneva Agreement and to negotiate in the absence of the Secretary-General's personal representative. President Pérez' move seemed to confirm earlier concerns of the personal representative that it might be difficult to maintain control over the group as a whole. It clearly demonstrated the limits of the Friends mechanism to act as a device at the exclusive request of the Secretary-General. The fading- out of national considerations is hard to maintain in the long run.

The immediate impact of the initiative was that the dealings of the Secretariat with the Group as a whole turned out to be much more guarded in terms of communication and exchange of documents.[167] Although the Presidents of Colombia, Mexico, Spain, and Venezuela later delivered a joint statement at the Ibero-American Summit in support of the peace process and in particular of the good offices of the Secretary-General,[168] the undercurrent of distrust remained. Seen from the UN Secretariat's perspective, the value of the informal mechanism seemed to fade with its formalization in 1991. Formalization meant in this context, according to Alvaro de Soto, that the personal representative started to meet the Group of Friends jointly in order to save time and to facilitate coordination.[169] In fact, it also constituted a safeguard to keep in control of the peace process. Although it is certainly an accurate statement that 'the informality of the Friends process allowed the mediators to expand or diminish their role as called for by the dynamics of a particular period in

---

[166] Yale–UN Oral History Interview Transcripts, Diego Arria, 5 September 1997.

[167] The question of access to documents evolved during the Guadalajara Summit from 17 to 20 July, when the Friends had demanded full information about the Secretary-General's talks with the parties. At that stage, Pérez de Cuéllar stressed the point that the countries were Friends of the Secretary-General, which implied that they had agreed to assist his efforts. He was therefore not the Secretary of the Friends. The countries were rather like-minded states in support of his good-offices functions; see Javier Pérez de Cuéllar Papers, Nota para el archivo, 12 August 1991.

[168] The joint statement of the Friends is mentioned in the report of the Secretary-General on the situation in Central America; see UN Doc A/46/713–S/23256, 2 December 1991.

[169] See de Soto, 'Ending Violent Conflict in El Salvador', 369.

the negotiations',[170] empirical evidence, as outlined earlier, suggests that the mechanism, comprising representatives of sovereign UN member states, also developed a life of its own which complicated peacemaking efforts under UN auspices. As de Soto has rightly observed:

If a government is spending diplomatic capital in assisting a peacemaking effort, it is unrealistic to ask it to do so indefinitely. Pressure to be in the picture increases as results begin to appear. In their messages to their national legislatures, in their campaigns for reelection, or in their speeches before the UN General Assembly, not unreasonably, leaders will be tempted to take credit for the role they are playing in support of a noble cause, particularly if it is bearing fruit.[171]

Those limits of the Friends mechanism have to be taken into account when drafting a strategy that draws upon the mobilization of international support from like-minded UN member states. Like-mindedness of sovereign states tends to have a relatively short half-life.

By August 1991, it was clear that the Democrats had secured a majority in the US Congress to cut military aid and to impose strict political conditions on any further assistance, which sent a signal to both the Salvadoran government as well as the Bush administration that the time had come to strike a final deal. The international pressure increased when the United States and the Soviet Union issued a joint letter by their Presidents that supported the peace process and demanded the direct involvement of the Secretary-General in the talks with the active support of the Group of Friends.[172] The letter came in response after the Secretary-General had sent them a number of proposals on how the governments could assist the UN to break the logjam. Looked at from the perspective of El Salvador's domestic opposition, the letter seemed however to be more important as a reassurance for the United States that the Soviet Union would not intervene. This reassurance was considered to be crucial to press the armed forces and President Cristiani to the conclusion of a final agreement.[173]

In September 1991, following earlier consultations at the first Ibero-American Summit with the GOES, the FMLN command, and the Presidents of Colombia, Mexico, Spain, and Venezuela that concluded with an agreement in principle, parties formally agreed at UN Headquarters in New York to compress the agenda into a single phase.[174] All substantive

---

[170] LeVine, 'Peacemaking in El Salvador', 249.
[171] De Soto, 'Ending Violent Conflict in El Salvador', 369.
[172] See UN Doc S/22947, 15 August 1991.
[173] Yale–UN Oral History Interview Transcripts, Ruben Zamora, 24 July 1997.
[174] See UN Doc A/46/502–S/23082, 26 September 1991; see also UN Doc A/46/502/Add.1–S/23082/Add.1, 7 October 1991.

questions would be dealt with before the commencement of the ceasefire. The meeting convened at the highest political level under participation of the Secretary-General, the High Command of the FMLN, and President Cristiani.[175] Negotiations in New York originated in a new proposal that the FMLN had presented in early summer, suggesting that all substantive issues should be settled in one single stage.[176] The future of the two military structures was considered the key problem to be solved. Although the FMLN favoured the dissolution of both structures, it left the option open for a profound reform of the Salvadoran armed forces, if dissolution was not politically viable. De Soto had personally conveyed the new proposal to President Cristiani and Assistant Secretary of State Aronson respectively. While Cristiani did not reject the proposal outright, he expressed reservations regarding the suggested participation of FMLN members in the armed forces and the political activities of the movement during the ceasefire. Aronson equally supported the new framework, as it suggested accelerating negotiations towards a final agreement. In a further step, the FMLN had approached the Group of Friends to support the new proposal and to convince the GOES to continue negotiations based upon the altered framework.

The compression of the negotiations in one phase had the advantage of dealing with a specified number of salient points at the same time, including the ceasefire, thereby preventing the subsequent introduction of additional demands on the agenda by the FMLN. In addition, the New York Agreement established a National Commission for the Consolidation of Peace (COPAZ), a mechanism that should monitor the implementation of the political agreements reached between the parties by drafting legislation once the ceasefire had started. The establishment of such a Commission had been suggested by Spain during a meeting between de Soto and the Permanent Representatives of the Friends on 5 September. It would aim at assisting the President to guarantee the pre-eminence of the civilian over the military power during the transition period.[177] The question of the integration of FMLN combatants in the

---

[175] See 'Letter dated 27 August 1991 from the Secretary-General to President Cristiani concerning consultations to be held at United Nations Headquarters on 16 and 17 September', in *The United Nations and El Salvador, 1990–1995*, 145 *et seq*. In fact, negotiations had to be extended until 25 September.

[176] See Javier Pérez de Cuéllar Papers, Estrictamente confidencial: Ayuda Memoria—El Salvador, Anexo, July 1991.

[177] See Javier Pérez de Cuéllar Papers, Estrictamente confidencial: nota para el archivo, 5 September 1991. Blanca Antonini of the UN Secretariat, who participated in the talks, under-

Salvadoran armed forces was settled by permitting them to participate in the national civilian police force. In support of the peace process and to keep up the momentum, the SC welcomed the New York Agreement of 25 September 1991 in Resolution 714 and urged the parties 'to reach at the earliest possible date a ceasefire and a peaceful settlement to the armed conflict'.[178] Furthermore, the Council appreciated 'the contributions of the Governments of the Group of Friends of the Secretary-General—Colombia, Mexico, Spain, and Venezuela—which have advanced the peace process in El Salvador'. This was the first time that the Friends appeared in an official document of the UN. Several rounds of negotiations from October to December sought to solve the outstanding issues. The announcement of the FMLN to suspend indefinitely military operations and the confirmation of the GOES to implement the constitutional reforms provided the mutual assurance to continue the process. However, in early December, the Secretary-General still expressed his concerns that '[t]here continue to be in El Salvador groups which, though increasingly isolated, are extremely strident in their opposition to the negotiation process, and which persist in issuing threatening statements against all whom they perceive as supporting it'.[179]

With Pérez de Cuéllar's term of office concluding, the GOES and the FMLN were pushed by the Group of Friends, the United States, and the Soviet Union to close a final deal. In close consultations with the Friends, the Secretary-General suggested continuing negotiations at UN Headquarters in New York from 16 December onwards. Salient issues on the agenda included provisions related to the civil police, the reduction of the army, socio-economic questions, and the ceasefire.[180] In order to prepare the final stage, de Soto requested the four Friends to convey three messages to Cristiani: firstly, that the Salvadoran President should come to New York; secondly, that he should present before the Secretary-General the plan for the reduction of the armed forces; and thirdly, that he should appoint, in consultation with the future members of COPAZ, the coordinator of the national police. In addition, the person in charge might also attend the talks to facilitate an agreement on the police forces.[181]

---

lines the key role of the Group of Friends in the successful conclusion of the New York agreement in September 1991; see Interview with Blanca Antonini, New York, 23 October 2002.

[178] See UN Doc S/RES/714, 30 September 1991, op. 4.
[179] UN Doc A/46/713–S/23256, 2 December 1991, para 15.
[180] See Tommie Sue Montgomery, *Revolution in El Salvador*, 225.
[181] Javier Pérez de Cuéllar Papers, Note for the Secretary-General, 7 December 1991.

In a last minute attempt to break the logjam, on 26 December, Pérez de Cuéllar invited Cristiani to participate in the final stage of the negotiations in New York, underlining that 'all efforts [had] been exhausted'.[182] Cristiani had faced considerable pressure from the Friends, the United States, the European Community, and the Church, both in San Salvador and in Rome, to follow this invitation.[183] At the same time, the direct talks between the FMLN and the US administration signalled to the GOES that leaving the negotiation table was not a politically viable option.[184]

The crucial importance of the four-plus-one mechanism came especially to the fore at the most critical stage of the negotiations in the final week of Secretary-General Pérez de Cuéllar's tenure. The pending departure constituted the final deadline and generated a pressure-cooker atmosphere that created the crucial momentum to strike the final deal. Parallel to ongoing negotiations at UN Headquarters, the Friends arranged separate meetings with President Cristiani and FMLN commanders without the participation of the UN intermediary to generate momentum for the conclusion of the final agreement.[185] The United States sent a high-level delegation to UN Headquarters offering political and financial support for the implementation of the agreement if the GOES would be prepared to reduce the Salvadoran armed forces.[186] Meetings took place either at President Cristiani's hotel residence, FMLN residences, or at the Permanent Missions of Mexico and Venezuela, with representatives of the US administration participating. Furthermore, in a joint effort, the four Friends, together with the Permanent Representative of the United States as well as the US Assistant Secretary for Inter-American Affairs, convened an emergency meeting with the Secretary-General, the Under-Secretary-General for Special Political Affairs, and the personal representative, urgently pressing for the Secretary-General's continued presence and the continuation of negotiations.[187] According to Jorge Montaño, the four-plus-one openly threatened to hold a press conference, exposing the Secretary-General in public and making him

---

[182] Letter dated 26 December 1991 from the Secretary-General to President Cristiani inviting the latter to UN Headquarters for negotiations, in *The UN and El Salvador, 1990–1995*, 186 et seq.

[183] See Juhn, *Negotiating Peace in El Salvador*, 117.

[184] Ibid., 118.

[185] See Yale–UN Oral History Interview Transcripts, Diego Arria, 5 September 1997; Yale–UN Oral History Interview Transcripts, Jorge Montaño, 1 October 1999.

[186] Juhn, *Negotiating Peace in El Salvador*, 119.

[187] This is confirmed by the Permanent Representatives of Spain and Venezuela as well as the US Assistant Secretary for Inter-American Affairs in separate interviews; see Yale–UN Oral History Interview Transcripts, Bernard Aronson, 9 October 1997; Yale–UN Oral History Inter-

responsible for the failure of the peace process, if he did not stay personally involved in the talks. Such robust diplomacy reflected the understanding that the success or failure of the negotiations depended on the Secretary-General's authority as he brought legitimacy to the process. It also reflected the concern that the priorities of the Organization would change under the leadership of his successor, Boutros Boutros-Ghali. Consequently, support by the four-plus-one countries, including their direct participation in the negotiations, was critical to push the parties to a final agreement, with the UN as the formal intermediary and informal mediator that provided legitimacy under the authority of the Secretary-General.

At midnight, the Act of New York completed negotiations on all substantive as well as the technical and military aspects of the ceasefire. The SC welcomed the New York Act in a Presidential Statement, adopted on 3 January 1992, commending the good offices of the Secretary-General and his personal representative, including the assistance of the four Friends within this process.[188] Procedures for the demobilization of the FMLN and the implementation of the agreements would be finalized in early January. The Peace Agreement was signed on 16 January 1992 at Chapultepec in Mexico, with a formal ceasefire between the GOES and the FMLN coming into effect on 1 February, and the armed conflict formally ending on 31 October 1992. Given the problems with the implementation of the peace agreement, as outlined later, the ceremony to mark the cessation of armed conflict would be held six weeks later on 15 December.[189]

At the centre of the accord was the calendar of implementation that linked the demobilization of the FMLN to reform steps taken by the GOES.[190] As David Moreno has observed, '[t]he gradual timetable was designed to build trust among the parties and permit phased implementation of other provisions.'[191] The agreements comprised, firstly, the purification, reform, and reduction of the armed forces of El Salvador to roughly 30,000; secondly, the establishment of a new national police; thirdly,

---

view Transcripts, Diego Arria, 5 September 1997; Yale–UN Oral History Interview Transcripts, Jorge Montaño, 1 October 1999.

[188] See UN Doc S/23360, 3 January 1992.

[189] For the first time, the four-plus-one-countries would issue a joint statement on this occasion 'to demonstrate their full support for the Agreements' and to express their commitment 'to assist the Secretary-General and Salvadorian institutions and political and social forces in their efforts to ensure that the Salvadorian Peace Agreements are fully implemented'; see UN Doc A/47/842–S/25007, 23 December 1992.

[190] See timetable for implementation in 1992, Table 5.

[191] Moreno, *The Struggle for Peace in Central America*, 145.

guarantees for the FMLN to participate in the elections; fourthly, the establishment of new institutions such as COPAZ or the Institute of Agrarian Reform as well as the Truth Commission. The distrust between the parties would lead to major problems in the implementation phase of the agreements. The GOES failed to implement the disbanding of the military police and to start the training of the new civilian police force on time, while some FMLN leaders failed to demobilize, maintaining some capacity to resume war.[192]

In close cooperation between the parties, the UN Secretariat, and the four-plus-one countries, the timetable for the implementation of the peace agreement had to be rescheduled in June and again in October 1992. It amended provisions for the concentration of armed forces of both sides at designated locations, the reintegration of former FMLN combatants into civilian life, and the abolition of the National Guard and the Treasury Police, which was to be replaced by the new National Civil Police. The timetable also amended terms and conditions for the transfer of land to

Table 5. New York Act I, Timetable for 1992

January	16	Signing of formal accords.
	24	Legal incorporation of COPAZ.
	25	Military to provide ONUSAL with complete arms and troops inventory.
February	1	D-Day: formal ceasefire starts; end of forced conscription; tabling of legislation to guarantee security of FMLN, COPAZ and other commissions; start of transfer of farms over 245 hectares.
	7	FMLN to start demobilization.
	16	Designation of Supreme Electoral Court.
	18	Deadline for FMLN inventory of land holdings in regions under its control.
March	2	Dissolution of Guardia Nacional and Policía de Hacienda; creation of state intelligence departments to replace DNI (to be dissolved by 15 June); designation of human rights ombudsman.
	31	Start of submission of land requests by veterans of both armies.
May	1	Start of demobilization and re-incorporation into civilian life of FMLN troops, to proceed at a monthly rate of at least twenty percent of fighters.
	16	Installation of Ad Hoc Commission to review records of military officers and recommend removal of human rights violators.
	31	Deadline for reform of electoral system.
June	30	Deadline for dissolution of all paramilitary defence units.
July	14	Legalisation of ownership of land in zones of conflict.
	17	Start of demobilization of army's five elite battalions.
October	13	Start of purge from armed forces of human rights violators.
	31	End of FMLN demobilization.
December	7	End of army's elite battalion demobilization.

Source: Dunkerley (1994), 73.

[192] See Goulding, *Peacemonger*, 239.

former combatants of both sides.[193] The SC supported this process by expressing public concern and urging the parties to comply with the provisions of the peace agreement.[194]

Another serious flaw concerned the lack of provisions related to the financing of the land distribution programme. Since horizontal inequalities regarding access to land had constituted one of the root causes of conflict, the conclusion of the New York Act was only the first step towards the consolidation of peace, which made a continued UN involvement indispensable, as Fen Osler Hampton has stressed: 'Once a settlement was reached, the UN's role in the peace process became even more important.'[195] With the deadline pending, the accords left many of the root causes of the conflict unsettled, in particular with reference to questions of poverty and social inequalities. Furthermore, the lack of transparency and coordination within the larger UN system, that is, between the International Monetary Fund (IMF), the World Bank, and the UN Secretariat, was a serious impediment during the implementation process.[196]

The rationale of the Group of Friends shifted accordingly. Now, the Friends mechanism primarily constituted a means to secure informal influence on SC decision-making, without being formally represented on the SC. Given its versatility that allows accommodating multiple functions at different stages of conflict, the rationale of the informal group shifted from a balancer towards an agenda setter of the Council. With the conclusion of the agreement, the perceived competition between Council and Friends had ceased to exist. The Friends continued to meet with both parties serving as a very important focal point for discussing and following up problems related to the implementation of the peace agreement. As has been pointed out earlier, forming a Group of Friends should ideally constitute a long-term commitment, since most peace agreements are prone to failure soon after they have been concluded.[197] The continued commitment of like-minded countries in the implementation of peace agreements is of utmost importance.[198]

In a sense, the Friends mechanism took over that role of the SC, which was often pronounced in resolutions following up the agreement, that is,

---

[193] See UN Doc S/23999/Add. 1, 19 June 1992 and UN Doc S/24688, 19 October 1992.
[194] See UN Doc S/24058, 3 June 1992.
[195] Hampson, 'The Pursuit of Human Rights: The United Nations in El Salvador', 96.
[196] See Alvaro de Soto and Graciana del Castillo, 'Obstacles to Peacebuilding', *Foreign Policy*, 94/1 (1994), 69–83.
[197] Given the multiplicity of factors (e.g. election campaigns, change of governments, budget constraints) that make the long-term commitment of like-minded countries difficult, continued engagement is not self-evident.
[198] See Stedman, 'Introduction', in *Ending Civil Wars*, 1–40.

to remain seized of the matter.[199] For this purpose, the Group of Friends received regular briefings by the UN Secretariat on the political situation on the ground. During the implementation phase, the Friends drafted virtually all SC resolutions and Presidential Statements that would be necessary in response to regular reports by the Secretary-General on El Salvador.[200] As the Friends mechanism was considered a kind of expert group that had been involved in the peace process from the very beginning, the SC did not perceive the informal group as acting in competition to the body.

Although the importance of the Group of Friends decreased with the subsequent implementation of the agreements, the mechanism did not cease to exist, even ten years after the signing of the peace agreement in Chapultepec. The collective efforts of the UN system, the continued engagement of the Friends, and the crucial support of the United States contributed to the largely successful transformation of El Salvador.

6.3 Conclusion: Exit, Voice, and Loyalty

This case study has illustrated the role and performance of the Group of Friends of the Secretary-General in settling the civil war in El Salvador. While the formation of the Western Contact Group in the case of Namibia could best be explained as part of an exit strategy, voice constituted the overarching rationale of the Friends mechanism. Although the Salvadoran case has often been referred to as a 'model' that illustrates the potential of the Group of Friends in UN-led negotiations, it also demonstrates its limits. The versatility of the informal device allowed the accommodation of several 'models' with mutually excludive functions, as this case study has shown.

The question of whether the Friends mechanism may serve as a model applicable to other crisis situations is therefore not entirely accurate. Instead of generally assuming that forming a Group of Friends contributes somehow to conflict resolution, it is of greater benefit to examine the diverse interests and perceptions that contribute to the formation and define the role and performance of the informal grouping. The greater the awareness of the multiple functions of the Group of Friends the better

---

[199] See, for example, UN Doc S/RES/784, 30 October 1992 and UN Doc S/RES/791, 30 November 1992.

[200] See Yale–UN Oral History Interview Transcripts, Manuel Tello and Gustavo Albin, 6 August 1997; also Yale–UN Oral History Interview Transcripts, Diego Arria, 5 September 1997.

the results in applying certain elements of the device to other conflict settings. This section summarizes the dynamics of exit, voice, and loyalty in the resolution of conflict in El Salvador.

6.3.1 *Parallelism of Exit and Voice*

The parallelism of exit and voice constituted a key pattern of the adaptation process of the UN to cope with the old and new challenges of the post-bipolar world. Both options proliferated in response to systemic change. They are flexible instruments to deal individually with specific conflict settings. While the voice option fosters conflict resolution with the strong engagement of the UN Secretariat assisted by UN member states, the exit option reflects an approach that is primarily driven by UN member states with the UN Secretariat playing a supportive role. The different approaches to deal with civil wars in Cambodia and El Salvador are indicative of this development.

6.3.2 *Voice as Amplifier*

Choosing the voice option, as epitomized in the Group of Friends of the Secretary-General on El Salvador, amplified the leverage of the UN intermediary in the negotiations with the parties to the conflict. As the UN Secretary-General himself cannot display any substantial leverage of his own, the assistance of like-minded governments is instrumental to keep the parties to the conflict engaged throughout the process. At the same time, countries participating in the Friends mechanism also amplify their leverage as they become part and parcel of the Secretary-General's good offices that bears the seal of UN legitimacy.

In the case of El Salvador, the UN Secretariat had to find a trade-off between generating maximum international support from governments with leverage in the process and restricting parallel initiatives by the same players. Controlling the dynamics between UN Secretariat, SC, and four-plus-one countries constituted the single most important factor that decided upon the success or failure of the Secretary-General's good offices. The Salvadoran peace process did not resemble a classic concert with the Secretary-General or his personal representative as the authoritative conductor orchestrating the players from the start to the conclusion of negotiations. The support of the Secretary-General's good offices clearly had its limits. The assistance of UN-led efforts by like-minded countries is hard to maintain in the long run, as the capability and willingness of sovereign governments to fade out national interests is restricted.

Furthermore, the notion of the United States as 'the UN's ultimate stick'[201] appears over-optimistic against the background of the strained relations between the UN Secretariat and the US administration. It also obfuscates cause and effects. Despite the US decision in early summer 1991 to keep military aid in a state of limbo, which displayed a conditioning effect at the negotiation table, this stick was not at the UN Secretariat's free disposal. In essence, the Salvadoran peace process and the Secretary-General's good offices rather resembled a jazz performance. The UN Secretariat, in cooperation with the Friends and the United States, played on a theme given by the SC. It adapted and interpreted the undercurrent theme as the process went along.

6.3.3 *Voice as Balancer*

Contrary to the process leading towards Namibian independence, the formation of the Group of Friends has to be explained in the context of the shifting balance of power between the UN Secretariat and the SC during the transformation of the bipolar system. The actual and perceived predominance of the P-5, especially of the United States, bore the danger of compromising the impartiality of the Secretary-General.

In this context, it is extremely important to distinguish between the cause and the effects of the Friends mechanism. While the grouping effectively constituted a device that lent leverage to UN intermediary efforts, the original function of providing a strategic balance to counter P-5/US predominance in the SC always remained in the background. The balancing function of the Group of Friends primarily accommodated the interest of the FMLN command to establish a political framework that would prevent potential micro-management of the Council.

Limiting the involvement of the SC to a minimum degree ultimately constituted a confidence-building measure that secured the continued participation of the FMLN at the negotiation table. The granting of voice to a group of like-minded states would strengthen the position of the Secretary-General vis-à-vis the Council and maintain his impartiality. With the pressure of the US administration growing, requesting assistance for the Secretary-General's good offices from like-minded UN member states gained greater currency in the UN Secretariat. Granting voice to a

---

[201] LeVine, 'Peacemaking in El Salvador', 252.

carefully selected group of countries with no direct stake in the outcome of the conflict reduced the Secretary-General's dependence on and vulnerability vis-à-vis the Council, including US dominance within that body.

6.3.4 Loyalty: The Group of Friends and US Hegemony

Viewed from the perspective of US foreign policy, the case of El Salvador demonstrates that 'support for multilateral negotiations can be more effective and less costly than the unilateral use of force'.[202] Despite the primary rationale of the Group of Friends to balance US preponderance inside and outside the SC, the United States adopted a very pragmatic approach by extending the Friends mechanism to an informal four-plus-one formula. Informal participation in the Group of Friends secured control over the peace process without becoming the protagonist. Choosing multilateral means with the assistance of a minilateral setting constituted the preferred strategy of the US administration for achieving its policy end of graceful exit from El Salvador.

Although the US administration sought to settle the civil war in El Salvador on its own terms, the peace process that rested firmly inside the UN framework restrained its room for manoeuvre. The joint efforts taken by the UN Secretariat, the Group of Friends, and the US administration reflected a productive mutual dependency that produced the momentum for an agreement that generated the perception of having achieved a 'peace without losers'.

---

[202] Karl, 'El Salvador's Negotiated Revolution', 164.

Foreign policy is not architecture .... In architecture, you make a plan down to the last nut, the last bolt, the last stress beam, and then you build the thing. Foreign policy, in my view, is more like jazz; it's an improvisation on a theme, and you change as you go along.[1]

Richard Holbrooke

[1] USIS (United States Investigations Services) Washington File, *Transcript: Special Kosovo Briefing By Special Envoy Holbrooke*, Washington, DC, 28 October 1998.

7
Kosovo: Quint, G-8, and Troika

The Kosovo crisis illustrates the extreme case of conducting crisis management outside the UN framework without the explicit authorization of the
Security Council (SC). The Western Alliance chose the exit option by
employing the North Atlantic Treaty Organization (NATO) because the SC
was or appeared to be deadlocked. After the failure of Contact Group efforts
from late 1997 to spring 1999 to negotiate a political settlement, the Group
of Eight (G-8) and Troika started to define the diplomatic response to the
ongoing crisis while NATO sustained the military pressure on the Milosevic
regime. The Quint provided the bridge between the political and military
tracks of conflict management. This chapter examines, in a first step, the
setting of the conflict by proceeding on two levels of analysis: firstly, the
dissolution process of former Yugoslavia in general and the crisis in the
Kosovo province in particular; secondly, governance in the SC at the time
of conflict. Analysis focuses especially on the dynamics between Contact
Group and SC in ending the war in former Yugoslavia as such interaction is
indicative of the changes in SC governance in the 1990s. In a second step,
the chapter sheds light on the resolution of the Kosovo conflict by analysing
the role and performance of the G-8, Quint, and Troika after the breakdown
of negotiations at the Rambouillet Conference in spring 1999. In this context, the rationale of these informal mechanisms as well as their relationship
to the SC is of particular concern. The chapter argues, firstly, that despite the
marginalization of the SC in the management of the crisis, the institution
continued to exert a pull on the players to seek *post hoc* legitimation of the
settlement. Loyalty mattered. The prospect of re-involving the UN constituted an important precondition for the resolution of conflict. Secondly,
ancillary to the first point, G-8 and Troika were instrumental in providing

a platform for the re-involvement of the UN. Thirdly, exiting the UN framework allowed to employ military force, which the Western Alliance considered necessary to achieve political outcomes. The retreat to informal mechanisms such as Quint, G-8, and Troika allowed merging the military and political track of conflict management that had become disconnected.

7.1 Conflict Setting

The dissolution of the Socialist Federal Republic of Yugoslavia (SFRY) has been part of a continuing transformation process of the international system that displayed a set of larger questions for the conduct of international relations. Firstly, it concerned the potential and limits of international institutions in general and the UN in particular to deal with conflict settings such as former Yugoslavia. Systemic change led to a situation where 'ill equipped and inappropriate institutions predicated on the Cold War division between East and West were clearly pitched against a multiplex problem'.[2] Secondly, the Kosovo conflict questioned the role of the SC as the primary instrument for the maintenance of international peace and security. Thirdly, and ancillary to the last point, it raised questions about the legitimacy of the threat or actual use of force to achieve policy goals. Fourthly, the dissolution process illustrated the change in the relative power of key international actors, as epitomized in the Contact Group that acted outside the framework of international institutions to manage the conflict. This section examines, firstly the setting of the conflict that re-emerged within the dissolution process of Yugoslavia. Secondly, it investigates the multiple crises the Council faced against the background of systemic change and their impact on governance in the SC. In this context, the Contact Group serves as a specific example to support the general argument.

7.1.1 Dissolution of Yugoslavia

The dissolution of the Yugoslav state originated in the failure to transform the socialist system into a democracy and a market economy. The process started prior to the breakdown of the bipolar system in the 1980s, with

---

[2] James Gow, *Triumph of the Lack of Will: International Diplomacy and the Yugoslav War* (London: Hurst & Company, 1997), 323.

economic decline and constitutional conflict as the most prominent indicators.[3] The conflict setting in Kosovo proper is defined by a complex set of parameters that comprise political, economic, and demographic factors with an external and internal dimension. Firstly, the conflict is to some extent the result of third-party interventions by external powers to impose peace settlements without achieving the policy goal of regional stability. Those interventions have raised questions about unanticipated, undesired, or even counterproductive effects of third-party engagement that perpetuates the state of conflict and instability instead of resolving it.[4] Secondly, at the domestic level, war in former Yugoslavia has been fuelled by historical myths that played an instrumental role to mobilize public support for the respective policies of regional leaders to mask their interests.[5] Thirdly, the conflict setting in Kosovo cannot be fully understood without taking into account its economic agenda.[6] This section argues that although the root causes of conflict constituted the underlying current, the escalation of the crisis followed situational rather than structural parameters.

The Kosovo province has long been considered the heartland of Serb nationalism and identity. During the middle ages, Serbs constituted the majority of Kosovars, which changed in the 500 years of the occupation by the Ottoman empire when an increasing number migrated to Croatia, Dalmatia, or Hungary.[7] Despite the repeated reference to the Kosovo province as the Serbian cradle, it has never been the heartland of the Serb people from the outset, that is, in the period from 850 until the great battle of Kosovo in 1389, when a united army under the leadership of Serb Prince Lazar confronted Ottoman troops at Kosovo Polje.[8] Serbian rulers have often misused the false assumptions, in order to support the argument of the historical importance of the territory for Serbian people, that the Turkish victory sealed the demise of the Serbian empire and resulted in the imposition of the Ottoman rule. As Noel Malcolm has

---

[3] See Susan L. Woodward, *Balkan Tragedy: Chaos and Dissolution after the Cold War* (Washington, DC: Brookings Institution, 1995), 47–81.

[4] For an elaboration of this argument, see the provocative article by Edward N. Luttwak, 'Give War a Chance', *Foreign Affairs*, 78/4 (1999), 36–51.

[5] See, for example, Laura Silber and Alan Little, *The Death of Yugoslavia*, rev. edn. (London: Penguin Books, 1996), 70–81.

[6] Despite the underdevelopment of the province, Kosovo was of strategic importance as it provided twenty per cent of the Serbian energy supply. The territory is rich in mineral resources such as nickel, zinc, lead, magnesium, and lignite; see Marie-Janine Calic, 'Kosovo in the Twentieth Century: A Historical Account', in *Kosovo and the Challenge of Humanitarian Intervention*, 26.

[7] See Tim Judah, 'Kosovo's Road to War', *Survival*, 41/2 (1999), 7.

[8] Noel Malcolm, *Kosovo: A Short History*, 2nd edn. (London: Pan Books, 2002), 41.

observed, '[t]he story of the battle of Kosovo has become a totem or talisman of Serbian identity, so that this event has a status unlike that of anything else in the history of the Serbs.'[9]

At the same time, the setting of the Kosovo conflict is embedded in the so-called Albanian question, which was brought for the first time to international attention in 1878 with the formation of the League of Prizren, comprising representatives from Albanian-inhabited districts of the region that articulated the interests and demands of the fragmented minorities under the Ottoman government.[10] With the breakdown of the Ottoman rule after the Balkan wars of 1912–13, Serbia rose to become the preponderant power of the region and occupied the Kosovo province and the western part of Macedonia. The mythic history of the Serbs would contribute to obfuscate the very nature of the Albanian–Kosovo question because it described the occupation as 'an act of liberation which rescued an oppressed people from a kind of alien, colonial rule'.[11] It virtually ignored the existence of an Albanian majority population. Repression of the Albanian majority would constitute the pattern of Serbian politics towards Kosovo for the next eight decades in order to retain control over the territory.

The London Conference of Ambassadors in May 1913 de-escalated the Balkan crisis by recognizing Albanian independence and rejecting Belgrade's demand for an Adriatic port.[12] The short-term success of the conference originated largely in the substantial cooperation and communication between Berlin and London. It is more than just an interesting footnote to recall that Kosovo's quest for independence constituted a direct result of the intervention of the Concert of Europe (Austria-Hungary, Britain, France, Germany, and Russia), including Italy, resulting in the creation of an Albanian rump state.[13] The borders of the new Albanian state were defined by a trade-off of diverging interests most visibly between Austria-Hungary on the one side and France as well as Russia on the other side. The prospect of including other Albanian-inhabited parts such

[9] Ibid., 58.

[10] By 1881, the League of Prizren had assumed full control over Kosovo and acted as the de facto government of the territory. The Ottoman government in late March 1881 crushed the League, after it had started forming an army to push for its claim of creating an Albanian state; ibid., 221–7.

[11] Ibid., 356.

[12] Albanian leaders had declared independence on 28 November 1912.

[13] The London Conference of Ambassadors of the European Concert; for the conference see Richard J. Crampton, *The Hollow Détente: Anglo–German Relations in the Balkans, 1911–1914* (London: Prior, 1980), 75–96; see also Jost Dülffer, Martin Kröger, and Rolf-Harald Wippich, *Vermiedene Kriege: Deeskalation von Konflikten der Großmächte zwischen Krimkrieg und Erstem Weltkrieg 1865–1914* (München, Germany: R. Oldenbourg Verlag, 1997), 641–55.

as Kosovo and western Macedonia had to yield to the interests of two key members of the European Concert. The conference destroyed Albanian hopes for achieving unity by ceding large parts of territory to Montenegro, Serbia, and Greece. The de-escalation of a conflict of interests between the great powers stood higher on the policy agenda than the achievement of a viable political solution for the region. In the long-term, the intervention of the past constituted the prologue for the crisis in Kosovo to which the Contact Group on former Yugoslavia (Britain, France, Germany, Russia, and the United States) would respond eighty-five years later.

The Paris Conference of 1919 that attempted to end the First World War brought about the creation of Yugoslavia comprising Serbia, including the Republic of Macedonia, and Montenegro. The new state furthermore comprised Bosnia and Herzegovina, Croatia, and Slovenia, which had formerly been entities of the Austro-Hungarian Monarchy.[14] The territory also included the province of Kosovo. During the World War II, after the German invasion of Yugoslavia in 1941, Albania, Kosovo, and western Macedonia became united under Italian tutelage. The greater Albanian state would however only last until when the SFRY was proclaimed. Then, Kosovo became a constituent of the Federal State of Serbia.

For some years of the post-war period, the Yugoslav government had imposed martial law upon the province. It would become a pattern of Yugoslav authorities to maintain control over Kosovo by suppressing Albanian insurrections and trying to alter the demographic balance of power in the territory. The deep-rooted, socio-economic problems remained unchanged until the dissolution of the Yugoslav state despite the attempts of its government to promote structural reforms in Kosovo.[15] It was not until 1968 that Tito somewhat relaxed his hard-line policy and granted Kosovo the status of an autonomous province, with substantial elements of self-government for the Kosovar Albanians.[16] By then, the province had turned into 'a Yugoslav republic in all but name'.[17]

---

[14] See Margaret MacMillan, *Peacemakers: The Paris Conference of 1919 and Its Attempt to End War* (London: John Murray, 2001), 119–33.

[15] The disparities of income between constituents with about the same population were considerable. For example, in 1989, the national income of Slovenia and Kosovo, with a population of roughly 1.9 million, totalled 36.55 million dinar in the former and 3.97 million dinar in the latter case; see Calic, 'Kosovo in the Twentieth Century'. 25.

[16] The process of amending the Yugoslav constitution commenced in 1968. The new constitution entered into force in 1974.

[17] Judah, 'Kosovo's Road to War', 8.

The political and cultural dominance of the Albanian majority in Kosovo became an issue and instrument in the 1980s that provoked Serb resistance under the guise of nationalism. Since the mid-1980s, the SFRY had been engaging in a political debate over reform of the federal constitution. Depriving Kosovo of its status as an autonomous province in 1989–90 changed the precarious balance of power among Yugoslav entities and furthered the process of disintegration and secession. The breakdown of the bipolar system resulted in another wave of self-determination. The process of dissolution forced external powers with an interest or stake in the region to think anew about the question of self-determination for the Yugoslav entities, including Kosovo.

One important reason that the question of Kosovo received less attention than other entities of former Yugoslavia was the fact that the Badinter Commission had made a formal distinction between republics and autonomous provinces as well as nations and nationalities respectively.[18] In consequence, despite Kosovo's appeal for independence in 1991, the maximum the European Union (EU) had been prepared to support was re-establishing Kosovo's autonomy.[19] Regional stability constituted the main concern of Western countries rather than the situation in Kosovo proper. In the period from 1991 to 1997, the key players displayed a 'pattern of neglect' towards the situation in the province.[20] Such neglect facilitated both the radicalization of the Kosovar Albanians as well as the Serbs, which led to a deterioration of the situation on the ground.[21] Furthermore, there was a widespread belief that a precedent of uncontained fragmentation of state entities might have had repercussions in other parts of the world such as Africa or the former Soviet Union. Such reasoning reflected tensions between fundamental principles of the international system, namely territorial

---

[18] This arbitration commission, called after its chair Robert Badinter, the president of the French Constitutional Court, dealt, *inter alia*, with questions pertaining to the legal status of the entities of the Yugoslav federation. On 29 November 1991, the Commission issued an opinion that the SFRY was in the process of dissolution; see 'Opinion No. 1 of the Arbitration Commission of the Peace Conference on Yugoslavia, 29 November 1991', in Snezana Trifunovska (ed.), *Yugoslavia through documents: From its Creation to its Dissolution* (Dordrecht, The Netherlands: Martinus Nijhoff, 1994), 415–17.

[19] Independent International Commission on Kosovo, *The Kosovo Report: Conflict, International Response, Lessons Learned* (Oxford: Oxford University Press, 2000), 58, quoted thereafter *The Kosovo Report*.

[20] Richard Caplan, 'International diplomacy and the crisis in Kosovo', *International Affairs*, 74/ 4 (1998), 747.

[21] Stefan Wolff, 'The Limits of Non-Military International Intervention: A case study of the Kosovo Conflict', in Florian Bieber and Zidas Daskalowski (eds.), *Understanding the War in Kosovo* (London: Frank Cass, 2003), 82.

unity versus self-determination.[22] While operational policy neglected the Kosovo province, in European capitals there was the prevailing sense that eventually the situation would arise when action became unavoidable.[23] With hostilities erupting in Croatia and Slovenia and the subsequent recognition of their independence, crisis management degenerated to a piecemeal approach. The International Conference on Former Yugoslavia (ICFY), established in 1992, dealt with the issue of Kosovo in the Working Group on Ethnic and National Communities, but it was removed from the agenda only one year later in order to secure the continued engagement of Milosevic in the ongoing negotiations on Bosnia. At the Dayton Peace Conference that ended the war in Bosnia and Herzegovina, the US administration rejected Milosevic's view to consider Kosovo an internal affair of the Federal Republic of Yugoslavia (FRY).[24]

However, the benevolent neglect of the issue clearly facilitated closing the final deal and its subsequent implementation. Participants in the conference underline that the inclusion of Kosovo on the agenda would have overfreighted negotiations that already had to address broad issues such as regional arms control and confidence-building measures.[25] As the hostilities in Kosovo had remained low key thus far, dealing with the question did not attain high priority. For the Kosovar Albanians, 'the effect of Dayton was little short of traumatic'.[26] As the International Independent Commission on Kosovo has rightly concluded: 'The decision to exclude the Kosovo question from the Dayton negotiations, and the lack of results achieved by the strategy of nonviolence, led many Kosovar Albanians to conclude that violence was the only way to attract international attention.'[27] After the conclusion of the Dayton Agreement, the European Union (EU) would formally recognize the FRY, with Kosovo being an autonomous province. The crisis in Kosovo re-emerged on the international agenda only in late September 1997 when violence erupted on the ground.

---

[22] See Marc Weller, 'The Rambouillet conference on Kosovo', *International Affairs*, 75/2 (1999), 213–16.

[23] This view is maintained by a senior advisor to French President Jacques Chirac; author interview, New York, 18 November 2000.

[24] See Richard Holbrooke, *To End A War* (New York: Modern Library, 1999), 234.

[25] Interview with Christian Clages, Berlin, 6 September 2000; for a useful analysis of the Dayton Accords and their implementation, see Elizabeth M. Cousens and Charles K. Cater, *Towards Peace in Bosnia: Implementing the Dayton Accords* (Boulder, CO: Lynne Rienner, 2001).

[26] See Judah, 'Kosovo's Road to War', 12. This was explicitly confirmed in the interview with a senior advisor to Jacques Chirac; author interview, New York, 18 November 2000.

[27] *The Kosovo Report*, 1.

7.1.2 *Systemic Change and Governance in the UN Security Council*

At the end of the 1990s, the SC faced the challenge of finding adequate responses to the systemic changes of the post-bipolar world and maintaining its role as the primary instrument for the maintenance of international peace and security. This 'Article 24 crisis' had essentially three dimensions.[28] Firstly, the crisis of representativeness pertained to the perception that the composition of the SC was neither geographically balanced nor did it reflect the current distribution of relative power among UN member states. Secondly, the crisis of effectiveness related to the growing mismatch in the SC between the willingness to take decisions and the allocation of resources for their implementation. Those problems had been most prominent in the cases of Srebrenica and Rwanda. Thirdly, the crisis of decision-making referred to the selectivity of the SC in addressing some conflicts while ignoring others. Especially after the failed intervention in Somalia, the Council had become increasingly reluctant to engage in conflict settings on the African continent. Exit and voice occurred in direct response to those crises, with informal group of states proliferating. Governance in the Council changed significantly, as much of the work was done within those informal frameworks, with minimal involvement of other SC members. The Contact Group on former Yugoslavia is indicative of how a group of UN member states chose the exit option while, at the same time, seeking *post hoc* legitimization of their action taken outside the UN framework. The task-sharing between informal group and Council had found little resistance at the level of the UN. From late 1997 onwards, the Contact Group would apply this model to manage the conflict in Kosovo.

EXIT AND LOYALTY: THE CONTACT GROUP ON FORMER YUGOSLAVIA, 1994–5

In April 1994, the Contact Group on former Yugoslavia—comprising France, Germany, Russia, the United Kingdom, with the United States assuming a leadership role from mid-1995 onwards—had started to define the parameters of settling the conflict in the Bosnian theatre, leading to the conclusion of the Dayton Accords. This informal setting had come into being to secure concerted and pragmatic action after efforts taken by international organizations such as the Conference on Security and Cooperation in Europe (CSCE), the EC/EU, as well as the UN had proven unsuccessful.[29]

---

[28] See Kühne and Prantl (eds.), *The Security Council and the G8 in the New Millennium*, 7–10.
[29] See Boidevaix, *Une Diplomatie Informelle Pour L'Europe*, 54.

The initiative sought to exit from the constraints of multilateral institutions that had been amidst a process of adapting themselves to the post-bipolar security environment. Furthermore, the ICFY had failed to produce any tangible results in the resolution of the conflict, as it comprised too many players with divergent interests at stake. According to Pauline Neville-Jones, the Contact Group would 'establish an informal but strong policy-making core around which the main international players could unite'.[30]

The formation of the Contact Group served in particular the interests of the United States to have a platform for cooperation with key European players beyond the institutional constraints of the EU. It also granted Russia a forum for continued involvement in the management of conflict. Lord Owen, then EU representative for former Yugoslavia, sought to circumvent those constraints by forming an informal mechanism that resembled the Contact Group on Namibia, in which he had been involved as foreign minister of the United Kingdom in the late 1970s.[31]

DYNAMICS BETWEEN CONTACT GROUP AND SECURITY COUNCIL

The Contact Group on former Yugoslavia acted within an area of tension between exit and loyalty. Its members followed the push to act outside the framework of multilateral institutions, while, at the same time, the SC exerted a pull on them to seek UN blessing for their action. In response to this tension, Contact Group members established the so-called 'Consultative and Co-ordination Process in New York relating to the work of the Contact Group' (CCP).[32] The CCP served as an interface to move the Contact Group policy upward to the level of the UN in order to receive the formal blessing of the SC. Genuinely, it constituted a device to transform the substance of Contact Group policies and politics into the process of the SC framework. One of the key functions of the CCP was 'to prevent problems in the Council' by settling differences to the greatest possible extent before

---

[30] Pauline Neville-Jones, 'Dayton, IFOR and Alliance Relations in Bosnia', *Survival*, 38/4 (1996), 46.

[31] See Lord Owen Interview Transcript, Liddel Hart Military Archives, 'The Death of Yugoslavia', King's College, London; see also David Owen, *Balkan Odyssey* (London: Victor Gollancz, 1995), 276 *et seq.*

[32] Interview with Francesco Talò, Counsellor, Permanent Mission of Italy to the UN, New York, 8 December 2000. This is confirmed by other interviewees such as Hans-Peter Kaul, formerly Political Counsellor, Permanent Mission of Germany to the UN, Bonn, 8 January 1999. In January 1999, the CCP was re-christened to the so-called CDG, the Consultation and Drafting Group on Kosovo.

a draft was introduced.[33] In essence, it acted as mediator between right process and substance.

The CCP was coordinated by a chair rotating on a monthly basis in alphabetical order according to the membership of the Contact Group. It prenegotiated and drafted all relevant resolutions on former Yugoslavia until they came under consideration in the Council's consultations of the whole.[34] Those resolutions usually reflected the consensual position of the Contact Group on the respective matter. The degree to which the CCP negotiated the substance of draft resolutions differed however. For example, it was the Contact Group members at Wright Patterson Air Force Base in Dayton/Ohio that negotiated the draft of what later should be adopted as SC Resolution 1031 (1995) legitimizing the outcome of the Dayton Accords. In this case, the UN Secretariat and the representatives of Permanent Missions in New York had been mostly excluded from the negotiations.[35] It had been only the fine-tuning of the resolution that was left to the CCP. The general working procedure provided that the respective coordinator of the CCP introduced the first text of a draft resolution or statement to the group. CCP members negotiated upon the draft until they arrived at a common position. In fact, later changes regarding the substance, and even the wording, of the draft resolution tended to be marginal once it had been introduced in the informal consultations of the Council. At the same time, the CCP reflected the interest of the UN Secretariat to have a high-level meeting on former Yugoslavia, a gathering that represented the most interested parties in dealing with the conflict. Although the Secretary-General himself did not usually participate in those meetings, he delegated the task to high-ranking senior officials.[36]

Initially, the CCP reflected the composition of the Contact Group. After complaints by EU partners about the 'exclusive' and 'undemocratic' nature of the gathering, the CCP in New York later included member states of

---

[33] Interview with Francesco Talò, New York, 8 December 2000.

[34] This view has been confirmed in various confidential interviews with participants.

[35] There was an explicit consensus among Contact Group representatives Richard Holbrooke, Igor Ivanov, Pauline Neville-Jones, Jacques Blot, and Wolfgang Ischinger that details about the conference should be kept strictly confidential. They agreed that it would not be possible to keep the SC informed about ongoing negotiations; see Auswärtiges Amt (ed.), *Deutsche Außenpolitik 1995. Auf dem Weg zu einer Friedensregelung für Bosnien und Herzegowina: 53 Telegramme aus Dayton* (Bonn, Germany: Auswärtiges Amt, 1998), 83 *et seq.*; Wolfgang Ischinger underlines that negotiations had been dominated by the US delegation that participated with over 100 representatives. In comparison, delegations of France, Germany, or Russia comprised only five to six delegates; author interview with Wolfgang Ischinger who led the German negotiation team in Dayton/Ohio, Washington DC, 24 January 2002.

[36] See exchange of letters with a senior official of the UN Secretariat, 27 February 2001.

the EU for the duration of their two-year term as non-permanent members on the Council.[37] A notable exception to this rotational principle was Italy, which had been forcefully demanding—and was finally rewarded with—full participation in meetings of the informal setting. When it started its term as non-permanent member on the SC in January 1995, Italy participated, first, in meetings of the CCP, and later in consultations of the Contact Group. Furthermore, the CCP illustrates how non-members as well as non-permanent members may amplify their voice before the Council and gain a kind of 'informal membership'.[38] While exit constituted the cause for forming the Contact Group, voice was a collateral side effect, emerging out of the workings of the informal setting. For example, Germany's informal participation in SC matters on former Yugoslavia via the CCP only became formalized with its non-permanent membership in 1995–6.[39] The combination of Contact Group and CCP membership elevated Germany to an 'informal permanent member' of the SC, given the circumstance that decisions were taken unanimously within the *ad hoc* grouping. In theory, every member had the power to prevent a decision from being taken, in essence, an 'informal veto'.[40] The Contact Group and the CCP revealed how the substance of conflict management had been decentralized to an informal grouping, while the Council secured the right process, that is, the legitimizing framework of action. Granting the seal of legitimacy by virtue of its formal decisions had been the only, though crucial, task left to the Council.

CONTACT GROUP AND US EXCEPTIONALISM

Any examination of the performance of the Contact Group on former Yugoslavia needs to take into account the leadership role of the United States from mid-1995 onwards, since it altered the original functions of the informal setting.[41] The diverging interests of its members limited the

[37] In October 1994, Spain had come forward with the complaint that EU member states serving on the Council should be included in the consultations of the CCP in New York; see interview with Hans-Peter Kaul, Bonn, 8 January 1999. By the end of 2002, the practice of inviting EU members being elected on the Council had stopped, which reflected the desire to keep the gathering as small as possible. The CDG is not even mentioned at coordination meetings of the EU; see interview with Vibeke Rovsing Jorgensen, New York, 19 November 2002; see also interview with Alexander Marschik, New York, 20 November 2002; telephone interview with Ana Jimenez, New York, 25 November 2002.

[38] See Ian Hurd, 'Security Council Reform: Informal Membership and Practice', in Bruce Russett (ed.), *The Once and Future Security Council* (New York: St. Martin's Press, 1997), 135–52.

[39] Interview with Tono Eitel, Münster, 5 August 2000.

[40] Hurd, 'Security Council Reform', 137.

[41] See Holbrooke, *To End A War*; also Ivo H. Daalder, *Getting To Dayton: The Making of America's Bosnia Policy* (Washington DC: Brookings Institution Press, 2000).

operational role of the Group from its beginning. Nevertheless, it was able to agree upon the basis for a negotiated settlement of the war in Bosnia-Herzegovina.[42] With the United States becoming more engaged in the conflict and defining the chain of action, the *ad hoc* grouping developed into, according to a former senior official of the Clinton administration, a 'sounding board'[43] both for providing feedback and approval for US policy initiatives. From the perspective of US foreign policy, the informal setting clearly reflected a trade-off between the interest of having maximum flexibility in the conduct of crisis management and the dependency on the support of key players.[44]

In essence, the Contact Group illustrated a further devolution of the exit strategy. Although the United States sought to escape from the constraints of the informal settings, at the same time, it was very keen to maintain its structure. The Contact Group should sanction US policy initiatives, which might have been criticized as unilateral otherwise. The Contact Group on former Yugoslavia is a striking example of how elements of unilateralism and multilateralism may coexist.[45] Analysing the attraction of institutional agreements for a leading state in general, John Ikenberry has observed that 'they potentially lock other States into stable and predictable policy orientations thereby reducing the need to use coercion to secure the dominant State's foreign policy aims'.[46] Extending Ikenberry's argument to the specific context of informal settings such as Contact Groups, his

---

[42] The Contact Group Plan, presented in July 1994, allocated forty-nine per cent of the territory to the Bosnian Serb side and fifty-one per cent to the Croat–Muslim Federation; see Carsten Giersch, *Konfliktregulierung in Jugoslawien 1991–1995. Die Rolle von OSZE, EU, UNO und NATO* (Baden-Baden, Germany: Nomos Verlag, 1998), 179 *et seq.*; also Melanie C. Greenberg and Margaret E. McGuinness, 'From Lisbon to Dayton: International Mediation and the Bosnia Crisis', in Melanie C. Greenberg, John H. Barton, and Margaret E. McGuinness (eds.) *Words Over War: Mediation and Arbitration to Prevent Deadly Conflict* (Lanham, Oxford: Rowman & Littlefield Publishers), 58 *et seq.*

[43] Author interview.

[44] Richard Holbrooke addressed this trade-off in a personal note to then US Secretary of State Warren Christopher on 23 August 1995: 'The Contact Group presents us with a constant conundrum. We can't live without it, we can't live with it. If we don't meet with them and tell them what we are doing, they complain publicly. If we tell them, they disagree and often leak—and worse. In the end, we must keep the Contact Group together, especially since we will need it later to endorse and legitimize any agreement'; Holbrooke, *To End A War*, 84.

[45] See David M. Malone and Yuen Foong Khong, 'Introduction', in David M. Malone and Yuen Foong Khong (eds.), *Unilateralism and U.S. Foreign Policy: International Perspectives* (Boulder, CO: Lynne Rienner, 2003), 3

[46] G. John Ikenberry, 'Multilateralism and U.S. Grand Strategy', in *Multilateralism and US Foreign Policy: Ambivalent Engagement*, 122; see also G. John Ikenberry, 'State Power and the Institutional Bargain: America's Ambivalent Economic and Security Multilateralism,' in Rosemary Foot, S. Neil MacFarlane, and Michael Mastanduno (eds.) *US Hegemony and International Organizations: The United States and Multilateral Institutions* (Oxford: Oxford University Press, 2003), 51–4.

observation becomes even more true: *ad hoc* groupings appear as a multilateral gathering with small numbers,[47] which might be described as a 'minilateral' setting. The minilateral solution offers a trade-off between inclusiveness and efficiency.

Although it is evident that 'the price that the leading State must pay for this institutionalized cooperation is a reduction in its own policy autonomy and unfettered ability to exercise power',[48] minilateral settings potentially reduce the political cost of action even further, since the number of players is restricted to key actors. The United States was able to keep France, Germany, the United Kingdom, and especially Russia under control, thus preventing the obstruction of stakeholders that might have complicated the efforts of the administration to end the conflict. Applying Henry Kissinger's definition of legitimacy to the specific context of the Contact Group, one could argue that the informal setting offered a platform for the articulation of legitimate concerns of the major powers, including those not permanently represented on the Council. The acceptance of the framework of crisis response by the key players, being stakeholders in the conflict, decreased the likelihood that one state was so dissatisfied that it expressed its dissatisfaction in a revolutionary foreign policy, that is, engaging in obstructionist activities.

In conclusion, the CCP was designed to generate formal legitimacy for actions taken by the Contact Group that acted outside the UN. It served as the executive body that translated the decisions taken on the Contact Group level into the framework of the UN. With the United States exercising leadership in the resolution of the conflict from mid-1995 onwards, the Contact Group transformed into a sounding board that granted feedback to US policy initiatives. The minilateral setting disguised US preponderance and avoided the appearance of unilateral action. Cooperation between stakeholders within the Contact Group framework was preferable to the SC, since minilateral settings tend to increase 'the likelihood and robustness of cooperation'.[49] The trade-off between inclusiveness and efficiency remains key. Finally, this case illustrates the limited explanatory power of typologies such as 'unilateralism' or 'multilateralism'. US foreign policy tends to focus strongly on policy ends while being flexible regarding the means to achieve them.

---

[47] See Miles Kahler, 'Multilateralism with Small and Large Numbers', *International Organization*, 46/3 (1992), 681–708.

[48] Ikenberry, 'Multilateralism and U.S. Grand Strategy', 122.

[49] Kenneth Oye, 'Explaining Cooperation Under Anarchy', in Kenneth Oye (ed.) *Cooperation Under Anarchy* (Princeton, NJ: Princeton University Press, 1986), 21.

7.2 Conflict Resolution

This section analyses international responses to the outbreak of the crisis in Kosovo from late 1997 onwards. It examines, firstly, the role and performance of the Contact Group to find a negotiated resolution to the conflict, which eventually failed at Rambouillet in spring 1999. Secondly, the section investigates the joint efforts taken by the G-8, Quint, and Troika after the failure of the Rambouillet Conference leading to the settlement of conflict.

7.2.1 Contact Group on Kosovo, 1997–9

With the hostilities on the ground escalating, the question of Kosovo re-emerged on the agenda in fall 1997. The Russian Federation had been particularly reluctant to address the issue within the Contact Group framework, as it considered the crisis an internal affair of the FRY.[50] At the same time, especially Western members of the informal group wanted to avoid the mistakes of protracted engagement that had been a key parameter of international crisis response in Bosnia. All players in the Contact Group concurred that only a concerted approach would have the desired effects on the FRY's policies towards Kosovo. However, as Daalder and O'Hanlon have observed, 'there was a conflict between the desire to act quickly and decisively, and the perceived need to forge a consensus on policy not only with key NATO allies but also with Russia'.[51]

At the margins of the annual General Debate of the UN General Assembly in September 1997, representatives of the Contact Group expressed concern over the rising tensions on the ground and demanded the creation of conditions that allowed for the return of refugees.[52] At the same time, the statement underlined somewhat ambiguously that the Group supported neither independence for Kosovo nor maintenance of the status quo, but an enhanced status within the FRY. Such constructive ambiguity should serve the purpose of opening a window for dialogue between the parties on the future status of Kosovo, which should be defined internally

---

[50] Oleg Levitin claims however that this reluctance had been a lost opportunity to engage in an early settlement of the conflict. Such engagement also might have preserved Russia's influence on the terms of any settlement; see Oleg Levitin, 'Inside Moscow's Kosovo Muddle', *Survival*, 42/1 (2000), 130–40.

[51] Daalder and O'Hanlon, *Winning Ugly*, 26.

[52] See 'Statement of the Contact Group Foreign Ministers, New York, 24 September 1997', in Marc Weller (ed.), *The Crisis in Kosovo 1989–1999* (Cambridge, MA: Documents & Analysis Publishing Ltd, 1999), 234.

and not by external powers. It was Milosevic in particular, quietly supported by the Russian Federation, who initially rejected any third-party intervention in the conflict.[53]

However, the subsequent escalation of conflict forced Contact Group representatives to develop common principles for the management of conflict. Those underlying principles reflected the understanding that the conflict basically constituted an internal affair of the FRY that had to be settled by authorities in Belgrade and the leadership of the Kosovar Albanian community themselves, with the Contact Group assuming a facilitating and supporting role in that process.[54] The political solution to the conflict 'should be based on the territorial integrity of the Federal Republic of Yugoslavia', with Kosovo being granted 'an enhanced status within the FRY' that includes 'meaningful self-administration'.[55] The acknowledgement that the conflict constituted an internal affair of the FRY, including the fact that the Contact Group considered the Kosovo Liberation Army (UCK) a terrorist group granted Milosevic a further pretext for using disproportionate force against the rebels.[56] Only after the further escalation of the crisis were Contact Group representatives able to agree upon specific measures in response to Belgrade's large-scale repression of non-violent demonstrations in Pristina, endorsing, *inter alia*, the consideration of a comprehensive arms embargo against the FRY by the SC.[57] At the meeting of the Contact Group on 9 March 1998 in London, it was US Secretary of State Albright in particular who pushed for assertive action in response to the growing violence.[58] The joint statement entailed a catalogue of specific actions to be taken by Milosevic that would lead to reconsidering the imposed measures. This catalogue comprised, *inter alia*, demands for the cessation of force against the civilian population, including the withdrawal of Serb special police units from Kosovo.

Furthermore, the government of the FRY should commit itself to a political dialogue with the Kosovar Albanian leadership. Contact Group representatives were not able to agree upon further action when the FRY

---

[53] See Daalder and O'Hanlon, *Winning Ugly*, 40. Later, Milosevic agreed to launch a political dialogue about the future status of Kosovo, mediated by US Ambassador to Macedonia, Christopher Hill.

[54] See 'Contact Group Statement on Kosovo, 8 January 1998', in *The Crisis in Kosovo 1989–1999*, 234.

[55] See 'Statement by the Contact Group on Kosovo, Moscow, Russia, 25 February 1998', in *The Crisis in Kosovo 1989–1999*, 235.

[56] See Caplan, 'International Diplomacy and the Crisis in Kosovo', 753 *et seq.*

[57] See 'Statement by the Contact Group, London, 9 March 1998', in *The Crisis in Kosovo 1989–1999*, 235.

[58] See Daalder and O'Hanlon, *Winning Ugly*, 28.

government failed to meet the demands. Those divisions prevented any more far-reaching action in the SC. SC Resolution 1160 of 31 March 1998 essentially reaffirmed previous demands of the Contact Group and imposed an arms embargo under Chapter VII of the UN Charter.[59] The draft resolution had been prepared within the CCP framework. The circumstance that Russia did not officially co-sponsor the draft resolution illustrated its reservations vis-à-vis the introduction of a military embargo.[60]

The situation further deteriorated over the summer, with the Serb security forces using disproportionate force against the UCK and fostering the deliberate displacement of tens of thousands of people.[61] The tentative approach of the Contact Group resulted, as Richard Caplan has argued, in 'the paradoxical effect of emboldening Belgrade and radicalizing the Albanian population, thus compounding the crisis in Kosovo'.[62] The Contact Group reiterated previous demands and urged the FRY government to facilitate the full return of refugees and displaced persons to their homes.[63] With the political talks stalling, Contact Group representatives recommended 'basic elements for a resolution of the question of Kosovo's status', accommodating the FRY's and Russian concerns regarding a too prominent role of the informal arrangement in the mediation of the conflict.[64] While the autonomy of Kosovo should be restored in the short term, the question of its future political status was left for negotiations in the long term.

At the level of the UN, discussions in the SC mirrored the divisions within the Contact Group and kept a precarious balance between acknowledging the implications of the crisis for the stability of the region and the territorial integrity of the FRY.[65] Nevertheless, the CCP was successful in achieving an endorsement of the Contact Group statement of 12 June in the Council.[66] The Russian Federation voted in favour of the resolution

---

[59] See UN Doc S/RES/1160, 31 March 1998, adopted by fourteen votes in favour, with China abstaining.

[60] See UN Doc S/PV.3868, 31 March 1998.

[61] By late August 1999, the number of internally displaced persons and refugees had reached 250,000; see Figure 2–1 in Daalder and O'Hanlon, *Winning Ugly*, 41.

[62] Caplan, 'International diplomacy and the crisis in Kosovo', 746.

[63] See 'Contact Group and the Foreign Ministers of Canada and Japan, Statement, London, UK, 12 June 1998', in *The Crisis in Kosovo 1989–1999*, 236 et seq.

[64] 'Contact Group Statement, 8 July 1998', in *The Crisis in Kosovo 1989–1999*, 237.

[65] See UN Doc S/PRST/1998/25, 24 August 1998. Despite US concerns the Permanent Representative of Slovenia to the UN, Danilo Türk, President of the SC for the month of August, had placed the Kosovo crisis on the SC agenda; see interview with Danilo Türk, New York, 6 November 2002.

[66] See UN DOC S/RES/ 1199, 23 September 1998, adopted by fourteen votes in favour, with China abstaining.

despite its concerns about 'the use of unilateral measures of force'.[67] Those concerns related to the pending adoption of Activation Warning (ACT-WARN) by NATO countries.[68]

By adopting ambiguous resolutions that stopped short of explicitly authorizing military action, France and Italy especially sought to achieve a semi-legal environment that made the use of force eventually acceptable.[69] At the military level, NATO defence ministers authorized the conduct of air exercises in Albania and Macedonia to demonstrate the power-projection capabilities of the Alliance. Furthermore, they requested the development of options for dealing with the crisis on the ground that would create the permissive environment for substantial negotiations towards a political settlement of the conflict.[70] At this stage however, despite ACTWARN there was no consensus within NATO either on the specific terms of the suggested intervention or the question of its legal basis. As Strobe Talbott has argued:

Through the summer and into the early fall of 1998, while Milosevic's security forces stepped up their rampage against the Kosovars, NATO was paralyzed by the West Europeans' unwillingness to contemplate military action without authorization from the UN Security Council. That gave the Russians (and Chinese) a veto that they repeatedly threatened to cast.[71]

The more NATO backed the concerted Russian–Western diplomacy by the threat of military force, the less valuable the Contact Group became. By October 1998, with Activation Order (ACTORD) pending, it became increasingly difficult to agree upon a common position within the framework of the informal setting. For example, Contact Group meetings in early October did not produce the habitual joint statement, which usually reflected the least common denominator. Instead, they ended only with 'Chairman's conclusions'. Despite the commitment to maintain a united stance, the conclusions could not gloss over Russia's isolation within the Contact Group.[72]

---

[67] See UN Doc S/PV.3930, 23 September 1998.

[68] ACTWARN constituted the first step in a three-phased procedure for the authorization of NATO military action, followed by the Activation Requirement (ACTREQ) and ACTORD; see General Wesley K. Clark, *Waging Modern War: Bosnia, Kosovo, and the Future of Combat* (New York: Public Affairs, 2001), 135.

[69] This was of secondary concern for the US administration, as a senior official in the US State Department confirms; author interview, Washington DC, 21 November 2000.

[70] See Daalder and O'Hanlon, *Winning Ugly*, 32.

[71] Strobe Talbott, *The Russia Hand* (New York: Random House, 2002), 301.

[72] See 'Chairman's Conclusions, Contact Group meeting on Kosovo in London, 2 October 1998', in *The Crisis in Kosovo 1989–1999*, 238.

Employment of NATO significantly increased the stakes as diplomacy was backed by the threat of military force.[73] Furthermore, the credibility of NATO proper became an overriding concern. The use of force would not only be contingent upon the conflict setting itself, but also be driven by considerations of the perceived strength or weakness of the Alliance. In consequence, the question of whether or not to employ NATO forces became somewhat detached from the actual conflict setting. The Western attempt to back international diplomacy by military force seriously affected the dynamics between Contact Group and SC.

Seen from the Russian point of view, exiting the UN framework via the Contact Group had reached its limits. The more the Russian Federation felt isolated within the Contact Group, the more attractive the SC became as the ultimate retreat for protecting its perceived vital interests. Discussions in the SC had illustrated very clearly that the Council would not authorize the use of force, given the reservations of the Russian Federation and China.

However, this stance appeared much more ambivalent than Russia's declaratory policy actually suggested.[74] In operational terms, Russia's policy remained cooperative rather than obstructive.[75] The country's neuralgia about NATO therefore resulted effectively into a separation of the political and military strategy to deal with the crisis in Kosovo. Those shifting parameters indicated that the interplay between Contact Group and SC was heading towards a dead end, if the parties, and Milosevic in particular, did not comply with the conditions presented to him.[76] The NATO Council presented the Western approach of diplomacy backed by the threat of military force in its purest form. It clearly spelled out the military threat that 'the NATO Secretary General may authorize air strikes

---

[73] See Clark, *Waging Modern War*, 131–61.

[74] At a meeting of Contact Group foreign ministers in fall 1998, Ivanov underlined that the Russian Federation would never support any SC resolution that supported NATO action. At the same time, he indicated however 'that Russia would not insist on the matter coming to the council;' Talbott, *The Russia Hand*, 302.

[75] For example, Ivanov was prepared to support Richard Holbrooke's ultimatum to Milosevic that explicitly included the threat of the use of force by NATO; Talbott, *The Russia Hand*, 302.

[76] Conditions included, 'first, an end to offensive operations and hostilities by both sides; secondly, the withdrawal of Belgrade's security forces...and the withdrawal of heavy weapons; thirdly, freedom of access for the humanitarian agencies...fourthly, full cooperation with the International War Crimes Tribunal...fifthly, the facilitation of the return of refugees to their homes without fear; and finally,...a start to negotiations on the Hill proposals....' Such an agreement would be incorporated in and endorsed by an SC resolution; see 'Contact Group Discussion on Kosovo, Statement by UK Foreign Secretary, 8 October 1998', in *The Crisis in Kosovo 1989–1999*, 238.

against any targets on FRY territory' to achieve the political outcome of a settlement between the parties.[77]

While any explicit reference to NATO was avoided in the official statements of the SC and the Contact Group, the UN Secretary-General's statement before the NATO Council in January clearly illustrated the dilemma vis-à-vis the use of force.[78] Recalling 'the lessons of Bosnia', Kofi Annan conceded that there might be 'the need to use force, when all other means have failed'.[79] After the commencement of air strikes on 24 March, he would further acknowledge that, while the SC had the primary responsibility for the maintenance of international peace and security, 'there are times when the use of force may be legitimate in the pursuit of peace'.[80]

The massacre of Racak in January 1999, which had left forty-five Kosovo Albanians dead, served as a further catalyst for a reassessment of the crisis response strategy. The SC responded with an ambiguous statement that strongly condemned the massacre without however considering further action.[81] In December, Contact Group countries had already explored the possibility of a Dayton-type conference to produce an interim settlement between the parties. Political Directors of the Contact Group set out the framework for negotiations between the parties, which foreign ministers adopted in a joint statement on 29 January 1999.[82] US Secretary of State Madeleine Albright had approached her Russian colleague Ivanov before to secure continued support from the Russian Federation. The statement included only an implicit threat to 'hold both sides accountable if they fail to take the opportunity now offered to them'.[83] From the Russian point of view, this threat did not include the use of military force. Others maintained that this statement contained at least a 'yellow light' for military

---

[77] 'Statement by North Atlantic Council on Kosovo, 30 January 1999'. in *The Crisis in Kosovo 1989–1999*, 416.

[78] The Russian Federation had strong concerns about Annan's 'pro-Western attitude'. Those issues would be addressed at the Secretary-General's visit to Moscow two months later, as a senior Russian diplomat confirms; author interview, Berlin, 26 September 2000.

[79] 'Statement by UN Secretary General to North Atlantic Council, NATO HQ Brussels, 28 January 1999', in *The Crisis in Kosovo 1989–1999*, 414 *et seq.*

[80] 'UN Sec-Gen Kofi Annan on Nato Air Strikes, March 24, 1999', in *USIS Washington File*, 24 March 1999. According to Edward Mortimer, who drafted the note, Kofi Annan considered this the most difficult statement he ever had to make thus far; see interview with Edward Mortimer, New York, 14 February 2001. This was however before the Iraq intervention of the United States in 2003.

[81] Instead, the Council confirmed 'its commitment to the sovereignty and territorial integrity of the Federal Republic of Yugoslavia'; see UN Doc S/PRST/1999/2, 19 January 1999.

[82] See 'Contact Group Statement, London, 29 January 1999', in *The Crisis in Kosovo 1989–1999*, 415 *et seq.*

[83] Ibid.

action.[84] Western members faced to a greater or lesser extent the dilemma of a paralysed SC. While the US administration seemed to be less affected by the deadlock, countries such as France maintained that 'it was of utmost importance not to violate the UN Charter'.[85] On the same day, the Consultation and Drafting Group in New York prepared a formal statement of the SC that welcomed and supported the decisions of Contact Group foreign ministers.[86]

The conference opening at Rambouillet on 6 February provided the framework for negotiations between the parties and was designed to produce an interim settlement of the conflict based upon two key documents, that is, the non-negotiable set of principles and the draft Interim Agreement for Peace and Self-government in Kosovo respectively.[87] The participation of the UCK illustrated the policy shift that effectively upgraded the UCK from a terrorist group to a conflict party with equal rights at the negotiation table. It also reflected the understanding that Ibrahim Rugova was no longer in the position to represent all Kosovar Albanians. With an official endorsement of the SC lacking, the conference was not only about reaching an agreement between the parties to the conflict. It also demonstrated that, in case of failure, the 'international community' had exhausted all political means for solving the conflict. Consequently, Rambouillet also served the purpose of mobilizing support for military action by NATO. As Daalder and O'Hanlon have observed, 'it was to create a consensus in Washington and among the NATO allies that force would have to be used'.[88]

However, it was also clear that the failure of the conference would not generate a sea change on the Russian side, resulting in an agreement over the engagement of NATO.[89] The Contact Group concluded in its statement on 20 February 1999 to undertake 'an ultimate effort to finalize

---

[84] Author interview with a senior advisor to French President Jaques Chirac, New York, 18 November 2000.

[85] Ibid.

[86] Author interview with Alfred Grannas, New York, 30 October 2000; author interview with Francesco Taló, New York, 8 December 2000; the SC statement is contained in UN Doc S/PRST/1999/5, 29 January 1999.

[87] 'Contact Group Non-negotiable Principles/Basic Elements, 30 January 1999', in *The Crisis in Kosovo 1989–1999*, 417; 'Interim Agreement for Peace and Self-Government in Kosovo, Initial Draft, 6 February 1999', in ibid., 421–8.

[88] Daalder and O'Hanlon, *Winning Ugly*, 85. The Independent International Commission on Kosovo argues in a similar vein; see *The Kosovo Report*, 153.

[89] The Russian Federation strongly rejected the military annex of the agreement that provided for the deployment of a NATO military presence on the ground (Kosovo Force (KFOR)). As long as the Serb delegation could count on Russian support, striking a deal was unlikely; see interview with a senior advisor to Jacques Chirac, New York, 18 November 2000.

as a whole the Interim Agreement and the proposed arrangements for an international military and civilian presence in Kosovo, if so agreed by the Parties, to implement and guarantee the Interim Agreement.'[90] After the failure of the conference, it was not the Contact Group as a whole but only its two co-chairs who clearly underlined that international diplomacy had reached a dead end. At that stage, the Contact Group had already ceased to be the primary forum for the management of the Kosovo crisis. The division of labour between Contact Group and NATO Council had worked as long as the Alliance would not deliver on the threat of using force. NATO air strikes without explicit approval of the SC illustrated that the initial strategy of international diplomacy backed by the threat of force had failed. With the Russian Federation being isolated on the question of whether or not to using force, the NATO Council took on the role as the primary actor in the military management of the conflict.

7.2.2 Quint, G-8, and Troika after the Rambouillet Conference

On 24 March, the NATO Alliance started to deliver on the military threat, without however having a roadmap for achieving the political settlement. This would be subject of negotiations within the Quint, G-8, and Troika framework. The last meeting of the Contact Group on 7 April 1999 in Brussels, held at the level of Political Directors, illustrated that the device could no longer serve as the forum for joint conflict management in Kosovo. Beyond the Russian rhetoric that strongly condemned NATO air strikes, on 1 April, President Yeltsin himself called for a special meeting of G-8 foreign ministers. Participation in such a meeting would not be contingent upon prior cessation of the bombardment.[91] His demand prepared the ground for transferring political cooperation and consultation from the Contact Group to the G-8.

In addition to the differences in the substance of policy, it is extremely important to understand that personalities constituted a decisive factor, too. Russian representatives on the Contact Group, Aleksandar Avdeyev, First Deputy Foreign Minister, and Boris Mayorski, Special Envoy for the Balkans, represented the hardliner fraction within the government, which genuinely excluded any pragmatic approach. It is also against this background that engaging the G-8 and establishing the Troika opened new opportunities for the resolution of conflict. This section analyses the

---

[90] 'Conclusions of the Contact Group, Rambouillet, 20 February 1999', in *The Crisis in Kosovo 1989–1999*, 449.
[91] See Joetze, *Der letzte Krieg in Europa?*, 104.

rationale and task-sharing of the various informal settings that were employed after the failure of the Rambouillet Conference. It examines the dynamics between the SC and those informal mechanisms.

RATIONALE OF INFORMAL GROUPS: EXIT VERSUS LOYALTY

Choosing the exit option without the explicit approval of the SC significantly raised the political costs of Western engagement in Kosovo. NATO air strikes raised questions about the legality of the military intervention. The use of force not only severely damaged diplomatic relations with the Russian Federation but also created divisions within the Alliance. The question at stake was how to create the broadest possible acceptance of the intervention in order to minimize political costs. Looked at from the perspective of the Western Alliance the question entailed an internal and external dimension. Internally, NATO faced the challenge of how to maintain the support of its member states for air strikes. Externally, there was the challenge of re-engaging the Russian Federation in the political settlement of the conflict.[92] Quint, G-8, and Troika would provide the platforms to deal with each dimension of this question. The Quint, comprising all Contact Group members except Russia, originally constituted a device for exchange of information and coordination between the United States and its key European allies.[93] Its primary purpose was to maintain the coherence within the NATO alliance. From the US point of view, such a mechanism turned out to be of special importance in cases where the domestic support for NATO air strikes had been extremely weak.[94]

Cooperation took place at various levels, with the foreign ministers of participating countries holding regular telephone conferences, backed up by consultations of Political Directors. The informal device also convened at the level of ministers of defence. In effect, the Quint developed into a mechanism that synchronized the political and military strategies into a single and coherent approach to terminate the conflict. As to the second challenge of re-engaging Russia, it should be borne in mind that beyond

[92] Western administrations would maintain a constant high-level dialogue with President Boris Yeltsin, Foreign Minister Ivanov, and Russian Envoy Victor Chernomyrdin. Looked at from the perspective of the US Secretary of State, Russia constituted 'the key to an acceptable outcome'; Madeleine Albright, *Madam Secretary* (New York: Miramax Books, 2003), 413; also author interview with Günter Joetze, Königswinter, 28 March 2003.

[93] See Madeleine Albright, *Madam Secretary*, 408–28.

[94] The case of Germany is a good example to support this argument. Good personal relations between Madeleine Albright and Joshka Fischer were extremely important to convince the US administration that the left Sozialdemokratische Partei Deutschlands (SPD)/ Green coalition in Germany would have enough stamina to continue its support for NATO's air strikes despite massive opposition at the domestic level and within the parties.

the specific question of how to address the Kosovo crisis loomed the larger problem of NATO–Russia relations in the post-Cold War era. This issue had not been fully resolved even after adopting the Founding Act in 1997 that established the NATO–Russia Permanent Joint Council for addressing security questions of common concern and providing an overall framework for cooperation. Previous experience of conflict management in former Yugoslavia from 1994 to 1995 suggested that despite strong reactions to the employment of force by NATO, the Russian Federation would ultimately go along with the Western approach.[95] At the same time, Russian policy reflected the desire to be recognized as a major power that cannot be ignored in international relations. This psychological moment had translated into the Western dealings with the situation in former Yugoslavia and especially affected the US strategy vis-à-vis the conflict.[96] Consequently, beyond the substantive issue of using force against the FRY, there was the more symbolic issue of restoring the sense of Russian power and influence. The G-8 provided the ideal platform to accommodate those concerns. As indicated earlier, President Yeltsin suggested only one week after the commencement of air strikes to convene a special meeting of the G-8 foreign ministers. Political Directors of the G-8 and foreign ministries were amidst preparations for the political declaration of the next summit of Heads of State and Government, to be held in Cologne in June 1999.

Employing the G-8 had several advantages. Firstly, it provided a flexible and informal framework for effective cooperation. The informal and high-level structure of the G-8 avoids the involvement of large administrations and allows for quicker decisions. Secondly, it granted Russia high-level participation in the political management of conflict.[97] Thirdly, it forced

---

[95] On the Russian side, there prevailed the sober assessment that any obstructionist operational policy might have jeopardized the continuation of Western financial and economic support and with it the recovery of the Russian economy. There was also the underlying fear of becoming isolated from Europe and the United States; see Paul Latowski and Martin A. Smith, *The Kosovo Crisis and the Evolution of Post-Cold War European Security* (Manchester, UK: Manchester University Press, 2003), 98.

[96] Richard Holbrooke underlines that such approach reflected 'a fundamental belief on the part of the Clinton Administration that it was essential to find the proper place for Russia in Europe's security structure, something it had not been part of since 1914'; Holbrooke, *To End A War*, 117. This policy approach was however highly ambivalent. While US foreign policy sought to accommodate Russian concerns by essentially symbolic means, this affected the substance of politics only in a marginal way. For example, NATO air strikes against Bosnian Serb positions in the summer of 1995, with the use of cruise missiles, 'the quintessential Cold War weapon', demonstrated that the accommodation of Russian interests clearly had its limits, especially when it was to be weighed against the credibility of post-Cold War NATO; ibid., 143.

[97] At the same time, the engagement reduced the possibility of military support for Milosevic by the Russian Federation. The delivery of SA10 missiles would have considerably

---

Russian representatives to compromise. In contrast to the SC, casting a veto was not an option. Furthermore, the Russian Federation cooperated with seven countries bound 'by a deep commonality of political values, notably democracy, human rights, and the rule of law'.[98] The outright rejection of those values by employing an obstructionist approach in the management of conflict would have led to Russian isolation within the Western community in general and the G-8 in particular.[99] Fourthly, the G-8 involved different personalities that facilitated cooperation.[100] For example, the representative of the Russian Federation, Deputy Foreign Minister Georgi Mamedov, represented a much more pragmatic policy line than Aleksandar Avdeyev and Boris Mayorski.

However, it should be kept in mind that the activation of the G-8 constituted the result of rather special circumstances. The Kosovo case is not necessarily a textbook case for supporting deterministic forecasts about the primary role of the G-8 in the maintenance of international peace and security. Although the G-8 certainly provides an indispensable forum for international cooperation, the Kosovo conflict is not the proper case for supporting the argument that this institution 'is emerging as a rival and effective, desirable replacement for the UN System in governing the global peace and security system'.[101] Firstly, it simply ignores the key role of the Troika. Secondly, it ignores the possibility that not all members might want to support this development, as the G-8 does not bear the same degree of legitimacy.[102] Thirdly, the thorough reading of empirical evidence suggests that the UN continued to display a strong pull on the key actors to seek legitimation of the policy outcomes, which the G-8 was unable to deliver.[103] The prospect of *post hoc* legitimation through the UN lent greater authority to the efforts made and created broader acceptance

upgraded the Serbian air defence system and seriously undermined NATO's air campaign. In addition, this would have triggered a large-scale international crisis.

[98] Kühne and Prantl (eds.), *The Security Council and the G8 in the New Millennium*, 12.

[99] This view is supported by interview with Martti Ahtisaari, Helsinki, 9 May 2000.

[100] Author interview with a senior official in the German Foreign Office, Berlin, 25 September 2000. However, Mayorski and Avdeyev would still remain involved in the negotiations, as a senior Russian diplomat maintains; author interview, Berlin, 26 September 2000.

[101] John J. Kirton, 'The G-8, the United Nations, and Global Security Governance', in John J. Kirton and Junichi Takase (eds.), *New Directions in Global Political Governance: The G-8 and International Order in the Twenty-first Century* (Aldershot, UK: Ashgate, 2002), 192.

[102] This view is maintained by a Japanese diplomat; author interview, Berlin, 13 September 2000.

[103] In fact, the so-called Shadow G-8, comprising C. Fred Bergsten, Leon Brittan, John Chipman, Richard N. Cooper, Wendy Dobson, Boris Fedorov, David Folkerts-Landau, Yoichi Funabashi, Paolo Guerrieri, Toyoo Gyohten, Karl Kaiser, Sergei Karaganov, Henry A. Kissinger, Barbara McDougall, Patrick Messerlin, Thierry de Montbrial, Joseph Nye, Richard Portes, Renato Ruggiero, and Paul Volcker, underlined in its recommendations for the Evian Summit

than would have been otherwise the case. China, the only permanent member of the SC not being represented at the G-8 level, would also be kept constantly informed. Such a scenario suggests that, despite bypassing the SC, loyalty mattered. The roles of G-8, Troika, and SC were complementary and mutually reinforcing, as it is demonstrated later.

However, Russian participation within the G-8 framework could not entirely resolve problems related to the fragmentation of the policymaking machinery of the Russian Federation. The appointment of Victor Chernomyrdin as President Yeltsin's Special Envoy for the FRY illustrated the desire to find a pragmatic solution to the conflict. The June summit of the G-8 constituted the deadline for such settlement. Any failure to strike a deal would have resulted in public isolation of the Russian President. The success of the summit constituted the primary, the settlement of the conflict the secondary goal of the Russian President. Chernomyrdin's appointment was ultimately a safeguard to avoid any accident.

The Troika, comprising Finnish President Martti Ahtisaari, Russian Special Envoy Victor Chenomyrdin, and US Deputy Secretary of State Strobe Talbott, provided a platform for the presentation of a joint position of the Western Alliance and Russia, which minimized Milosevic's options for 'forum shopping'.[104] It closed the gaps between the parallel efforts by the international community to achieve a settlement. Viewed from the Western perspective, this format limited the direct influence of other agencies of the Russian government such as the foreign ministry or the military on defining the specific terms of the third-party intervention. The informal mechanism allowed reducing the widely fragmented Russian foreign policy machinery to a single focal point. In addition, Chernomyrdin enjoyed the full backing of his President at all stages of negotiations that provided him with the full authority and flexibility to strike a deal.[105] Support of the highest authorities constituted a sine qua non for containing, though not excluding, obstructionist behaviour of hardliners in the Russian foreign

in 2003 that the G-8 itself faced a 'crisis of legitimacy'. The institution 'has come to appear both ineffective and illegitimate'; see *Restoring G-8 Leadership of the World Economy: Recommendations for the Evian Summit from the Shadow G-8*. Available at www.iie.com/publications/papers/g8-2003.pdf. Accessed on 23 April 2005, 10; see also Shadow G-8, 'Pour une nouvelle légitimité du G-8', *Politique Etrangere*, 68/2 (2003), 245–58.

[104] Interview with Strobe Talbott, New Haven, Connecticut, 26 September 2001. He refers in particular to the EU, G-8, NATO, the UN, and a 'de-facto continuation of the Contact Group' that even after Rambouillet still remained in the background.

[105] At all stages of negotiations, Chernomyrdin could rely on written instructions signed by the President Yeltsin, which presented the bottom line of the Russian position. However, those instructions must be balanced against Yeltsin's overriding policy goal: the cessation of NATO air strikes and the resolution of conflict before the start of the G-8 summit in Cologne; see Joetze, *Der letzte Krieg in Europa?*, 154 *et seq.*

ministry and the military apparatus. For Ahtisaari, the full backing of Germany, holding the Presidency of the EU, was extremely important to protect him from criticism by other EU member states.[106]

It may be useful to distinguish between the inward and outward functions of the Troika, as it sheds some light especially on the varying degrees of US involvement. The Troika's inward functions included the trilateral effort to agree upon a paper that would reflect the common position of the Russian Federation and EU–NATO countries. It is important to understand that it was the Troika and not the G-8 that would resolve the key differences in the positions between NATO and Russia. The role of the G-8 remained limited as to the drafting of the SC resolution, which would endorse the final settlement of the conflict. The Troika conducted the actual management of conflict and defined the terms of its settlement.[107]

Originally, Chernomyrdin perceived his role in the Troika as the mediator between Milosevic and Ahtisaari/Talbott. However, Ahtisaari's decision to wait for a direct meeting in Belgrade until Russian and Western positions had converged altered the strategic balance within the informal group. Ahtisaari would eventually assume the key role of mediating between Russian and US positions. The Troika's outward functions comprised the very act of imposing the conditions on Milosevic in Belgrade. Here, the US administration would keep a very low profile.

In conclusion, Quint, G-8, and Troika provided a set of informal frameworks to merge the military and political tracks of conflict management in Kosovo.

DYNAMICS BETWEEN INFORMAL GROUPS AND THE SECURITY COUNCIL

At the beginning of the air campaign, there were widespread expectations that the intervention would be rather short, following an apparent 'mythologizing' on the side of the Western alliance about the effectiveness of

[106] At some stage, France demanded Ahtisaari's resignation, which reflected concerns that the Finnish President had assumed a too-powerful role in settling the conflict. This was however averted by an intervention of the German EU Presidency; author interview with Günter Joetze, Königswinter, 28 March 2003.

[107] In consequence, the importance of the G-8 proper during the Kosovo crisis has often been overrated; see Kirton, 'The G-8, the United Nations, and Global Security Governance', 198 et seq.; Risto E. J. Penttilä, The Role of the G-8 in International Peace and Security, Adelphi Paper 355, International Institute for Strategic Studies (Oxford: Oxford University Press, 2003), 44–6; Barry R. Posen, 'The War for Kosovo: Serbia's Political–Military Strategy', International Security, 24/4 (2000), 69–78; Christoph Schwegmann, 'Modern Concert Diplomacy: The Contact Group and the G7/8 in Crisis Management', in John J. Kirton, Joseph P. Daniels, and Andreas Freytag (eds.), Guiding Global Order: G-8 Governance in the Twenty-first Century, (Aldershot, UK: Ashgate, 2001), 113–16.

NATO's Operation Deliberate Force in Bosnia in the summer of 1995 that facilitated the eventual acceptance of a ceasefire by the Serbs.[108] Milosevic seemed to share the assumption of the limited duration and severity of NATO air strikes, although for completely different reasons. In essence, he counted on two factors that would constrain NATO's use of force. Firstly, he counted on the continued support from the Russian Federation. Secondly, he anticipated an early erosion of Western unity against the background of an intensification of the humanitarian crisis on the ground and casualties on the Serb civilian and NATO's side.[109]

With the perceived deadlock of the Council as the primary institution for the maintenance of international peace and security, the NATO Council attempted to fill the vacuum by conducting a military campaign without having a comprehensive political strategy of how to settle the actual conflict. The NATO Council maintained a fragile consensus that the conduct of air strikes was not legal but legitimate.[110] The question whether the Alliance was the appropriate and legitimate framework to work out a political strategy had been a highly contentious issue even prior to the intervention. France, Germany, Italy, and the United Kingdom especially had argued that the Contact Group should remain the steering committee for the political management of conflict, as it included Russia. Despite the fact that the use of force was not explicitly sanctioned by a SC resolution, there was not enough support within the Council to agree upon an unequivocal

[108] However, this was a false analogy. The re-taking of the Croatian Krajina prior to the air strikes of Serb targets in Bosnia had changed the military balance on the ground and put the Serbs in the defensive; see Adam Roberts, 'NATO's "Humanitarian War" over Kosovo', *Survival*, 41/3 (1999), 110.

[109] See Stephen T. Hosmer, *The Conflict over Kosovo: Why Milosevic Decided to Settle when He Did* (Santa Monica, CA: Rand, 2001), xii.

[110] On the question of the legality versus legitimacy of NATO's intervention see Catherine Guicherd, 'International Law and the War in Kosovo', *Survival*, 41/2 (1999), 19–34; Ruth Wedgwood, 'NATO's Campaign in Yugoslavia', *American Journal of International Law*, 93/4 (1999), 828–34; on the wider questions of legitimacy in international relations see Clark, *Legitimacy in International Society*; on intervention in international affairs in general and humanitarian intervention in particular see Martha Finnemore, *The Purpose of Intervention: Changing Beliefs About the Use of Force* (Ithaca, NY: Cornell University Press, 2003); J. L. Holzgrefe and Robert O. Keohane (eds.), *Humanitarian Intervention: Ethical, Legal and Political Dilemmas* (Cambridge, Cambridge University Press, 2003); S. Neil MacFarlane, *Intervention in Contemporary World Politics*, Adelphi Paper 350, International Institute for Strategic Studies (Oxford: Oxford University Press, 2002); Edward Mortimer, *A Few Words on Intervention: John Stuart Mill's Principles of International Action applied to the Post Cold War World* (London: John Stuart Mill Institute, 1995); Simon Chesterman, *Just War or Just Peace? Humanitarian Intervention and International Law* (Oxford: Oxford University Press, 2001); Schnabel and Thakur (eds.), *Kosovo and the Challenge of Humanitarian Intervention*; Jennifer M. Welsh (ed.), *Humanitarian Intervention and International Relations* (Oxford: Oxford University Press, 2004); and Nicholas J. Wheeler, *Saving Strangers: Humanitarian Intervention in International Society* (Oxford: Oxford University Press, 2000); on the implications of the NATO air campaign for the rule of non-intervention see Roberts, 'NATO's "Humanitarian War" over Kosovo', *Survival*, 41/3 (1999), 102–23.

condemnation either. When Belarus and the Russian Federation, co-sponsored by India, submitted a resolution to call for an immediate cessation of the air strikes and the urgent resumption of negotiations, it was only China and Namibia that supported the draft.[111] In late March, it seemed that the bombing constituted less a forward-looking political strategy than a backward-looking policy. Such a strategy was developed only after the air strikes had actually started. In this context, Quint, G-8, and Troika would play an indispensable role to merge the use of force with a viable political strategy for conflict resolution.

Especially from the perspective of the newly elected German coalition government, NATO air strikes could be justified only if there were clearly articulated policy goals that defined the ends and means of the campaign. The development of a political strategy would be the sine qua non for the maintenance of domestic support for the air campaign and eventually secure the survival of the left coalition in Germany. This circumstance had implications for the timing of the political initiative. While France and the United Kingdom wanted to await the effects of the air campaign before they would launch a new political initiative, Germany could not afford any diplomatic vacuum given its constraints at the domestic table.

In close cooperation with, and supported by, US Secretary of State Madeleine Albright, German Foreign Minister Fischer took the initiative and suggested a joint paper of the Quint that would define a set of political conditions which the regime in Belgrade had to meet to achieve the cessation of air strikes.[112] Such criteria included, firstly, an immediate end of violence in Kosovo; secondly, the withdrawal of military forces and police units; thirdly, the disarmament and withdrawal of Serb paramilitary forces; fourthly, the free return of refugees and displaced persons; fifthly, negotiations on the future status of Kosovo based upon the Rambouillet Agreement; and sixthly, a robust international military presence. In addition to that, the proposal foresaw a key role for the G-8 as the forum that would lay out the terms for a settlement offer to Milosevic. The final package, including provisions for implementing the agreement, should be legitimized by an enabling resolution of the SC. The German paper suggested furthermore that NATO air strikes would be suspended for twenty-four hours as soon as Serb forces had started to withdraw from Kosovo.[113]

[111] See UN Doc S/1999/328, 24 March 1999; Un Doc S/PV.3989, 26 March 1999.

[112] On 30 March, Fischer suggested the paper for the first time during a telephone conference of the Quint. In addition to the close consultations between Fischer and Albright, the German Chancellery had sought the backing of the White House; see Joetze, *Der letzte Krieg in Europa?*, 101–03.

[113] Ibid., 100.

Although the proposal for suspending air strikes did not meet the approval of the US administration, the key elements of the German initiative subsequently found acceptance at the levels of the EU and NATO. Furthermore, the projected prominent role of the G-8 as well as the prospect of an SC resolution constituted strong incentives for the Russian Federation to stay engaged in the political process of conflict management.

With NATO air strikes failing to produce the immediate effect of forcing Milosevic to return to the negotiation table, those conditions developed into the political framework that defined the rationale of the campaign and the conditions under which it would be terminated. The NATO Council approved the criteria on 4 April and confirmed it subsequently.[114] Political Directors of the Quint had drafted the declaration prior to the meeting. In attendance of UN Secretary-General Annan, the EU endorsed the conditions at a special summit on 14 April.[115] With the quasi-legitimation of the political process by NATO, the EU, and the UN Secretary-General providing an additional aura of legitimacy, the criteria set the political agenda for the resolution of conflict in Kosovo. The EU's invitation reflected the desire to keep the UN engaged in the political process of conflict management. Heads of state and government expressed support for the Secretary-General's statement of 9 April that called upon Yugoslav authorities to commit themselves to the Western demands.[116]

The meeting of G-8 Political Directors, held from 8 to 9 April in Dresden, constituted the beginning of a multilateral process that sought to bring international diplomacy back on track by orchestrating the political and military strategies of the Western alliance, including Russia. The joint paper approved the conditions for the cessation of NATO air strikes.[117] Furthermore, the paper outlined a sequence that reflected the later course of action. It called, firstly, for a meeting of G-8 foreign ministers to adopt the common approach. Secondly, G-8 ministers would seek approval of those political conditions by the SC. At this stage, it turned out however that Mamedov did not have the full backing of the Russian foreign ministry that still struggled to reconcile the hard- and soft-line strands within the Russian foreign policy machinery.[118] The Russian foreign minister

---

[114] See NATO Press Release M-NAC-1(99)51, 12 April 1999, and NATO Press Release S-1(99)62, 23 April 1999.

[115] See Chairman's Summary of the Deliberations on Kosovo at the Informal Meeting of the Heads of State and Government of the EU in Brussels on 14 April 1999 (on file with author).

[116] See UN Doc S/1999/402, 9 April 1999.

[117] See Joetze, *Der letzte Krieg in Europa?*, 106.

[118] This view is maintained by a senior German diplomat who participated in the meeting; author interview.

especially resented the robust military presence on the ground, while supporting the role of the G-8 as the preferred forum for the management of the Kosovo conflict. He also favoured the adoption of an SC resolution for the formal cessation of conflict. At this stage, there seemed to exist a common understanding that the conflict could not be terminated by closing another deal with Milosevic. The resolution of conflict had to be imposed by a joint Russian–Western effort and legitimized by a resolution of the SC. With the activation of the G-8 in early April, the management of conflict rested upon the military pillar of NATO and the political pillar of the G-8, with the Quint providing a bridge between both institutions. The Washington Summit of NATO adopted the political strategy while, at the same time, deciding to continue and intensify the air strikes.[119]

President Yeltsin's appointment of Victor Chernomyrdin as his Special Envoy for the FRY constituted another decisive shift of policy, which, firstly, aimed at altering the Russian inter- and intradepartmental balance of power and, secondly, offered the United States a suitable counterpart for cooperation. Chernomyrdin had established a large network of contacts in Central and South-eastern Europe as the chief executive of Gazprom, the Russian oil and gas enterprise. His relations with US Vice-President Al Gore and other members of the Clinton administration were excellent. The nomination reflected Yeltsin's strong disagreement with the handling of the Kosovo crisis by Prime Minister Primakov. It illustrated the strong interest of the Kremlin to find a pragmatic solution to the conflict before the G-8 summit in June.

In early May, Chernomyrdin met in Washington DC with Vice-President Al Gore, National Security Advisor Sandy Berger, US Secretary of State Madeleine Albright, as well as her deputy Strobe Talbott. Discussions centred on the political strategy of how to force Milosevic to accept the conditions. The idea to form the Troika developed during that meeting. Chernomyrdin proposed the appointment of a counterpart who would work together with him 'to accept the sword of surrender from Milosevic'.[120] Finnish President Martti Ahtisaari was the compromise candidate after the proposal of UN Secretary-General Kofi Annan had been rejected by the US side.[121] Initially, Chernomyrdin favoured the idea of Ahtisaari representing the UN, as he wanted to have a counterpart who enjoyed maximum support from the international community. The appearance of

---

[119] See NATO Press Release S-1(99)62, 23 April 1999, para 5. After the Washington Summit, the Alliance doubled and later even quadrupled the number of sorties.

[120] Chernomyrdin is quoted in Talbott, *The Russia Hand*, 314.

[121] Interview with Strobe Talbott, New Haven, Connecticut, 26 September 2001.

a high degree of legitimacy would facilitate the selling of the final settlement to the Russian audience. However, Annan had already appointed Carl Bildt and Eduard Kukan as his two Special Envoys for the Kosovo conflict in an attempt to re-involve the Organization. He was therefore rather lukewarm in his support for the suggested appointment.[122] With Finland assuming the Presidency of the EU in the second half of 1999, the Council of Ministers adopted a mandate for Ahtisaari that formalized his role as the EU's Special Envoy.[123]

When the Troika started to meet, there were three questions which needed to be solved among the representatives.[124] The first contentious issue constituted the question of the specific terms of the withdrawal of Serb forces. While Talbott demanded the complete withdrawal of the forces, Chernomyrdin wanted to concede the right to the FRY of maintaining a considerable security presence on the ground. The second contentious issue related to the timing of the cessation of the air campaign. At the Washington Summit, NATO countries had agreed to suspend the air strikes only after the FRY had 'unequivocally accepted the . . . conditions and demonstrably begun to withdraw its forces from Kosovo according to a precise and rapid timetable'.[125] The third contentious issue centred on the question of the composition and command structure of the international security presence. Chernomyrdin rejected the idea of a NATO-unified command along the lines of the already existing military presence in Bosnia. Furthermore, the force should not comprise of those countries that had participated in the air campaign, which was unacceptable to both Ahtisaari and Talbott. Those questions were discussed in detail at subsequent meetings of the Troika in Helsinki, Moscow, and on the Petersberg near Bonn.[126] Chernomyrdin seemed to have calculated that Ahtisaari would support the Russian position vis-à-vis the Serb withdrawal and limiting NATO's role within the international security force. However, after the first Troika

[122] Ahtisaari, Chernomyrdin, and Talbott were therefore a bit concerned that the two UN envoys might act in competition to the Troika. Any prominent role of Bildt and Kukan might have undermined the rationale of the Troika, that is, to minimize Milosevic's options for forum shopping; ibid.

[123] Ahtisaari has repeatedly underlined that this nomination by the EU was crucial for his authority as mediator. Without any institutional background, he would not have had the necessary legitimacy and political clout in dealing with Milosevic as well as the foreign ministry of the Russian Federation; author interview with Martti Ahtisaari, Helsinki, 9 May 2000.

[124] See Daalder and O'Hanlon, *Winning Ugly*, 169 *et seq.*

[125] NATO Press Release S-1(99)62, 23 April 1999, para 6.

[126] Between May and June, the Troika met four times in total, having more than fifty hours of substantive sessions; see Judah, *Kosovo: War and Revenge*, 276. The first meeting took place in Helsinki on 13 May; see Talbott, *The Russia Hand*, 316.

meeting it had been clear that the Finnish President would stay firm on 'the zero option' and 'hard core NATO'.[127]

From May onwards, conflict management proceeded on four levels. Members of the NATO Council consulted on the conduct of air strikes, with the Quint acting as the bridge for the synchronization of military and political strategies. Troika and G-8 conducted diplomacy on a double track. While the former sought agreement on the conditions of Milosevic's surrender, the latter prepared the ground for an SC resolution that would legitimize the terms of conflict resolution. What may appear at first sight as a model for interlocking informal *ad hoc* groupings creating synergies for the effective management of crisis settings had serious shortcomings as well. While Chernomyrdin rather represented the pragmatic strand of Russia's new foreign policy, Ivanov, Avdeyev, and Mayorski stood, with varying degrees, for the hard-line approach of the former Soviet empire.

Substantial negotiations on the resolution started at the level of Political Directors on 3 May and continued on 6 May with the participation of G-8 foreign ministers. The Russian Federation presented a four-page paper, which aimed at maintaining the sovereignty of the FRY to a maximum degree.[128] Russian negotiators rejected a separate security presence, demanding a civilian mission of the UN with a military component. The German G-8 Presidency presented a one-page counterproposal that avoided any premature details and emphasized instead the need for the deployment of a separate international civilian and security presence authorized by the UN. This provision raised two major concerns on the side of the US administration.[129] Firstly, the United States rejected the wording of an overall authority of the UN, as it seemed to imply the subordination of NATO vis-à-vis the Organization. The British delegation proposed therefore a compromise formula, with the UN endorsing and adopting the deployment of the operation, which eventually found acceptance by G-8 foreign ministers. Secondly, the US administration insisted on changing the wording to 'presences' in the plural in order to underline that the mission in Kosovo would rest on two separate pillars, that is, a civilian and a military presence. Further details related to the command structure had been deliberately avoided in order to obtain Russian approval. It constituted however a central Western demand that the core of the security

---

[127] These were Ahtisaari's shorthand notions for the two compulsory elements of the joint paper to be presented to Milosevic, quoted in Talbott, *The Russia Hand*, 318.

[128] See Joetze, *Der letzte Krieg in Europa?*, 142.

[129] Author interview with a senior official in the US State Department who participated in the negotiations, Washington DC, 21 November 2000.

presence would comprise countries of the NATO alliance. The meeting of G-8 foreign ministers concluded with the adoption of general principles on the political solution to the Kosovo crisis, which mirrored the core demands of the joint paper of the Quint and the decision of the NATO Council of April.[130] In addition to the points already mentioned, 'G-8 foreign ministers instructed their Political Directors to prepare elements of a United Nations Security Council resolution.'[131] This decision clearly illustrated, firstly, the prevalence of loyalty in the conduct of conflict management. Secondly, the prospect of SC legitimation accommodated the interest of minimizing the political costs of an imposed settlement. Finally, the seal of UN legitimacy would facilitate the mobilization of international support for peace-building. At the same time, the statement anchored the political process firmly into the G-8 framework by emphasizing that Political Directors would work out a roadmap on further steps to be taken. Finally, the Chinese government would be informed about the results of the meeting in view of the SC resolution that had to be adopted at a later stage.

SC Resolution 1239, originally dealing with the humanitarian catastrophe on the ground, implicitly endorsed the G-8 principles as it emphasized 'that the humanitarian situation will continue to deteriorate in the absence of a political solution to the crisis consistent with the principles adopted...on 6 May 1999'.[132] This illustrates, firstly, that loyalty remained an essential concern. It also contributed to the broader acceptance of the political process of conflict management that was conducted outside the UN framework but now within the objectives of the SC. Secondly, exit from the UN framework had been particularly humiliating for the Russian Federation that had lost its lever, that is the possibility of casting a veto, to prevent any military intervention in Kosovo. Reference to the G-8 framework ultimately reflected the commitment of Western countries to keep Russia involved in the management of the conflict.

Negotiations on the specific terms of an SC resolution continued on 19 and 21 May, reflecting diverging Western positions vis-à-vis the implementing agency of the international civilian mission. While the United States favoured a civilian presence under the authority of the Organization for Security and Cooperation in Europe (OSCE), Germany and the United Kingdom called for a UN operation and France for a mission under EU

---

[130] See Statement by the Chairman on the conclusion of the meeting of the G-8 Foreign Ministers held at the Petersberg Centre on 6 May 1999, UN DOC S/1999/516, 6 May 1999.
[131] Ibid, para 2.
[132] UN Doc S/RES/1239, 14 May 1999, op. 5.

authority. For the representative of the Russian Federation, Mayorski, those divisions were rather of a theoretical nature as he rejected any discussion about an international administration of Kosovo at this stage.[133]

However, consultations within the Troika framework would eventually set the pace for the G-8 representatives. During meetings in Moscow on 20 and 26–27 May, the Troika consulted on talking points for Ahtisaari's and Chernomyrdin's joint mission to Belgrade that the US delegation had drafted for them. The Finnish President insisted on a single text that he would jointly present with his Russian counterpart to Milosevic.[134] Given Russia's strong opposition with respect to Western demands for a total withdrawal of Serb forces, the US administration originally did not see a great chance to achieve a three-way common position.[135] Also participating in the meetings of the Troika, Mayorski signalled that he might concede a separate UN peacekeeping force under Chapter VI mandate. The meetings produced agreement on the substance of the international force, which would have NATO countries at the core.

The presence of Chernomyrdin forced the Russian hardliner to take much more accommodating positions than at the level of the G-8. Troika consultations clearly facilitated the rapprochement of Western and Russian interests within the G-8 framework. On the one hand, the Russian Federation gained the high-level attention it needed as recognition that it still had a role to play in international affairs. Looked at from the perspective of Russian domestic politics, it secured the high-level influence of the President at the expense of the foreign ministry and the military respectively. On the other hand, seen from a Western point of view, it avoided the problem of dealing with the highly fragmented foreign policy apparatus of the former Soviet empire. Victor Chernomyrdin was the focal point whose decisions were backed at the highest political level, that is, the President of the Russian Federation. The Troika also served as a confidence-building exercise aimed at preventing any obstructionist measures by Russia such as the delivery of sophisticated anti-aircraft systems, which would have raised the political and military stakes for NATO's intervention.[136]

---

[133] See Joetze, *Der letzte Krieg in Europa?*, 146.

[134] Author interview with Martti Ahtisaari, Helsinki, 9 May 2000; see also Talbott, *The Russia Hand*, 321.

[135] This view is maintained by Ahtisaari, ibid.; Talbott confirmed this view; author interview with Strobe Talbott, New Haven, Connecticut, 26 September 2001.

[136] Tim Judah underlines that the US administration told the Russian Federation 'repeatedly and explicitly' to refrain from any military assistance to the FRY; Judah, *Kosovo: War and Revenge*, 272.

Chernomyrdin's mission to Belgrade on 28 May prepared the ground for the presentation of the joint paper. In eleven-hour consultations with Milosevic, he sought to convince the President to concede.[137] Based upon information from Russian intelligence, Chernomyrdin furthermore sketched out in detail the state of the discussion within the Western Alliance about the potential deployment of ground forces.[138] One day earlier, the Quint had discussed options for a ground war at the level of defence ministers, without however taking a decision.[139] Despite the differences between key member states, NATO had started planning the ground option as a measure of last resort after the Washington Summit in late April.[140] Bowing to the prospect of a pending ground invasion and the perception of increasing isolation, Milosevic agreed to the NATO presence in Kosovo if it was not composed of states participating in the air campaign. He also demanded a separate sector for Russia and other non-NATO forces in the northern part of Kosovo, operating not under NATO but UN command.[141] In this context, it was not a coincidence that Milosevic's concessions regarding the deployment of NATO forces accommodated in particular Russian interests. Furthermore, he emphasized that the Serbian Parliament would accept any solution as long as it was subject to an affirmative vote of the SC, including the approval of the Russian Federation.[142] In effect, Milosevic would not surrender to NATO but to the UN.

Despite the ripe moment for the joint intervention by Ahtisaari and Chernomyrdin, the Troika still needed to finalize negotiations on the conditions to be presented to Milosevic. The most contentious issue constituted US demands of a security force under unified NATO command and the total withdrawal of Serb forces. Instead, Russia demanded that the entire operation would act under the authority of the UN, with a separate sector for the Russian contingent, which would not answer to NATO command.[143] During its meeting on 1–2 June in the Petersberg near Bonn, the Troika agreed upon an elaborate formula that essentially

---

[137] At this stage, the trilateral diplomacy with Milosevic as the point of reference faced another obstacle, as the President of the FRY had become indicted by the International War Crimes Tribunal because of his responsibility for atrocities against civilians in Kosovo.

[138] See Joetze, *Der letzte Krieg in Europa?*, 151. Joetze bases his claims upon extensive discussions with Vladimir Markov who served as Chernomyrdin's personal advisor and was present at the talks.

[139] See Judah, *Kosovo: War and Revenge*, 270 *et seq.*

[140] At the summit, there were no public discussions about the ground option in order to avoid an open split of the NATO Alliance; see Albright, *Madam Secretary*, 415 *et seq.*

[141] See Daalder and O'Hanlon, *Winning Ugly*, 171.

[142] See Joetze, *Der letzte Krieg in Europa?*, 152.

[143] See Talbott, *The Russia Hand*, 324; also Albright, *Madam Secretary*, 420.

accommodated the US position.[144] Negotiations remained limited to the Troika core and did not include other G-8 representatives.[145] Ahtisaari and Chernomyrdin would demand from Milosevic the withdrawal of all military, paramilitary, and police forces. At the same time, they would concede the return of a small number of Serb military and police personnel at a later stage to perform certain functions such as holding liaison with the international security and civil presence, marking and clearing of minefields, and maintaining a presence at key border crossings as well as Serb patrimonial sites. As for the command structure of the security presence, Chernomyrdin conceded an international force with substantial participation of NATO countries under unified command. The details of the command structure as well as the question of the respective responsibilities for the troop sectors on the ground were excluded from negotiations with Milosevic. These contentious items remained reserved for subsequent bilateral US–Russian talks.[146] The paper that Ahtisaari and Chernomyrdin presented to Milosevic therefore did not contain any reference to those pending issues.[147] Unable to open further negotiations on the text of the joint proposal, Milosevic accepted the conditions on 2 June.

Sequencing became the cardinal issue for ultimately achieving the termination of conflict. The problems at stake resembled a classical catch-22 scenario. The Serbian forces would not withdraw prior to the adoption of the SC resolution. China and Russia would not adopt the resolution prior to the cessation of NATO air strikes. NATO would not cease the air strikes prior to the withdrawal of Serbian forces. The synchronization of events constituted the key feature to accommodate the diverging interests of the players. In this context, the drafting of the resolution within the G-8 setting and its subsequent adoption by the SC provided the indispensable legitimizing framework that kept the process going. The prospect of a UN resolution drafted by the G-8, which included the Russian Federation, accommodated the Serbian interest not to surrender to NATO.

---

[144] See UN Doc S/1999/649, 7 June 1999.

[145] This had been a deliberate decision by the Troika, see interview with Strobe Talbott, New Haven, Connecticut, 26 September 2001. The proposal that was finally presented to Milosevic was therefore the product of negotiations between Troika representatives and not the G-8 as a whole.

[146] Those questions were discussed during a meeting of US Secretary of Defence Cohen and Russian Defence Minister Sergeyev on 17 June in Helsinki, with President Ahtisaari acting as facilitator.

[147] In fact, when Milosevic asked for a copy of the joint paper, Ahtisaari advised his personal assistant not to photocopy the footnote that referred to open questions related to the international security force; see interview with Martti Ahtisaari, Helsinki, 9 May 2000.

The core of the SC resolution contained key elements of the Troika paper, as agreed upon on the Petersberg. However, it turned once more to be extremely difficult to obtain agreement from Russian representatives at the G-8 level for decisions that had already been taken at the Troika level. During a meeting with representatives of the G-8 Presidency on 5 June in Moscow, Mayorski rejected the German draft that contained the Petersberg and Belgrade Agreements because Chernomyrdin had not acted as the representative of the government but of President Yeltsin.[148] In fact, Mayorski sought to return to the state of G-8 negotiations as of 6 May. Such an obstructionist approach had been caused by the strong criticism the Russian government faced in the Duma and in reports of the media. On the other hand, at this stage, the G-8 remained the Russian Federation's only platform to keep actively involved in the process. It reflected a gambling rather than substantive concern. The loss of prestige would be more substantial if the SC, and with it Russia, was bypassed again and President Yeltsin isolated at the upcoming G-8 summit in Cologne.

At the meeting of G-8 foreign ministers on 7–8 June, the Russian Federation ultimately accepted the Western draft. After intense consultations with President Yeltsin, Ivanov eventually signalled acceptance of the proposal that included the provisions that had already been agreed upon at the Petersberg meeting. Progress in the simultaneous talks at Kumanovo on the military-technical agreement made the continuation of the entire process contingent upon the agreement on the draft resolution.[149] The agreement reflected the Russian position that the cessation of NATO air strikes remained its overriding concern.

With the withdrawal of Serb forces commencing, NATO Secretary-General declared the suspension of air strikes on 10 June, whose continuation would be subject to compliance with the provisions of the military-technical agreement. On the same day, and without any further involvement of the Consultation and Drafting Group (CDG) in New York, the SC adopted the draft resolution of G-8 foreign ministers.[150] The draft

---

[148] Author interview with a senior German diplomat, Berlin, 26 September 2000.

[149] The military–technical agreement between the international security force and the FRY, signed on 9 June, laid out the details of the withdrawal of Serb forces from Kosovo and the deployment of KFOR.

[150] The Permanent Representative of Germany to the UN confirmed that the draft resolution included all technical details, which made any further deliberation by the CDG unnecessary; see interview with Dieter Kastrup, New York, 14 November 2000. A senior official in the US State Department claims that the genesis of SC Resolution 1244 was 'an aberration'; author interview, Washington, DC, 21 November 2000. A former senior advisor to Jacques Chirac also maintains that SC Resolution 1244 might well be 'the least negotiated' inside the SC framework; author interview, New York, 18 November 2000.

remained almost unchanged, with the exception of two minor changes introduced by the Chinese delegation, which underlined the principles of the UN Charter as well as the SC's primary responsibility for the maintenance of international peace and security.[151] Deviating from previous wording, the resolution determined that the situation in the region posed and continued to be a threat to *international* peace and security, which could be read as a *post hoc* legitimation for NATO air strikes. Resolutions 1199 and 1203 had affirmed only that the situation posed a threat to peace and security *in the region*, while reaffirming the territorial integrity of the FRY. In effect, Resolution 1244 established a protectorate, with the UN Mission in Kosovo (UNMIK) and the international security presence (KFOR) as its two pillars. The resolution provided the establishment of the presences 'for an initial period of 12 months, to continue thereafter unless the Security Council decides otherwise'. Such a provision constituted a peculiarity, as the mission was, in effect, open-ended in order to prevent the possibility that extension of the mission became subject to the veto of the Russian Federation or China.[152] It also responded to the bad precedent the Chinese delegation had set in February 1999 when it blocked the extension of the UN's preventive deployment force in Macedonia by casting its veto.[153]

The circumstance that fifteen countries, not being members of the Council, had requested participation in the SC meeting under Article 31 demonstrated that the adoption of the draft resolution constituted more than just a formal procedure to provide the form for the already existing substance of the settlement.[154] In essence, this was an expression of loyalty. The Council provided the platform for creating the perception of legitimacy, while voice played a supportive role to achieve broader acceptance of the settlement that had been reached outside the UN framework. In this regard, the complementary functions of loyalty and voice became further illustrated with the creation of the so-called Friends of the Secretary-General for Kosovo.[155] The informal group originated in the desire to

---

[151] See UN Doc S/RES/1244, 10 June 1999.

[152] It is not entirely clear why the Russian delegation accepted this provision. Some have suggested that the early cessation of air strikes constituted Russia's overriding concern, and for this reason, they did not pay very much attention to this detail; author interviews with various participants in the negotiations.

[153] The United Nations Preventive Deployment Force (UNPREDEP) had been deployed in March 1995. China opposed the further extension of the operation as Macedonia had accepted economic assistance from Taiwan.

[154] See UN Doc S/PV.4011, 10 June 1999.

[155] In its formative stage, the Group of Friends comprised Austria, Belgium, Canada, China, Denmark, Finland, France, Germany, Greece, Italy, Japan, Netherlands, Russia, Spain, Sweden, Turkey, the United Kingdom, the United States; OSCE, EU, and (Organization of Islamic Conferences) OIC.

mobilize international support for the implementation of the civilian aspects of SC Resolution 1244. It developed into a kind of donors' meeting.[156] The engagement of such a large number of key actors served symbolic rather than operational purposes.[157] It enhanced the perception of the legitimacy of the peace process, which would be crucial for maintaining long-term support for the implementation of peace.

7.3 Conclusion: Exit, Voice, and Loyalty

This case study investigated the role and performance of Quint, G-8, and Troika in settling the Kosovo war. Crisis management raised important questions whether the SC still stood at the centre or had slipped to the periphery of international security in the post-bipolar era. Some have argued that the Kosovo war bore the potential 'to be a defining moment in post-Cold War history'.[158] In order to evaluate this potential, it is necessary to analyse conflict response in Kosovo in the wider context of conflict management in former Yugoslavia as a whole, which had already changed governance in the SC.

In addition to that, it is important to realize that UN responses to other crisis settings such as East Timor, which occurred in parallel, offered different conclusions about the actual and perceived severity of the Article 24 crisis.[159] This section summarizes the dynamics of exit, voice, and loyalty in the context of settling the Kosovo conflict.

7.3.1 Parallelism of Exit and Voice

Any proper evaluation of the impact of conflict management in Kosovo on the primary responsibility of the SC to maintain international peace and security needs to take into account the parallelism of exit and voice. Those findings essentially confirm the conclusions pertaining to the El Salvador case.[160] While East Timor illustrated the Council's potential, Kosovo

---

[156] See interview with Alexander Marschik, Counsellor, Permanent Mission of Austria to the UN, New York, 20 November 2002.

[157] The mandate of the group was rather broad in order to avoid competition with the CDG; author interview with a senior official of the UN Secretariat, UN, New York, 4 October 2002.

[158] Albrecht Schnabel and Ramesh Thakur, 'Kosovo, the changing contours of world politics, and the challenge of world order', in *Kosovo and the Challenge of Humanitarian Intervention*, 1.

[159] See section 7.1.2

[160] See chapter 6.

demonstrated its limits. Conclusions about the ability of the Council to meet its responsibilities according to Article 24 are therefore much more ambiguous than the single evaluation of the Kosovo war may suggest. Looking at the ways and means of crisis response in East Timor illustrates a very successful case of cooperation between Core Group and Council that contained striking similarities. It was the perception of the deadlocked SC that contributed to the perception of failure in the Kosovo case.

7.3.2 Loyalty and the Containment of Exit

Since 1994, with the establishment of the Contact Group on former Yugoslavia, conflict management had been conducted outside the UN framework. Despite choosing the exit option, Contact Group members had also formed the CCP and the CDG in New York as an interface to move policy upward to the level of the UN in order to receive the formal blessing of the SC. The interaction between Contact Group, CCP/CDG, and SC had established a semi-formal framework to create wider acceptance within the UN framework. Seen from this perspective, intervention in Kosovo without authorization of the SC did not constitute an entirely new policy but pushed the exit option to its extreme.

The Kosovo case illustrates the importance and persistence of the 'symbolic life'[161] of the SC. Despite the marginalization of the institution in shaping the outcome of the political settlement of the Kosovo conflict, the SC continued to exert a strong pull on states to seek its *post hoc* blessing. The decoupling of the substance of conflict management in Kosovo from the process of its legitimation significantly increased the political costs of intervention. Consequently, loyalty contained the negative repercussions of exit. The prospect and the eventual adoption of SC Resolution 1244 helped to create broader acceptance and the perception of legitimacy.

While Quint, G-8, and Troika delivered substantial outcomes, the SC produced legitimacy through its formal decisions. The adoption of SC Resolution 1244 merged process and substance of conflict settlement. Maintaining the right process was of crucial importance to achieve legitimacy based on both procedure and output. In the final analysis, the dynamics between Quint, G-8, and Troika on the one side and the SC on the other side were mutually reinforcing. If exit resulted in a deprivation of legitimacy, loyalty contributed to its restoration.

---

[161] See Ian Hurd, 'Legitimacy, Power, and the Symbolic Life of the UN Security Council', *Global Governance*, 8/1 (2002), 35–51.

Conclusions: Implications for Governance of the UN Security Council

In March 2005, UN Secretary-General Kofi Annan introduced his report 'In Larger Freedom: Towards Development, Security and Human Rights for All', in which he sought to forge a new consensus on how to address the security challenges of the twenty-first century. Changes in the formal membership of the Security Council (SC) were considered a sine qua non 'to make it more representative . . . and thereby more legitimate in the eyes of the world'.[1] In the report, the Secretary-General underlined that the Council 'must be not only more representative but also more able and willing to take action when action is needed. Reconciling these two imperatives is the hard test that any reform proposal must pass.'[2] At the same time, Annan raised the caveat that reform 'should not impair the effectiveness of the Security Council'.[3] Adaptations needed to result in an increase of 'the democratic and accountable nature of the body'.[4] While those arguments have been exchanged back and forth for more than a decade, they tend to overemphasize the importance of formal membership and to ignore the actual workings of the Council, which have undergone profound changes in the post-Cold War era.

This book has established the importance of informal groups of states as part and parcel of SC governance. In order to understand the variables that define the performance of the SC, we need to extend our analysis to levels of informal cooperation. Informal groups have reshaped

---

[1] UN Doc A/59/2005, 21 March 2005, para 168.
[2] Ibid.
[3] Ibid.
[4] Ibid.

international diplomacy and altered the balance of power within the UN. Seen from the perspective of principal-agent theory, UN member states have re-delegated tasks away from the SC to informal arrangements that allow for the better management of multiple policy externalities. The findings suggest that we need to qualify the claim that the functions of centralization and independence enhance the efficiency of international organizations (IOs). Such a pattern may alter when IOs are challenged to adapt to systemic change. The synergistic framework of analysis underlying this book has helped to explain why decentralization through informal groups of states may enhance efficiency. *Ad hoc* arrangements are instrumental to escape from the structural constraints of IOs. Decentralization results in a new and rather peculiar structure of international diplomacy, in which the functions of diplomatic problem-solving and legitimation have become decoupled.

The dynamics between informal groups of states and the SC can best be captured by applying the analytical framework of exit, voice, and loyalty. This appears to be particularly useful to understand variations in the level of cooperation, which constitutes a key challenge to institutional theory. The importance of exit, voice, and loyalty originates in the explanatory leverage it provides to analyse the institutional effects of the SC under conditions of systemic change. This book is a starting point to qualify answers to the question of why states act through formal IOs.[5]

Future research desiderata would include therefore extending the database by conducting a comparative analysis of international institutions such as the European Union (EU), the International Monetary Fund (IMF), the North Atlantic Treaty Organization (NATO), the UN, or the World Trade Organization (WTO). Exit, voice, and loyalty do not conceptualize the role of informal groups of states as mediators or facilitators in the making of peace. This would be subject to further research by integrating the phenomenon into the body of literature on international mediation and bargaining.

This final section summarizes the causes of informal groups of states and their effects on SC governance. It argues that those informal mechanisms are changing the role of the SC in the international system. The functions of diplomatic problem-solving and its collective legitimation become separate from one another. This has implications for our understanding of power, legitimacy, and change in the theory of international relations.

---

[5] See Abbott and Snidal, 'Why States Act Through Formal International Organizations'.

1. Exit, Voice, and Loyalty: Causes

Causes for exit and voice are twofold (see Figure 4). Firstly, exit and voice emerged as policy alternatives in response to systemic change. The *Janus*-faced structure of the SC makes it sensitive to changing structural conditions while the restrictive provisions of the Charter of the UN limit the possibilities for formal adaptations. Secondly, multiple strategic constraints inhibit the efficient running of the Council's conflict-resolution machinery. Such problems include the varying capacity and resources of UN member states to contribute to the Council's work programme, the biannual rotation

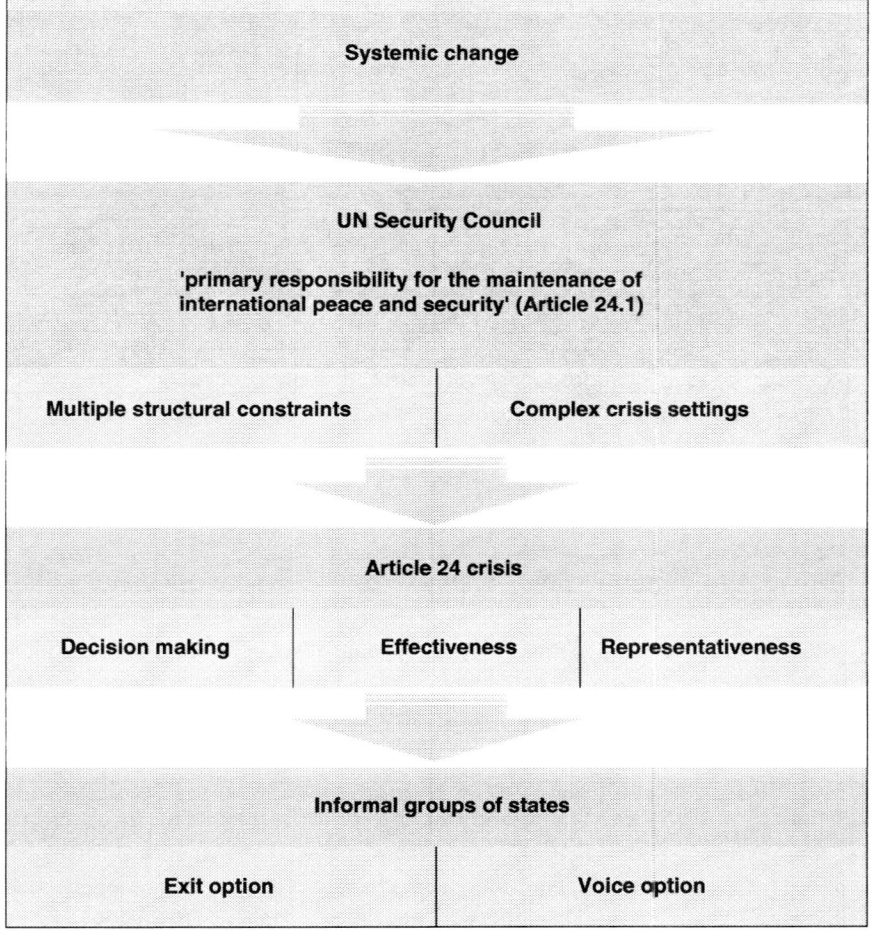

Figure 4 Proliferation of Informal Groups in the post-Cold War Era: Causes

of elected members of the SC, lack of political will to address conflicts, lack of support from permanent and elected members to implement resolutions that have been adapted by themselves, or SC working methods and practices. Systemic change generated the Article 24 crisis of the SC, raising questions about its representativeness, effectiveness, and decision-making.

Exit and voice constitute different answers to different conflict settings accommodating specific needs. While Groups of Friends of the Secretary-General developed to assist the UN in the making of peace on a consensual basis, Contact Groups were rather engaged in cases of peace enforcement. While the voice option implies conflict resolution with the strong engagement of the UN Secretariat assisted by UN member states, the exit option reflects an approach that is primarily driven by a coalition of states. Depending on the specific case, the UN Secretariat may play a supportive role. In this context, loyalty displayed two decisive functions: firstly, it pushed those players acting outside the UN framework to seek *post hoc* legitimation by the SC; secondly, loyalty contained the extent of exit and limited the damage created by the marginalization of the Organization. The different approaches of managing conflicts in Namibia, El Salvador, and Kosovo are indicative of the varying dynamics of exit, voice, and loyalty.

The case study of Namibia has illustrated a case of exit in response to deficiencies in the working methods and procedures of the SC. The growing recourse to Article 31 of the UN Charter that granted non-members the possibility of participation in formal meetings of the Council effectively transformed the body into a mini-Assembly, with negative repercussions for dealing effectively with the conflict. The increased institutionalization of so-called informal consultations of the SC, in itself an exit strategy to deal with the effects of systemic change, did not necessarily solve the structural deficiencies.

The formation of the Group of Friends on El Salvador originated in the fact that the UN Secretary-General does not display any leverage of his own in negotiations with the parties to the conflict. The assistance of like-minded governments was instrumental to amplify the leverage of the UN intermediary. Furthermore, and contrary to the process leading towards Namibian independence, the formation of the Group of Friends occurred in response to the shifting balance of power between Secretariat and SC during the transformation period of the bipolar system. The impartiality of the Secretary-General had been compromised by the actual and perceived predominance of the P-5, especially of the United States. The strategic balance between Secretariat and SC constituted the primary concern of the Group of Friends on El Salvador. Strengthening the role of the

Table 6. Informal Groups of States: Effects

Power	• Amplifying the relative influence and power of stakeholders in a conflict setting; • Balancing P-5 preponderance in the SC; • Disguising US hegemony.
Legitimacy	• Decoupling the processes of diplomatic problem-solving and collective legitimation; • Strengthening SC procedural and output legitimacy; • Embedding US foreign policy in a minilateral framework.
Incremental change	• Ameliorating the Article 24 crisis of the SC; • Complementing SC governance.

Secretary-General was the manifest interest of the *Frente Farabundo Marti para la Liberación Nacional (FMLN)* to prevent micromanagement of the conflict by the Council.

The Kosovo case has illustrated the Article 24 crisis of the SC at the end of the 1990s, which raised further questions about the ability to meet its responsibilities in cases when the body appears to be deadlocked. NATO intervention in Kosovo without the authorization of the SC pushed the exit option to its extreme, while generating a maximum pull on the key actors to seek *post hoc* legitimation for their action taken. The Kosovo case constituted a textbook example for the strong symbolic power of the SC that remained prevalent throughout the management of the crisis. The substance of conflict management in Kosovo and the process of legitimation became decoupled.

2. Exit, Voice, and Loyalty: Effects

Informal groups of states incrementally change the workings of the SC. They affect SC governance in multiple ways (see Table 6). Firstly, process and substance of conflict resolution become decoupled. Secondly, ancillary to the first point, functions of diplomatic problem-solving and its collective legitimation are separable but not separate processes (see Table 6).

2.1 Decoupling the Process and Substance of Legitimation

Ideally, the work of informal groups and the SC is complementary and mutually reinforcing. They narrow the operational and participatory gap growing out of the multiple incapacities that prevents the SC from formulating an effective response to crisis situations. The output legitimacy of the Council is strengthened, while actions taken by informal arrangements become more acceptable. Any positive impact on SC governance is however dependent upon the ability to strike a balance between the competing demands of inclusiveness, efficiency, informality, accountability, and transparency. In the worst case, informal groups of states operate in competition to the SC. Then, the legitimacy of the Council is weakened, with the process and substance of conflict resolution becoming mutually excluding.

2.2 Loyalty and the Containment of Exit

There is a tendency that the further UN member states push for exit, the greater the pull of loyalty. The Kosovo case enhances our understanding of the post-Cold War role of the SC in the conduct of international affairs. Intervention in Kosovo without the authorization of the SC pushed the exit option to its extreme, while loyalty prevented the long-term marginalization of the Organization. Despite the Article 24 crisis of the SC that relates to problems of representativeness, effectiveness, and decision-making, the international institution is perceived to be 'ineffective but indispensable'.[6]

Seen from this perspective, the Kosovo case illustrates the importance and persistence of the symbolic life of the SC. Despite the marginalization of the institution in shaping the outcome of the political settlement of the Kosovo conflict, loyalty prevented further damage by seeking the re-involvement of the UN at a relatively early stage. In addition, the degree to which the UN became re-involved in administering the transitional authority in Kosovo may suggest that this constituted a direct effect of its marginalization. The pendulum swung back from the one extreme of marginalization to the other extreme of establishing a UN protectorate. The decoupling of the substance of conflict management in Kosovo from the process of its legitimation significantly increased the political costs of intervention. Consequently, loyalty contained the negative repercussions of exit.

2.3 Accommodating US Exceptionalism

Looked at from the perspective of US foreign policy, the cases of Namibia and El Salvador demonstrate that choosing multilateral means with the assistance of minilateral settings constitutes a promising strategy for achieving policy ends at a relatively low cost. US exceptionalism has to

[6] Mats Berdal, 'The UN Security Council: Ineffective but Indispensable', *Survival*, 45/2 (2003), 7–30.

be taken into account and cannot be ignored in the resolution of conflicts with US involvement.

In the case of Namibia, the adoption of the linkage approach had the effect that Western partners as well as the UN Secretariat could only try to limit the damage growing out of this policy change. Engaging the US administration via the Contact Group prevented complete exit that would have resulted in a loss of control by the UN Secretariat and Western partners. Even the degradation of the Contact Group into a sounding board for approval of US policy seemed to be the least bad option as it maintained semi-formalized communication between US administration and Western partners beyond the dividing lines. Ultimately, this contributed to the predictability of US foreign policy. At the same time, the seal of UN legitimacy exerted a strong pull factor at least on the wiser heads in the Reagan administration.

In the case of El Salvador, the peace process rested inside the UN framework and restrained the United States' room for manoeuvre. Nevertheless, joint efforts taken by the UN Secretariat, the Group of Friends, and the US administration helped to generate the momentum for an agreement. The minilateral solution offers US foreign policy a trade-off between inclusiveness and efficiency. In the long run, it may prevent a shift towards revolutionary policies that undermine the stability of the international system. Minilateral settings ultimately play into the pattern of US foreign policy to seek maximum flexibility while securing an aura of legitimacy.

2.4 Generating Incremental Change: Informal Groups and Security Council Membership

This study has illustrated that informal groups of states have taken on certain functions as agents of incremental change, without formally changing membership on the SC. Exit, voice, and loyalty allow for an incremental change of international institutions. It is part and parcel of 'an evolutionary process in which continual adjustments are made to accommodate the shifting interests and power relations of groups and states'.[7] Informal groups serve as flexible agents of incremental change. Change is incremental because the Charter of the UN remains unaltered. Consequently, those agents are able to alleviate tensions generated by systemic change in combination with the inability of the SC to adapt. In effect, they constitute a safety valve to divert the inner-institutional pressure for SC

---

[7] Gilpin, *War and Change in World Politics*, 45.

reform. They display the role of being stabilizing elements for international institutions in transition. This leads to the crucial question whether the engagement of key players through informal devices may serve as compensation for lack of SC reform. Although agents of incremental change lend stability to a dynamic process, it is unlikely that the calls for substantial reform of the SC will fade. SC reform is about form rather than substance. Enlarging the membership will help to perceive the institution as geographically balanced and, at the same time, more legitimate. It is, however, important to understand that enlarging the SC will not solve its problems of output legitimacy, that is, effectiveness and decision-making. In consequence, SC reform will have the effect of raising, not decreasing, the significance of informal groups of states. And this view is even shared by candidate countries with aspirations for a permanent seat on the Council.[8]

3. Conclusion

This study focused on the dynamics between formal and informal institutions in the making of peace. However, it is an underlying feature of the case studies that success or failure of institutions depends a great deal on the personalities involved. They breathe life into those bodies. Individuals display the endurance, determinism, leadership, and vision to end conflicts. In their aim to reconcile the mutually incompatible elements of utopia and reality, morality and power, they ultimately move the utopian element of the UN closer to reality.

[8] Author interview.

Appendix
Interviews Conducted (in alphabetical order)

Martti Ahtisaari, former President of Finland, Helsinki, 9 May 2000.

Günter Altenburg, former Director-General for UN, Human Rights, Humanitarian Affairs, and Global Issues, Foreign Office, Berlin, 25 September 2000.

Blanca Antonini, former Assistant to the Personal Representative of the Secretary-General for the Central American Peace Process, New York, 23 October 2002.

Diego Arria, former Permanent Representative of Venezuela to the UN, New York, 28 November 2000.

Neylan Bali, former Director of the SC Affairs Division, UN, New York, 1 December 2000.

Christian Clages, Assistant to the Foreign and Security Policy Advisor of the German Chancellor, Federal Chancellery, Berlin, 6 September 2000.

Chester Crocker, former US Assistant Secretary of State for African Affairs, Washington, DC, 21 November 2000.

William Durch, Senior Associate, Stimson Center, Washington, DC, 11 September 2001.

Interview with Ambassador Tono Eitel, former Permanent Representative of Germany to the UN, Münster, 5 August 2000.

Alfred Grannas, Counsellor, Permanent Mission of Germany to the UN, 30 October 2000.

Alexej Grigorjew, First Counsellor, Embassy of the Russian Federation, Berlin, 26 September 2000.

Wolfgang Ischinger, former State Secretary, German Foreign Office, Washington, DC, 24 January 2002.

Ana Jimenez, First Secretary, Permanent Mission of Spain to the UN, New York, 25 November 2002.

Günter Joetze, formerly German Foreign Office and Author of *Der letzte Krieg in Europa?*, Königswinter, 28 March 2003.

Dieter Kastrup, former Permanent Representative of Germany to the UN, New York, 14 November 2000.

Hans-Peter Kaul, formerly Counsellor, Permanent Mission of Germany to the UN, Bonn, 8 January 1999.

John Kornblum, former US Assistant Secretary for European and Canadian Affairs, Berlin, 18 September 2000.

Jean-David Levitte, former Diplomatic Advisor to the President of France, Jacques Chirac, New York, 18 November 2000.

Alexander Marschik, Counsellor, Permanent Mission of Austria to the UN, New York, 20 November 2002.

Aleksandre Matsouka, Desk Officer Kosovo, UN, New York, 4 October 2002.

Michael Moller, Director of Political, Peacekeeping and Humanitarian Affairs, Executive Office of the UN Secretary-General, UN, New York, 24 October 2002.

Edward Mortimer, Director of Communications, Executive Office of the UN Secretary-General, New York, 14 February 2001.

Gunter Pleuger, State Secretary, Foreign Office, Berlin, 26 September 2000.

Robert Rosenstock, Minister Counsellor, Permanent Mission of the United States to the UN, New York, 24 November 2000.

Alvaro de Soto, former Personal Representative of the Secretary-General for the Central American Peace Process, New York, 17 November 2000.

Vibeke Rovsing Jorgensen, Counsellor, Permanent Mission of Denmark to the UN, New York, 19 November 2002.

Yusuke Shindo, First Secretary, Embassy of Japan, Berlin, 13 September 2000.

Francesco Talò, Counsellor, Permanent Mission of Italy to the UN, New York, 8 December 2000.

Strobe Talbott, former US Deputy Assistant Secretary of State, New Haven, Connecticut, 26 September 2001.

Danilo Türk, Assistant-Secretary-General for Political Affairs, UN, New York, 6 November 2002.

Sir Brian Urquhart, former Under-Secretary-General for Special Political Affairs of the UN, 7 February 2001 and 21 February 2001.

Sergio Vento, Permanent Representative of Italy to the UN, New York, 8 December 2000.

Hans-Joachim Vergau, formerly German representative in the Western Contact Group on Namibia, Berlin, 9 January 2001.

Abiodun Williams, Director of the Strategic Planning Unit, Executive Office of the UN Secretary-General, UN, New York, 29 October 2002.

William Wood, Principal Deputy Assistant Secretary of State for International Organizations, US State Department, Washington DC, 21 November 2000.

Bibliography

1. Archives

LIDDELL HART MILITARY ARCHIVES, KING'S COLLEGE
The Death of Yugoslavia

UNITED NATIONS, ARCHIVES, AND RECORDS MANAGEMENT SECTION
Advisory Committee on the United Nations Emergency Force, 1957–1959
United Nations Advisory Committee on the Congo, 1961–1963
Papers of Secretary-General Kurt Waldheim, 1972–1981

YALE UNIVERSITY, MANUSCRIPTS AND ARCHIVES, STERLING MEMORIAL LIBRARY
Javier Pérez de Cuéllar Papers, 1980–1992, Manuscript Group ⌐768

UNITED NATIONS STUDIES PROGRAM AT YALE
UN-Oral History Interview Transcripts:
Bernard Aronson, former US Assistant Secretary of State for Inter-American Affairs, 9 October 1997.
Diego Arria, former Permanent Representative of Venezuela to the United Nations, 5 September 1997.
Roelof Botha, former Foreign Minister of South Africa, 5 March 2001.
Alfredo Cristiani, former President of El Salvador, 25 July 1997.
Chester Crocker, former US Assistant Secretary of State for African Affairs, 20 July 1998.
David Escobar Galindo, former negotiator for the Government of El Salvador, 21 June 1997.
Arthur Lall, former Permanent Representative of India to the United Nations, 27 June 1990.
Jorge Montaño, former Permanent Representative of Mexico to the United Nations, 1 October 1999.
Geoffrey Murray, formerly in the Middle East Section of the European Division, Department of External Affairs, Ottawa, 10 January 1991.
Beatrice Rangel, former Chief of Staff for President Péres of Venezuela, 16 September 1997.

Alvaro de Soto, former Personal Representative of the UN Secretary-General for the Central American Peace Process, 9 April 1996.

Manuel Tello (with Gustavo Albin), former Permanent Representative of Mexico to the United Nations, 6 August 1997.

Brian Urquhart, former Under Secretary-General for Special Political Affairs, United Nations, 27 June 1984, 20 July 1984, 15 October 1984, and 10 December 1985.

Francesc Vendrell, former Deputy to the Personal Representative of the UN Secretary-General for the Central American Peace Process, 18 April 1996.

Rubén Zamora, Opposition Presidential Candidate in El Salvador, 24 July 1997.

2. Documents

NATO Press Release M-NAC-1(99)51, 12 April 1999.

NATO Press Release S-1(99)62, 23 April 1999.

UN Document S/RES/84, 7 July 1950.

UN Document A/RES/377, 3 November 1950.

UN Document A/RES/230, 4 December 1954.

UN Document A/2967, 14 September 1955.

UN Document A/RES/334, 3 December 1955.

UN Document A/RES/119, 31 October 1956.

UN Document A/RES/998(ES-I), 4 November 1956.

UN Document A/3302, 6 November 1956.

UN Document A/RES/1001(ES-I), 7 November 1956.

UN Document GAOR, First Emergency Special Session, 567th Plenary Meeting, 7 November 1956.

UN Document A/2253, 10 November 1956.

UN Document A/3375, 20 November 1956.

UN Document GAOR, 690th plenary meeting, 26 September 1957.

UN Document A/RES/1145, 14 November 1957.

UN Document S/RES/128 (1958), 11 June 1958.

UN Document SCOR, 837th Meeting, 22 July 1958.

UN Document SG/709, 24 July 1958.

UN Document S/RES/129, 7 August 1958.

UN Document A/3943, 9 October 1958.

UN Document A/3949, 16 October 1958.

UN Document A/RES/1344 (XIII), 13 December 1958.

UN Document S/RES/143, 14 July 1960.

UN Document S/RES/146, 9 August 1960.

UN Document A/4592 (Annexes), 24 November 1960.

UN Document A/RES/1514(XV), 14 December 1960.

UN Document S/RES/161, 21 February 1961.

UN Document A/RES/1991(XVIII), 17 December 1963.

UN Document GA/RES/2145(XXI), 27 October 1966.

UN Document GA/RES/2248(S-V), 19 May 1967.

UN Document A/6730, Add. 3, 26 June 1967.

UN Document A/RES/2372(XXII), 12 June 1968.

UN Document S/RES/301, 20 October 1971.

UN Document S/PV/1627, 28 January 1972.

UN Document S/PV/1630, 31 January 1972.

UN Document S/PV/1631, 31 January 1972.

UN Document S/PV/1635, 2 February 1972.

UN Document S/PV/1637, 3 February 1972.

UN Document SCOR, 27th year, 1637th meeting, 3 February 1972.

UN Document S/PV/1638, 4 February 1972.

UN Document S/RES/310, 4 February 1972.

UN Document S/RES/309 (1972), 9 February 1972.

UN Document S/10738, 17 July 1972.

UN Document S/RES/323, 6 December 1972.

UN Document GAOR, 27th session, 4th Committee, 2018th meeting, 11 December 1972.

UN Document S/PV/1684, 16 January 1973.

UN Document S/10921, 30 April 1973.

UN Document S/10921/Corr. 1, 30 April 1973.

UN Document SCOR, 28th year, 1747th, 1748th, and 1750th meeting, 21–23 October and 25 October 1973.

UN Document S/11052, 26 October 1973.

UN Document SCOR, 1752nd meeting, 27 October 1973.

UN Document S/RES/342, 11 December 1973.

UN Document SCOR, 28th year, 1758th meeting, 11 December 1973.

UN Document A/RES/3111(XXVIII), 12 December 1973.

UN Document S/RES/366 (1974), 17 December 1974.

UN Document S/RES/385 (1976), 30 January 1976.

UN Document S/11713, 6 June 1975.

UN Document S/12211, 15 October 1976.

UN Document S/PV/1963, 19 October 1976.

UN Document A/31/PV/40, 21 October 1976.

UN Document A/RES/7(XXXI), 5 November 1976.

UN Document A/RES/146(XXXI), 20 December 1976.

UN Document A/RES/148(XXXI), 20 December 1976.

UN Document S/PV.1988–99, 21–31 March 1977.

UN Document S/12309–12, 30 March 1977.

UN Document E/C/10/26, 6 April 1977.

UN Document S/RES/417, 31 October 1977.

UN Document S/RES/418, 4 November 1977.

UN Document S/RES/421, 9 December 1977.

UN Document S/12636, 10 April 1978.

UN Document A/RES/S-9/2, 3 May 1978.

UN Document S/12791, 27 July 1978.

UN Document S/PV/2082, 27 July 1978.

UN Document S/RES/431, 27 July 1978.

UN Document S/RES/432, 27 July 1978.

UN Document S/12853, 20 September 1978.

UN Document S/12868, 27 September 1978.

UN Document S/PV/2087, 29 September 1978.

UN Document S/RES/435, 29 September 1978.

UN Document S/PV/2095, 2 November 1978.

UN Document S/RES/439, 13 November 1978.

UN Document S/13120, 26 February 1979.

UN Document S/13935, 12 May 1980.

UN Document S/RES/473, 13 June 1980.

UN Document S/RES/475, 27 June 1980.

UN Document S/PV/2268–77, 22–27 April 1981.

UN Document S/14459, 27 April 1981.

UN Document S/14461–63, 27 April 1981.

UN Document S/PV/2277, 27 April 1981.

UN Document S/14460/Rev. 1, 29 April 1981.

UN Document S/PV/2298, 29 August 1981.

UN Document S/14664/Rev. 2, 31 August 1981.

UN Document S/PV/2300, 31 August 1981.

UN Document ES-8/2, 14 September 1981.

UN Document GAOR, Eighth Special Emergency Session, Verbatim Records of Meeting, 12th meeting, 14 September 1981.

UN Document S/15287, 12 July 1982.

UN Document S/15757, 29 April 1983.

UN Document S/15776, 19 May 1983.

UN Document S/RES/530, 19 May 1983.

UN Documents S/PV/2439–2451, 23 May–1 June 1983.

UN Document S/RES/532, 31 May 1983.

UN Document S/PV/2451, 1 June 1983.

UN Document S/15943, 29 August 1983.

UN Document S/PV2485, 25 October 1983.

UN Document S/RES/539, 28 October 1983.

UN Document A/RES/38/36, 2 December 1983.

UN Document S/16237, 29 December 1983.

UN Document A/RES/39/50, 12 December 1984.

UN Document S/RES/567, 20 June 1985.

UN Document S/RES/569, 26 July 1985.

UN Document S/17354/Rev. 1, 26 July 1985.

UN Document S/RES/571, 20 September 1985.

UN Document S/RES/574, 7 October 1985.

UN Document S/PV/2602; S/17633, 15 November 1985.

UN Document A/RES/40/56, 2 December 1985.

UN Document S/RES/577, 6 December 1985.

UN Document S/PV/2629, 18 June 1986.

UN Document S/18087/Rev. 1, 18 June 1986.

UN Document A/RES/41/39, 20 November 1986.

UN Document S/PV/2693, 2 February 1987.

UN Document S/18705, 2 February 1987.

UN Document S/PV/2738, 9 April 1987.

UN Document S/PV/2747, 9 April 1987.

UN Document S/18785, 9 April 1987.

UN Document A/RES/42/14, 6 November 1987.

UN Document A/42/844, 1 December 1987.

UN Document A/RES/43/26, 17 November 1988.

UN Document S/RES/628, 16 January 1989.

UN Document S/RES/629, 16 January 1989.

UN Document S/20635, 15 May 1989.

UN Document S/RES/637, 27 July 1989.

UN Document A/44/872 12 December 1989.

UN Document S/21019, 12 December 1989.

UN Document A/45/706, 8 November 1990.

UN Document S/21931, 8 November 1990.

UN Document S/RES/678, 29 November 1990.

UN Document S/22031, 21 December 1990.

UN Document S/RES/693, 20 May 1991.

UN Document S/22947, 15 August 1991.

UN Document A/46/502, 26 September 1991.

UN Document S/23082, 26 September 1991.

UN Document S/RES/714, 30 September 1991.

UN Document A/46/502/Add.1, 7 October 1991.

UN Document S/23082/Add.1, 7 October 1991.

UN Document A/46/553, 9 October 1991.

UN Document S/23130, 9 October 1991.

UN Document A/46/713, 2 December 1991.

UN Document S/23256, 2 December 1991.

UN Document S/23360, 3 January 1992.

UN Document S/24058, 3 June 1992.

UN Document A/47/277–S/24111, 17 June 1992.

UN Document S/23999/Add. 1, 19 June 1992.

UN Document S/24688, 19 October 1992.

UN Document S/RES/784, 30 October 1992.

UN Document S/RES/791, 30 November 1992.

UN Document A/47/842, 23 December 1992.

UN Document S/25007, 23 December 1992.

UN Document S/1994/653, 1 June 1994.

UN Document A/50/60–S/1995/1, 3 January 1995.

UN Document SG/SM/5624, 1 May 1995.

UN Document S/RES/1034, 19 December 1995.

UN Document S/1995/1051, 21 December 1995.

UN Document S/PV/3612, 21 December 1995.

UN Document Supplement to Reports A/50/332 and A/51/512 on Democratization, 17 December 1996.

UN Document A/51/761, 20 December 1996.

UN Document S/PV.3868, 31 March 1998.

UN Document S/RES/1160, 31 March 1998.

UN Document S/1998/318, 13 April 1998.

UN Document S/PRST/1998/25, 24 August 1998.

UN Document S/PV/3930, 23 September 1998.

UN Document S/RES/1199, 23 September 1998.

UN Document S/PRST/1999/2, 19 January 1999.

UN Document S/PRST/1999/5, 29 January 1999.

UN Document S/1999/328, 24 March 1999.

UN Document S/PV/3989, 26 March 1999.

UN Document S/1999/402, 9 April 1999.

UN Document S/1999/516, 6 May 1999.

UN Document S/RES/1239, 14 May 1999.

UN Document S/1999/649, 7 June 1999.

UN Document S/PV/4011, 10 June 1999.

UN Document S/RES/1244, 10 June 1999.

UN Document S/1999/1008, 25 September 1999.

UN Document S/1999/1257, 16 December 1999.

UN Document S/2000/809, 21 August 2000.

UN Document S/PV/4257, 16 January 2001.

UN Document S/2001/574, 7 June 2001.

United Nations. Report of the Security Council, 16 June 2000–15 June 2001, GAOR, Fifty-sixth Session, Supplement No. 2 (A/56/2).

UN Document S/RES/1353 (2001), 13 June 2001.

UN Document A/56/371, 18 September 2001.

UN Document A/56/PV/27, 16 October 2001.

UN Document S/PV/4432, 30 November 2001.

UN Document S/PV/4445, 21 December 2001.

UN Document E/2002/12, 2 April 2002.

UN Document S/2002/603, 6 June 2002.

UN Document A/59/2005, 21 March 2005.

3. Books and Articles

Abbott, Kenneth W. and Snidal, Duncan (1998). 'Why States Act Through Formal International Organizations', *Journal of Conflict Resolution*, 42/1: 3–32.

Abbott, Kenneth W. and Snidal, Duncan (2001). 'Why States Act Through Formal International Organizations', in P. F. Diehl (ed.), *The Politics of Global Governance: International Organizations in an Interdependent World*. London: Lynne Rienner, pp. 9–43.

Aguilar Zinzer, Adolfo (1986). 'Obstacles to Dialogue and a Negotiated Solution in Latin America', in J. Child (ed.), *Conflict in Central America*. London: Hurst & Co., pp. 55–68.

Albright, Madeleine (2003). *Madam Secretary: A Memoir*. New York: Miramax Books.

Annan, Kofi A. (1998). 'Challenges of the New Peacekeeping', in O. A. Otunnu and M. W. Doyle (eds.), *Peacemaking and Peacekeeping for the New Century*. Lanham, MD: Rowman & Littlefield, pp. 169–87.

—— (2000). *We The Peoples: The Role of the United Nations in the 21st Century*. New York: United Nations.

Antonini, Blanca (2000). 'Scenarios for Multilateral Approaches to Political Transitions in the Western Hemisphere', in T. S. Montgomery (ed.), *Peacemaking and Democratization in the Western Hemisphere*. University of Miami, FL: North South Center Press, pp. 303–14.

Arnson, Cynthia J. (1999). 'Introduction', in C. J. Arnson (ed.), *Comparative Peace Processes in Latin America*. Stanford, CA: Stanford University Press, pp. 1–28.

—— (1984). 'The Salvadoran Military and Regime Transformation', in W. Grabendorff, H.-W. Krumwiede, and J. Todt (eds.), *Political Change in Central America: Internal and External Dimensions*. Boulder, CO: Westview Press, pp. 97–113.

Aust, Anthony (1993). 'The Procedure and Practice of the Security Council Today', in Hague Academy of International Law (ed.), *Peacekeeping and Peacebuilding: The Development of the Role of the Security Council*. Dordrecht, The Netherlands: Martinus Nijhoff, pp. 365–74.

Auswärtiges Amt (ed.) (1998). *Deutsche Außenpolitik 1995. Auf dem Weg zu einer Friedensregelung für Bosnien und Herzegowina: 53 Telegramme aus Dayton*. Bonn: Auswärtiges Amt.

Bailey, Sydney D. (1969). *Voting in the Security Council*. Bloomington, IN: Indiana University Press.

—— and Daws, Sam (1998). *The Procedure of the UN Security Council*, 3rd edn. Oxford: Oxford University Press.

Barnett, Michael and Finnemore, Martha (1999). 'The Politics, Power, and Pathologies of International Organizations', *International Organization*, 53/4: 699–732.

—— —— (2004). *Rules for the World: International Organizations in Global Politics*. Ithaca, NY: Cornell University Press.

Barratt, John (1976). 'Southern Africa: A South African View', *Foreign Affairs*, 55/1: 147–86.

Bibliography

Berdal, Mats (2003). 'The UN Security Council: Ineffective but Indispensable', *Survival*, 45/2: 7–30.

—— (1993). *Whither UN Peacekeeping?* Adelphi Paper 281, International Institute for Strategic Studies. Oxford: Oxford University Press.

Berridge, G. R. (1989). 'Diplomacy and the Angola/Namibia Accords', *International Affairs*, 65/3: 463–79.

Bley, Helmut (1978). 'Die Bundesrepublik, der Westen und die internationale Lage um Namibia', in H. Bley and R. Tetzlaff (eds.), *Afrika und Bonn*. Reinbek bei Hamburg, Germany: Rowohlt, pp. 145–68.

Boidevaix, Francine (1997). *Une Diplomatie Informelle Pour L'Europe: Le Groupe de Contact Bosnie*. Paris: Fondation pour les Etudes de Défense.

Boutros-Ghali, Boutros (1996). 'Global Leadership After the Cold War', *Foreign Affairs*, 75/2: 86–98.

Brandt, Hartmut et al. (eds.) (1980). *Perspectives of Independent Development in Southern Africa: The Cases of Zimbabwe and Namibia*. Berlin: German Development Institute.

Brenke, Gabriele (1989). *Die Bundesrepublik Deutschland und der Namibia-Konflikt* München, Germany: Oldenbourg.

Browning, David (1971). *El Salvador: Landscape and Society*. Oxford: Clarendon Press.

Byrne, Hugh (1996). *El Salvador's Civil War: A Study of Revolution*. Boulder, CO: Lynne Rienner.

Calic, Marie-Janine (2000). 'Kosovo in the Twentieth Century: Historical Account', in A. Schnabel and R. Thakur (eds.), *Kosovo and the Challenge of Humanitarian Intervention: Selective Indignation, Collective Action, and International Citizenship*. Tokyo: United Nations University Press, pp. 19–31.

Caplan, Richard (2005). *International Governance of War-Torn Territories: Rule and Reconstruction*. Oxford: Oxford University Press.

—— (2002). *A New Trusteeship? The International Administration of War-torn Territories*. Adelphi Paper 341, International Institute for Strategic Studies. Oxford: Oxford University Press.

—— (1998). 'International Diplomacy and the Crisis in Kosovo', *International Affairs*, 74/4: 745–61.

Carnegie Commission on Preventing Deadly Conflict (1997). *Preventing Deadly Conflict*, Final Report. New York: Carnegie Corporation.

Caron, David D. (1993). 'The Legitimacy of the Collective Authority of the Security Council', *American Journal of International Law*, 87/4: 552–88.

Carr, Edward Hallett (1981). *The Twenty Years' Crisis 1919–1939: An Introduction to the Study of International Relations*, 2nd edn. Reissued with a new preface. London: Macmillan.

Chesterman, Simon (2001). *Just War or Just Peace? Humanitarian Intervention and International Law*. Oxford: Oxford University Press.

Child, Jack (1992). *The Central American Peace Process, 1983–1991: Sheathing Swords, Building Confidence*. Boulder, CO: Lynne Rienner.

Clark, General Wesley K. (2001). *Waging Modern War: Bosnia, Kosovo, and the Future of Combat.* New York: Public Affairs.

Clark, Ian (2005). *Legitimacy in International Society.* Oxford: Oxford University Press.

Claude, Inis L. (1964). *Swords into Plowshares: The Problems and Progress of International Organization,* 3rd edn. New York: Random House.

—— (1966). 'Collective Legitimization as a Political Function of the United Nations', *International Organization,* 20/3: 367–79.

Coleman, Kenneth M. and Herring, George C. (eds.) (1985). *The Central American Crisis: Sources of Conflict and the Failure of U.S. Policy.* Wilmington, DE: SR Scholarly Resources.

Collier, Paul et al. (2003). *Breaking the Conflict Trap: Civil War and Development Policy.* Washington, DC: World Bank.

Cordier, Andrew W. and Foote, Wilder (1969). *Public Papers of the Secretaries-General of the United Nations,* vol. I: Trygve Lie, 1946–53. New York: Columbia University Press.

—— —— (1974). *Public Papers of the Secretaries-General of the United Nations,* vol. IV: *Dag Hammarskjöld, 1958–60.* New York: Columbia University Press.

—— —— (1975). *Public Papers of the Secretaries-General of the United Nations,* vol. V: *Dag Hammarskjöld, 1960–61.* New York: Columbia University Press.

Cousens, Elizabeth M. and Cater, Charles K. (2001). *Towards Peace in Bosnia: Implementing the Dayton Accords.* Boulder, CO: Lynne Rienner.

Cox, Robert W. and Jacobson, Harold K. (1973). 'The Framework for Inquiry', in R. W. Cox and H. K. Jacobson (eds.), *The Anatomy of Influence: Decision-Making in International Organisation.* New Haven, CT: Yale University Press, pp. 371–436.

Crampton, Richard J. (1980). *The Hollow Détente: Anglo-German Relations in the Balkans, 1911–1914.* London.

Crocker, Chester A. (1980). 'South Africa: Strategy for Change'. *Foreign Affairs,* 59/2: 323–51.

—— (1992). *High Noon in Southern Africa: Making Peace in a Rough Neighborhood.* New York: W.W. Norton.

—— (1994). 'Statement', in H. Weiland and M. Braham (eds.), *The Namibian Peace Process: Implications and Lessons for the Future.* Freiburg, Germany: Arnold Bergstraesser Institut, pp. 37–45.

—— (ed.) (1999). *Herding Cats: Multiparty Mediation in a Complex World.* Washington, DC: United States Institute of Peace Press.

Czempiel, Ernst-Otto and Schweitzer, Carl-Christoph (eds.) (1984). *Weltpolitik der USA.* Opladen: Leske & Budrich.

Daalder, Ivo H. (2000). *Getting To Dayton: The Making of America's Bosnia Policy.* Washington, DC: Brookings Institution Press.

—— and O'Hanlon, Michael E. (2000). *Winning Ugly: NATO's War to Save Kosovo.* Washington, DC: Brookings Institution Press.

Dahl, Robert A. (1997). *Toward Democracy: A Journey, Reflections, 1940–1997.* University of California, Berkeley, CA: Institute of Governmental Studies Press.

Bibliography

Delon, Francis (1993). 'La concertation entre les membres permanents du Conseil de sécurité', *Annuaire français de droit international*, 39, 53–69.

Domínguez, Jorge I. (1999). 'US–Latin American Relations During the Cold War and its Aftermath', in V. B. Thomas and J. Dunkerley (eds.), *The United States and Latin America: The New Agenda*. Cambridge, MA: Harvard University Press, pp. 33–50.

Doyle, Michael W., Johnstone, Ian, and Orr, Robert (eds.) (1995). *Multidimensional Peacekeeping: Lessons from Cambodia and El Salvador*. New York: International Peace Academy.

Doyle, Michael (2001). 'War Making and Peace Making: The United Nations' Post-Cold War Record', in C. A. Crocker, F. O. Hampson, and P. Aall (eds.), *Turbulent Peace: The Challenges of Managing International Conflict*. Washington, DC: United States Institute of Peace Press, pp. 529–60.

Dugard, John (ed.) (1973). *The South West Africa/Namibia Dispute: Documents and Scholarly Writings on the Controversy Between South Africa and the United Nations*. Berkeley, CA: University of California Press.

Dülffer, Jost, Kröger, Martin, and Wippich, Rolf-Harald (1997). *Vermiedene Kriege: Deeskalation von Konflikten der Großmächte zwischen Krimkrieg und Erstem Weltkrieg 1865–1914*. München, Germany: Oldenbourg-Verlag.

Dunbabin, J. P. D. (1994). *International Relations Since 1945: A History in Two Volumes, 2: The Post-Imperial Age: The Great Powers and the Wider World*. Harlow, UK: Longman.

Dunkerley, James (1994). *The Pacification of Central America: Political Change in the Isthmus, 1987–1993*. London: Verso.

Economist Intelligence Unit (1986). *Country Profile: Namibia, 1986–87*. London: The Economist Publications.

—— (1987). *Country Profile: Namibia, 1987–88*. London: The Economist Publications.

Eldon, Stewart (2004). 'East Timor', in D. Malone (ed.), *The UN Security Council: From the Cold War to the 21st Century*. Boulder, CO: Lynne Rienner, pp. 551–74.

Elmandjra, Mahdi (1998). *The United Nations System: An Analysis*. London: Faber & Faber.

Fassbender, Bardo (1998). *UN Security Council and the Right of Veto: A Constitutional Perspective*. The Hague: Kluwer Law International.

Feuerle, Loie (1985). 'Informal Consultation: A Mechanism in Security Council Decision-Making', *New York University Journal of International Law and Politics* 18/1: 267–308.

Finnemore, Martha (2003). *The Purpose of Intervention: Changing Beliefs About the Use of Force*. Ithaca, NY: Cornell University Press.

Franck, Thomas M. (1990). *The Power of Legitimacy Among Nations*. Oxford: Oxford University Press.

Freudenschuß, Helmut (1993). 'Article 39 of the UN Charter Revisited: Threats to Peace and Recent Practice of the UN Security Council', *Austrian Journal of International Law* 46/1: 1–39.

Freuding, Christian (2000). *Deutschland in der Weltpolitik: Die Bundesrepublik Deutschland als nicht-ständiges Mitglied im Sicherheitsrat der Vereinten Nationen in den Jahren 1977/78, 1987/88 und 1995/96.* Baden-Baden, Germany: Nomos-Verlag.

Gallarotti, Guilio M. (1991). 'The Limits of International Organization: Systematic Failure in the Management of International Relations', *International Organization*, 45/2: 183–220.

Geldenhuys, Deon (1984). *The Diplomacy of Isolation: South African Foreign Policy Making.* Johannesburg: Macmillan for the South African Institute of International Affairs.

Giersch, Carsten (1998). *Konfliktregulierung in Jugoslawien 1991–1995. Die Rolle von OSZE, EU, UNO und NATO.* Baden-Baden, Germany: Nomos-Verlag.

Gilpin, Robert (1981). *War and Change in World Politics.* Cambridge: Cambridge University Press.

Glennon, Michael J. (2003). 'Why the Security Council Failed', *Foreign Affairs*, 82/3: 16–35.

Goulding, Marrack (1993). 'The Evolution of United Nations Peacekeeping', *International Affairs*, 69/3: 451–64.

—— (2002). *Peacemonger.* London: John Murray.

Gow, James (1997). *Triumph of the Lack of Will: International Diplomacy and the Yugoslav War.* London: Hurst & Co.

Greenberg, Melanie C. and McGuinness, Margaret E. (2000). 'From Lisbon to Dayton: International Mediation and the Bosnia Crisis', in M. C. Greenberg, J. H. Barton and M. E. McGuinness (eds.), *Words Over War: Mediation and Arbitration to Prevent Deadly Conflict.* Oxford: Rowman & Littlefield pp. 35–75.

Guicherd, Catherine (1999). 'International Law and the War in Kosovo', *Survival*, 41/2: 19–34.

Gurirab, Theo-Ben (1994). 'Statement', in H. Weiland and M. Braham (eds.), *The Namibian Peace Process: Implications and Lessons for the Future.* Freiburg, Germay: Arnold Bergstraesser Institut, pp. 45–50.

Hague Academy of International Law (ed.) (1993). *Peacekeeping and Peacebuilding: The Development of the Role of the Security Council.* Dordrecht, The Netherlands: Martinus Nijhoff.

Halperin, Maurice (1980). 'The Cuban Role in Southern Africa', in J. Seiler (ed.), *Southern Africa Since the Portuguese Coup.* Boulder, CO: Westview Press, pp. 25–43.

Hampson, Fen Osler (1997). 'The Pursuit of Human Rights: The United Nations in El Salvador', in W. J. Durch (ed.), *UN Peacekeeping, American Politics, and the Uncivil Wars of the 1990s.* London: Macmillan, pp. 69–102.

Heideking, Jürgen (1983). 'Völkerbund und Vereinte Nationen in der internationalen Politik', *Aus Politik und Zeitgeschichte*, 36/83: 3–16.

Hellmann, Gunther (1988). 'The Collapse of "Constructive Engagement": U.S. Foreign Policy in Southern Africa', in H. Haftendorn and J. Schissler (eds.), *The*

Reagan Administration: A Reconstruction of American Strength? Berlin: Walter de Gruyter, pp. 265–83.

Herbst, Jeffrey (1989). 'The United States in Africa 1988–89: A Very Good Year for Constructive Engagement', in M. E. Doro (ed.), *Africa Contemporary Record*. New York/London: Africana Publishing, pp. A134–145.

Hinsley, Francis Harry (1963). *Power and the Pursuit of Peace: Theory and Practice in the History of Relations Between States*. Cambridge: Cambridge University Press.

—— (1987). 'Peace and War in Modern Times', in R. Väyrynen (ed.), *The Quest for Peace: Transcending Collective Violence and War among Societies, Cultures and States*. London: Sage, pp. 63–79.

Hirschman, Albert O. (1970). *Exit, Voice, and Loyalty: Responses to Decline in Firms, Organizations, and States*. Cambridge, MA: Harvard University Press.

Hiscocks, Richard (1973). *The Security Council: A Study in Adolescence*. New York: Free Press.

Holbrooke, Richard (1999). *To End A War*. New York: Modern Library.

Holland, Martin (1987). 'Three Approaches for Understanding European Political Co-operation: A Case Study of EC-South African Policy', *Journal of Common Market Studies*, 25/4: 295–313.

Holzgrefe, J. L., and Keohane, Robert O. (eds.) (2003). *Humanitarian Intervention: Ethical, Legal and Political Dilemmas*. Cambridge: Cambridge University Press.

Hoopes, Townsend and Brinkley, Douglas (1997). *FDR and the Creation of the U.N.* New Haven, CT: Yale University Press.

Hosmer, Stephen T. (2001). *The Conflict Over Kosovo: Why Milosevic Decided to Settle When He Did*. Santa Monica, CA: Rand.

Hume, Cameron R. (1994). *The United Nations, Iran, and Iraq: How Peacemaking Changed*. Bloomington, IN: Indiana University Press.

Hughes, Thomas L. (1969). 'On the Causes of Our Discontents', *Foreign Affairs*, 47/4: 653–67.

Hurd, Ian (1997). 'Security Council Reform: Informal Membership and Practice', in B. Russett (ed.), *The Once and Future Security Council*. New York: St Martin's Press, pp. 135–52.

—— (1999). 'Legitimacy and Authority in International Politics', *International Organization*, 53/2: 379–408.

—— (2002). 'Legitimacy, Power, and the Symbolic Life of the UN Security Council', *Global Governance*, 8/1: 35–51.

Hurrell, Andrew and Fawcett, Louise (1995). 'Conclusion: Regionalism and International Order?', in L. Fawcett and A. Hurrell (eds.), *Regionalism in World Politics: Regional Organization and International Order*. Oxford: Oxford University Press, pp. 309–27.

Ikenberry, G. John (2002). 'Multilateralism and U.S. Grand Strategy', in S. Patrick and S. Forman (eds.), *Multilateralism and US Foreign Policy: Ambivalent Engagement*. London: Lynne Rienner, pp. 121–40.

—— (2003). 'State Power and the Institutional Bargain: America's Ambivalent Economic and Security Multilateralism', in R. Foot, S. N. MacFarlane, and M. Mastanduno (eds.), *US Hegemony and International Organizations: The United States and Multilateral Institutions*. Oxford: Oxford University Press, pp. 49–70.

Independent International Commission on Kosovo (2000). *The Kosovo Report*. Oxford: Oxford University Press.

International Commission on Intervention and State Sovereignty (2001). *The Responsibility to Protect*. Ottawa: International Development Research Centre.

International Court of Justice (1966). *South-West Africa Cases (Ethiopia v. South Africa; Liberia v. South Africa)*, Judgment of 18 July 1966. The Hague: International Court of Justice.

Jabri, Vivienne (1990). *Mediating Conflict: Decision-Making and Western Intervention in Namibia*. Manchester: Manchester University Press.

Jaster, Robert S. (1985). *South Africa in Namibia: The Botha Strategy*. Lanham, MD: University Press of America.

Joetze, Günther (2001). *Der letzte Krieg in Europa? Das Kosovo und die deutsche Politik*. Munich: DVA.

Johnstone, Ian (1995). *Rights and Reconciliation: UN strategies in El Salvador*. London: Lynne Rienner.

Jones, Bruce D. (2001). *The Challenges of Strategic Coordination: Containing Opposition and Sustaining Implementation of Peace Agreements in Civil Wars*, IPA Policy Paper Series on Peace Implementation. New York: International Peace Academy.

Judah, Tim (1999). 'Kosovo's Road to War', *Survival*, 41/2: 5–18.

—— (2002). *Kosovo: War and Revenge*. New Haven, CT: Yale University Press.

Juhn, Tricia (1998). *Negotiating Peace in El Salvador: Civil-Military Relations and the Conspiracy to End the War*. London: Macmillan.

Kahler, Miles (1992). 'Multilateralism with Small and Large Numbers', *International Organization*, 46/3: 681–708.

Karl, Terry Lynn (1992). 'El Salvador's Negotiated Revolution', *Foreign Affairs*, 71/2: 147–64.

Karns, Margaret P. (1987). 'Ad Hoc Multilateral Diplomacy: The United States, the Contact Group, and Namibia', *International Organization*, 41/1: 93–123.

Kaufman Purcell, Susan (1985). 'Demystifying Contadora', *Foreign Affairs*, 64/1: 74–95.

Kaul, Hans-Peter (1998). 'Arbeitsweise und informelle Verfahren des Sicherheitsrates: Beobachtungen eines Unterhändlers', *Vereinte Nationen*, 46/1: 6–13.

Keohane, Robert O. (1984). *After Hegemony: Cooperation and Discord in the World Political Economy*. Princeton, NJ: Princeton University Press.

—— (1989). *International Institutions and State Power: Essays in International Relations Theory*. Boulder, CO: Westview Press.

—— and Nye, Joseph S. (2000) 'Introduction', in J. S. Nye and J. D. Donahue (eds.), *Governance in a Globalizing World*. Washington, DC: Brookings Institution Press, pp. 1–41.

Keohane, Robert O. and Martin, Lisa L. (2003). 'Institutional Theory as a Research Program', in C. Elman and M. F. Elman (eds.), *Progress in International Relations Theory: Appraising the Field.* Cambridge, MA: MIT Press, pp. 71–107.

Kirton, John J. (2002). 'The G-8, the United Nations, and Global Security Governance', in J. J. Kirton and J. Takase (eds.), *New Directions in Global Political Governance: The G-8 and International Order in the Twenty-first Century.* Aldershot, UK: Ashgate, pp. 191–207.

Kissinger, Henry A. (1957). *A World Restored—Metternich, Castlereagh and the Problems of Peace 1812–22.* Boston, MA: Houghton Mifflin.

Koremenos, Barbara, Lipson, Charles, and Snidal, Duncan (eds.) (2004). *The Rational Design of International Institutions.* Cambridge: Cambridge University Press.

Krasno, Jean E. (1996). *The Group of Friends of the Secretary-General: A Useful Diplomatic Tool.* Washington, DC: Carnegie Commission on Preventing Deadly Conflict.

—— (ed.) (2004). *The United Nations: Confronting the Challenges of a Global Society.* Boulder, CO: Lynne Rienner.

Krauss, Clifford (1991). 'U.N. Aide Assailed in Salvadoran Talks: Washington Says a Mediator Accedes to Rebel Delaying Tactics', *New York Times*, 1 February, A3.

Kühne, Winrich (1985). *Südafrika und seine Nachbarn: Durchbruch zum Frieden?* Baden-Baden, Germany: Nomos-Verlag.

—— (1989). 'Frieden im südwestlichen Afrika? Der Durchbruch bei den Verhandlungen um die Unabhängigkeit Namibias', *Europa-Archiv*, 44/4: 105–14.

—— 'Völkerrecht und Friedenssicherung in einer turbulenten Welt: Eine analytische Zusammenfassung der Grundprobleme und Entwicklungsperspektiven', in W. Kühne (ed.), *Blauhelme in einer turbulenten Welt.* Baden-Baden, Germany: Nomos-Verlag, pp. 17–100.

—— and Prantl, Jochen (eds.) (2000). *The Security Council and the G8 in the New Millennium: Who is in Charge of International Peace and Security?* Report of the 5th International Berlin Workshop. Ebenhausen, Germany: Research Institute for International Affairs.

Langenhove, Fernand van (1958). *La Crise du Système de Sécurité Collective des Nations Unies, 1946–1957.* The Hague: M. Nijhoff.

Latowski, Paul and Smith, Martin A. (2003). *The Kosovo Crisis and the Evolution of Post–Cold War European Security.* Manchester: Manchester University Press.

Legum, Colin (1979). *The Western Crisis Over Southern Africa. South Africa, Rhodesia, Namibia.* London: Africana Publishing Co.

Leigh-Phippard, Helen (1996). *Coalitions and Contact Groups in Multilateral Diplomacy*, Centre for the Study of Diplomacy, Discussion Paper No. 21. Leicester: Leicester University.

Leonhard, Richard (1983). *South Africa at War: White Power and the Crisis in Southern Africa.* Westport, CT: Lawrence Hill & Co.

LeVine, Mark (1997). 'Peacemaking in El Salvador', in M. W. Doyle, I. Johnstone, and R. C. Orr (eds.), *Keeping the Peace: Multidimensional UN*

Operations in Cambodia and El Salvador. Cambridge: Cambridge University Press, pp. 227–54.

Levitin, Oleg (2000). 'Inside Moscow's Kosovo Muddle', *Survival*, 42/1: 130–40.

Lindo-Fuentes, Héctor (1990). *Weak Foundations: The Economy of El Salvador in the Nineteenth Century.* Berkeley, CA: University of California Press.

Lippmann, Walter (1922). *Public Opinion.* New York: Simon & Schuster.

Luck, Edward (2002). The United States, 'International Organization, and the Quest for Legitimacy', in S. Patrick and S. Forman (ed.), *Multilateralism and US Foreign Policy: Ambivalent Engagement.* London: Lynne Rienner, pp. 47–74.

Luttwak, Edward N. (1999). 'Give War a Chance', *Foreign Affairs*, 78/4: 36–51.

MacFarlane, Neil S. (1998). 'On the Front Lines in the Near Abroad: The CIS and the OSCE in Georgia's Civil Wars', in T. G. Weiss (ed.), *Beyond UN Subcontracting: Task-Sharing with Regional Security Arrangements and Service-Providing NGOs.* New York: St Martin's Press, pp. 115–36.

—— (2002). *Intervention in Contemporary World Politics.* Adelphi Paper 350, International Institute for Strategic Studies. Oxford: Oxford University Press.

MacMillan, Margaret (2001). *Peacemakers: The Paris Conference of 1919 and Its Attempt to End War.* London: John Murray.

Malcolm, Noel (2002). *Kosovo: A Short History*, 2nd edn. London: Pan Books.

Malone, David M. (1998). *Decision-Making in the Security Council: The Case of Haiti, 1990–1997.* Oxford: Oxford University Press.

—— (1998). 'The UN Security Council in the Post-Cold War World: 1987–97', *Security Dialogue*, 28/4: 393–408.

—— (1999). 'The Security Council in the Post-Cold War Era', in M. Alagappa and T. Inoguchi (eds.), *International Security Management and the United Nations.* Tokyo: United Nations University Press, pp. 394–408.

—— (2000). 'Eyes on the Prize: The Quest for Nonpermanent Seats on the UN Security Council', *Global Governance*, 6/1: 3–23.

—— (2003). 'L'affrontement Nord-Sud aux Nations Unies: Un Anachronisme sur le Déclin?', *Politique Étrangère*, 68/1: 149–64.

—— (ed.) (2004). *The UN Security Council: From the Cold War to the 21st Century.* Boulder, CO: Lynne Rienner.

—— and Wermester, Karen (2001). 'Boom and Bust? The Changing Nature of UN Peacekeeping', in A. Adebajo and C. L. Sriram (eds.), *Managing Conflicts in the 21st Century.* London: F. Cass, pp. 37–54.

—— and Khong, Yuen Foong (2003). 'Introduction', in D. M. Malone and Y. F. Khong (eds.), *Unilateralism and U.S. Foreign Policy: International Perspectives.* Boulder, CO: Lynne Rienner, pp. 1–17.

May, Ernest R. (1975). *The Making of the Monroe Doctrine.* Cambridge, MA: Harvard University Press.

Mayall, James (1971). *Africa: The Cold War and After.* London: Elek Books.

McCarthy, Patrick A. (1997). 'Positionality, Tension, and Instability in the UN Security Council', *Global Governance*, 3/2: 147–69.

Bibliography

McCarthy, Patrick A. (1998). *Hierarchy and Flexibility in World Politics: Adaptation to Shifting Power Distributions in the United Nations Security Council and the International Monetary Fund*. Aldershot, UK: Ashgate.

McHenry, Donald (1994). 'Statement', in H. Weiland and M. Braham (eds.), *The Namibian Peace Process: Implications and Lessons for the Future*. Freiburg, Germany: Arnold Bergstraesser Institut, pp. 13–17.

Mearsheimer, John J. (1994/95). 'The False Promise of International Institutions', *International Security*, 19/3: 5–49.

—— (2001). *The Tragedy of Great Power Politics*. New York: W. W. Norton.

Messing, Barbara (2000). 'El Salvador', in M. C. Greenberg, J. H. Barton, and M. E. McGuinness (eds.), *Words Over War: Mediation and Arbitration to Prevent Deadly Conflict*. Oxford: Rowman & Littlefield, pp. 161–81.

Miller, Nicola (1989). *Soviet relations with Latin America, 1959–1987*. Cambridge: Cambridge University Press.

Mingst, Karen A. and Karns, Margaret P. (2000). *The United Nations in the Post–Cold War Era*, 2nd edn. Oxford: Westview Press.

Montgomery, Tommie Sue (1995). *Revolution in El Salvador: From Civil Strife to Civil Peace*, 2nd edn. Boulder, CO: Westview Press.

Moreno, David (1994). *The Struggle for Peace in Central America*. Gainesville, FL: University Press of Florida.

Mortimer, Edward (1995). *A Few Words on Intervention: John Stuart Mill's Principles of International Action Applied to the Post–Cold War World*. London: John Stuart Mill Institute.

Neville-Jones, Pauline (1996). 'Dayton, IFOR and Alliance Relations in Bosnia', *Survival*, 38/4: 45–65.

Nicholas, Herbert George (1975). *The United Nations as a Political Institution*, 5th edn. Oxford: Oxford University Press.

Nicol, Davidson (1982). *The United Nations Security Council: Towards Greater Effectiveness*. New York: UNITAR.

Novosseloff, Alexandre (1995). 'Le Processus de Décision au Sein du Conseil de Sécurité des Nations Unies: Une Approche Historique', *Revue d'histoire diplomatique*, 109/3: 273–304.

Nye, Joseph S. (2002). *The Paradox of American Power: Why the World's Only Superpower Can't Go It Alone*. Oxford: Oxford University Press.

Osgood, Robert E. (1981). *The Revitalization of Containment, Foreign Affairs*, 60/3: 465–502.

Owen, David (1995). *Balkan Odyssey*. London: Victor Gollancz.

Oye, Kenneth A. (1986). 'Explaining Cooperation Under Anarchy: Hypotheses and Strategies', in K. A. Oye (ed.), *Cooperation Under Anarchy*. Princeton, NJ: Princeton University Press, pp. 1–24.

Parsons, Anthony (1995). *From Cold War to Hot Peace: UN Interventions 1947–1995*. London: Michael Joseph.

Parsons, Talcott (1977). *The Evolution of Societies.* Edited and with an introduction by Jackson Toby. Englewood Cliffs, NJ: Prentice-Hall.

Penttilä, Risto E. J. (2003). *The Role of the G-8 in International Peace and Security.* Adelphi Paper 355, International Institute for Strategic Studies. Oxford: Oxford University Press.

Pérez de Cuéllar, Javier (1997). *Pilgrimage for Peace: A Secretary-General's Memoir.* Basingstoke: Macmillan.

Pisani, André du (1985). *SWA/Namibia: The Politics of Continuity and Change.* Johannesburg: Jonathan Ball Publishers.

Posen, Barry R. (2000). 'The War for Kosovo: Serbia's Political-Military Strategy', *International Security*, 24/4: 69–78.

Prantl, Jochen (2005). 'Informal Groups of States and the UN Security Council', *International Organization*, 59/3: 559–92.

—— and Krasno, Jean E. (2004). 'Informal Groups of Member States', in J. E. Krasno (ed.), *The United Nations: Confronting the Challenges of a Global Society.* Boulder, CO: Lynne Rienner, pp. 311–57.

Price, Robert M. (1990). 'Pretoria's Southern African Strategy', in S. Chan (ed.), *Exporting Apartheid: Foreign Policies in Southern Africa 1978–1988.* London: Macmillan, pp. 145–69.

Prinsloo, D. S. (1977). *SWA/Namibia: Towards A Negotiated Settlement.* Pretoria: Foreign Affairs Association.

Pugh, Michael and Sidhu, Waheguru Pal Singh (eds.) (2003). *The United Nations and Regional Security: Europe and Beyond.* Boulder, CO: Lynne Rienner.

Rajan, M. S. (1987). 'The Role of the Nonaligned States in the United Nations', in M. S. Rajan, V. S. Mani, and C. S. R. Murthy (eds.), *The Nonaligned and the United Nations.* New Delhi: South Asian Publishers, pp. 294–348.

Reinicke, Wolfgang and Deng, Francis (2000). *Critical Choices: The United Nations, Networks, and the Future of Global Governance.* Ottawa: International Development Research Centre.

Rich, Paul (1993). 'The United States, Its History of Mediation and the Chester Crocker Round of Negotiations Over Namibia in 1988', in S. Chan and V. Jabri (eds.), *Mediation in Southern Africa.* London: Macmillan, pp. 75–99.

Richardson, James L. (1994). *Crisis Diplomacy: The Great Powers since the Mid-Nineteenth Century.* Cambridge: Cambridge University Press.

Roberts, Adam (1996). 'The United Nations: Variants of Collective Security', in N. Woods, *Explaining International Relations Since 1945.* Oxford: Oxford University Press, pp. 309–36.

—— (1999). 'NATO's "Humanitarian War" over Kosovo', *Survival*, 41/3: 102–23.

—— (2003). 'Order/Justice Issues at the United Nations', in R. Foot, J. Gaddis, and A. Hurrell (eds.), *Order and Justice in International Relations.* Oxford: Oxford University Press, pp. 49–79.

Roberts, Adam and Kingsbury, Benedict (1994). *Presiding Over a Divided World: Changing UN Roles, 1945–1993*, International Peace Academy, Occasional Paper Series. Boulder, CO: Lynne Rienner.

—— —— (eds.) (1993). *United Nations, Divided World: The UN's Roles in International Relations*, 2nd edn. Oxford: Clarendon Press.

Rocha, Geisa Maria (1984). *In Search of Namibian Independence: The Limitations of the United Nations*. Boulder, CO: Westview Press.

Rogers, William D. (1985). 'The United States and Latin America', *Foreign Affairs*, 63/3: 560–80.

Russett, Bruce (1997). 'Ten Balances For Weighing UN Reform Proposals', in B. Russett (ed.), *The Once And Future Security Council*. New York: St Martin's Press, pp. 13–28.

Saint-Exupéry, Antoine de (1946). *Le Petit Prince*. Paris: Gallimard.

Schild, Georg (1995). *Bretton Woods and Dumbarton Oaks: American Economic and Political Post-war Planning in the Summer of 1944*. Basingstoke: Macmillan.

Schnabel, Albrecht and Thakur, Ramesh (eds.) (2000). *Kosovo and the Challenge of Humanitarian Intervention: Selective Indignation, Collective Action, and International Citizenship*. Tokyo: United Nations University Press.

Schwegmann, Christoph (2001). 'Modern Concert Diplomacy: The Contact Group and the G7/8 in Crisis Management', in J. J. Kirton, J. P. Daniels, and A. Freytag (eds.), *Guiding Global Order: G-8 Governance in the Twenty-first Century*. Aldershot, UK: Ashgate, 113–6.

Seiler, John (ed.) (1980). *Southern Africa Since the Portuguese Coup*. Boulder, CO: Westview Press.

—— (1976). 'Which Way in Southern Africa?', *Africa Report*, 26/3: 17–22.

Serfontein, J. H. P. (2003). *Namibia?* London: Fokus Suid Publishers.

Shadow G-8 (2003). 'Pour une Nouvelle Légitimité du G-8', *Politique Etrangère*, 68/2: 245–58.

Silber, Laura and Little, Alan (1996). *The Death of Yugoslavia*, rev. edn. London: Penguin Books.

Simma, Bruno (ed.) (2002). *The Charter of the United Nations: A Commentary*, 2nd edn. Oxford: Oxford University Press.

Simmons, Beth A., and Martin, Lisa L. (2002). 'International Organization and Institutions', in W. Carlsnaes, T. Risse and B. A. Simmons (eds.), *Handbook of International Relations*. London: Sage, pp. 192–234.

SIPRI (ed.) (2001). *SIPRI Yearbook 2001*. Oxford: Oxford University Press.

Soto, Alvaro de. (1999). 'Ending Violent Conflict in El Salvador', in C. Crocker, F. Osler Hampson, and P. Aall (eds.), *Herding Cats: Multiparty Mediation in a Complex World*. Washington, DC: United States Institute of Peace Press, pp. 345–85.

—— and Castillo, Graciana del (1995). 'Implementation of Comprehensive Peace Agreements: Staying the Course in El Salvador', *Global Governance*, 1/2: 189–203.

—— —— (1994). 'Obstacles to Peacebuilding', *Foreign Policy*, 94/1: 69–83.

Stanley, William (1996). *The Protection Racket State: Elite Politics, Military Extortion and Civil War in El Salvador.* Philadelphia, PA: Temple University Press.

Stedman, Stephen John (2001). *Implementing Peace Agreements in Civil Wars: Lessons and Recommendations for Policymakers,* IPA Policy Paper Series on Peace Implementation. New York: International Peace Academy.

—— and Rothchild, Donald and Cousens, Elizabeth M. (eds.) (2002). *Ending Civil Wars: The Implementation of Peace Agreements.* Boulder, CO: Lynne Rienner.

Steele, Jonathan (1983). *World Power: Soviet Foreign Policy Under Brezhnev and Andropov.* London: Michael Joseph.

Stevens, Christopher (1980). 'The Soviet Role in Southern Africa', in J. Seiler (ed.), *Southern Africa Since the Portuguese Coup.* Boulder, CO: Westview Press, pp. 45–52.

Stoessinger, John G. (1970). *The United Nations and the Superpowers: United States–Soviet Interaction at the United Nations,* 2nd edn. New York: Random House.

Study Commission on U.S. Policy Toward Southern Africa (1981). *Southern Africa: Time Running Out.* Berkeley, CA: University of California Press.

Sutterlin, James S. (1995). *The United Nations and the Maintenance of International Peace and Security: A Challenge To Be Met.* Westport, CT: Praeger.

—— (1997). 'The Past as Prologue', in B. Russett (ed.), *The Once and Future Security Council.* New York: St Martin's Press, pp. 1–11.

Talbott, Strobe (2002). *The Russia Hand.* New York: Random House.

Torres-Rivas, Edelberto (1997). 'Insurrection and Civil War in El Salvador', in M. W. Doyle, I. Johnstone and R. C. Orr (eds.), *Keeping the Peace: Multidimensional UN Operations in Cambodia and El Salvador.* Cambridge: Cambridge University Press, pp. 209–26.

Traub, James (2000). 'Inventing East Timor', *Foreign Affairs,* 79/4: 74–89.

Trifunovska, Snezana (ed.) (1994). *Yugoslavia Through Documents: From Its Creation to Its Dissolution.* Dordrecht, The Netherlands: Martinus Nijhoff.

Ungar, Sanford J. and Vale, Peter (1985). 'South Africa: Why Constructive Engagement Failed', *Foreign Affairs,* 64/2: 234–58.

United Nations (ed.) (1951). *Yearbook of the United Nations 1950.* New York: UN Department of Public Information.

United Nations (1954). *Permanent Missions to the United Nations.* New York: United Nations.

—— (1965). *Repertoire of the Practice of the Security Council: Supplement 1959–1963.* New York: United Nations.

—— (1973–83). *Index to Proceedings of the Security Council.* New York: United Nations.

—— (1988–93). *Index to Proceedings of the Security Council: Forty-second to Forty-seventh year, 1987–92.* New York: United Nations.

—— (1995). *The United Nations and El Salvador: 1990 – 1995.* New York: United Nations.

United Nations Institute for Namibia (1986). *Namibia: Perspectives for National Reconstruction and Development.* Lusaka: United Nations Institute for Namibia.

Bibliography

Urquhart, Brian (1973). *Hammarskjöld*. New York/London: W.W. Norton.

—— (1998). *A Life In Peace And War*. London: Weidenfeld & Nicolson.

USIS Washington File (1998). *Transcript: Special Kosovo Briefing by Special Envoy Holbrooke*. Washington, DC, 28 October.

Vance, Cyrus R. (1983). *Hard Choices: Critical Years in America's Foreign Policy*. New York: Simon & Schuster.

Vergau, Hans-Joachim (1994). 'Statement', in H. Weiland and M. Braham (eds.), *The Namibian Peace Process: Implications and Lessons for the Future*. Freiburg, Germany: Arnold Bergstraesser Institut, pp. 18–26.

—— (2002). *Genscher und das südliche Afrika*, in H.-D. Lucas (ed.), Genscher, Deutschland und Europa. Baden-Baden, Germany: Nomos-Verlag, pp. 223–39.

Wedgwood, Ruth (1999). 'NATO's Campaign in Yugoslavia', *American Journal of International Law*, 93/4: 828–34.

Weiland, Heribert and Braham, Mathew (eds.) (1994). *The Namibian Peace Process: Implications and Lessons for the Future*. Freiburg, Germany: Arnold Bergstraesser Institut.

Weiss, Thomas G. (ed.) (1998). *Beyond UN Subcontracting: Task-Sharing with Regional Security Arrangements and Service-Providing NGOs*. New York: St Martin's Press.

—— (1999). 'UN Military Operations in the 1990s: "Lessons" from the Recent Past and Directions for the near Future', in M. Alagappa and T. Inoguchi (eds.), *International Security Management and the United Nations*. Tokyo: United Nations University Press, pp. 417–22.

—— Forsythe, David P., and Coate, Roger A. (2004). *The United Nations and Changing World Politics*, 4th edn. Boulder, CO: Westview Press.

Wedgwood, Ruth (2002). 'Unilateral Action in a Multilateral World', in S. Patrick and S. Forman (eds.), *Multilateralism and US Foreign Policy: Ambivalent Engagement*. London: Lynne Rienner, pp. 167–89.

Weller, Marc (ed.) (1999). *The Crisis in Kosovo 1989–1999: International Documents and Analysis*, vol. 1. Cambridge: Documents & Analysis Publishing.

—— (1999). 'The Rambouillet Conference on Kosovo', *International Affairs*, 75/2: 211–51.

Welsh, Jennifer M. (ed.) (2004). *Humanitarian Intervention and International Relations*. Oxford: Oxford University Press.

Weston, Burns H. (1991). *Security Council Resolution 678 and Persian Gulf Decision-Making: Precarious Legitimacy, American Journal of International Law*, 85/3: 516–35.

Wheeler, Nicholas J. (2000). *Saving Strangers: Humanitarian Intervention in International Society*. Oxford: Oxford University Press.

Whitfield, Teresa (1994). *Paying the Price: Ignacio Ellacuría and the Murdered Jesuits of El Salvador*. Philadelphia, PA: Temple University Press.

—— (1999). 'The Role of the United Nations in El Salvador and Guatemala: A Preliminary Comparison', in C. J. Arnson (ed.), *Comparative Peace Processes in Latin America*. Stanford, CA: Stanford University Press, pp. 257–90.

—— (2001). 'The UN's Role in Peace-Building in El Salvador', in M. S. Studemeister (ed.), *El Salvador: Implementation of the Peace Accords*. Washington: United States Institute of Peace, pp. 33–57.

—— (2004). 'Group of Friends', in D. Malone (ed.), *The UN Security Council: From the Cold War to the 21st Century*. Boulder, CO: Lynne Rienner, pp. 311–24.

Wight, Martin (1978). *Power Politics*. London: Leicester University Press.

Winkelmann, Ingo (1998). 'Bringing the Security Council into a New Era: Recent Developments in the Discussion on the Reform of the Security Council', in J. A. Frowein and R. Wolfrum (eds.), *Max Planck Yearbook of United Nations Law*, 1/ 1997. The Hague: Kluwer Law International, pp. 35–90.

Wolff, Stefan (2003). 'The Limits of Non-Military International Intervention: A Case Study of the Kosovo Conflict', in F. Bieber and Z Daskalowski (eds.), *Understanding the War in Kosovo*. London: Frank Cass, pp. 79–100.

Wood, Elisabeth Jean (2003). *Insurgent Collective Action and Civil War in El Salvador*. Cambridge: Cambridge University Press.

Wood, Michael C. (1996). 'Security Council Working Methods and Procedure: Recent Developments', *The International and Comparative Law Quarterly*, 45/1: 150–61.

Woods, Ngaire (1999). 'Good Governance in International Organizations', *Global Governance*, 5/1: 39–61.

Woodward, Susan L. (1995). *Balkan Tragedy: Chaos and Dissolution after the Cold War*. Washington, DC: Brookings Institution.

Young, Andrew (1980). 'The United States and Africa: Victory for Diplomacy', *Foreign Affairs*, 59/3: 648–66.

Zartman, William (1995). 'Dynamics and Constraints in Negotiations in Internal Conflicts', in W. Zartman (ed.), *Elusive Peace: Negotiation an End to Civil Wars*. Washington, DC: The Brookings Institution, pp. 3–29.

Index

Notes and tables are indexed as **n** and **t** in bold.